SAMS Teach Yourself JavaServer Pages™ 2.0 WITH APACHE TOMCAT in 24 Hours

Mark Wutka
Alan Moffet
Kunal Mittal

SAMS 800 East 96th Street., Indianapolis, Indiana, 46240 USA

Sams Teach Yourself JavaServer Pages 2.0 with Apache Tomcat in 24 Hours

International Standard Book Number: 0-672-32597-7

Library of Congress Catalog Card Number: 2003111831

Printed in the United States of America

First Printing: December 2003

06 05 04 03 4 3 2 1

Trademarks

All terms mentioned in this book that are known to be trademarks or service marks have been appropriately capitalized. Sams Publishing cannot attest to the accuracy of this information. Use of a term in this book should not be regarded as affecting the validity of any trademark or service mark.

Warning and Disclaimer

Every effort has been made to make this book as complete and as accurate as possible, but no warranty of fitness is implied. The information provided is on an "as is" basis. The authors and the publisher shall have neither liability nor responsibility to any person or entity with respect to any loss or damages arising from the information contained in this book or from the use of the CD or programs accompanying it.

Bulk Sales

Sams Publishing offers excellent discounts on this book when ordered in quantity for bulk purchases or special sales. For more information, please contact

U.S. Corporate and Government Sales

1-800-382-3419

corpsales@pearsontechgroup.com

For sales outside of the U.S., please contact

International Sales

1-317-428-3341

international@pearsontechgroup.com

Associate Publisher
Michael Stephens

Acquisitions Editor
Todd Green

Development Editor
Sean Dixon

Managing Editor
Charlotte Clapp

Senior Project Editor
Matthew Purcell

Copy Editor
Publication Services, Inc.

Indexer
Publication Services, Inc.

Proofreader
Publication Services, Inc.

Technical Editor
Marc Goldford
Mark Wutka
Jeff Linwood
Jeff Pajor

Publishing Coordinator
Cindy Teeters

Multimedia Developer
Dan Scherf

Interior Designer
Gary Adair

Cover Designer
Alan Clements

Page Layout
Publication Services, Inc.

Contents at a Glance

Introduction 1

1 Getting Started with JavaServer Pages 5
2 JavaServer Pages Behind the Scenes 25
3 Creating HTML Forms 49
4 How the Browser Interacts with the Server 65
5 JSP and Servlet Lifecycles 81
6 Looking Under the Hood—Core Servlet Components 101
7 Servlet Filters 135
8 Core JavaServer Page Components 153
9 JSP Directives 171
10 Using JSP Standard Actions to Organize Your Web Application 187
11 Debugging and Error Handling 213
12 Saving Data Between Requests 235
13 More About Saving Data 261
14 Interacting with JavaBeans 293
15 The JSP Expression Language 315
16 Extending JSP with New Tags 325
17 The JSP Standard Tag Library 355
18 Working with Databases and JSTL Database Actions 373
19 Creating an XML Application 387
20 Building Web Applications with JavaServer Pages and Servlets 411
21 Using Struts and JavaServer Faces 429
22 Internationalization 445
23 Security 471
24 Performance 487

Index 501

Appendixes (on CD-ROM)

A Apache Tomcat PDF:501
B Packaging a Web Application PDF:513

Table of Contents

Introduction **1**

Who Should Read This Book ... 1

How This Book Is Organized ... 2

In Every Hour ... 3

Conventions Used in This Book ... 3

Apache Tomcat ... 4

HOUR 1: Getting Started with JavaServer Pages **5**

A "Hello World" JavaServer Page ... 6

Using the `<% %>` Tags in a JavaServer Page ... 9

Displaying a Value with `<%= %>` ... 11

Inserting Comments ... 13

Declaring Methods and Variables with `<%! %>` ... 15

Handling Multiple Threads in a JSP ... 17

Summary ... 21

Q&A ... 23

Workshop ... 24

HOUR 2: JavaServer Pages Behind the Scenes **25**

Introducing Servlets ... 25

A "Hello World" Servlet ... 26

Using the `invoker` to Run a Servlet ... 30

Packaging, Deploying, and Running a Servlet ... 32

The Anatomy of a Servlet ... 37

Sending a Response to the Browser ... 40

The `HttpServlet` Class ... 42

Choosing Between JavaServer Pages and Servlets ... 42

Summary ... 45

Q&A ... 46
Workshop ... 46

HOUR 3: Creating HTML Forms 49
A Simple HTML Form ... 49
Using the `request` Object ... 52
Retrieving Form Variables in a Servlet ... 57
Different Ways to Do Forms ... 59
Summary ... 61
Q&A ... 63
Workshop ... 63

HOUR 4: How the Browser Interacts with the Server 65
The Hypertext Transfer Protocol ... 66
Common Request Headers ... 71
Common Response Headers ... 73
The HTTP `POST` Command ... 74
`GET` versus `POST` ... 75
HTTPS: Secure HTTP ... 76
Summary ... 77
Q&A ... 78
Workshop ... 78

HOUR 5: JSP and Servlet Lifecycles 81
Servlet Lifecycle ... 82
JavaServer Page Lifecycle ... 87
Reloading Other Classes ... 89
Application Lifecycle Events ... 92
Summary ... 96
Q&A ... 98
Workshop ... 99

HOUR 6: Looking Under the Hood—Core Servlet Components 101
The ServletRequest Class 101
The HttpServletRequest Class 112
The ServletContext Class 116
The ServletResponse Class 119
The HttpServletResponse Class 121
The ServletInputStream Class 123
The ServletOutputStream Class 124
The HttpSession Class 124
The Cookie Class 127
Creating a New Cookie 127
Summary 131
Q&A 132
Workshop 132

HOUR 7: Servlet Filters 135
The Filter Interface 135
An Example Filter—JSP/Servlet Timings 139
An Example Filter—Session Logging 145
Summary 151
Q&A 152
Workshop 152

HOUR 8: Core JavaServer Page Components 153
Built-in JSP Objects 153
The JspWriter Class 156
Working with the pageContext Object 159
The JspEngineInfo Class 165
Summary 166
Q&A 168
Workshop 168

HOUR 9: JSP Directives 171
An Overview of JSP Directives 171
The page Directive 172

The `include` Directive 183
The `taglib` Directive 183
Summary 184
Q&A 185
Workshop 186

HOUR 10: Using JSP Standard Actions to Organize Your Web Application **187**
Including Other Files 188
Forwarding to Another Page 196
Passing Java Objects Between JSPs and Servlets 199
Making Your Application More Modular 200
Using an Applet in Your Form 207
Summary 209
Q&A 211
Workshop 211

HOUR 11: Debugging and Error Handling **213**
Why Debugging Is Tough 213
Compile Versus Runtime Errors 214
Using Log Files to Debug an Application 215
Using a Debugger 221
Error Handling 228
Summary 231
Q&A 232
Workshop 232

HOUR 12: Saving Data Between Requests **235**
Storing Data in Hidden Form Variables 235
Storing Data in a `session` Object 240
How Sessions Work 244
Forcing a New Session 245
Handling Session Termination 247
Handling Sessions Without Cookies 252
Storing Application-Wide Data 255

Summary 257
Q&A 258
Workshop 258

HOUR 13: More About Saving Data **261**
Using Sessions to Save Data in a Shopping Cart Application 261
Storing Data in a Cookie 287
Q&A 291
Workshop 291

HOUR 14: Interacting with JavaBeans **293**
The `jsp:useBean` Action 293
A Bean-Based Web Application 307
Summary 311
Q&A 312
Workshop 313

HOUR 15: The JSP Expression Language **315**
Basic Syntax 315
Variables 316
Literals and Operators 316
Implicit Objects 320
Functions 321
Q&A 322
Workshop 322

HOUR 16: Extending JSP with New Tags **325**
"Hello World" Tag 325
Packaging and Installing a Tag 328
Conditionally Including the Body of a Custom Tag 330
Processing Body Content with a Custom Tag 332
Handling Exceptions 334
Accessing Tag Attributes 335
Using Dynamic Attributes 337

Adding Scripting Variables ... 338
The JSP 2.0 `SimpleTag` Interface ... 342
Tag Files—Tag Extensions Without Java ... 347
Tag File Directives ... 348
Summary ... 351
Q&A ... 352
Workshop ... 353

HOUR 17: The JSP Standard Tag Library **355**
Installing and Using JSTL ... 355
Core Tag Library ... 357
Functions ... 366
Q&A ... 371
Workshop ... 371

HOUR 18: Working with Databases and JSTL Database Actions **373**
A Brief Overview of Databases ... 373
What Is SQL? ... 374
Getting Started with Cloudscape ... 376
What Is JDBC? ... 377
Using JDBC from JavaServer Pages and Servlets ... 379
JSTL SQL Tag Library ... 380
Summary ... 383
Q&A ... 384
Workshop ... 384

HOUR 19: Creating an XML Application **387**
A "Hello World" XML Page ... 388
A Few Simple Rules for XML ... 391
Why Use XML with JSP and Servlets? ... 392
XML Tag Library ... 405
Summary ... 408
Q&A ... 409
Workshop ... 409

HOUR 20: Building Web Applications with JavaServer Pages and Servlets **411**
Web Application Architecture 411
The Model 1 and Model 2 Architectures 412
Using Model-View-Controller in Your Web Applications 414
Calling Multiple Controllers and Views 421
Summary 425
Q&A 426
Workshop 426

HOUR 21: Using Struts and JavaServer Faces **429**
An Overview of Struts 429
Setting Up Struts 436
An Overview of JavaServer Faces (JSF) 437
Summary 443
Q&A 444
Workshop 444

HOUR 22: Internationalization **445**
Setting the Page Encoding 445
Detecting the Browser's Preferred Locale 446
Using Locale-Based Text Formatters 448
Using Resource Bundles in Web Pages 455
The Format Tag Library 461
Summary 469
Q&A 470
Workshop 470

HOUR 23: Security **471**
Role-Based Security 471
BASIC Authentication 472
Creating a Custom Login Form 476
Checking Security Roles Programmatically 479
Using Client Certificates for Authentication 483

Summary 484
Q&A 485
Workshop 485

HOUR 24: Performance **487**
Buffering Pages to Improve Performance 488
Use Static Content Where Possible 488
Caching Objects to Reduce Setup Time 489
Choosing the Right Session Mechanism 489
Precompiling JSPs 490
Setting the JSP Reload Time 493
Simple Java Optimizations 493
Making JSPs and Servlets Thread-Safe 495
Using Thread Pools 497
Summary 498
Q&A 499
Workshop 499
Appendixes 500

Index 501

APPENDIXES (ON THE CD-ROM)

APPENDIX A: Apache Tomcat **PDF:501**
Where to Get Tomcat PDF:501
Installing Tomcat on Windows PDF:502
Running Tomcat PDF:505
Tomcat Configuration PDF:505
Logging PDF:506
Setting the Classpath PDF:506
Authentication PDF:506
Tomcat Web Server Administration Tool PDF:508
Tomcat Manager PDF:509

APPENDIX B: Packaging a Web Application PDF:513

A Simple WAR File Example PDF:513

Installing a WAR File Under Tomcat PDF:515

WAR Configuration Options PDF:516

About the Authors

Mark Wutka has been programming since the Carter administration and considers programming to be a relaxing pastime. He managed to get a computer science degree while designing and developing networking software for Delta Airlines. Although he has been known to delve into areas of system and application architecture, he isn't happy unless he's writing code . . . usually in Java.

As a consultant for Wutka Consulting, Mark enjoys solving interesting technical problems and helping his coworkers explore new technologies. He has taught classes, written articles and books, and given lectures. His first book, *Hacking Java*, outsold Stephen King at the local technical bookstore. He's also known for having a warped sense of humor.

He plays a mean game of Scrabble and a lousy game of chess, and he is the bane of every greenskeeper east of Atlanta. He is also a women's gymnastics judge.

He can be reached via e-mail at `mark@wutka.com`. You can also visit his company Web site at `http://www.wutka.com`.

Alan Moffet is a consultant with over 20 years of experience in software development and management. He specializes in software architecture and design, and development practice. His work has focused on applying emerging technologies, updating legacy systems, and improving organizational effectiveness. His programming experience includes a variety of systems and programming languages. He began to work with Java professionally while it was a beta product and continues to follow its development and use it in his projects. He is a member of the JCP.

Kunal Mittal is a consultant for implementation and strategy for WebServices and Services Oriented Architectures. He has co-authored and contributed to several books on Java, WebLogic, and Web Services. Over the past several years, Kunal has worked on numerous projects using different BEA products ranging from WebLogic Server 4.5 to 8.1, BEA Portal, BEA Integration, Liquid Data for WebLogic and WebLogic Workshop. His projects have ranged in verticals such as Finance, Real-Estate, Supply Chain, Broadband, Entertainment, and ISV's in the Web Services space.

Dedication

from Mark Wutka:

To my Mom, Dr. Patricia Brown Graham

It is both an honor and an absolute joy to be your son and friend.

from Alan Moffet:

To my wonderful family, Tricia, Kyle, Ryan, and Kalyn

Acknowledgments

from Mark Wutka:

Writing a book like this is more than just a team effort. The team members are more than just the people whose names you see in the credits; they are also our family and friends.

The first person I would like to thank is you, the reader. Without you, there would be no need for this book. I sincerely hope that you enjoy and learn from this book and that you find it useful enough to refer to it frequently.

I can't give enough thanks to my wife, Ceal. You have put up with me all these years and supported me in everything that I do. Your love and encouragement help get me through every day.

I owe such a huge debt to my Mom for all that she has done for me. She always gave me encouragement and served as a wonderful role model. While I was working all day and writing in my spare time, my Mom was making me look like a slacker by working, writing a book, *and* writing her dissertation. I can't say enough to thank you, but . . . thank you! Thank you also to Dr. John Graham for supporting both of us!

I'd like to thank several of my colleagues. First, Alan Moffet, who is incredibly sharp and thorough. I wish I had his depth of knowledge. I would also like to thank Chuck Cavaness and Cliff McCartney for their assistance over the years. It is great to have such top-notch gurus to bounce ideas off of. It's like having a personal think-tank. Thanks to Mike "Dot-Com" Connor for his suggestions and also for several of the menu images I used in the book. Thanks also to Mike Bates of the John H. Harland company for his suggestions and support. I'd also like to thank Joe Weber for his excellent input on the original outline for this book. I put a lot of stock in what Joe says.

The folks at Sams have been a pleasure to work with. I'd especially like to thank Todd Green for his patience with my bizarre schedule and frequent trips out of town and for getting me to do this book in the first place. Thanks also to Sean Dixon and Jan Fisher. I know there are a lot more people working on this book that I have never talked to and whose names I don't know. Thank you, too. I couldn't have done any of this if it weren't for you folks.

Finally, I would like to thank the multitudes of developers out there who are working on open-source projects—especially those working on OpenOffice. Thanks to your excellent work, I did much of the work on this book with OpenOffice running on Mandrake Linux. The folks on the Jakarta project are doing a fantastic job as well, not just with Tomcat, but with Ant, Struts, and a number of other tools.

from Alan Moffet:

During the course of writing this book, I became very busy with work. Several projects demanded most of my time. Fortunately for me, the people at Sams have been very patient and great to work with. I'm particularly grateful for Todd Green and Sean Dixon, whose encouragement and support haven't wavered. Thanks, Todd and Sean.

It's also been a pleasure to work with Mark Wutka. Mark's a sharp developer with a lot of experience. He understands how to use Java and its platforms in real-world applications. His practical writing and examples have made the book what it is.

Kunal Mittal stepped in and helped with several chapters. Marc Goldford and Jeff Linwood helped us to stay on track technically. I appreciate your work and expertise.

I also need to thank my parents. They helped me develop a love for learning and the discipline that has served me so well.

Finally, I have to thank my family and friends. Your smiles, teasing, hugs, and occasional games of "horse" put everything into perspective. You make it all possible.

from Kunal Mittal:

I would like to dedicate this book to my wife, Neeta, and my dog, Dusty, for their patience as I chose to bail on their weekend plans to work on completing chapters for this book. I could not have done it without their support and understanding.

I would also like to acknowledge Todd Green, who introduced me into this book and gave me the opportunity to contribute to it. I would also like to thank the entire Sams team that has made this book a reality.

We Want to Hear from You!

As the reader of this book, *you* are our most important critic and commentator. We value your opinion and want to know what we're doing right, what we could do better, what areas you'd like to see us publish in, and any other words of wisdom you're willing to pass our way.

As an associate publisher for Sams Publishing, I welcome your comments. You can e-mail or write me directly to let me know what you did or didn't like about this book—as well as what we can do to make our books better.

Please note that I cannot help you with technical problems related to the topic of this book. We do have a User Services group, however, where I will forward specific technical questions related to the book.

When you write, please be sure to include this book's title and author as well as your name, e-mail address, and phone number. I will carefully review your comments and share them with the author and editors who worked on the book.

E-mail: feedback@samspublishing.com

Mail: Michael Stephens
Associate Publisher
Sams Publishing
800 East 96th Street
Indianapolis, IN 46240 USA

For more information about this book or another Sams Publishing title, visit our Web site at `www.samspublishing.com`. Type the ISBN (excluding hyphens) or the title of a book in the Search field to find the page you're looking for.

Introduction

The JavaServer Pages JSP 2.0 specification is one of the most exciting Java Community Process (JCP) releases of the year. Chances are you picked this book to learn more about the new features of JSP 2.0. Or you may be interested in using JSPs for the first time in your next project. Regardless of your interest, we've put together a book that tries to bring you up to speed fast.

The goal of JSP 2.0 has been to make it easier to create sophisticated, well-designed Web applications. We feel that the authors of the specification have achieved their goal. Working with databases or XML has never been simpler. Your applications can be functionally well-organized. You can create your own reusable components.

Because JSPs have become easier to use, we're able to put more into the 24 hours you'll spend reading this book. Each hour will introduce you to a topic and help you to understand it well enough to be able to do something useful with it. We've created hands-on tasks to make sure that you can exercise your new skills.

By the time you've finished the book, you'll feel comfortable using JavaServer Pages and servlets to create Web applications. You will also have been introduced to the important features of JSP 2.0 and to complimentary technologies such as Struts and JavaServer Faces. And you will have learned about debugging, internationalization, security, and performance.

Who Should Read This Book

Sams Teach Yourself JavaServer Pages 2.0 with Apache Tomcat in 24 Hours is written for developers who have experience building Web applications using HTML. You don't need to be a guru, but you need to understand how to write a Web page.

You'll get the most out of this book if you know some Java. You'll learn how to use JSP features by implementing them using Java and by using newer alternatives. Additionally, most Web applications are a combination of JSPs and servlets. You'll need to know some Java to be able to use servlets. If you aren't familiar with Java or need to brush up on the language, there are some great books that can help you, such as *Sams Teach Yourself Java 2 in 24 Hours* (ISBN: 0-672-32460-1).

You don't need to know anything about JSPs or servlets to start. We'll help you through the basics of JSPs and servlets, the new Expression Language, JSTL and custom tags, and other topics you'll need to understand to build Web applications.

How This Book Is Organized

Getting Started

The first 4 hours are your basic training. When you finish these chapters, you'll know almost everything you need to know to create JSPs and servlets and use them in simple applications. The concepts introduced in this first part are applied throughout the rest of the book.

Core Components In-Depth

Hours 5 through 14 give you more background into JavaServer Pages and servlets. You'll learn how to work with JSPs and servlets by exploring the APIs and runtime environments. In addition, you'll extend your knowledge of how to use them in more advanced applications.

JSP Key Features

Hours 15 through 19 introduce you to many of the features of JSP 2.0, including the Expression Language, custom tags, and JSTL. Here, you will also learn how to use databases and XML in dynamic Web applications.

Advanced Topics

The last 5 hours will teach you how to use JSPs and servlets together in Web applications. It covers Struts and JavaServer Faces. It also addresses application-wide topics such as internationalization, security, and performance.

Appendixes

Appendix A, "Apache Tomcat," will help you get started with Apache Tomcat. Appendix B, "Packaging a Web Application," reveals the details of how to package and deploy your Web applications. The appendixes are available only on the included CD.

In Every Hour

In every hour, we've provided a Q&A section designed to help you troubleshoot potential problems you might encounter when working with what you have learned. Additionally, each hour contains a workshop that is designed to help reinforce the topics discussed in that hour. The workshop consists of the following elements.

Quiz

The Quiz presents a few questions from the material covered in the hour that are designed to test your understanding of the material. They can help you determine if you need to reread or study an important subject.

Answers

The Answers section contains the answers to each of the quiz questions.

Activities

The Activities are suggested activities that you can pursue to get practice in the topics explained in an hour.

Conventions Used in This Book

This book uses the following typographic conventions to make reading easier:

- New terms appear in boldface. The italic attribute is used for emphasis.
- All code listings and commands appear in a special `monospace` font.
- Replaceable elements and placeholders use *`italic monospace`*.

By the Way

By the Way elements explain interesting or important points that can help you understand significant concepts and techniques. This isn't necessarily information you need to know, but it can be useful and interesting if you take the time to read it.

By the Way

Did you Know?

Did You Know?

Did You Know? elements describe shortcuts and alternative approaches to gaining an objective. They often give you a real-world, practical perspective on the topic or task at hand.

Watch Out!

Watch Out!

Every Watch Out! offers a warning about something you must look out for to avoid potentially costly and frustrating problems. Don't ignore these, because they can save you time and frustration.

Apache Tomcat

Apache Tomcat is the reference implementation of JavaServer Pages and Servlets. Although you can run JSP and Servlet applications in other application servers, such as BEA WebLogic Server or IBM WebSphere Application Server, Tomcat is all you need for basic applications. Tomcat is an open source project available for free from `http://jakarta.apache.org/tomcat`.

Because this book covers JSP 2.0, you need the current version of Tomcat 5.0. We've included Tomcat 5.0.x on the CD-ROM with this book, but by the time you read this a later version may be available, so be sure to check the Web site for an update.

Although Tomcat 5.0 is currently a beta version, it's relatively stable. All of the examples in this book work with it. If future versions of Tomcat 5.0 break an example, you'll find updated source code on the book's Web site at `http://samspublishing.com`. You can also begin to develop your own JSP 2.0 Web applications in anticipation of the final release. It is likely that a production quality release is close. As with all beta software, you should not place Tomcat 5 into a production system.

HOUR 1

Getting Started with JavaServer Pages

What You'll Learn in This Hour:

- What JavaServer Pages are
- How to write simple JavaServer Pages to create dynamic Web pages
- The basics of how JavaServer Pages work
- About JavaServer Pages scripting elements, including scriptlets, expressions, and declarations

With the release of the JavaServer Pages 2.0 specification, a new milestone has been reached. Looking backward, we see that using JavaServer Pages has become a time-tested way to develop Web pages with dynamic content. JSPs are the technology of choice in many Web-based applications. Developers know that, because JavaServer Pages have Java at their foundation, they can build upon all that the platform provides, including a robust and rich set of technologies. If you are a Java programmer, chances are you may already be familiar with some of them and want to begin to develop Web applications that leverage your knowledge.

Beginning with JavaServer Pages 2.0, it's become easier to create Web applications. In fact, even if you are new to Java or don't have any Java experience at all, you'll be able to build sophisticated sites that use databases or work with XML documents—things that used to require an intermediate knowledge of the Java programming language and its platforms. The road ahead is full of opportunity.

A "Hello World" JavaServer Page

JavaServer Pages (JSPs) are, in the most basic sense, Web pages with embedded Java code. The embedded Java code is executed on the server before the page is returned to the browser. If a picture is worth a thousand words, in this case an example is worth a thousand explanations. Listing 1.1 shows a basic JSP.

LISTING 1.1 HelloWorld.jsp

```
<html>
<body>
<%
    out.println("<h1>Hello World!</h1>");
%>
</body>
</html>
```

As you can see, the page is composed of standard HTML with a dash of Java contained between the <% and %> character sequences. The <% and %> along with the code inside is called a **scriptlet**.

Although you can probably guess what the browser will display when this page runs, Figure 1.1 should remove any doubt because it shows the output from this page.

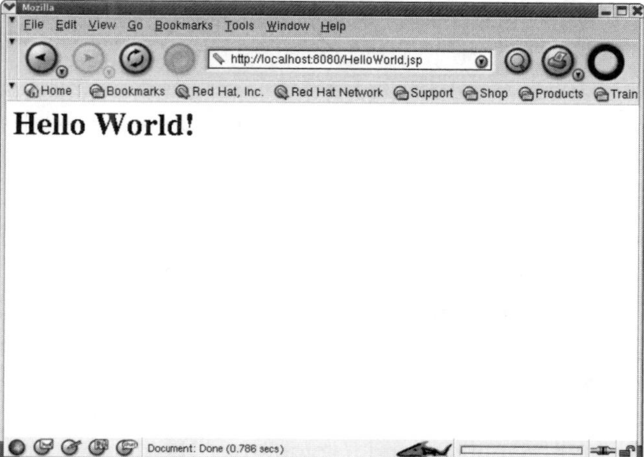

FIGURE 1.1
A JavaServer Page can generate HTML output.

By the Way

Trying Out the Example

If you want to try out the "Hello World" JSP, put it in the same place that you would put an HTML page and point your browser to it. You also need to install a JSP-capable Web server, such as Tomcat. Appendix A, "Apache Tomcat," provides instructions on how to install Tomcat. If you already have an installation of Tomcat, you can save this example as a file named `HelloWorld.jsp` and place it in the `webapps/ROOT` folder located in your Tomcat installation directory. Then enter `http://localhost:8080/HelloWorld.jsp` into your browser as the address. You should obtain the same results as shown in Figure 1.1.

By the Way

In Case of Trouble

If you are having trouble displaying the "Hello World" JSP, see the "Q&A" section at the end of this hour.

When the browser asks the Web server for a JSP, the Web server passes control to a JSP container. A **container** works with the Web server to provide the runtime environment and other services a JSP needs. It knows how to understand the special elements that are part of JSPs. Because this is the first time this JSP has been invoked, the JSP container converts it into an executable unit called a **servlet**. The entire page, including the parts that are in HTML, is translated into source code. After the code has been translated, the JSP container compiles the servlet, loads it automatically, and then executes it. Typically, the JSP container checks to see whether a servlet for a JSP file already exists and whether the modification date on the JSP is older than the servlet. If the JSP is older than its generated servlet, the JSP container assumes that the JSP hasn't changed and that the generated servlet still matches the JSP's contents. Because it takes some time to generate a servlet and compile it, the JSP container wants to minimize the number of compiles it has to perform, so it tries to avoid unnecessary compiles. We will discuss servlets in some more detail later in the book.

The other interesting piece of this equation is the actual HTML code that was sent to the browser. Most browsers enable you to view the HTML source for the Web page you are viewing. Listing 1.2 shows you the HTML code generated by the JSP in Listing 1.1.

LISTING 1.2 HTML Output from `HelloWorld.jsp`

```
<html>
<body>
<h1>Hello World!</h1>
</body>
</html>
```

As you can see, the text from the out.println statement in the JSP file is inserted directly into the HTML output. Of course, printing out a text string is not a practical use for JSP. Typically, you want to print out things that might change every time you run the JSP. The current time and date are trivial examples of items more suited for JSP.

The out object used to write the "Hello World" string is an object of type JspWriter. For now, you just need to know that this out object has approximately the same methods as the standard Java class PrintWriter. There are print and println methods for writing out various types of data. One word of caution, however: JspWriter is not a PrintWriter, so you cannot pass the out object to methods that expect a PrintWriter. You'll learn more about the JspWriter object in Hour 8, "Core JavaServer Page Components."

As mentioned earlier, when the browser asks the Web server for HelloWorld.jsp, the JSP container first checks to see whether HelloWorld.jsp has already been compiled into a servlet. If not, it creates a servlet that prints out the HTML in your JSP file and executes the code contained within the JSP file. Listing 1.3 shows the portion of the generated servlet that produces the HTML code in Listing 1.1.

LISTING 1.3 Java Code to Produce the HTML from Listing 1.2

```
out.write("<html>\r\n");
out.write("<body>\r\n");

out.println("<h1>Hello World!</h1>");

out.write("\r\n");
out.write("</body>\r\n");
out.write("</html>\r\n");
```

Typically, you won't need to look at the generated servlet; however, sometimes it is useful. If your JSP throws an exception and you print out the Java stack trace from the exception, the line numbers displayed in the stack trace will be line numbers from the generated servlet. There is no standard indicating where the generated servlets must be placed. It varies from JSP container to JSP container. In Tomcat you will find the generated source code and the servlet binary class files under the work subdirectory of your Tomcat installation directory. In the current release of Tomcat 5.0, they are usually in the work/Catalina/localhost/_/org/apache/jsp subdirectory.

By the Way

What's a Stack Trace?

Stack traces are usually produced with an exception when an error occurs. They're helpful in determining what caused the problem. A stack trace shows the methods as they were called by the application, from the point where the exception was thrown to the genesis, in reverse order.

Using the <% %> Tags in a JavaServer Page

As you saw in the `HelloWorld.jsp` example, the `<%` and `%>` tags in a JSP file are used to indicate the presence of Java code within the HTML. The JSP specification allows for languages other than Java to be used for scripting; at the present time, however, few servers support languages other than Java. Eventually there will be more support for other scripting languages, but until that time, and certainly for the rest of this book, the focus is on Java as the JSP scripting language.

Let's take a look at another example of a JavaServer Page in Listing 1.4.

LISTING 1.4 Source Code for `Greeting.jsp`

```
<html>
<body>
Good
<%
    java.util.Calendar currTime = new java.util.GregorianCalendar();

    if (currTime.get(currTime.HOUR_OF_DAY) < 12)
    {
%>
        Morning!
<%
    }
    else if (currTime.get(currTime.HOUR_OF_DAY) < 18)
    {
%>
        Afternoon!
<%
    }
    else
    {
%>
        Evening!
<%
    }
%>
</body>
</html>
```

If you are unfamiliar with either Active Server Pages or JavaServer Pages, the code in Listing 1.4 probably looks absolutely bizarre to you. First, remember that the code outside of the <% %> tag pair is sent verbatim. Of course, that might lead you to conclude that the three strings, `Morning!`, `Afternoon!`, and `Evening!`, should all be sent in the response. What really happens is that items outside of the <% %> tag pair are converted into Java statements that print out the HTML verbatim. Because the `Morning!`, `Afternoon!`, and `Evening!` strings occur within an `if` statement, they are printed only when their section of the `if` block is true.

Listing 1.5 shows you a portion of the Java code generated by the JSP in Listing 1.4. (Don't worry, you won't have to look at the Java code for every JSP in this book or even in this hour.)

LISTING 1.5 Java Code Generated by Listing 1.4

```
    out.write("<html>\r\n");
    out.write("<body>\r\nGood\r\n");

  java.util.Calendar currTime = new java.util.GregorianCalendar();
  if (currTime.get(currTime.HOUR_OF_DAY) < 12)
  {
    out.write("\r\n        Morning!\r\n");
  }
  else if (currTime.get(currTime.HOUR_OF_DAY) < 18)
  {
    out.write("\r\n        Afternoon!\r\n");
  }
  else
  {
    out.write("\r\n        Evening!\r\n");
  }

    out.write("\r\n");
    out.write("</body>\r\n");
    out.write("</html>\r\n");
```

Comparing Listing 1.5 to Listing 1.4, you should begin to get the idea of how the code within <% and %> relates to the rest of the file.

Did you Know?

Reading through JSPs

It's easier to read through a JSP if you remember that any text outside the <% and %> tags is really just shorthand for an `out.write` statement containing that text.

Listing 1.4 illustrates how scriptlets and HTML can be intermixed. However, it is not a good example of how to make a clear, readable JSP file.

Displaying a Value with <%= %>

The earlier example in Listing 1.4 could have been written in a much more compact way that determined the time of day first and printed out its greeting near the end of the file. Listing 1.6 shows a much more compact version.

LISTING 1.6 Source Code for `Greeting1.jsp`

```
<html>
<body>
<%
    java.util.Calendar currTime = new java.util.GregorianCalendar();

    String timeOfDay = "";

    if (currTime.get(currTime.HOUR_OF_DAY) < 12)
    {
        timeOfDay = "Morning!";
    }
    else if (currTime.get(currTime.HOUR_OF_DAY) < 18)
    {
        timeOfDay = "Afternoon!";
    }
    else
    {
        timeOfDay = "Evening!";
    }
%>
Good <% out.write(timeOfDay); %>
</body>
</html>
```

As you can see, Listing 1.6 is much easier to read because it doesn't jump back and forth between Java and HTML so rapidly. Down at the bottom of the file, you can see where the `timeOfDay` variable is written out as part of the display. Notice that even though it is a single statement on the same line as some HTML text, `out.write(timeOfDay)` must still end with a semicolon because it must be a legal Java statement.

JSP provides a shorthand for printing out variables to save you from having to put `out.write()` all over the place. The line that prints out the greeting in Listing 1.6 can be replaced with the following line:

```
Good <%= timeOfDay %>
```

The `<%=` tag indicates that you want to write out a Java expression as part of the output sent back to the browser. Notice that you still close the tag with `%>` and not `=%>`. You can include any Java expression. Just make sure you don't put a semicolon after the expression—the semicolon is automatically generated for you. The following line shows you a more complex expression:

```
<%= 2*3+4-5*6+7*8-9 %>
```

As you can see, it's just as valid to print out a numerical expression as it is to print out a string. In fact, you can also print out an entire object. For example, you can use the following line to print out the string representation of a calendar object:

```
<%= new java.util.GregorianCalendar() %>
```

Of course, the result of printing out an object might not be what you expect. Figure 1.2 shows how the `GregorianCalendar` object looks when the <%= tag is used to display it.

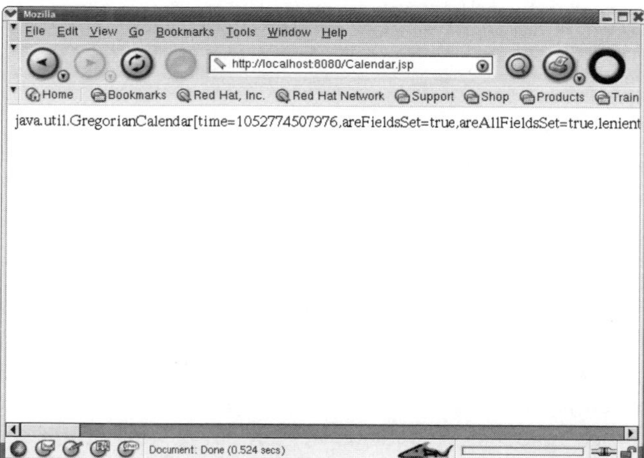

FIGURE 1.2
The <%= tag can print out an entire object.

Watch Out!

> **<%= Is Not <% =**
>
> Make sure you don't put any space between the <% and the = sign.

When you use the <%= tag to display an object, the result is the same kind of output you would see if you wrote out the object to `System.out` in a regular program. Basically, the output routine calls the `toString` method in the object and displays the results of the method call.

By the Way

It's All `out.write`

Anything you put between the `<%=` and `%>` ends up inside an `out.write()` expression. In other words, think of `<%=` as shorthand for `out.write(` and its closing `%>` as shorthand for `);`.

Listing 1.7 shows a somewhat more practical combination of `<%` and `<%=` used to display the current date.

LISTING 1.7 Source Code for `ShowDate.jsp`

```
<html>
<body>
<% java.util.Calendar currDate = new java.util.GregorianCalendar();
   // add 1 to month because Calendar's months start at 0, not 1
   int month = currDate.get(currDate.MONTH)+1;
   int day = currDate.get(currDate.DAY_OF_MONTH);
   int year = currDate.get(currDate.YEAR);
%>
The current date is: <%= month %>/<%= day %>/<%= year %>
</body>
</html>
```

The `<%=` tag is often useful when graphic designers are creating the Web page and Web programmers are adding the server-side Java code. Typically, the Web programmers encase their code in `<% %>` tags somewhere near the beginning of the JSP file. They put all the interesting data (the data interesting to the graphic designers) into Java variables. Then the graphic designers can lay out the page the way they want it and use the `<%= %>` tags to insert the data where they want without having to write any Java code. Listing 1.7 is a basic example of this very concept. The graphic designers can insert the `month`, `day`, and `year` variables anywhere they want.

JavaServer Pages make it possible to separate the roles of authors who develop the look and feel of the content, and developers who create reusable software components. As you will see later in this book, there are additional ways that JSPs help to make it easier to develop Web pages when different groups must work on the same JSP.

Inserting Comments

Comments are generally used for two things: making notations about the code and removing sections of code. There are at least four different ways to add comments to a JavaServer Page, each with its own advantages and disadvantages. If your JSP is generating HTML, you can use HTML comments, which use the <!-- and --> tags, shown here:

```
<!-- This is an HTML comment. -->
```

In general, use HTML comments in a JSP only if you want the comment to be visible on the browser. Most of the time, you don't care whether the user can see any of your comments, so HTML comments are usually not used in a JSP. You might find yourself using HTML comments if you have a large section of HTML in your JSP and you want to remove a section temporarily. Although you can remove it with JSP comment tags (which you will learn about in a moment), it's nicer to keep the block pure HTML rather than turn it into a mixture of HTML and JSP tags. It will be easier to identify the source of a problem if you accidentally remove a comment start or end tag later on in your development.

Did you Know?

Debugging with Comments

HTML comments can be useful if you want to include debugging information in the output of a page, without showing it to users. However, don't put anything sensitive in the comments.

Because any code you place inside the <% %> tags is Java code, you can use both of Java's commenting mechanisms. For example, you can do a one-liner comment, such as

```
<% // This is a one-line JSP comment. %>
```

You can also use the /* */ comment tags within separate <% %> tag pairs. This method is difficult to follow, and fortunately, there is a better way. Here is an example of using the /* and */ comment tags:

```
<% /* %>
  This is actually commented out.
<% */ %>
```

Not only is the commenting method confusing; it's also wasteful. When the JSP is translated, the text within the /* */ is still converted into Java statements that emit the text. However, because the Java statements are surrounded by /* */, they are ignored by the compiler.

JavaServer Pages have a special comment tag pair recognized by the JSP compiler. You can surround your comments with <%-- --%> to place a comment in your JSP code. The <%-- --%> prevents text from even being placed into the Java source generated by the JSP container. Here is an example of a JSP comment:

```
<%-- This comment will not appear in the servlet source code. --%>
```

If you need to remove a section of code from a JSP, the `<%-- --%>` tags are the best way to do it. They take priority over the other tags. In other words, if a `<% %>` tag pair occurs within the comment tags, the `<% %>` tag pair is ignored, as the following example shows:

```
<%--
<%
    out.println("You will never see this.");
%>
--%>
```

Declaring Methods and Variables with `<%! %>`

So far you have seen how to insert Java statements and expressions into your code. In case you haven't realized it yet, all the code within the `<% %>` tags and all the expressions within the `<%= %>` tags belong to one big Java method in the generated servlet. That is why you can use the `<%= %>` tags to display a variable that was declared inside the `<% %>` tags.

You might want to put an entire Java method into a JSP. If you try to declare a method within the `<% %>` tags, the Java compiler reports an error. After all, Java doesn't like it if you try to declare a method within another method. Use the `<%! %>` tags to enclose any declarations that belong outside the big method that generates the page. Listing 1.8 shows a JSP file that declares a separate method and then uses the `<%= %>` tags to display the result of calling the method.

LISTING 1.8 Source Code for `DeclareMethod.jsp`

```
<html>
<body>
<%!
    public String myMethod(String someParameter)
    {
        return "You sent me: "+someParameter;
    }
%>
<%= myMethod("Hi there") %>
</body>
</html>
```

Because it may not be obvious, Figure 1.3 shows the results of the `DeclareMethod.jsp` as they are displayed on the browser.

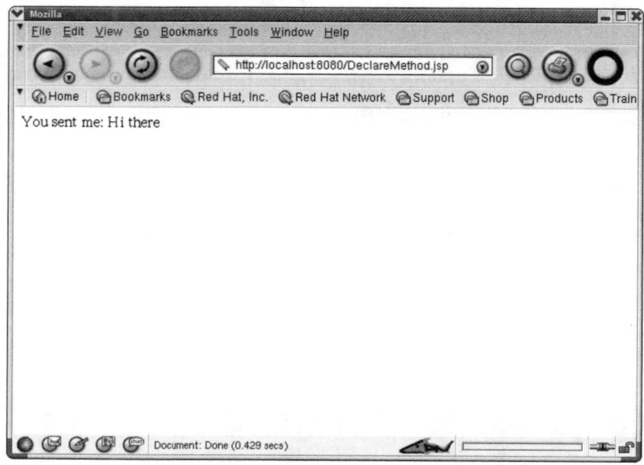

FIGURE 1.3 You can declare Java methods in a JSP and display results returned by those methods.

Did you Know?

Writing to `out` **Inside of <%! %>**

The `out` variable is not available inside any methods you declare with the `<%!` tag. If you need to send data back to the browser from within a method, you must pass the `out` variable in as a parameter of type `JspWriter`.

In addition to declaring methods, you can also use the `<%! %>` tags to declare instance variables. These instance variables are visible to any methods you declare, and also to the code within the `<% %>` tags. Declaring an instance variable is as simple as this:

```
<%! int myInstanceVariable = 10; %>
```

After this variable has been declared, you can use it in other methods declared with `<%! %>` or within the `<% %>` and `<%= %>` tags. For example, you can display the value of `myInstanceVariable` this way:

```
<%
    out.println("myInstanceVariable is "+ myInstanceVariable);
%>
```

Likewise, you can use the `<%= %>` tags to display the variable this way:

```
MyInstanceVariable is <%= myInstanceVariable %>
```

Skip

Handling Multiple Threads in a JSP

Even though Java is a fairly thread-friendly language, many Java developers are not comfortable dealing with a threaded application. If you are developing JavaServer Pages for a production system, you need to be comfortable with threading. By default, the JSP container assumes that your JSPs are thread-safe, so it might invoke the same page from multiple threads.

If all your Java code is enclosed within the `<% %>` tags and you don't use any external objects, your code is probably already safe. Remember, because each Java thread has its own execution stack (where local variables are stored), any method that uses only local variables should already be thread-safe. If you do use external variables, or if you declare instance variables with the `<%! %>` tags, you might run into threading issues.

By the Way

JspWriter Is Thread-Safe

Just in case you're worried, the `JspWriter` class (that is, the `out` variable) is properly synchronized. You don't have to worry that your `out.print` and `out.println` statements will fail when multiple threads try to call them at the same time.

Listing 1.9 shows an abbreviated example of a real-life situation in which threading issues became an ugly problem. In this example, the JSP is formatting name and address information for a customer. As you look it over, see whether you can spot where the threading issues occur.

LISTING 1.9 Source Code for `Address.jsp`

```
<html>
<body>

<%!
// Holders for the various portions of the address
    String firstName;
    String middleName;
    String lastName;
    String address1;
    String address2;
    String city;
    String state;
    String zip;
%>

<%
// Copy the information passed into the JSP.
    firstName = request.getParameter("firstName");
    middleName = request.getParameter("middleName");
```

```
    lastName = request.getParameter("lastName");
    address1 = request.getParameter("address1");
    address2 = request.getParameter("address2");
    city = request.getParameter("city");
    state = request.getParameter("state");
    zip = request.getParameter("zip");

// Call the formatting routine.
    formatNameAndAddress(out);
%>
</body>
</html>

<%!
// Print out the name address.
    void formatNameAndAddress(JspWriter out)
        throws java.io.IOException
    {
        out.println("<PRE>");
        out.print(firstName);
// Print the middle name only if it contains data.
        if ((middleName != null) && (middleName.length() > 0))
        {
            out.print(" "+middleName);
        }
        out.println(" "+lastName);
        out.println(address1);

// Print the second address line only if it contains data.
        if ((address2 != null) && (address1.length() > 0))
        {
            out.println(address2);
        }
        out.println(city+", "+state+" "+zip);
        out.println("</PRE>");
    }
%>
```

By the Way

Trying Out This Example

If you would like to try this out, you'll need to place `address.jsp` in the `webapps/ROOT/` subdirectory of your Tomcat installation. Then, you can exercise the example by using a URL like this:

`http://localhost:8080/address.jsp?firstname=`*`fill-in`* `&middlename=`*`fill-in`*`&lastname=`*`fill-in`*`&address1=`*`fill-in`*`&address2=`*`fill-in`*`&city=`*`fill-in`*`&state=`*`fill-in`*`&zip=`*`fill-in`*

You need to provide data in place of *`fill-in`*. This example uses the `request` object and HTTP parameters, which we haven't discussed yet. We'll get to them a little later in the book.

Can you see the problem? If you can't, don't feel too bad. In the real-life program, the error was not discovered until the program was being tested with multiple users. The problem is that the variables holding the name and address information are instance variables. Typically, only one instance of the servlet used to service a JSP request is loaded at one time. Each time a browser requests a JSP, the Web server spawns another thread to handle the request. It's possible to have multiple threads executing the same servlet at the same time.

In the case of Listing 1.9, the problem is that the instance variables are shared across all the threads. One thread might set all the variables, and then before it has a chance to call the formatting routine, another thread comes along and changes the values. Figure 1.4 illustrates how this happens.

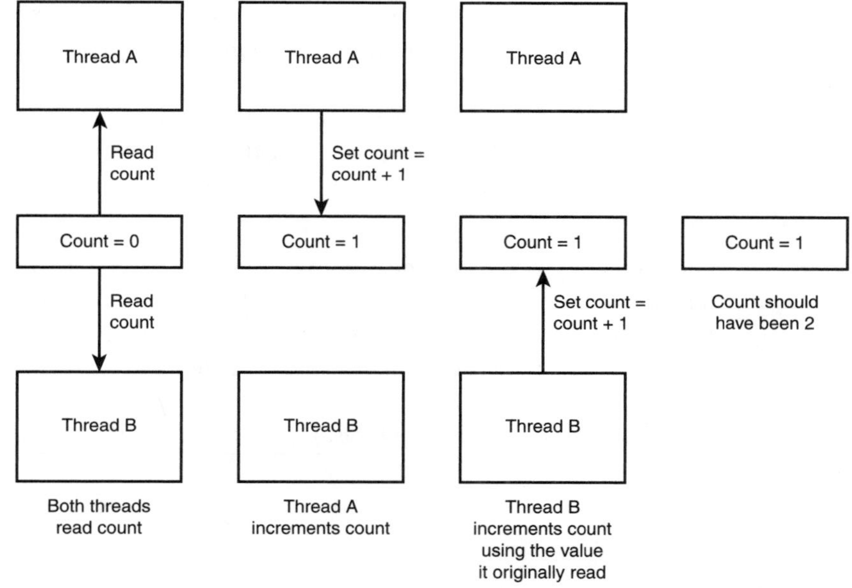

FIGURE 1.4 Multiple threads can modify the same member variable in a JSP.

As I said before, the root of the problem is that the data is being passed to `formatNameAndAddress` via instance variables instead of as parameters to the method. Although it seems like an obvious thing to just pass parameters, in the real-life program from which this example was pulled, the formatting routine needed about 30 different values. It is more than a little cumbersome to pass 30 parameters around, especially if they must be passed to several different methods. One solution for this problem is to synchronize the variable assignments and the method call, as in this example:

```
// Copy the information passed into the JSP.
    synchronized (this)
    {
        firstName = request.getParameter("firstName");
        middleName = request.getParameter("middleName");
        lastName = request.getParameter("lastName");
        address1 = request.getParameter("address1");
        address2 = request.getParameter("address2");
        city = request.getParameter("city");
        state = request.getParameter("state");
        zip = request.getParameter("zip");

// Call the formatting routine.
        formatNameAndAddress(out);
    }
```

Although synchronization can prevent threading problems, it does so at the cost of performance. The server tries to use multiple threads so that it can service as many requests as possible in a short amount of time. If you suddenly create a bottleneck in which a large amount of work can be done only one thread at a time, you are defeating the performance enhancements of threading. There is nothing wrong with using the `synchronized` keyword here and there to prevent errors, but synchronizing all or even a majority of the work in one large block is usually not a good idea.

The solution for the problem posed in Listing 1.9 involves passing the data as method parameters rather than through instance variables. All the parameters can be encapsulated in a Java class, and the Java class can be declared within the JSP as a nested class. Listing 1.10 shows the thread-safe solution.

LISTING 1.10 Source Code for `AddressGood.jsp`

```
<html>
<body>

<%
// Allocate a holder for the data.
    NameAndAddress data = new NameAndAddress();

// Copy the information passed into the JSP.
    data.firstName = request.getParameter("firstName");
    data.middleName = request.getParameter("middleName");
    data.lastName = request.getParameter("lastName");
    data.address1 = request.getParameter("address1");
    data.address2 = request.getParameter("address2");
    data.city = request.getParameter("city");
    data.state = request.getParameter("state");
    data.zip = request.getParameter("zip");

// Call the formatting routine.
    formatNameAndAddress(data, out);
```

```
%>
</body>
</html>

<%!
// The holder for the formatting data
    class NameAndAddress
    {
        public String firstName;
        public String middleName;
        public String lastName;
        public String address1;
        public String address2;
        public String city;
        public String state;
        public String zip;
    }

// Print out the name address.
    void formatNameAndAddress(NameAndAddress data, JspWriter out)
        throws java.io.IOException
    {
        out.println("<PRE>");
        out.print(data.firstName);
// Print the middle name only if it contains data.
        if ((data.middleName != null) &&
            (data.middleName.length() > 0))
        {
            out.print(" "+data.middleName);
        }
        out.println(" "+data.lastName);
        out.println(data.address1);

// Print the second address line only if it contains data.
        if ((data.address2 != null) &&
            (data.address1.length() > 0))
        {
            out.println(data.address2);
        }
        out.println(data.city+", "+data.state+" "+data.zip);
        out.println("</PRE>");
    }
%>
```

The example in Listing 1.10 avoids thread collisions by allocating an object to hold the data it passes to another routine. Because each thread allocates its own copy of the data object, the threads cannot overwrite one another's data.

Summary

In this hour you learned that JavaServer Pages can use the Java programming language and all of its component technologies to develop Web applications. JSPs mostly consist of scriptlets, which are fragments of Java code that can be mixed with HTML to produce Web pages with dynamic content. Writing to the current output stream occurs frequently, so JSP provides an abbreviated method to produce text output that is inserted into the resulting document. Java expressions can be enclosed in `<%=` and `%>` tags, and the results will automatically be output as a string. Code generated from scriptlets and expressions belong to a single method that handles requests on behalf of a JSP. You can also declare methods and variables outside of the scope of that method by enclosing your declarations inside of `<%!` and `%>` tags. Scriptlets and expression and declaration elements are ultimately all part of a servlet that is produced by a JSP container when a request for a JSP is made. By default, a JSP container uses a single servlet to handle multiple requests by using multithreading, making it important to be aware of issues related to concurrency. These problems are often easily solved by using Java's mechanisms for synchronization or by good design.

Q&A

Q. ***Why do I get a*** `404 (File Not Found)` ***error when I access the JavaServer Page?***

A. You are probably putting the JSP in a directory that the Web server can't get to. If you have an HTML page that you can access from the Web server, put the JSP in the same directory and see whether you can get to it.

Q. ***Why do I get a*** `500 (Internal Server Error)` ***error when I access the JSP?***

A. Usually, a 500 error is caused by a miscommunication between the Web server and the JSP container, or by an error in the JSP container. Check to make sure that you have configured your JSP container properly. Another possibility is that you are having problems compiling the source code produced by the container. Inspecting the resulting page or error logs will usually provide a clue as to where your code is faulty. Often, the information includes line numbers.

Q. ***Why do I get an error saying*** `No Compiler Available or unable to locate "com.sun.tools.javac.Main`***?***

A. The JSP container converts your JSPs into Java classes and then compiles them. To compile them, it needs a Java compiler. You need to install either a full JDK or at least get the `tools.jar` file from an existing JDK installation and put it in your classpath. This error occurs mostly when you have installed only the JRE (Java Runtime Environment), which does not come with a Java compiler.

Q. ***Why do I see bizarre compiler errors, such as*** `expected }` ***or*** `no catch/finally clause`***?***

A. You probably forgot an opening `<%` or a closing `%>`.

Q. ***Instead of seeing an HTML page, why do I see the source code for my JSP?***

A. You don't have the JSP container set up correctly. The Web server doesn't understand that the JSP container is supposed to handle filenames ending in `.jsp`. You might need to reinstall your JSP container.

Workshop

The Workshop is designed to help you review what you have learned, and help you to further increase your understanding of the material covered in this hour.

Quiz

1. What file extension is used to identify JavaServer Pages?
2. What is the name of the method that performs most of the work servicing a JSP?
3. Why won't the following code work?

```
<%! public void printName() {
    out.print("My Name")
} %>
```

Answers

1. Top-level JSP files are identified by the use of the .jsp extension. JSPs may also be divided into segments that are statically included into top-level files. The JSP 2.0 standard suggests that you use a .jspf extension for these in order to maintain consistency with earlier specifications that referred to files with partial JSPs in them as fragments. In addition, JSPs can be delivered as XML documents, in which case the extension .jspx is used.
2. The method `jspService()` is used to do most of the work. This method contains the scriptlets and expressions found in your JSP. Declarations from your JSP occur outside of this method.
3. The `out` variable is available only within the scope of `jspService()`. Since this is a method declaration, the method `printName()` occurs outside of the scope of `jspService`, and it does not have access to `out`.

Activity

Write a simple JavaServer Page using a scriptlet, an expression, and a declaration. Access the page from a Web browser to make sure it works and to produce the source code for the servlet that handles your request. Take a moment to examine the generated source code.

HOUR 2

JavaServer Pages Behind the Scenes

Introducing Servlets

What You'll Learn in This Hour:

- What servlets are
- How to create and deploy simple servlets
- The basics of how servlets work
- How to choose between servlets and JSPs when developing an application

As you learned in the last hour, servlets are an underlying technology behind JavaServer Pages. Because of the close relationship, it's useful to learn something about servlets. Understanding servlets will help you in your study of JSPs by helping you understand what is going on under the hood. Even if you do most of your work with JSPs, you will be more effective at writing JSPs and debugging problems if you can understand the servlet code. In addition, JSPs and servlets have distinct and complementing roles in Web applications. More often than not, you will find yourself using a combination.

Servlets allow the programmer to work directly with requests made to a Web server and to form responses that include content that is returned to a client. Unlike JSPs, which are oriented toward presentation, with their combination of HTML and scriptlets or other elements, servlets are composed entirely with Java. As you might expect, servlets are great for performing lower-level functions that work with data or implement business models.

A "Hello World" Servlet

Servlets are a little more involved than JSP, but in simple cases they aren't too bad. Listing 2.1 shows you the "Hello World" program in servlet form.

LISTING 2.1 Source Code for `HelloWorldServlet.java`

```
package examples;

import javax.servlet.*;
import javax.servlet.http.*;
import java.io.*;

public class HelloWorldServlet extends HttpServlet
{
    public void doGet(HttpServletRequest request,
                    HttpServletResponse response)
        throws IOException
    {
// Tell the Web server that the response is HTML.
        response.setContentType("text/html");

// Get the PrintWriter for writing out the response.
        PrintWriter out = response.getWriter();

// Write the HTML back to the browser.
        out.println("<html>");
        out.println("<body>");
        out.println("<h1>Hello World!</h1>");
        out.println("</body>");
        out.println("</html>");
    }
}
```

The HTML portion of `HelloWorldServlet` is probably the most recognizable part. The browser's view of `HelloWorldServlet` is shown in Figure 2.1.

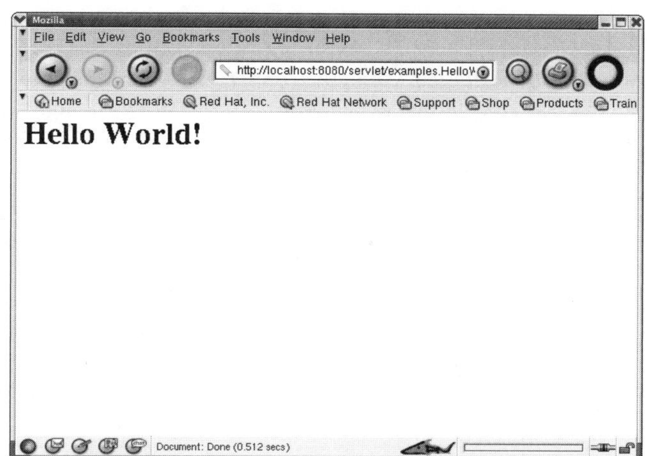

FIGURE 2.1
A servlet can generate HTML code.

As mentioned earlier, unlike JSPs, servlets are pure Java classes. The good news is that you don't have to learn any additional syntax to create a servlet; the bad news is that you have to do a bit more work in your programs. Although, as you can see from the "Hello World" servlet, the amount of work isn't really that great.

Compiling the Servlet

Before you compile the servlet, make sure the servlet classes are in your classpath. The location of the servlet classes varies depending on which servlet container you are using. For example, if you are using the Apache Tomcat server, the `servlet-api.jar` file is located in the `common\lib` directory underneath your main Tomcat installation. To compile `HelloWorldServlet.java` on a system where you have Tomcat installed, you might set your `CLASSPATH` variable this way under Windows:

```
set CLASSPATH=.;c:\jakarta-tomcat\common\lib\servlet-api.jar;%CLASSPATH%
```

Under Unix or Linux, you might set it this way:

```
export CLASSPATH=.:/usr/local/jakarta-tomcat/common/lib/servlet-api.jar:$CLASSPATH
```

Of course, you can also add the classpath to the command line using the `-classpath` option of `javac`, the java compiler.

By the Way

Where Are the Classes in Tomcat 5?

In past versions of Tomcat, the classes that support servlet development have been located in `servlet.jar`, located in the `common\lib` directory. For Tomcat 5.0, which includes support for the Servlet 2.4 and JSP 2.0 specifications, the class is named `servlet-api.jar`—at least for the moment.

By the Way

Where Are the Classes in the J2EE SDK?

If you are using the J2EE SDK, the JAR file that includes support for servlets and JSPs is named `J2EE.jar` and is located in the `lib` directory off of the J2EE home directory. This book will be using Tomcat for its examples, so if you decide to use the J2EE SDK, you may have to adjust the procedures slightly for compiling and running the examples.

By the Way

Tomcat Is Part of the Standard

Tomcat is the official playground for servlet and JSP reference implementation development. Once the specifications start to firm up, development on a new version of Tomcat begins right away. A release of Tomcat is ultimately bundled with Sun's J2EE SDK when the SDK is finalized. Tomcat itself is a production quality implementation and is continually refined. Tomcat 5.0 supports the Java Servlet 2.4 and JavaServer Pages 2.0 specifications; it is the version used throughout this book.

Then, to compile the servlet, enter the following command:

```
javac -d . HelloWorldServlet.java
```

The reason for the `-d .` in the `javac` command is that the source for `HelloWorldServlet.java` specifies a Java package. When you specify a destination directory with the `-d` option, Java creates the necessary package directories. For example, when you compile `HelloWorldServlet.java`, you won't see a `HelloWorldServlet.class` file in your current directory, but you should see a directory named `examples` (corresponding to the package that `HelloWorldServlet` belongs to), which should contain the `HelloWorldServlet.class` file.

By the Way

Having Trouble with the Example?

If you are having trouble compiling `HelloWorldServlet`, see the "Q&A" at the end of this hour.

HelloWorldServlet In-Depth

The first thing your servlet must do is implement the Servlet interface. There are two ways to do it: Create a subclass from a class that implements the Servlet interface or implement the Servlet interface directly in the servlet. HelloWorldServlet, shown earlier in Listing 2.1, takes the easier approach by subclassing an existing class, HttpServlet, which implements Servlet. Other classes also implement the Servlet interface, and they will be discussed shortly.

When a request comes in for a particular servlet, the servlet container loads the servlet (if it has not yet been loaded) and invokes the servlet's service method. The method takes two arguments: an object containing information about the request from the browser and an object containing information about the response going back to the browser. The HttpServlet class provides the implementation of this method for us. Looking at the HTTP request header, it will determine that the HTTP request method was GET and will invoke the method doGet, which has been overridden in the example.

As you will see in Hour 3, "Creating HTML Forms," there are actually several different methods that handle incoming requests. The doGet method is specific to the HttpServlet class and handles HTTP GET requests. The GenericServlet class provides a more general service method that handles all kinds of requests.

Next the servlet must tell the Web browser what kind of content is being returned. Most of the time, you are returning HTML content, so the content type is set to text/html. As you will see in Hour 19, "Creating an XML Application," you can also set the content type to text/xml to return data in XML. In the example we set the response's content type by invoking setContentType in the response object that was passed to us as a parameter of doGet.

After you have set the content type, you are ready to start sending text back to the browser. Of course, you need some sort of output object to send the text back. Again the response object has the methods necessary to get an output stream for writing a response. Because the "Hello World" servlet is writing out text, it needs only a PrintWriter object, so it calls the getWriter method in the response object. If you need to send binary data back to the browser, you should use the getOutputStream method in the response object.

Having read Hour 1, "Getting Started with JavaServer Pages," the final part of HelloWorldServlet probably looks familiar to you by now. HelloWorldServlet uses the println method in the PrintWriter to send HTML back to the browser. Remember, in Hour 1 you saw a portion of the servlet code generated by the

"Hello World" JSP. Aside from some extra comments, that code is almost identical to the code at the end of `HelloWorldServlet`. After all, JSPs eventually become servlets, and there are only so many ways to send output from a servlet, so why shouldn't they be similar?

Using the `invoker` to Run a Servlet

There are several ways to run a servlet, but the easiest is to use the `invoker` servlet. Although it's not a part of servlet specification, most servlet containers make the `invoker` servlet available, so that you don't have to do anything special for the container to recognize your servlets. As you go through the examples in the book, you may find that's it's convenient to use this feature.

By default, Tomcat does not enable the `invoker` servlet; it's considered a security risk. You'll need to enable it. Looking at `web.xml` in the `conf/` directory of your Tomcat installation, you will see the following:

```
<!--
    <servlet>
        <servlet-name>invoker</servlet-name>
        <servlet-class>
          org.apache.catalina.servlets.InvokerServlet
        </servlet-class>
        <init-param>
            <param-name>debug</param-name>
            <param-value>0</param-value>
        </init-param>
        <load-on-startup>2</load-on-startup>
    </servlet>
-->
```

All that needs to be done is to uncomment the servlet declaration so that it looks like this:

```
<servlet>
    <servlet-name>invoker</servlet-name>
    <servlet-class>
      org.apache.catalina.servlets.InvokerServlet
    </servlet-class>
    <init-param>
        <param-name>debug</param-name>
        <param-value>0</param-value>
    </init-param>
    <load-on-startup>2</load-on-startup>
</servlet>
```

That makes Tomcat aware of the invoker servlet's configuration. Then, you'll need to uncomment the servlet mapping for the `invoker`. Uncomment this mapping:

```
<!-- The mapping for the invoker servlet -->
<!--
<servlet-mapping>
    <servlet-name>invoker</servlet-name>
    <url-pattern>/servlet/*</url-pattern>
 </servlet-mapping>
-->
```

It should look like this when you are done:

```
<!-- The mapping for the invoker servlet -->

<servlet-mapping>
    <servlet-name>invoker</servlet-name>
    <url-pattern>/servlet/*</url-pattern>
</servlet-mapping>
```

At this point, a servlet can be invoked by using a URL that includes the path `servlet/`. The `invoker` will try to match whatever follows servlet/ to a servlet class in the container's classpath and execute it. The URL for this example is

```
http://localhost:8080/servlet/examples.HelloWorldServlet
```

Watch Out!

Using `invoker` in a Production Environment Is Unsafe

Although the `/servlet/` pattern is useful for development, you should never use it on a production server. The `/servlet/` pattern can arbitrarily load Java classes regardless of whether or not they are servlets. (It must first load them before it can determine whether they implement the `Servlet` interface.) A malicious person could force your container to load a class and potentially harm or compromise your server. You should always remove the `/servlet/` pattern from your production servers.

The method for adding to a container's classpath varies with the container you are using. For some containers, you must edit the container's startup script, whereas others enable you to add to the classpath through an administration tool. Tomcat has a nice alternative to modifying the classpath: It gives you a place to store your class files that is already in the classpath. You copy them to `common\classes\` underneath the main Tomcat directory. (If you want to add JAR files, copy them to `common\lib\`.) Because `HelloWorldServlet` is packaged in `examples`, you must create a directory under `common\classes\` called `examples\`.

We will try out our servlet by placing `HelloWorldServlet.class` in common\classes\examples\.

By the Way

Sharing Classes Between Web Applications

Both `common\classes` and `common\lib` are actually reserved as places where you can put classes and libraries that are shared by all Web applications.

After copying `HelloWorldServlet`, starting Tomcat, and pointing your browser to it, you should see the result shown in Figure 2.1.

If, when trying to access your servlet, the container fails to locate your servlet the first time you try to run it, try restarting the container. If it still doesn't work, your modification to the classpath may not have worked.

Did you Know?

Redeploying a Changed Servlet

Some servlet containers don't automatically reload a servlet after it has been loaded. If you make changes to your servlet and redeploy it, you might not see the changes. If your servlet container doesn't reload servlets, you might need to restart the servlet container to pick up the changes.

By the Way

In Case of Trouble

If you are having trouble running `HelloWorldServlet`, see "Q&A" at the end of this hour.

Packaging, Deploying, and Running a Servlet

Although using the `invoker` is great for experimentation, you should really use a proper technique for deploying and running a servlet. You should package your servlets into WAR (Web Archive) files. A WAR file is similar to a JAR file, but it is specific to Web applications. You can mix servlets, JSPs, HTML files, and even other classes and JAR files within a WAR file. A *deployment descriptor* named `web.xml` contains all the necessary definitions for the application, including the list of servlets and their pathnames. Appendix B, "Packaging a Web Application," contains a detailed description of WAR files and their structure. For now, you need to know just a few things to include in the deployment descriptor and how to package your servlets in a WAR file.

Creating a Deployment Descriptor

A deployment descriptor describes a Web application, which may consist of servlets, JSPs, Java classes and JARs, HTML files, and other resources. For the moment, you only need to include servlets in the file. In later hours, you'll see how to add additional items. Listing 2.2 shows a deployment descriptor for `HelloWorldServlet`.

LISTING 2.2 Source Code for `web.xml`

```
<?xml version="1.0" encoding="ISO-8859-1"?>
<web-app xmlns="http://java.sun.com/xml/ns/j2ee"
    xmlns:xsi="http://www.w3.org/2001/XMLSchema-instance"
    xsi:schemaLocation="http://java.sun.com/xml/ns/j2ee
    http://java.sun.com/xml/ns/j2ee/web-app_2_4.xsd"
    version="2.4">
    <display-name>Hello World</display-name>
    <description>A Hello World Web Application</description>

    <servlet>
        <servlet-name>HelloWorld</servlet-name>
        <servlet-class>examples.HelloWorldServlet</servlet-class>
    </servlet>

    <servlet-mapping>
        <servlet-name>HelloWorld</servlet-name>
        <url-pattern>/hello</url-pattern>
    </servlet-mapping>
</web-app>
```

The `<?xml?>` tag in `web.xml` defines the file as an XML file. All XML files should contain this tag. For Java Servlet specification version 2.4, deployment descriptors are defined in terms of an XML schema document. Earlier versions were based on DTDs. Servlet containers are required to be backward compatible to version 2.2.

The `<web-app>` tag defines the main element for this file; it says that this XML file describes a Web application. The next two tags, `<display-name>` and `<description>`, provide brief descriptions of the application. The `<display-name>` tag defines a short name for the application that may be displayed by the servlet container's management interface, or possibly in log files. The `<description>` tag provides a longer text description of the application.

A `web.xml` file can contain any number of servlet definitions, each specified by a `<servlet>` tag that must contain at least a servlet name and a classname. In Listing 2.2, you see a single servlet definition giving the servlet a name of `HelloWorld` and specifying the classname as `examples.HelloWorldServlet`.

Defining the servlet is not enough, however, you must also specify a servlet mapping, which maps a URL to a servlet. The `<servlet-mapping>` tag requires a `<servlet-name>` and a `<url-pattern>`. The `<servlet-name>` element identifies the name of a previously declared servlet. The `<url-pattern>` element defines the pattern that is used to determine which servlet should be invoked.

To properly understand how to create a `url-pattern`, it's helpful to look at the parts of the URL that the servlet container receives from the Web server. The following equation is helpful:

```
requestURI = contextPath + servletPath + pathInfo
```

When you issue a request to a Web server to invoke a servlet, you include the protocol for the request, the name or IP address of the machine you're directing the request to, and possibly a TCP/IP port if the Web server isn't running on the well-known port 80 for HTTP. The rest of the URL is an identifier used by the container to locate the servlet; it's the part that's the `requestURI` in the previous equation.

By the Way

URI Versus URL

You might be wondering what the difference between a URI (Uniform Resource Identifier) and a URL (Uniform Resource Locator) is. Simply put, a URI identifies some kind of an object or resource by name. A URL includes specific information about how to access the resource, such as a scheme (http or ftp) or location. Because a name can include locator information, a URL is a kind of URI. `http://www.ietf.org/rfc/rfc2396.txt` defines both in detail.

Every application has a **context**. You'll learn more about contexts in later hours, but they're basically a way to distinguish one application and its resources from another. The `contextPath` part of the `requestURI` identifies the context for the application. The `contextPath` is also sometimes called the **application prefix**.

The `servletPath` is the part that we're mostly concerned about when we are defining a `url-pattern`. It's this part that the `url-pattern` tries to match. If the `url-pattern` successfully matches something here, the container has identified the servlet it's going to invoke. The syntax for `url-pattern` defines these mappings:

- A string beginning with "/" and ending with "/*" is used for path-mapping. The container will examine the portion of the URI following the `contextPath` and attempt to make the longest possible match to determine which servlet is invoked. The part of the URI that follows the matched portion is the `pathInfo`. A servlet can use this for its own purposes.
- A string beginning with "*." is an extension mapping.

- A string containing only a "/" character maps to an application's default servlet.
- Any other string requires an exact match.

Let's look at a few brief examples. We'll use Listing 2.2 as a basis for each mapping. Just picture the URL-mapping element changing while the rest remains the same.

If we used a `url-pattern` of "/myservlet/*" we could invoke our servlet with any URL whose `servletPath` started with "/myservlet/". These include

```
http://localhost:8080/myservlet/

http://localhost:8080/myservlet/onemorelevel/
```

If we then changed to an extension mapping by using the `url-pattern` "*.bar", we could invoke our servlet with

```
http://localhost:8080/foo.bar
```

Changing the `url-pattern` to "/" makes our servlet the default servlet, which means that it will be invoked whenever a match for a URL cannot be found.

Finally, looking at the example as-is, we see that the `url-pattern` is "/hello", meaning that the URL for `HelloWorldServlet` will have to end with "/hello".

By the Way

`url-pattern`, `servletPath`, and `pathInfo`

In actuality, the `url-pattern` is what defines `servletPath` and `pathInfo`. The portion of the URI that matches the `url-pattern` becomes the `servletPath`. Anything that's left over becomes the `pathInfo`. However, when designing a `url-pattern`, it's easier to think of it the other way around, as we have in the text.

Creating the WAR File

You have created the `web.xml` file, and you are ready to package the Web application into a WAR file. The structure of the WAR files looks like this:

```
WEB-INF/
WEB-INF/web.xml
WEB-INF/classes/
WEB-INF/lib/
```

JSP, HTML, and Other Files and Directories

The WEB-INF directory contains the deployment descriptor and directories containing any class files (WEB-INF/classes) or JAR files (WEB-INF/lib). If you have any additional JSP, HTML, or other files, you can add them to the WAR file as well, outside of the WEB-INF directory. Under Windows, you can use the following statements to create a helloworld.war file for the HelloWorld application:

```
mkdir WEB-INF
copy web.xml WEB-INF
mkdir WEB-INF\classes
javac -d WEB-INF\classes HelloWorldServlet.java
jar cvf helloworld.war WEB-INF
```

Under Unix or Linux, the procedure is similar:

```
mkdir WEB-INF
cp web.xml WEB-INF
mkdir WEB-INF/classes
javac -d WEB-INF/classes HelloWorldServlet.java
jar cvf helloworld.war WEB-INF
```

Be Careful with Case

Depending on the platform, the case of directory names is significant. To be certain that your application works, make sure that WEB-INF/ is capitalized.

Deploying the WAR File

Different servlet containers use different procedures to install WAR files. If you are using Tomcat, you can simply copy the WAR file to the webapps directory under Tomcat's main directory and then restart Tomcat. When Tomcat starts, it looks for any WAR files in the webapps directory and then automatically unpacks them and makes the applications available for use. Tomcat won't install a WAR file that is already unpacked, so if you redeploy a WAR file, you must delete the old unpacked directory and restart Tomcat.

When you deploy a WAR file, you must specify the application context somehow. Tomcat uses the name of the WAR file as the name of the application context. For example, if you copy a WAR file named helloworld.war to the webapps directory, the application context is /helloworld/. If Tomcat is running on port 8080 on your local machine, then the full URL for the HelloWorld servlet is http://localhost:8080/helloworld/hello.

Although this packaging process seems a little cumbersome, you will see its usefulness in later hours. You can add additional information to the `web.xml` file that makes it easier to configure and manage your application.

To make the deployment process easier, you can use Apache's Ant configuration tool (`http://jakarta.apache.org/ant`) to automatically package a WAR file (you still need to create `web.xml` manually) and even deploy it to some servlet containers, including Tomcat. Or you can use the Web application manager provided with Tomcat to deploy and manage your applications. You can bring the manager up in a Web browser by using the address `http://localhost:8080/manager/html`—it is simple to use and is least error-prone.

Using Tomcat Manager

Tomcat's manager application isn't enabled with a default user and password. To use it (and the Administration tool), you'll have to add users with the appropriate rights to `tomcat-users.xml` in the `conf/` subdirectory of your Tomcat installation. See Appendix A, "Apache Tomcat," for instructions.

By the Way

The Anatomy of a Servlet

As you just saw in `HelloWorldServlet`, a **servlet** is a Java class that implements a few important methods. You can choose to implement these methods yourself or to create a subclass of an existing servlet class that already implements them. The `Servlet` interface defines the methods that are required for a Java class to become a servlet. The interface definition is shown in Listing 2.3.

LISTING 2.3 The Definition of the `Servlet` Interface

```
package javax.servlet;

public interface Servlet
{
    public void destroy();
    public ServletConfig getServletConfig();
    public String getServletInfo();
    public void init(ServletConfig config)
        throws ServletException;
    public void service(ServletRequest request,
        ServletResponse response)
        throws ServletException, java.io.IOException;
}
```

By the Way

For More Information on the Servlet 2.4 API

The complete servlet 2.4 API documentation is included in the Tomcat documentation (`http://jakarta.apache.org/tomcat/`) or in the J2EE 1.4 documentation (`http://java.sun.com/j2ee/1.4/docs/`).

Most of the time, you will create a servlet by subclassing either `GenericServlet` or `HttpServlet`. Both of these classes implement the `Servlet` interface, but they provide a few handy features that make them preferable to implementing the `Servlet` interface yourself.

The `service` Method

The heart of any servlet is the `service` method. As you just learned, the servlet container calls the `service` method to handle each request from a browser. By using `HttpServlet`, we avoided having to implement the `service` method because `HttpServlet` did it for us. However, this method is one you should know about. When calling the `service` method, the container passes in references to two objects: `ServletRequest` contains information about the request that invoked the servlet, and `ServletResponse` provides the mechanisms for sending back a response.

The `init` Method

Many times, a servlet needs to perform some initialization one time before it begins to handle requests. The `init` method in a servlet is called just after the servlet is first loaded, but before it begins to handle requests. Listing 2.4 shows a simple `init` method that initializes a database connection.

LISTING 2.4 `init` **Method from** `JDBCServlet.java`

```
protected Connection conn;

public void init()
{
    try
    {
// Make sure the JdbcOdbcDriver class is loaded.
        Class.forName("sun.jdbc.odbc.JdbcOdbcDriver");

// Try to connect to a database via ODBC.
        conn = DriverManager.getConnection(
            "jdbc:odbc:examples");
    }
    catch (Exception exc)
    {
```

LISTING 2.4 Continued

```
// If there's an error, use the servlet logging API.
        getServletContext().log(
            "Error making JDBC connection: ", exc);
    }
}
```

Notice that the `init` method in Listing 2.4, unlike the `init` method in the `Servlet` interface, does not take a parameter. One of the convenient features of the `GenericServlet` and `HttpServlet` classes is that they have an alternate version of `init` that doesn't take any parameters. In case you're wondering why it even matters, the `init` method in the `Servlet` interface takes a `ServletConfig` object as a parameter. The servlet is then responsible for keeping track of the `ServletConfig` object. The `GenericServlet` and `HttpServlet` classes perform this housekeeping chore and then provide the parameterless `init` method for you to do any servlet-specific initialization.

Watch Out!

Be Careful When Overriding `init`

If you override the `init(ServletConfig config)` method of `GenericServlet` or `HttpServlet`, make sure you call `super.init(config)` as the first statement in your `init` method so that the housekeeping will still be performed.

The `destroy` Method

Sometimes, the servlet container decides that it doesn't need to keep your servlet loaded anymore. This could happen automatically, or as the result of you deactivating the servlet with an administration tool. Before the servlet container unloads your servlet, it calls the `destroy` method to enable the servlet to perform any necessary cleanup. The cleanup usually involves closing database connections, open files, or network connections. Listing 2.5 shows the `destroy` method that is a companion to the `init` method in Listing 2.4.

LISTING 2.5 `destroy` Method from `JDBCServlet.java`

```
public void destroy()
{
    try
    {
// Try to close the connection only if it's non-null.
        if (conn != null)
        {
            conn.close();
        }
```

LISTING 2.5 Continued

```
    }
    catch (SQLException exc)
    {
// If there's an error, use the servlet logging API.
        getServletContext().log(
            "Error closing JDBC connection: ", exc);
    }
}
```

The `getServletInfo` and `getServletConfig` Methods

If you are subclassing `GenericServlet` or `HttpServlet`, you probably don't need to override the `getServletInfo` or `getServletConfig` methods. The Servlet API documentation recommends that you return information such as the author, version, and copyright from the `getServletInfo` method. Although there is no specific format for the string returned by the method, you should return only plain text, without any HTML or XML tags embedded within it.

The `getServletConfig` method returns the `ServletConfig` object that was passed to the servlet in the `init` method. Unless you are keeping track of the `config` object yourself, your best bet is to leave this method alone and let the superclass handle it.

Sending a Response to the Browser

Probably the biggest difference between a JSP and a servlet is in the way responses are sent back to the browser. In a JSP, most of the response is embedded in the JSP in the form of static text in a template. In the servlet, however, the response is usually in the form of code—mostly calls to `out.print` and `out.println`.

A minimal servlet needs to do two things to send a response: Set the content type and write the response. The `ServletRequest` and `ServletResponse` objects help out in these areas. References to these objects are provided to the servlet as parameters of the `service` method.

If you are new to Web programming, you are probably unfamiliar with the notion of **content type**. Even though every request you make to a Web server involves a content type, it has probably been invisible to you. Whenever a browser asks the server for a file, the server sends back a content type along with the file. The content type tells the Web browser how it should display the file. For instance, if the file is an HTML file, the content type is `text/html`, whereas a JPEG image file has a content type of `image/jpeg`.

Most Web servers determine the content type by looking at the extension on the filename (for example, `.htm` and `.html` indicate HTML files, whereas `.jpg` indicates a JPEG image). In the case of a servlet, however, the Web server can't guess what the servlet is going to send back. It could be sending back HTML, XML, WML, or even a JPEG image! Instead, the Web server relies on the servlet to tell it what is being returned.

As you saw earlier in Listing 2.1, you set the content type by calling the `setContentType` method in the `ServletResponse` object. If you already know the exact length of the response, you can also call the `setContentLength` method. If you are just sending an HTML response, you don't need to send the content length. The browser can figure it out.

Watch Out!

Set the Content Type Before Getting a `Writer`

Make sure you set the content type before you call `getWriter`. Because the servlet container depends on the content type when it modifies the character set mapping, it needs to know the content type before it creates the `Writer`.

After you have set the content type, you are ready to send the response. If you are sending a text response, as is the case with HTML and XML, you should use the `PrintWriter` object returned by `response.getWriter()`. If you are sending a binary file, such as a JPEG image, an audio file, or an animation file, you should use the `ServletOutputStream` returned by `response.getOutputStream()`.

By the Way

Use `PrintWriter` with Character Data

Although the `ServletOutputStream` class also contains `print` and `println` methods like the `PrintWriter` class, you should use the `PrintWriter` object when sending text output. Some content types require a slightly different character set, and the `PrintWriter` object automatically adjusts the character set based on the content type. In fact, the general rule of thumb with Java I/O is that you should always use a `Writer` object when writing character data.

You don't need to worry about closing the output stream when you finish writing out the response; the servlet container knows you are through when the `service` method has finished executing. In addition to giving you the output streams, the `ServletResponse` object performs other interesting tasks. You can control the amount of buffering, flush the output stream, and even clear the output stream.

ServletResponse is discussed in detail in Hour 6, "Looking under the Hood—Core Servlet Components."

The HttpServlet Class

You've seen that two prebuilt servlet classes are available for you to subclass, but so far you may not know why you would choose HttpServlet over GenericServlet. The main difference between the two is that HttpServlet has extra methods and special request-and-response objects that are geared toward HTTP. HttpServlet provides separate methods for handling the different types of HTTP requests (GET, POST, PUT, and so on). The two most common types of HTTP requests are GET and POST, which are handled by the doGet and doPost methods, like so:

```
protected void doGet(HttpServletRequest request,
    HttpServletResponse response)
    throws ServletException, java.io.IOException;

protected void doPost(HttpServletRequest request,
    HttpServletResponse response)
    throws ServletException, java.io.IOException;
```

As you can see, the doGet and doPost methods are of the same general form as the service method (you saw the doGet method in an earlier example). The service method of HttpServlet looks at the type of the HTTP request and then calls the appropriate handler methods. The HttpServletRequest and HttpServletResponse classes contain extra methods for dealing with HTTP. These classes are introduced more fully in the next few hours and discussed in detail in Hour 6.

Choosing Between JavaServer Pages and Servlets

Although you've just barely scratched the surface of JSPs and Servlets, now is a good time to talk about when to use servlets, when to use JSPs, and when to use both. To make such decisions, you need to weigh the advantages and disadvantages of each. Remember, too, that because JSPs are translated into servlets, they can't be all that different when you get right down to it.

The Advantages and Disadvantages of JSPs

The biggest strength of a JSP is that it looks like HTML (or XML or whatever kind of content you are generating). You can give a JSP to someone who is familiar with HTML and expect that person to be able to make changes fairly quickly. It is also quite obvious what the HTML will look like when it is sent to the browser. It is not always so obvious when Java code generates the HTML.

JSPs were developed to better separate content from code. Such separation makes it easier for Web page authors and software developers to do their jobs somewhat independently. The division better leverages the skills required for either job and makes it easier to develop reusable components. With JSP 2.0, significant improvements have been made that make it possible for authors and developers to be even more effective. Later in the book, you'll learn more about these.

A much more subtle advantage of JSPs, one that you may not have really encountered yet, is that when the JSP is turned into a servlet, that servlet is automatically loaded into the servlet container. When the JSP changes, its corresponding servlet is automatically regenerated and reloaded. When you are doing rapid development, it's great to be able to make quick changes and see them without having to restart the server. If you make a lot of changes to a lot of files, you don't have to worry about reloading all the changed files; the JSP container picks them up automatically.

Because JSPs eventually become servlets, it's difficult to point to any technical disadvantages of a JSP that aren't also present in servlets. The greatest disadvantage I've seen in practice is related to the greatest strength of JSPs: the capability to mix in Java code with HTML. If you aren't careful in organizing your code, you can end up with an ugly mess: huge JSP files with HTML interspersed between huge blocks of Java code. Things only get worse if you do a lot of JavaScript in the page, too. It can be terribly confusing to look at a page and not know whether you are looking at server-side Java code or client-side JavaScript. Fortunately, you will learn ways around this in the next few hours.

The Advantages and Disadvantages of Servlets

For the most part, the advantages of servlets are the disadvantages of JSP and vice versa. Because servlets are Java classes, you don't end up with a huge mess of Java, HTML, and JavaScript. Everything in your servlet is Java. Of course, when the servlet is generating HTML or XML, you might find that you still have a huge mess in the form of many `out.print` and `out.println` statements.

You were probably impressed by the differences in deployment. Most of the time, servlets must be packaged to be deployed. You needed to specify a special URL or at least a URL pattern (such as `/servlet/`) for executing a servlet, when for a JSP all you need to have is a filename that ends with `.jsp`. This makes your site configuration a little more tedious to maintain. However, as you develop Web applications that include many elements, you will find that packaging is actually a great thing. Finally, servlets are not always automatically reloaded by the servlet container, although most popular servlet containers do reload them automatically.

It probably sounds as if I'm biased in favor of JSPs, and I can't really dispute that—at least for early development. Because a JSP eventually becomes a servlet, you have the entire servlet API available to you from within the JSP. When it comes to deploying a full production system, however, it is often easier to manage servlets. Most of the configuration options in the JSP/Servlet deployment file (that is, `web.xml`) are oriented to servlets.

An interesting combination of servlets and JSPs that builds upon the strengths of each has become popular with developers. When the initial request comes in, it is handled by a servlet. The servlet performs any business logic, such as fetching data from the database, doing computations, or pulling data in from other sources. When it's time to send a response back to the browser, the servlet calls a JSP to render the output. This uses the strength of each of these technologies: The servlet is a simple Java class, whereas the JSP is a template geared toward generating output. You will learn more about this technique in Hour 20, "Building Web Applications with JavaServer Pages and Servlets" and in Hour 21, "Using Struts and JavaServer Faces."

Did you Know?

When Should I Use a Servlet for Output?

One rule of thumb that many Web developers use is that if you generate binary data like JPEG or audio files, use a servlet; if you generate text, use a JSP. Furthermore, use a JSP if you want to edit generated text directly. If you generate the text completely automatically (running an external command and displaying the output, for example), use a servlet.

If you take a little extra time, you can create a JSP that doesn't contain any Java code at all. It might seem a little strange to make a JSP with no Java code, but throughout the rest of this book, you will learn about built-in JSP tags that enable you to access Java objects as well as a tag extension mechanism that enables you to create new JSP tags. In addition, for those times when you do require some control within a JSP, JSP 2.0 adds the Expression Language as a higher-level programming feature. Using these features, you can easily eliminate embedded Java code, which some would argue is the best way to use JSPs.

It probably sounds a little too simplistic, but you should use the technology that best fits your requirements. If you have a lot of static HTML, XML, WML, or another textual markup language, use a JSP. If you are sending back binary data, such as an image or an audio file, a servlet is probably a better bet (not from a technical standpoint, just an aesthetic one).

Summary

Servlets are the foundation for JavaServer Pages. Whereas JSPs are composed mostly of HTML, servlets are pure Java. They use the Java class libraries and other platform libraries to perform functions, such as writing output, that are related to working with HTTP requests and responses. They must be compiled and then deployed into a container. Usually, they are accompanied by a deployment descriptor that provides the container with information such as how the servlet can be accessed by a Web browser.

A servlet, as might be expected, implements the `Servlet` interface. `Servlet` has a few methods for initializing and deactivating a servlet, for obtaining information about the servlet or its environment, or for servicing requests. The `service` method is the workhorse method and is invoked each time a servlet is used. When writing a servlet, programmers can extend `GenericServlet` or `HttpServlet` to take advantage of built-in functionality such as managing the `ServletConfig` object or methods that make working with HTTP requests easier.

Deciding when to use JSPs or servlets can be made easier by determining whether you are working primarily on producing “template” output, such as an HTML page, or whether you need to be more programmatic. It’s also valuable to try to reduce the mingling of presentation and low-level code as much as possible.

Q&A

Q. ***Why won't my servlet compile? The compiler reports that it can't find the*** `javax.servlet` ***package.***

A. Your classpath isn't set up correctly. You need to locate the `servlet-api.jar` file (it might have a different name) and add it to your classpath.

Q. ***I put my WAR file in Tomcat's*** `webapps` ***directory; why isn't Tomcat unpacking it?***

A. If Tomcat doesn't unpack the WAR file in the `webapps` directory, look in Tomcat's `logs` directory for an error or output file. If you are using Tomcat 4.0 or 5.0, look at the `catalina.out` file. It may contain errors relating to your WAR file. Also, make sure that the file is named `.war` and not `.jar`.

Q. ***Why does the Web server give me a*** `404` ***(***`File Not Found`***) error or a*** `500` ***(***`Internal Server Error`***)?***

A. This is usually either an installation problem or a classpath issue. One way to check the installation is to run one of the default servlets that comes with the servlet container. If you can't run one of the defaults, you need to check your servlet container's configuration and possibly reinstall it. If you can run the default servlet, but not your own, your classpath probably doesn't point to your servlet. Also, if you change the classpath after you have started the servlet container, you need to restart the servlet container to pick up the changes.

Workshop

The Workshop is designed to help you review what you have learned and help you to further increase your understanding of the material covered in this hour.

Quiz

1. What are the methods that the `Servlet` interface declares?
2. Why did the example use `HttpServlet`?
3. Where do the object references used to work with requests and responses come from?
4. How do you obtain a reference to an object that can be used to output to?

Answers

1. The `Servlet` interface declares the following methods: `init`, `destroy`, `service`, `getServletConfig`, and `getServletInfo`.

2. `HttpServlet` is an implementation of `Servlet` that provides methods that manage the `ServletConfig` object, and it is specialized to work with HTTP. It allows a servlet to handle `GET` or `POST` requests and works with other operations specific to HTTP. Using `HttpServlet`, the example only needed to implement `doGet` (overriding a method of `HttpServlet`) to be able to produce a response to an HTTP `GET` request from a browser.

3. References to instances of the classes `ServletRequest` and `ServletResponse` are passed as parameters to the `service` method. In the case of an `HttpServlet` object, references to instances of `HttpServletRequest` and `HttpServletResponse` are passed to the `doGet` method (as well as other methods that may need to interact with these objects).

4. The `getWriter` method of the `ServletResponse` or `HttpServletResponse` objects will return a Print`Writer` that you can output text to. If you need to obtain a stream to perform binary output, you can use `getOuputStream`.

Activities

1. Write another simple servlet that produces a slightly more complicated output. For example, produce a servlet that outputs an "address card" that consists of your name, an HTML horizontal rule (<HR>), your address and phone number.

2. Use the Tomcat application manager to deploy the servlet above.

HOUR 3

Creating HTML Forms

What You'll Learn in This Hour:

- How to use a JSP to receive form data
- How to work with form parameters
- How servlets interact with forms
- How to use a single JSP to present a form and handle its submission

By now you are probably comfortable with the fundamentals of JavaServer Pages and servlets. In the examples presented so far, you have learned how to send output back to the browser. One of the advantages of the Web is that you can create forms to send data from the browser to the server. You are finally ready to begin creating forms with JSP and servlets, and that's where the fun really begins!

A Simple HTML Form

To start off the exploration of HTML forms, it's best to start with a small form and expand from there. Also, it's better to start with a JSP rather than a servlet, because it is easier to write out the HTML. Most of the form handling for JSPs and servlets is identical, so after you know how to retrieve form information from a JSP, you know how to do it from a servlet. Listing 3.1 shows an HTML file containing a simple input form that calls a JSP to handle the form.

LISTING 3.1 Source Code for `SimpleForm.html`

```
<html>
<body>

<h1>Please tell me about yourself</h1>

<form action="SimpleFormHandler.jsp" method="get">

Name:  <input type="text" name="firstName">
    <input type="text" name="lastName"><br>
Sex:
    <input type="radio" checked name="sex" value="male">Male
    <input type="radio" name="sex" value="female">Female
<p>
What Java primitive type best describes your personality:
<select name="javaType">
    <option value="boolean">boolean</option>
    <option value="byte">byte</option>
    <option value="char" selected>char</option>
    <option value="double">double</option>
    <option value="float">float</option>
    <option value="int">int</option>
    <option value="long">long</option>
</select>
<br>
<input type="submit">
</form>
</body>
</html>
```

The `<form>` tag in Listing 3.1 sends the input from the form to a JSP called `SimpleFormHandler.jsp`. Figure 3.1 shows this form running in a browser.

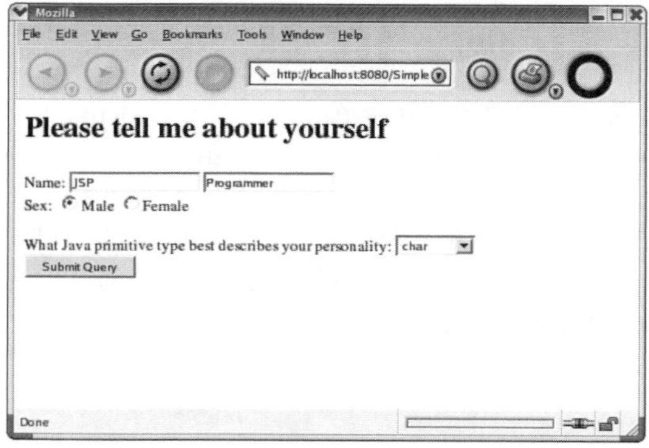

FIGURE 3.1 HTML forms frequently serve as the front end for a JSP.

The `SimpleFormHandler` JSP does little more than retrieve the form variables and print out their values. Listing 3.2 shows the contents of `SimpleFormHandler.jsp`, which you can see is pretty short.

LISTING 3.2 Source Code for `SimpleFormHandler.jsp`

```
<html>
<body>

<%

// Grab the variables from the form.
    String firstName = request.getParameter("firstName");
    String lastName = request.getParameter("lastName");
    String sex = request.getParameter("sex");
    String javaType = request.getParameter("javaType");
%>
<%-- Print out the variables. --%>
<h1>Hello, <%=firstName%> <%=lastName%>!</h1>
I see that you are <%=sex%>. You know, you remind me of a
<%=javaType%> variable I once knew.

</body>
</html>
```

By the Way

In Case of Trouble

If you are having trouble displaying the form, or some of the form results, see the "Q&A" at the end of this hour.

Most of `SimpleFormHandler.jsp` should seem pretty familiar to you. It is very similar to an example in Hour 1, "Getting Started with JavaServer Pages," that used the `<%= %>` tags to assign some variables and print out their values. The only new thing introduced in Listing 3.2 is the built-in `request` object. Every JSP has a few built-in objects. The most common ones are `out` and `request`.

The `out` object was introduced in Hour 1 and is the output stream used to send data back to the browser. The `request` object contains information about the request from the browser, and although it contains quite a bit of information, the `request` object is most commonly used for retrieving the values of form variables.

By the Way

The True Identity of `request`

The `request` object is really just an instance of `HttpServletRequest`. After you know how to use the `request` object in a JSP, you are ready to use the `HttpServletRequest` object in a servlet.

As you look at the `SimpleFormHandler` JSP, it should be pretty obvious what the output would look like. Just to make sure you've got it, Figure 3.2 shows how `SimpleFormHandler` looks when displayed in a browser.

FIGURE 3.2
A JSP can read form input and embed the form data in its output.

Using the `request` Object

As you saw in Listing 3.2, the `getParameter` method in the `request` object retrieves the values of the form variable. The lone argument to `getParameter` is the name of the form variable as it was defined in the HTML form, and must match the case exactly. In other words, if you called a form variable `firstName` in the HTML file, you must pass `firstName` to `getParameter` and not `firstname` or `FIRSTNAME`.

If you ask the `request` object for the value of a form variable that does not exist, it returns `null`. Note that `getParameter` always returns a string. If you are expecting a number, you have to convert it yourself.

Did you Know?

Form Variables: Empty or Null?

There is a difference between a form variable that is empty and a form variable that does not exist. The value of an empty text box is `""` (a string with a length of `0`). The `getParameter` method should return `null` only if a form variable does not exist at all.

Although the term **form variable** has been used here to describe the parameters passed to the JSP, these parameters technically have nothing to do with forms. When you press the Submit button on an HTML form, the browser encodes the form variables and uses one of two commands to pass them: an HTTP GET command or an HTTP POST command. Without getting down into the nitty-gritty of HTTP, parameters in a GET command are passed in the actual URL, whereas in a POST command they are passed in a different part of the request.

You may notice while surfing the Web that the URL displayed by the browser has a ? and some values of the form name=value separated by & characters. In fact, if you run the example and look at the URL in your browser's address textbox, you can see exactly that. The URL will look something like:

```
http://localhost:8080/SimpleFormHandler.jsp?firstName=JSP
      &lastName=Programmer&sex=male&javaType=char
```

If you wanted to, you could run SimpleFormHandler.jsp directly without going through the initial HTML form. All you would need to do is add the parameters to the end of the URL for your JSP or servlet.

By the Way

How Special Characters Are Encoded in URLs

URLs have a special encoding for many characters. For example, a space is represented by +. Many characters are represented by % followed by the character's ASCII value in hex. The = sign, for instance, is represented by %3D because its ASCII value is 61 decimal, or 3D hex. You may want to stick to characters and numbers when entering parameters by hand.

Why is this important? Well, it's often necessary to test a form handler, and it is much quicker to manually pass the parameters straight to the form handler than it is to type in the form values every time. Also, because all the form variables are encoded directly into the URL, you can bookmark the JSP in your browser and display the form output whenever you select that bookmark.

Bookmarking a JSP is not always useful, especially when the JSP is just accepting form input. But when the JSP is displaying updated information such as sports scores, weather, stock quotes, or other frequently changing data, bookmarking the page is quite useful. Unfortunately, if the data is sent to the server via an HTTP POST request, bookmarking doesn't work. The bookmark contains only the URL, and when form data is sent via POST, the URL does not include the form data. In the next hour, "How the Browser Interacts with the Server," you'll learn more about the GET and POST request methods.

Handling Multiple Form Values

The browser passes parameters to the server as a series of `name=value` pairs, as in `firstname=Sam` or `lastname=Tippin`. When there are multiple values for the same form variable name, the browser sends multiple `name=value` pairs. Listing 3.3 shows a simple input form with several text input fields.

LISTING 3.3 Source Code for `MultiForm.html`

```
<html>
<body>

<h1>Please enter a list of names</h1>

<form action="MultiFormHandler.jsp" method="get">
    <input type="text" name="names"><br>
    <input type="text" name="names"><br>
    <input type="text" name="names"><br>
    <input type="text" name="names"><br>
    <input type="text" name="names"><br>

    <input type="submit">
</form>
</body>
</html>
```

Figure 3.3 shows the form running inside a browser.

FIGURE 3.3
You can prompt the user with multiple values for the same form variable.

Notice that in Listing 3.3 the names of the fields are the same. If you were to use the getParameter method to fetch the names, you would get only the first one. When you need to fetch multiple parameters, use the getParameterValues method. Listing 3.4 shows a JSP that retrieves the values from the page in Listing 3.3.

LISTING 3.4 Source Code for MultiFormHandler.jsp

```
<html>
<body>
The names you entered are:
< pre>
<%
// Fetch the name values.
    String names[] = request.getParameterValues("names");

    for (int i=0; i < names.length; i++)
    {
        out.println(names[i]);
    }
%>
</ pre>

</body>
</html>
```

You need to know two things about the getParameterValues method:

- If the parameter value doesn't exist at all (that is, there was no form variable with that name), getParameterValues returns null.
- If there is exactly one parameter value, you still get back an array. The length of this array is 1.

You usually know the names of all the parameters you are expecting, but for cases where you need to discover the names of all the parameters passed in you can use the getParameterNames method. The method signature for getParameterNames in the request object is

```
java.util.Enumeration getParameterNames()
```

The getParameterNames method returns an enumeration of the string objects. Each of these strings is the name of a parameter and can be used as an argument to getParameter or getParameterValues. Listing 3.5 shows a JSP that dumps out the names and values of all the parameters passed to it, including multiple values.

LISTING 3.5 Source Code for ShowParameters.jsp

```
<html>
<body>
You passed me the following parameters:
< pre>
<%

// Find out the names of all the parameters.
    java.util.Enumeration params = request.getParameterNames();

    while (params.hasMoreElements())
    {
// Get the next parameter name.
        String paramName = (String) params.nextElement();

// Use getParameterValues in case there are multiple values.
        String paramValues[] =
            request.getParameterValues(paramName);

// If there is only one value, print it out.
        if (paramValues.length == 1)
        {
            out.println(paramName+"="+paramValues[0]);
        }
        else
        {
// For multiple values, loop through them.
            out.print(paramName+"=");

            for (int i=0; i < paramValues.length; i++)
            {
// If this isn't the first value, print a comma to separate values.
                if (i > 0) out.print(',');

                out.print(paramValues[i]);
            }
            out.println();
        }
    }
%>
</pre>
</body>
</html>
```

Figure 3.4 shows the output from the JSP shown in Listing 3.5. You can easily play around with the ShowParameters JSP by passing parameters without an input form by entering them in the browser's address line. Figure 3.4 illustrates the result of using two parameters in the URL

http://localhost:8080/ShowParameters.jsp?param1=One¶m2=Two

FIGURE 3.4
You can pass parameters to the JSP manually by adding them to the end of the URL.

Retrieving Form Variables in a Servlet

Up to this point, the discussion has centered around the `request` object in JSPs. The `request` object in a JSP is an instance of `HttpServletRequest`.

In Hour 2, "JavaServer Pages Behind the Scenes," you saw servlets that received requests via the `doGet` method. This works fine for receiving form data via an HTTP `GET` request, but it will not work for data sent via an HTTP `POST` request. There are at least two other ways to receive a request in a servlet. First, you can implement a `doPost` method, which is invoked only if the browser posts data to the servlet. Second, you can implement the `service` method, which receives data whether it was sent via a `GET` or a `POST` request. It is best to receive form data via the service method, because it lets you send data to the servlet via `GET` or `POST`. By implementing only `doGet` or only `doPost`, you limit the ways to access the servlet. The `service` method, just like `doGet` and `doPost`, takes an `HttpServletRequest` and an `HttpServletResponse` as parameters. The `HttpServletRequest` is the same object as the `request` object in a JSP. This means, of course, that you already know how to retrieve form variables in a servlet because you do it the same way you do in a JSP.

Did you Know?

Handling GET and POST with doPost

If you extend `HttpServlet` and want to neatly handle both GETs and POSTs using the same code, you can override `doPost` this way:

```
public void doPost(HttpServletRequest req, HttpServletResponse res)
                            throws ServletException, IOException
{
doGet(req, res);
}
```

Listing 3.6 shows a servlet version of the `ShowParameters` JSP you saw in Listing 3.5. Again, you can test it out by passing parameters directly in the URL.

LISTING 3.6 Source Code for ShowParametersServlet.java

```
package examples;

import javax.servlet.*;
import javax.servlet.http.*;
import java.io.*;
import java.util.*;

public class ShowParametersServlet extends HttpServlet
{
    public void service(HttpServletRequest request,
        HttpServletResponse response)
        throws IOException
    {
// Tell the Web server that the response is HTML.
        response.setContentType("text/html");

        PrintWriter out = response.getWriter();

        out.println("<html>");
        out.println("<body>");
        out.println("You passed me the following parameters:");
        out.println("<pre>");

// Find out the names of all the parameters.
        Enumeration params = request.getParameterNames();

        while (params.hasMoreElements())
        {
// Get the next parameter name.
            String paramName = (String) params.nextElement();

// Use getParameterValues in case there are multiple values.
            String paramValues[] =
                request.getParameterValues(paramName);

// If there is only one value, print it out.
            if (paramValues.length == 1)
            {
                out.println(paramName+
```

LISTING 3.6 Continued

```
                    "="+paramValues[0]);
            }
            else
            {
// For multiple values, loop through them.
                out.print(paramName+"=");

                for (int i=0; i < paramValues.length; i++)
                {
// If this isn't the first value, print a comma to separate values.
                    if (i > 0) out.print(',');

                    out.print(paramValues[i]);
                }
                out.println();
            }
        }

        out.println("</pre>");
        out.println("</body>");
        out.println("</html>");
    }
}
```

The output from `ShowParametersServlet` is identical to the output from the `ShowParameters` JSP. In fact, the core part of both programs is the same. The only difference is the code to print out the beginning and ending HTML tags.

Different Ways to Do Forms

As with most flexible programming tools, you can arrange your JSP form handling code in a number of ways. Three of the most common arrangements of forms and their handlers are

- A static HTML input form calling a JSP form handler
- A JSP input form calling a separate JSP form handler
- A single JSP page that displays the form and handles the input

By the Way

Adding to the Mix—Using JSP and Servlets Together

You can organize your JSPs in many other ways, especially when you mix servlets with JSPs. Hour 20, "Building Web Applications with JavaServer Pages and Servlets," provides several other examples.

The HTML page shown way back in Listing 3.1 and the JSP in Listing 3.2 are examples of a static HTML form calling a JSP form handler. This form of Web programming has been the most popular for years—dating back to the origin of CGI programs. Many developers prefer to keep their Web sites as pure HTML, using JSP, servlets, or other server-side technologies only for handling form data.

Using a JSP input form isn't much different than a static HTML input form. However the possibilities are greatly expanded by the dynamic nature of JSPs. For example, instead of having fixed text or fields, you could read in a file or access a database to define the text or fields. Remember that, using JSPs, you have all of the facilities of the Java platform at your disposal.

The last commonly used arrangement is a little trickier, so we'll spend a moment discussing it.

Using the Same JSP for the Input Form and Form Handler

You might think it's a little strange, but putting the input form and the form handler in the same JSP page is sometimes a good idea. Typically, you combine the input form and form handler when the user needs to use the form multiple times, possibly seeing the results of the previous form submission.

For example, you might have a page for entering an order where you display the current order and allow the user to enter new items for the order. At the beginning of the page you handle the new order items entered by the user and then display the current order. At the end of the page you display the form to add new entries.

The first time the user hits the page, you can detect that there is no form data to process and just present the initial input form. After that, when you detect the presence of previous form data you can process it. There are a few different techniques you can use to detect the form data:

- Look for the presence of form variables.
- Pass a special variable indicating that this is a form submission.
- Submit the form using the HTTP `POST` method and examine the request method in your form.

Looking for the form variables is the easiest of these methods. You may occasionally find times when it doesn't suit you, though. For example, you may pass in a set of form variables to the input form the first time it is displayed. The seed values might be embedded in the URL and passed from the Web page that led the user to the current input form. You wouldn't be able to tell the difference between the initial seed values and a form submission. Even so, this method should work for you most of the time.

In the case where you pass initial values to the input form, you can create a hidden variable on the form with an additional parameter, like `"isSubmitted"`. The declaration in HTML would look like this:

```
<input type="hidden" name="isSubmitted" value="yes">
```

When the user accesses the form for the first time, you don't see this variable because the user hasn't submitted the input form. You can check to see whether `request.getParameter("isSubmitted")` returns `null` or not. If it returns `null`, the form was not submitted.

Sometimes you don't even want to go through the hassle of testing to see whether the form variables are there. You want to know right away whether the form was submitted. If a hyperlink is used to access the initial form (that is, the browser accesses the form with an HTTP `GET`) and you declare the method for the `<form>` tag to be `POST`, you can use `request.getMethod()` to determine whether the user actually submitted the form.

In other words, you set up your form like this:

```
<form action="someaction.jsp" method="POST">
```

You then use `request.getMethod` to see whether the form was submitted:

```
if (request.getMethod().equals("POST"))
```

Summary

Forms are an important aid to making the Web interactive. With JavaServer Pages, handling forms is easy—they do most of the work required to get to the information submitted with a form. Sometimes, constructing the form itself is more work than writing the handler.

Information from forms is submitted using either the `GET` or `POST` request methods. You can construct the equivalent of a `GET` request by appending a "?" along with the name-value pairs for each variable. This is very useful for testing handlers and can save you quite a bit of time.

JSPs and servlets can give you information about form parameters, including their name and values. If a parameter name occurs more than once in a submission, you can use the method `getParameterValues` to get to each instance. As you would naturally expect, the way you use servlets to handle form submissions is fundamentally the same. Several combinations of forms and handlers are available for you to use in your application. Now that you have some experience with using JSP and servlets to build and handle forms, you can select the most appropriate for your needs and preferences.

Q&A

Form and Form Variable Names

Q. ***I press the Submit button, but the form won't load. What am I doing wrong?***

A. Aside from checking for spelling errors in the action attribute of the `<form>`, you must also make sure that the capitalization action attribute matches the name of the form JSP. Even if you are running under Windows, Java is case sensitive, so you can run into problems if you use capitalization that is different from the actual filename when you try to invoke a JSP.

Q. ***Why are the form variable values null?***

A. If you can't get the value of a form variable, the reason is usually because the name of the variable in the form doesn't exactly match the name you use in the `getParameter` method, either because of a spelling difference or a capitalization difference.

Workshop

The Workshop is designed to help you review what you have learned and to help you to further increase your understanding of the material covered in this chapter.

Quiz

1. What are the names of the two objects discussed in this hour that are "built into" JSPs?
2. The `getParameter` method is used to obtain the value of a form variable. What object is this method part of?
3. Explain the difference between the `doGet` and `doPost` methods of `HttpServlet`.

Answers

1. Several objects are made available to JSPs. The two implicit objects that are discussed in this chapter are

   - `out`, which provides a stream to write output content to.
   - `request`, which is a reference to an instance of `HttpRequest`. It's used to access many of the attributes of the HTTP request that triggered the service invocation, including the names of any form names and values.

2. `getParameter` is a method of `HttpRequest` and is available through the `request` implicit object.

3. These methods are used to handle HTTP `GET` and `POST` request methods, respectively. The default implementation for either indicates that the method is not supported. You must override the methods in order to be able to work with the request types you are interested in handling.

Activities

1. Write an HTML form that includes a checkbox and other HTML form elements. Make the form use the `GET` request method. Write a JSP handler that returns the values for each element.

2. Change the form above to use the form `POST` method. Discover whether any changes are required to handle a `POST`. Look at the generated source code for the JSP.

HOUR 4

How the Browser Interacts with the Server

What You'll Learn in This Hour:

- What HTTP is
- About HTTP request and response headers and their component pieces
- What the differences between the `GET` and `POST` request methods are
- What Secure HTTP is

Even if you didn't realize it, you have used some form of a response or request object in every example thus far. In the simplest JavaServer Pages you have studied, the operations that use these objects were hidden from you. For example, the implicit `out` object is acquired behind the scenes using the `getWriter` method from an instance of `HttpServletResponse`. In the last hour, you used the implicit `request` object to discover the values of form variables. Requests and their responses are at the heart of most JSP and servlet operations.

All servlets and JSPs use a request-response programming model. Servlets are capable of working with any kind of request—making them suitable for servicing quite a few Internet protocols based on the request-response model. Servlets are commonly used to work with the Hypertext Transfer Protocol, or HTTP, and so there is a specialized class, `HttpServlet`, designed to make it easier for you. JSPs almost always work exclusively with HTTP. Because so much of what is done with JSPs and servlets revolves around HTTP, it's worth spending an hour exploring the protocol.

The Hypertext Transfer Protocol

Most of the time, a browser uses HTTP to communicate with the Web server. In some cases the browser uses File Transfer Protocol (FTP) and communicates with an FTP server, but overall, HTTP carries the bulk of Web traffic. Most people wouldn't recognize the HTTP protocol if it bit them, and there's really nothing wrong with that. Even as a Java programmer, you don't need to know the specifics of HTTP because you have the `URL` and `URLConnection` classes to handle communications from the client side, and servlets and JSP to handle the server side of things.

However, it's almost always better to know more than you absolutely need to, especially in the computer industry. That little extra bit of understanding can help you diagnose problems faster, understand the implications of architectural decisions better, and use all the capabilities a system has to offer.

An HTTP connection is a simple network socket connection. The Web server usually listens for incoming connections on port 80. After the connection is established, the browser sends a few lines of text indicating which Web page it wants to see, some request headers telling the Web server what kind of browser is making the request, and a few other interesting items, such as the browser user's preferred language, the kinds of data the browser accepts, and even the kind of browser (Netscape, Internet Explorer, Opera, and so on).

The only part of the request that is required is the first line, which tells the server what file the browser wants. The rest is optional. Each line in the request is a human-readable text line, separated by a newline character. The request header ends with a blank line. The protocol is so simple that you can even use the `telnet` command to interact manually with a Web server.

For example, you can view the "Hello World" JSP from Hour 1, "Getting Started with JavaServer Pages," by telneting to port 80 on your Web server (or whatever port your Web server is running on, like Tomcat's default of 8080), entering `GET` *`path`* `HTTP/1.0`, and pressing Enter twice. The *`path`* in an HTTP request is the portion of the URL that comes after the hostname and includes the leading `/`. Thus, if you access `HelloWorld.jsp` with `http://localhost:8080/HelloWorld.jsp`, you enter `/HelloWorld.jsp` as the path.

Figure 4.1 shows a Telnet session requesting and receiving the HelloWorld JSP.

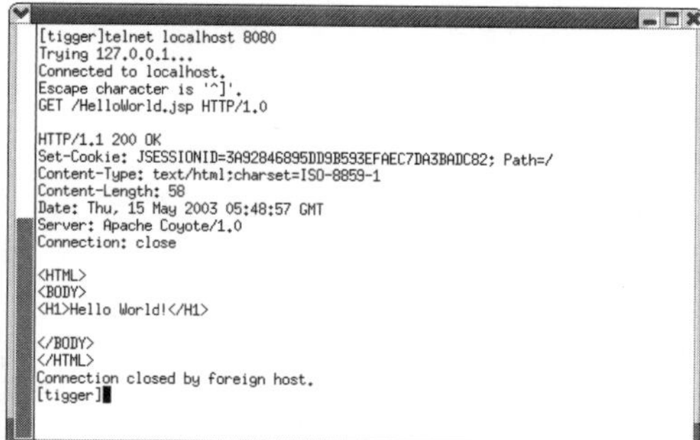
[tigger]telnet localhost 8080
Trying 127.0.0.1...
Connected to localhost.
Escape character is '^]'.
GET /HelloWorld.jsp HTTP/1.0
HTTP/1.1 200 OK
Set-Cookie: JSESSIONID=3A92846895DD9B593EFAEC7DA3BADC82; Path=/
Content-Type: text/html;charset=ISO-8859-1
Content-Length: 58
Date: Thu, 15 May 2003 05:48:57 GMT
Server: Apache Coyote/1.0
Connection: close
<HTML>
<BODY>
<H1>Hello World!</H1>
</BODY>
</HTML>
Connection closed by foreign host.
[tigger]

FIGURE 4.1
You can interact with a Web server directly by using the `telnet` command.

By the Way

Why Can't I See What I'm Typing?

You might need to turn on local echo in your Telnet window to see what you are typing. Also, if you make any typing errors, don't be surprised if the Web server doesn't understand the Backspace key and complains that you sent it a garbled command.

Turning local echo on or off varies depending on the client you use. If you are using the Microsoft Telnet Client, you can type "set LOCALECHO" at the telnet command prompt. If you have already connected to a host, you'll need to move to the command prompt by typing ctrl-]. To leave the command prompt, press the "Enter" key at the command prompt.

Many command line telnet clients allow you to turn local echo on by typing "toggle echo" at the command prompt. If that doesn't work, consult your documentation.

Notice that the request to the server said that it was using version 1.0 of HTTP (the `HTTP/1.0` at the end of the `GET` request), and that the server responded with version 1.1 of HTTP. HTTP version 1.1 adds a number of options that can optimize Web access and enable the browser to retrieve multiple pages over a single connection.

Under HTTP 1.1, an additional line must be present in each request. You must specify the name of the host you are accessing. This is important in multihomed hosts in which a single Web server supports many host names.

Figure 4.2 shows a Telnet session that again fetches the `HelloWorld.jsp` file, this time using HTTP 1.1.

[tigger]telnet localhost 8080
Trying 127.0.0.1...
Connected to localhost.
Escape character is '^]'.
GET /HelloWorld.jsp HTTP/1.1
Host: localhost
HTTP/1.1 200 OK
Set-Cookie: JSESSIONID=946552507CB49A570CE32F5E66A51E9D; Path=/
Content-Type: text/html;charset=ISO-8859-1
Content-Length: 58
Date: Thu, 15 May 2003 05:50:42 GMT
Server: Apache Coyote/1.0
<HTML>
<BODY>
<H1>Hello World!</H1>
</BODY>
</HTML>

FIGURE 4.2
HTTP 1.1 requires you to specify a hostname in the request.

Notice that the Web server did not automatically close down the connection as it did when you used HTTP/1.0. One of the optimizations of HTTP 1.1 is that a browser can use the same connection to make multiple requests. Setting up a connection is a time-consuming process, so leaving a connection open can be a real time-saver. You can force the server to close the connection by specifying `Connection: close` in the request. Figure 4.3 shows a Telnet session that asks the server to close the connection.

```
[tigger]telnet localhost 8080
Trying 127.0.0.1...
Connected to localhost.
Escape character is '^]'.
GET /HelloWorld.jsp HTTP/1.1
Host: localhost
Connection: close

HTTP/1.1 200 OK
Set-Cookie: JSESSIONID=D08F6097592EB166803D1F6565869ABF; Path=/
Content-Type: text/html;charset=ISO-8859-1
Content-Length: 58
Date: Thu, 15 May 2003 05:51:56 GMT
Server: Apache Coyote/1.0
Connection: close

<HTML>
<BODY>
<H1>Hello World!</H1>

</BODY>
</HTML>
Connection closed by foreign host.
[tigger]
```

FIGURE 4.3
If you want the server to automatically close the connection in HTTP 1.1, you must explicitly say so.

Viewing the Request Headers Made by a Browser

A browser sends quite a bit more information than the minimum. The request object has methods that enable you to retrieve all the header values the browser sends. Listing 4.1 shows a JSP file that displays all the headers sent to it.

LISTING 4.1 Source Code for DumpHeaders.jsp

```
<html>
<body>
<pre>
<%
    java.util.Enumeration e = request.getHeaderNames();

    while (e.hasMoreElements())
    {
        String headerName = (String) e.nextElement();
        out.print(headerName+": ");

        java.util.Enumeration h = request.getHeaders(headerName);

        while (h.hasMoreElements())
        {
            String header = (String) h.nextElement();
            out.print(header);
            if (h.hasMoreElements()) out.print(", ");
        }
        out.println();
    }
%>
</pre>
</body>
</html>
```

Figure 4.4 shows the headers sent to `DumpHeaders.jsp`.

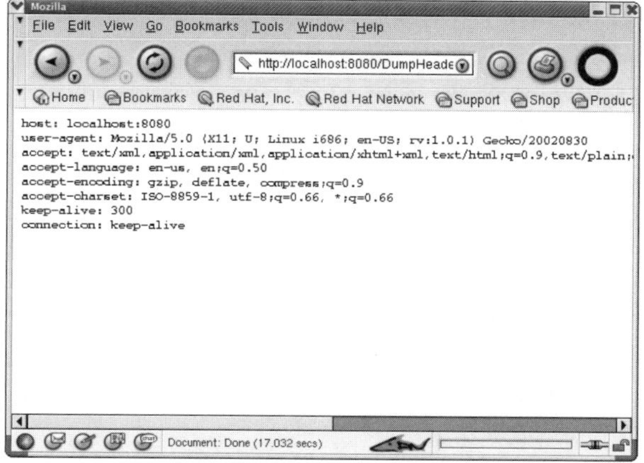

FIGURE 4.4
A JSP or servlet can examine all the request headers.

How can you be sure that you are really seeing all the header values? Because HTTP works over a simple socket connection, you can create a program that accepts an incoming connection and dumps out anything sent to it.

Listing 4.2 shows the `Dumper.java` program you can use to verify that you are seeing all the header values.

LISTING 4.2 Source Code for `Dumper.java`

```
import java.net.*;
import java.io.*;

public class Dumper
{
    public static void main(String[] args)
    {
        try {
            int portNumber = 1234;
            try {
                portNumber = Integer.parseInt(System.getProperty("port"));
            } catch (Exception e) {
            }
            ServerSocket serv = new ServerSocket(portNumber);

            for (;;) {
                Socket sock = serv.accept();
                InputStream inStream = sock.getInputStream();
                int ch;
                while ((ch = inStream.read()) >= 0) {
                    System.out.print((char) ch);
                }
                sock.close();
            }
        } catch (Exception e) {
            e.printStackTrace();
        }
    }
}
```

Figure 4.5 shows the output from the Dumper program. When you run Dumper on your local machine, point the browser to the URL `http://localhost:1234`. Because the Dumper program doesn't understand HTTP and doesn't know to shut down the connection, you need to either click the Stop button on your browser or terminate the Dumper program.

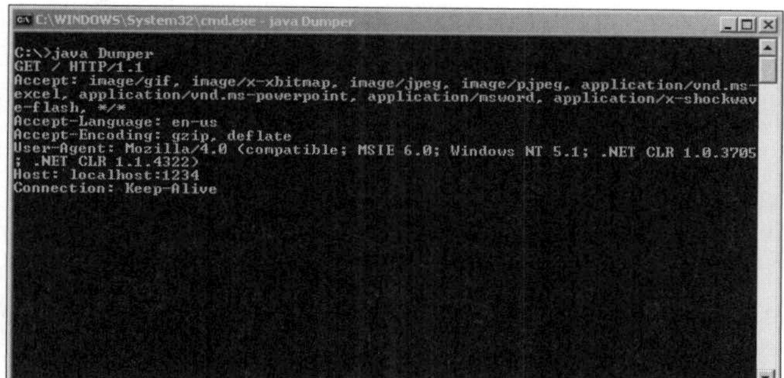

FIGURE 4.5
You can use a simple socket program to view the headers sent by a browser.

By the Way

In Case of Trouble

If you are having trouble accessing the Dumper program, see the "Q&A" at the end of this hour.

Common Request Headers

The headers you saw in Figures 4.4 and 4.5 represent the most common set of request headers you'll receive. Netscape browsers might also send an `Accept-Charset` request header. This section explains those headers in a little more detail.

The `Accept` Header

The `Accept` header indicates the kind of content the browser can accept. The order of the items is typically the order the browser prefers. In other words, when the browser lists `text/xml` before `text/html` it says that it prefers XML documents to HTML documents. Usually, you'll see `*/*` at the end of the list, meaning that the browser accepts anything, but it prefers those it has already listed.

By the Way

Values and Options Vary Between Browsers

Figure 4.4 was produced using Mozilla and Figure 4.5 using Internet Explorer. Although the browsers won't vary from the protocol requirements, the values and optional elements are quite a bit different. For example, notice all of the Microsoft applications Internet Explorer is willing to accept.

If you look at the `Accept` header sent by a wireless phone, you'll see that it lists HTML text and bitmap images after the `*/*`, indicating that it prefers just about anything to HTML or bitmaps! Here is the `Accept` header sent from a wireless phone:

```
Accept: application/x-hdmlc, application/x-up-alert, application/x-up-cacheop,
   application/x-up-device, application/x-up-digestentry, text/x-hdml;
           version=3.1,
   text/x-hdml;version=3.0, text/x-hdml;version=2.0, text/x-wap.wml,
   text/vnd.wap.wml, */*, image/bmp, text/html
```

The `Accept-Language` Header

The `Accept-Language` header gives you a hint as to what language the browser prefers (actually, the browser's user, because the browser doesn't speak human languages). For English, you might see just `en` or you might see `en-us` or `en-uk` specifying English for a particular locale such as the United States or the United Kingdom. You can use this header to provide language-specific content automatically. You'll learn more about this idea in Hour 22, "Internationalization."

The `Accept-Charset` Header

If present, the `Accept-Charset` header indicates the preferred character set(s) that the browser accepts. For Netscape running in an English-speaking locale, you'll most likely see this kind of header:

```
Accept-Charset: iso-8859-1,*,utf-8
```

The `User-Agent` Header

Of all the headers sent by the browser, the `User-Agent` header is probably the most useful because it indicates what kind of browser is making the request. Oddly, both Netscape and Internet Explorer identify themselves as Mozilla, which was the nickname for the early Netscape browser. (There is now a browser called Mozilla, which was born from the code for Netscape 5.)

By the Way

Mozilla—A Monster Browser

In case you're wondering where the name *Mozilla* came from, Netscape was founded by the folks who wrote the old Mosaic Web browser. Netscape Navigator was intended to be a monstrous version of Mosaic: the Godzilla Mosaic, or Mozilla.

When Internet Explorer (IE) first came out, it lagged behind Netscape in usage, and gradually added features to become a reasonable alternative by the time IE version 3 came along. By identifying itself as Mozilla-compatible, IE is telling the Web server that it can handle anything Mozilla can.

If you want to figure out whether the browser is Netscape or IE, only IE sends the `MSIE` string as part of its `User-Agent` header. Thus, you can do the following test in your JSP or servlet:

```
if (request.getHeader("USER-AGENT").
    indexOf("MSIE") >= 0)
{
    // do Internet Explorer specific stuff here
}
else
{
    // do Netscape specific stuff here
}
```

You can perform similar tests to detect other browsers, such as Opera.

By the Way

In Case of Trouble

If you are having trouble seeing request headers you are expecting, see the "Q&A" at the end of this hour.

Common Response Headers

If you look all the way back to Figure 4.1, you'll see a typical response sent by a Web server. There are many variations of response headers, but relatively few that you need to worry about when you write Java Web applications.

The `Content-Type` Header

The `Content-Type` header is the most important response header. It tells the browser how to interpret the data it receives. A JSP has a default content type of `text/html`, although you can use a JSP page directive to change the content type. If you are returning XML data, for instance, you use a content type of `text/xml`.

The `Content-Length` Header

The `Content-Length` header is important for many types of content that contain binary data. It tells the browser exactly how many bytes are in the body of the response. That way the browser can read the full response without worrying about whether it has received everything.

The `Cache-Control` Header

The `Cache-Control` header allows you to control how long the browser keeps a particular page cached. As you saw in Figure 4.1, a JSP normally isn't cached at all. You can request that a page be cached for 5 minutes (300 seconds) by using the following response header:

```
Cache-Control: maxage=300
```

By the Way

Should I Remember You?

The `Cache-Control` header controls only whether the browser uses the cache the next time it loads a page; it does not force the browser to reload the page when it expires. To reload a page after a specific period of time, include the tag

```
<META HTTP-EQUIV="Refresh" Content = "30; URL=YourJSPUrlHere.jsp">
```

in your JSP or HTML file. The `30` in the tag is the number of seconds to wait before refreshing.

The HTTP `POST` Command

So far, the only HTTP command you have seen in this hour is the `GET` command. You are aware that another command, the `POST` command, is frequently used to send form information to the Web server. Technically, the `POST` command might be used for more than just form data, but form data is by far the most common kind of data sent via `POST`.

When a browser sends a `POST` command, the first line of the request looks just like the `GET` request, except that instead of `GET`, the command is `POST`. The difference comes about just after the request header. In a `GET` request, there is no data after the request header. After the server sees the blank line indicating the end of the header, it processes the request. In a `POST` request, the browser sends the form data after the header. The format of the data is a series of `name=value` pairs separated by &s. In addition, the data values are URL-encoded, just like the values in a `GET` request. Notice, also, that the content type for a `POST` request is `application/x-www-form-urlencoded`.

Listing 4.3 shows a bare-bones form that posts its data to the Dumper program so you can see what a POST request looks like.

LISTING 4.3 Source Code for PostForm.html

```
<html>
<body>
<form action="http://localhost:1234" method="post">
<input type="text" name="foo" value="Foo!"><br>
<input type="text" name="bar" value="Bar?"><br>
<input type="text" name="baz" value="<<BAZ>>"><br>
<input type="submit">
</form>
</body>
</html>
```

Figure 4.6 shows the output from the Dumper program after it receives a POST request.

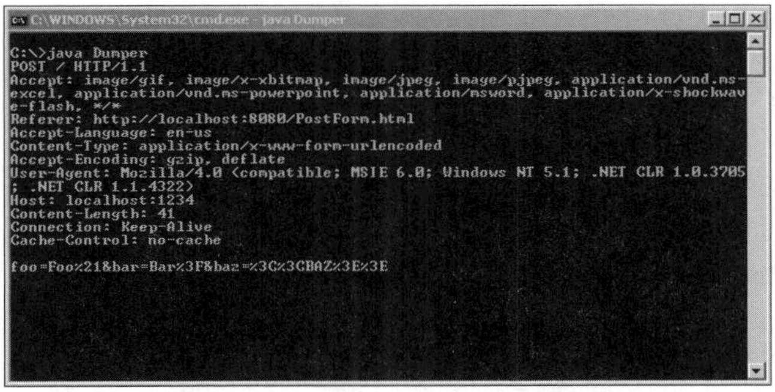

```
C:\WINDOWS\System32\cmd.exe - java Dumper
C:\>java Dumper
POST / HTTP/1.1
Accept: image/gif, image/x-xbitmap, image/jpeg, image/pjpeg, application/vnd.ms-
excel, application/vnd.ms-powerpoint, application/msword, application/x-shockwav
e-flash, */*
Referer: http://localhost:8080/PostForm.html
Accept-Language: en-us
Content-Type: application/x-www-form-urlencoded
Accept-Encoding: gzip, deflate
User-Agent: Mozilla/4.0 (compatible; MSIE 6.0; Windows NT 5.1; .NET CLR 1.0.3705
; .NET CLR 1.1.4322)
Host: localhost:1234
Content-Length: 41
Connection: Keep-Alive
Cache-Control: no-cache

foo=Foo%21&bar=Bar%3F&baz=%3C%3CBAZ%3E%3E
```

FIGURE 4.6
A POST request sends form data in the body of the request.

By the Way

In Case of Trouble

If you are having trouble accessing the Dumper program, see the "Q&A" at the end of this hour.

Notice that a content type and content length are in the request. No matter which direction the data is going, if you are sending content, you need to specify a content type and usually a content length.

GET Versus POST

You might wonder why someone would choose to do a GET rather than a POST or vice-versa. Why is there even a choice? When you use the GET request to send form data, you're really taking advantage of a performance hack. By appending the form variables to the end of the pathname, you simplify the work that the server needs to do, because it takes a little more work to read posted data. For example, the corresponding `GET` request for the form data posted from the `PostForm` page looks like this:

```
GET /?foo=Foo%21&bar=Bar%3F&baz=%3C%3CBAZ%3E%3E HTTP/1.1
```

There is a limit to the length of the pathname for a `GET` request, however. So if the total length of your form variables is fairly long, more than 4KB, you can't use a `GET` request at all. Some servers won't even accept 2KB in a pathname. If you think the total length of your form data could be anywhere near the limit, you should use a `POST` rather than a `GET`.

In addition to the size limitations, there are other reasons to choose `POST` over `GET` or vice-versa. If you use the `GET` request to submit a form, and then bookmark the resulting page, the bookmark contains the form variables because they are part of the URL. You might consider this a good thing because it saves the user from having to type in the data. It might also be a bad thing, though, if one of the form items is a password. Not only is the password now saved as a bookmark, defeating the purpose of requiring a password, but also the password is visible in the browser's address window.

Did you Know?

Protecting Your Form Data

If your form contains sensitive data, such as a password, use `POST` rather than `GET`. Although it does not protect the information as it goes across the wire, at least sensitive information does not appear in an address in a browser window, or even as a bookmark.

HTTPS: Secure HTTP

You might notice that when you visit a Web site that wants you to enter a credit card, the URL usually begins with `https` instead of `http`. The browser recognizes `https` as a request to use secure sockets to pass the data. The Secure Sockets Layer (SSL) enables you to send encrypted data back and forth between the browser and the server. (Technically, it just provides encrypted traffic between any two endpoints, not specifically between browsers and servers.)

The nice thing about using HTTP over SSL is that the HTTP protocol is still the same—it's just the transport layer that has changed. For example, if you have an

SSL library that you can use with the Dumper program, you can connect to the dumper with `https` and still see the HTTP headers exactly as you see them with an unencrypted connection. Figure 4.7 shows the relationship between the HTTP protocol and the SSL protocol as compared to an unencrypted HTTP connection.

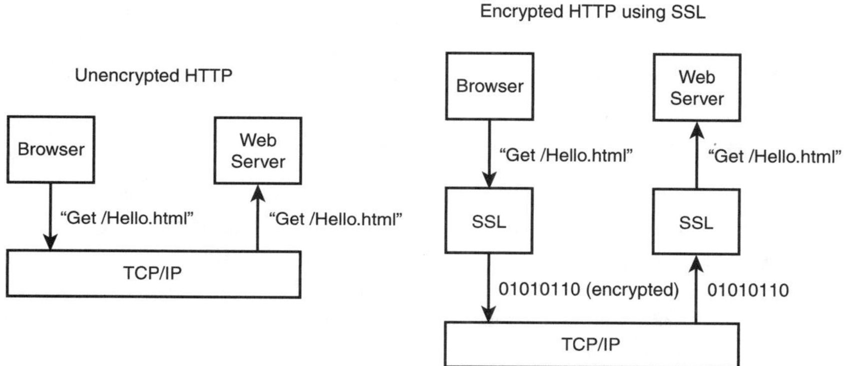

FIGURE 4.7
The SSL takes the place of a regular TCP/IP socket connection when sending encrypted HTTP traffic.

Summary

As you can see, HTTP is not terribly complicated. However, it is important. JSPs and servlets are designed to make working with HTTP easier. Although much of the handling of the details isn't immediately visible to you, knowing something about HTTP is useful. Many of the concepts in the coming hours will be clearer to you.

HTTP, like many other Internet protocols, is based on a request-response model. You've seen that the protocol is human-readable and now have an understanding of most of the elements of HTTP headers. You also understand the difference between HTTP `GET` and `POST` request methods.

Secure HTTP, or HTTPS, makes it possible to send and receive HTTP over a secure communications channel, so that information is not compromised. Yet, HTTP still operates the same and can be dealt with by JSPs or servlets in the usual way.

Q&A

Q. ***Why don't I see the same headers coming from Netscape as I do from Internet Explorer?***

A. Request headers are more like hints than required fields. The browsers aren't required to send any headers (although for HTTP `POST` they must send a content type). Therefore, there's no way to guarantee that different vendors will send the same information. You should write your application so it works even if there are no headers.

Q. ***Why does Internet Explorer identify itself as Mozilla?***

A. When Internet Explorer first appeared on the scene, the Netscape browser was the most popular browser. Because many Web sites checked for the Netscape browser, Internet Explorer originally identified itself as "Mozilla-compatible" so it could take advantage of all the Netscape-oriented features. Although it is now more popular than Netscape, Internet Explorer still identifies itself as Mozilla compatible. Look for the string MSIE in the User-Agent header and you'll be able to identify Internet Explorer.

Q. ***I started the Dumper program; why can't my browser access it?***

A. Did you remember to put the :1234 after the hostname? The Dumper program operates on a port number other than 80 (the default HTTP port).

Q. ***I remembered the :1234 in the URL, so why can I still not access the Dumper program?***

A. Make sure you aren't using a Web proxy from your browser. Some proxies won't access nonstandard ports. If the Dumper program is running on a separate host from your browser, make sure there isn't a firewall between your browser and the program. If you're running this from home, you probably don't have a firewall.

Workshop

The Workshop is designed to help you review what you have learned and help you to further increase your understanding of the material covered in this hour.

Quiz

1. Which TCP/IP port does an HTTP server listen on?
2. When using a servlet to produce an HTML response, which header field must be set prior to writing to the output stream?
3. Give one reason to use an HTTP `GET` request method rather than a `POST` request method to submit information.

Answers

1. HTTP servers typically use the well-known port 80. Tomcat's internal Web server listens on port 8080 by default. Web Servers that support HTTPS use port 443.
2. When using a servlet, you must set the content-type header field like this:

   ```
   response.setContentType("text/html");
   ```

   It isn't necessary to do this for a JSP—it defaults to this.
3. A common reason for using the `GET` request method is because URLs are almost always completely parsed. Using `POST`, programs have to do some additional work to get to the posted data. However, the performance loss is negligible. A better reason to use `GET` is so that the URL can be bookmarked.

Activities

1. Write a JSP that examines the HTTP header to detect which browser made a request. Output text to indicate your finding.
2. Using the software you created for the exercises in Hour 3, "Creating HTML Forms," change the form targets to `DumpHeaders.jsp` and look at the headers.

HOUR 5

JSP and Servlet Lifecycles

What You'll Learn in This Hour:

- How servlets are created, used, and destroyed
- How JSPs are created, used, and destroyed
- How containers manage "live" changes to JSPs, servlets, and other classes
- How to use the servlet application events facilities

Now that you understand the major features of JSPs and servlets, it's time to drill down into some of the underlying structure. So far, you have learned how to use JSPs and servlets to service requests or create responses as part of an application.

Unlike ordinary Java objects, where you control when an object is created and destroyed, JSPs and servlets are created and managed by containers that interact with a Web server. When the Web server determines that a request is destined for a Web component such as a JSP or servlet, it passes control to the container, which then causes the appropriate component to take care of the request. The container is responsible for instantiating, using, and destroying objects. Leaving these functions to the container relieves you from considerable overhead. The container can create and use or reuse as many objects as required to service the workload, resulting in enhanced scalability—and you don't have to worry about anything other than writing the next great application.

It is important to understand the JSP and servlet lifecycle: when and how servlets and JSPs are loaded, executed, and unloaded. Because JSPs are also servlets, it makes sense to start with servlets.

Servlet Lifecycle

A servlet goes through four phases:

1. Loading
2. Initialization
3. Execution
4. Cleanup

Servlet Loading

A servlet can be loaded at three different times:

- When the server starts up
- When the system administrator asks the server to load the servlet
- When a browser tries to access the servlet

Servlet engines provide a way for you to list the servlets you want to load during startup. Although the actual loading of the servlet might take a reasonably short time, the servlet might have a costly initialization phase. By loading and initializing a servlet early, you can improve the server's response time.

For example, suppose your servlet creates several database connections during initialization and then reads and caches some data from the database. If you wait until a browser first accesses the servlet, users will experience a much longer wait than usual while the servlet performs its initialization. If you load the servlet when the server starts, the server might take a little more time to start, but users will not see any delays after everything starts. If you restart the server during periods of low usage, users might never see the slowdown from initialization.

To load a servlet, the server needs to know the classname for the servlet. Normally, the classname is the name of the servlet for which the browser asks. When a servlet is within a Java package, the servlet name contains the fully qualified Java classname. For example, a servlet class named `HelloWorldServlet` in the package `examples` would have a servlet name of `examples.HelloWorldServlet`.

But how does the servlet engine know that you are asking it to run a servlet? In the examples you have seen so far, the URL was `http://localhost:8080/servlet/examples.HelloWorldServlet`. It's not the word "Servlet" at the end of the classname that gives the server its cue; it's the `/servlet/` right before the servlet name.

About halfway through Hour 2, "JavaServer Pages Behind the Scenes," you learned about servlet mapping using a URL pattern. A typical servlet container recognizes a special servlet name called `invoker`. The container might not actually have a servlet named invoker; it's just a special name that the container recognizes. When configuring the container, you set up the `/servlet` path by mapping `/servlet/*` to the servlet named `invoker`. Then whenever the servlet engine sees a URL starting with `/servlet/`, it extracts the servlet name from the URL and invokes the servlet.

By the Way

Getting to Know `web.xml`

If you're using Tomcat, you may have made a change to `web.xml` in the `conf/` directory of your Tomcat installation to enable this mapping for the examples in Hour 2. It's a great idea to take a moment to review that change and become reacquainted with that portion of `web.xml`.

You can also map specific URLs to specific servlets. For example, you could map the URL `/HelloWorld` to run the `HelloWorldServlet` program. You can save a little time by mapping servlet names directly, because the server doesn't have to extract a servlet name from the URL as it does when you use the invoker.

After the servlet engine knows it needs to run a servlet, it checks to see whether that servlet is already loaded in memory. If not, the servlet engine uses Java's class loading features to load the servlet into memory. After the servlet is loaded, the servlet engine initializes it and the servlet is ready to go.

Servlet Initialization

When the servlet engine initializes a servlet, it calls the servlet's `init` method, passing it a `ServletConfig` object. The `init` method is declared like this:

```
public void init(ServletConfig config)
    throws ServletException
```

The `ServletConfig` object contains initialization parameters and a `ServletContext` object. The initialization parameters are items that you can configure within your servlet engine that are specific to a servlet. They are set up in the deployment descriptor as part of the definition of the servlet itself. Adding an initialization parameter to the deployment descriptor is as easy as adding one or more init-param elements as children to the servlet element. Here's an example:

```
<servlet>
…
<init-param>
    <param-name>parameter</param-name>
    <param-value>value</param-value>
</init-param>
…
</servlet>
```

The following methods in ServletConfig enable you to find out what initialization parameters exist and the value of each parameter:

```
public java.util.Enumeration getInitParameterNames()
public String getInitParameter(String name)
```

Servlet initialization parameters can be used for a number of things, such as providing a path to a resource that the servlet uses.

The ServletConfig object also gives you access to the ServletContext object. ServletContext provides the servlet with a view of its runtime environment within a Web application. All of the components associated with a Web application have a view of the same context, making the context a place that is frequently used to exchange information or provide access to common services. You will frequently use the context to provide access to logs or databases. More information about ServletContext will be provided in Hour 6, "Looking Under the Hood—Core Servlet Components."

Understanding Default Context

If you don't explicitly define a context, such as when you drop a JSP into the webapps/ or webapps/ROOT/ folder without any deployment descriptor, your JSP belongs to a "default" context.

Although a Web container provides initial access to ServletContext object, a servlet is responsible for keeping track of its ServletContext object. Rather than dealing with the ServletConfig object and keeping track of the ServletContext yourself, you can just make your servlet a subclass of GenericServlet or HttpServlet (which itself is a subclass of GenericServlet). These objects perform the housekeeping for you.

`GenericServlet` and `HttpServlet` provide an additional `init` method that doesn't take any arguments:

```
public void init() throws ServletException
```

This simplified `init` method is provided as a convenience for servlets that need to perform initialization. Without this `init` method, you would need to override the normal `init` method and then call `super.init`, like this:

```
public void init(ServletConfig config)
    Throws ServletException
{
    super.init(config);

    // Perform servlet-specific initialization here.
}
```

Did you Know?

Override the Simplified `init` Method

You should override the simplified `init` method to perform any servlet-specific initialization.

In Case of Trouble

If you are having trouble with a servlet when there is an `init` method, see the "Q&A" section at the end of this hour.

Servlet Execution

A servlet spends most of its time in the execution phase of its lifecycle. When a request comes in, the servlet engine invokes the servlet's `service` method, passing references to `ServletRequest` and `ServletResponse` objects as parameters.

Although the lifecycle's execution phase is fairly obvious, the full path of the request from browser to servlet might not be so obvious. Figure 5.1 shows the path a request takes from the browser all the way to the service method.

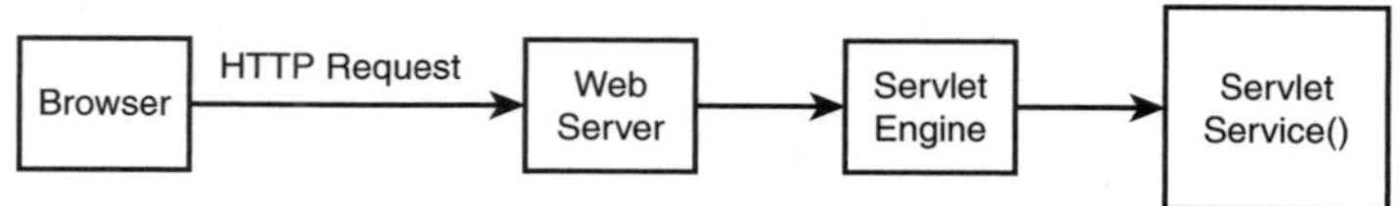

FIGURE 5.1
The Web server handles the communications with the browser while it passes data to the servlet.

The fact that the Web server handles the communications with the browser might seem insignificant, but there is one interesting point. Until recently, there hasn't been an official Secure Sockets Layer (SSL) API from Sun, yet servlets and JSPs have been able to support SSL since the Servlet API first came out. As long as your Web server supports SSL, you don't need SSL support in your Java environment. By the time requests get to your application, they don't look any different than requests that arrived using an insecure channel.

However, just because you are able to access your JSPs and servlets through SSL, don't automatically assume that you have an SSL API available for use from your Java code. If you have a servlet that must make a direct SSL request to another server somewhere, you may need to install the SSL package from Sun. As of JDK 1.4, SSL has been a part of Java 2 Standard Edition. If you use an earlier version of Java, you must install the Java Secure Sockets Extension (JSSE), available at http://java.sun.com/products/jsse.

Servlet Cleanup

When the servlet engine decides to unload a servlet (by administrator request, for performance reasons, or for system shutdown), it invokes the servlet's `destroy` method. The `destroy` method is a courtesy method to give servlets a chance to release any allocated resources that might be so precious that you can't afford to wait for garbage collection to reclaim them. For example, if your servlet allocates a large number of database connections, you should release them when the servlet is destroyed. Otherwise, it might take a while before the system reclaims them.

Although you probably don't need to worry about cleanup if the whole servlet engine is shutting down, you still need to provide for the possibility that the servlet engine will want to unload the servlet, or that you might want to manually unload it.

JavaServer Page Lifecycle

A JSP has an extra phase in its lifecycle, because it must also be compiled. The phases of a JSP's lifecycle are

1. Compilation
2. Loading
3. Initialization
4. Execution
5. Cleanup

JSP Compilation

When a browser asks for a JSP, the JSP engine first checks to see whether it needs to compile the page. If the page has never been compiled, or if the JSP has been modified since it was last compiled, the JSP engine compiles the page. The compilation process involves first parsing the JSP, turning the JSP into a servlet, and then compiling the servlet.

You can circumvent the compilation process by manually generating a servlet for the JSP and compiling it by hand. In Hour 24, "Performance," you'll learn how to do this.

By the Way

Changing JSP Source After Hand Compilation

If you compile the JSP by hand but then change the JSP source file later, the JSP engine will recognize that the JSP must be recompiled. If you want to control the compilation totally, you must deploy your application with a Web Archive file (WAR), which is discussed in detail in Appendix B, "Packaging a Web Application." You can also set up a URL mapping that forces `YourPageName.jsp` to run a specific servlet, avoiding the JSP compiler altogether.

JSP Loading

Because a JSP becomes a servlet before it is actually loaded, the loading process for a JSP is similar to the loading process for a servlet. The main difference between a JSP and a servlet is that the class file for the JSP may be reloaded, if a newer version of a JSP source file is found.

Reloading Associated Classes

Although a JSP class may be reloaded, any associated classes, such as JavaBeans or utility classes, are not always reloaded automatically. Some JSP engines might automatically reload other classes, but don't count on it.

JSP Initialization

Although a JSP is compiled into a servlet, JSP developers should not override the underlying servlet `init` and `destroy` methods. If you need to perform JSP-specific initialization, override the `jspInit` method:

```
public void jspInit()
```

As with the servlet `init` method, you generally initialize database connections, open files, and create lookup tables in the `jspInit` method.

You might wonder if there's something similar to the `ServletConfig` object available to a servlet. After all, it does seem pretty useful to be able to access initialization parameters or the Web application context. In fact, there are a few implicit objects available to you: `config` is a reference to the `ServletConfig` object for the JSP, and `application` is a reference to the `ServletContext` object.

Only one problem remains: How do you associate initialization parameters with a JSP? From Hour 2, recall that a servlet has an entry in a deployment descriptor that looks like this:

```
<servlet>
    <servlet-name>HelloWorldServlet</servlet-name>
    <servlet-class>examples.HelloWorldServlet</servlet-class>
...
</servlet>
```

Any properties that are specific to a servlet will be defined as part of the servlet element. So far, we've only named the servlet and identified the class file. Earlier in this chapter you saw how to associate an initialization parameter with a servlet by adding an `init-param` element.

Fortunately, you don't have to try and guess what the name of the class that is produced by compiling a JSP will be. There's an alternate form especially for JSPs:

```
<servlet>
    <servlet-name>HelloWorldJSP</servlet-name>
    <jsp-file>/HelloWorld.jsp</jsp-file>
…
</servlet>
```

You use this exactly as you would a servlet declaration; that is, you can add an `init-param` element.

JSP Execution

Whenever a browser requests a JSP and the page has been loaded and initialized, the JSP engine invokes the `jspService` method in the JSP. The `jspService` method takes an `HttpServletRequest` and an `HttpServletResponse` as its parameters.

Never Override the `jspService` Method

Because the JSP compiler generates the `jspService` method, you should never try to override this method yourself.

Watch Out!

JSP Cleanup

The `jspDestroy` method is the JSP equivalent of the `destroy` method for servlets. Override `jspDestroy` when you need to perform any cleanup, such as releasing database connections or closing open files. The `jspDestroy` method is declared this way:

```
<%!
    public void jspDestroy()
    {
        // Your cleanup code goes here.
    }
%>
```

Reloading Other Classes

When you change a JSP, the JSP engine automatically reloads it the next time a browser requests it. Some servlet engines even reload a servlet when it changes. Many engines, however, do not automatically reload associated classes. In other words, when you create a Java class that is a companion to a JSP and you change that companion class, it isn't reloaded even if the JSP itself is reloaded.

For example, the JSP in Listing 5.1 calls a static method in an external class to retrieve a message.

LISTING 5.1 Source Code for `ReloadTest.jsp`

```
<%@ page language="java" import="examples.*" %>
<html>
<body>

The message is: <%= ReloadedClass.getMessage() %>
</body>
</html>
```

Listing 5.2 shows the `ReloadedClass` class that returns the message.

LISTING 5.2 Source Code for `ReloadedClass.java`

```
package examples;

public class ReloadedClass
{
   public static String getMessage()
    {
         return "This is the original message";
    }
}
```

Now when you run `ReloadTest.jsp`, you get the kind of result shown in Figure 5.2.

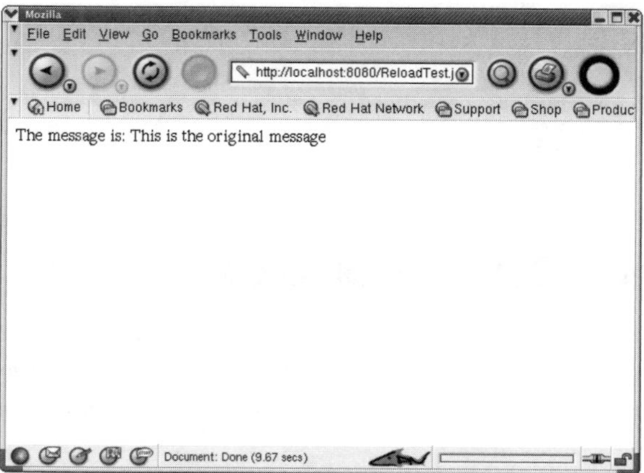

FIGURE 5.2 The JSP engine automatically loads the `ReloadedClass` Java class.

Now suppose you change the message to return a different message, like this:

```
return "This is the new message";
```

When you recompile the Java class and reload the JSP, you will not notice any change because the JSP engine is still holding on to the original.

Now suppose you change the `ReloadTest` class to have a slightly different message, like:

```
The new message is: <%= ReloadedClass.getMessage() %>
```

When you reload the JSP, the JSP engine recompiles the page, but the screen still looks the same. When the JSP engine loads the recompiled servlet into memory, it sees that it already has ReloadedClass in memory, so it doesn't bother to reload it again.

Now, if you restart the JSP engine and display the page again, you can see that the changed `ReloadedClass` class finally gets reloaded as shown in Figure 5.3.

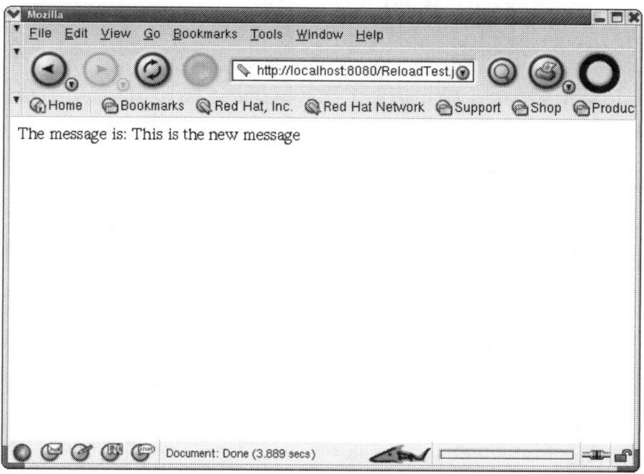

FIGURE 5.3
When the JSP engine is restarted, it picks up the changed `ReloadedClass` class.

Did you Know?

Using WAR Files

If you package your application in a WAR file and deploy it to the server using a deployment tool, the server usually refreshes all the classes in the WAR file automatically. It's a great idea to use Apache's ANT tool to automate the compiling, repackaging, and deploying of a Web application.

In Case of Trouble

If you are having trouble reloading classes, see the "Q&A" section at the end of this hour.

Application Lifecycle Events

You can imagine that there are resources that are shared among JSPs and servlets. For example, there might be a common facility to perform logging, or perhaps some global initialization data. The `ServletContext` object is frequently used to provide access to shared services or resources. Using it, Web application developers can obtain initialization parameters, store attributes by name, and access resources such as GIFs that have been packaged in the WAR file.

During the lifecycle of an application, other objects come into play also. You have worked with the `ServletRequest`, for example. Although, so far you've only worked with short-lived requests that are serviced by a single JSP or servlet, a `ServletRequest` can interact with a number of Web application components. And, although we haven't discussed it yet, the `HttpSession` object is another that may persist beyond the service methods of a JSP or servlet.

In particular, you can monitor changes in attributes or the lifecycle of these objects. Collectively, the objects and operations that provide this capability are known as the **application event facilities**.

Using Listeners

A servlet context is created by a container when an application starts up. By implementing `ServletContextListener`, you can perform actions relating to the initialization and closing of the application. The methods of `ServletContextListener` are

```
public void contextInitialized ( ServletContextEvent sce );
public void contextDestroyed ( ServletContextEvent sce );
```

A container will invoke `contextInitialized` when the application is created and `contextDestroyed` when it is shut down. The parameter, `ServletContextEvent`, provides access to the servlet context.

Listing 5.3 is an example of a `ServletContextListener` that records information to a system log when an application starts up or is shut down.

LISTING 5.3 **Source Code for** `MyAppListener.java`

```
package examples;

import java.io.*;
import javax.servlet.*;
import javax.servlet.http.*;

public class MyAppListener
        implements ServletContextListener {

    public void contextInitialized(ServletContextEvent event) {
        ServletContext context = event.getServletContext();
        context.log("***ShowLifecycles - Created the servlet context");
    }

    public void contextDestroyed(ServletContextEvent event) {
        ServletContext context = event.getServletContext();
        context.log("***ShowLifecycles - Destroyed the servlet context");
    }
}
```

In each case this simple example obtains the servlet context from the `ServletContextEvent` and outputs text into one of the container's logs.

Listing 5.4 is a companion JSP that logs its own lifecycle events.

LISTING 5.4 **Source Code for** `ShowLifecycles.jsp`

```
<html>
<body>

<%!
    public void jspInit()
    {
        log("***ShowLifecycles.jsp  - Invoked jspInit()");
    }
%>
<%!
    public void jspDestroy()
    {
        log("***ShowLifecycles.jsp - Invoked jspDestroy()");
    }
%>

```

LISTING 5.4 Continued

```
    log("***ShowLifecycles.jsp - Invoked jspService()");
%>

The current date is: <%= new java.util.Date() %>
</body>
</html>
```

The only thing tricky about this JSP is the `log` method itself. Reading the JSP specification, you might note that there is no specific mention of the `log` method. However, remember that a JSP ultimately becomes a servlet; `log` is a method of `GenericServlet`, which in most cases is a superclass of the servlet generated by the JSP container.

By the Way

For Your Convenience

The `log` method is actually a **shortcut** method. It's usually equivalent to the `log` method that is part of the `ServletContext` and saves you the trouble of having to call getServletContext().log().

Since the container must somehow know about a `ServletContextListener` that is defined for an application, you would expect that you have to add an entry into the application deployment descriptor. Listing 5.5 show the content of `web.xml` for this application:

LISTING 5.5 Source Code for `web.xml`

```
<?xml version="1.0" encoding="ISO-8859-1"?>
<web-app xmlns="http://java.sun.com/xml/ns/j2ee"
    xmlns:xsi="http://www.w3.org/2001/XMLSchema-instance"
    xsi:schemaLocation="http://java.sun.com/xml/ns/j2ee
    http://java.sun.com/xml/ns/j2ee/web-app_2_4.xsd"
    version="2.4">
    <display-name>ShowLifecycles</display-name>
    <description>An example of how to use lifecycle events</description>

    <listener>
        <listener-class>
            examples.MyAppListener
        </listener-class>
    </listener>
</web-app>
```

This is the first time you've seen a deployment descriptor associated with a JSP. It's necessary because we're defining a Web application that includes a JSP and a `ServletContextListener`. Fortunately, the deployment descriptor doesn't look terribly different. The only part of it that is new to you is the listener element, which defines the class that responds to lifecycle events for the application.

After compiling `MyAppListener.java`, the WAR file is created by placing the files in the directories as shown:

```
ShowLifecycles.jsp
WEB-INF/web.xml
WEB-INF/classes/examples/MyAppListener.class
```

The `jar` utility neatly packages these into a WAR file using the command

```
jar cfv ShowLifecycles.war *
```

The application can now be deployed. If you use Tomcat's application manager, it's easy to deploy the application; and you will be able to stop the application so that you can see the results when the servlet context is destroyed.

To start the application, point your browser to

```
http://localhost:8080/ShowLifecycles/ShowLifecycles.jsp
```

By the Way

Understanding Context Paths

Remember that Tomcat adds a URL prefix. In this case, because the WAR file was named `ShowLifecycles.war`, the URL prefix is `/ShowLifecycles`. This is actually a **context path**, which is used to identify the context programmatically.

What we are interested in is in the container's log files. For Tomcat you'll find them in `logs/`. The particular file will be named `localhost_log.`*`date`*`.txt`, where *`date`* is the date the log was created. Of course, you'll want the most recent one. Other servlet containers put logs in different places. Check your documentation for the location and names.

If you examine the log for your JSP/servlet container, you will see entries that look like this:

```
2003-05-16 12:45:08 HTMLManager: install: Installing web application at 'null'
     from  'jar:file:/opt/jakarta-tomcat-5/webapps/ShowLifecycles.war!/'
2003-05-16 12:45:08 ***ShowLifecycles - Created the servlet context
2003-05-16 12:45:58 jsp: ***ShowLifecycles.jsp - Invoked jspInit()
2003-05-16 12:45:58 jsp: ***ShowLifecycles.jsp - Invoked _jspService()
2003-05-16 12:46:08 HTMLManager: stop: Stopping web application at
        '/ShowLifecycles'
```

```
2003-05-16 12:46:08 ***ShowLifecycles - Destroyed the servlet contex
2003-05-16 12:46:08 jsp: ***ShowLifecycles.jsp - Invoked jspDestroy()
```

Here you can see that the following steps occurred:

1. The `ShowLifecycles` application was installed.
2. The servlet context was created at the same time.
3. The JSP was loaded and initialized.
4. The JSP's `jspService` method was invoked.
5. If you stopped the application, the servlet context was destroyed.
6. `jspDestroy` was invoked in the JSP.

In addition to receiving notifications about application lifecycle events, you can also find out when an attribute that is associated with the application is added, changed, or removed. Simply implement the `ServletContextAttributeListener` and add the listener to the deployment descriptor in the same way you did for the example. Attributes are discussed in additional detail in Hour 6.

Following the same pattern, you can observe lifecycle events and attribute changes for `ServletRequest` and `HttpSession` objects.

Using a `ServletRequestListener`, you can discover when a request has started to be processed by your application.

A `ServletRequestAttributeListener` will let you know when an attribute is added, modified, or deleted from a `ServletRequest`.

An `HttpSession` object is used to create a session between an HTTP client and server that lasts across multiple requests. In essence, it provides a way to store the state of an application or user while using the stateless HTTP protocol. You'll learn more about HTTP sessions in the next hour. Like its siblings, you can use `HttpSessionListener` and `HttpSessionAttributeListener` to track the creation and destruction of a session, or changes to attributes associated with a session.

Summary

In this hour you learned that servlets and JavaServer Pages have distinct phases that they go through during their existence as part of a Web application. Containers are responsible for loading, instantiating, initializing, using, and destroying Web application components. As part of these activities, the container will invoke lifecycle methods, such as `jspInit` or `jspDestroy`, to allow you the opportunity to perform component specific operations.

JSPs must be compiled by a container before they can be used. A JSP container will compile a JSP when necessary. On the other hand, some containers will not update servlets, even if their class files have changed. In any case, classes that are part of the Web application and are not servlets are usually not reloaded. To be certain that all of the components are refreshed, package them in a WAR and redeploy the application rather than replacing individual pieces. Tools like Apache's Ant make this process much easier.

You can also monitor events that occur at the application level by writing a listener and registering it with a container. This is useful for managing resources that are shared by all of the Web application components. Several interfaces for listeners exist that permit you to know when an application is loaded or unloaded, when it begins to process a request, or when sessions are created or destroyed. In addition, you can learn about changes to attributes that are associated with a servlet context, request, or HTTP session.

Q&A

Q. ***I added an* `init` *method to my servlet; why can't I run it now?***

A. If your servlet was working before and the only thing you changed was the `init` method, there's a pretty good chance your `init` method is throwing an exception. If the `init` method throws an exception, the servlet engine stops loading it and it won't run. Check your server's error logs to see whether any exceptions are there.

Q. ***Why does my servlet act strangely when I have defined an* `init` *method?***

A. If you override the `init(ServletContext ctx)` method rather than the simpler `init()` method, and you forget to call `super.init(ctx)`, your servlet won't be properly initialized and might act strangely.

Q. ***My JSP recompiled; why do I still see old data?***

A. If your JSP depends on other classes that have changed, you must reload these classes. Most JSP engines must be restarted before they pick up changed classes.

Q. ***I restarted my JSP engine; why didn't it pick up the changed classes?***

A. Make sure that the class file the JSP engine is using has been changed. If you copy class files from one place to another, you might have an old copy of the class file somewhere that is closer to the front of the classpath than the class file you just regenerated. Your operating system probably has a utility to search for files with a particular name (`Start->Search->"For Files or Folders...` under Windows, or `find` in Unix). Also, if you left any `.java` files in the directory where your JSP is, the JSP engine might have compiled those files and put them in its own class file directory. Again, searching for class files should locate any such files.

Q. ***Why isn't my listener working even though I added it to the deployment descriptor?***

A. The listener element in the deployment descriptor is a subelement of the `web-app` element. Also, it must be placed prior to any servlet elements. Listeners will be invoked in the order they are declared.

Workshop

The Workshop is designed to help you review what you have learned and help you to further increase your understanding of the material covered in this chapter.

Quiz

1. What is the purpose of the `ServletConfig` object?
2. When is a servlet or JSP destroyed?
3. Which interface in the application event facilities is best used to initialize resources that are used for the duration of a request?

Answers

1. A `ServletConfig` object provides access to JSP or servlet specific initialization parameters and to a servlet context. It can also give you the name of the servlet or JSP as defined in the deployment descriptor.
2. A servlet or JSP is only destroyed when the application or container is shut down, or when the container decides to unload the JSP or servlet for some reason. (It may do this for performance.) They are not destroyed at the end of processing a request; remember that Web components are often reused.
3. An object that implements `ServletRequestListener` is appropriate. This interface will let you know when servicing a request begins and when the request is about to be destroyed.

Activities

1. Write a JSP that reads several initialization parameters and outputs them to a Web page.
2. Run the listener example and reload the browser page so that the JSP is invoked more than once. Note which events occur each time the JSP is invoked.
3. Extend the example to use a `ServletRequestListener` so that you can see when requests begin to be processed.

HOUR 6

Looking Under the Hood—Core Servlet Components

What You'll Learn in This Hour:

- The ServletRequest and HttpServletRequest classes
- The ServletResponse and HttpServletResponse classes
- How to use the ServletInputStream and ServletOutputStream classes to perform input and output
- How to use the application-wide classes `ServletContext` and `HttpSession`

It may have become pretty apparent that it's tough to separate JavaServer Pages from servlets if you are building Web applications. Although this is true to some degree, later in the book you will learn how to build fairly sophisticated applications without having to know much about servlets. JavaServer Pages 2.0 has made impressive gains in this area by giving the JSP developer some higher-level programming capability and built-in components to work with databases, for example.

Still, if you want to be a programmer extraordinaire, or even if you want to just be effective, knowing more about servlets is essential.

The `ServletRequest` Class

A `ServletRequest` object contains information about the request from the browser. In addition to obvious things such as access to form variables, the `request` object can give you information about the kinds of languages that the browser accepts and the character encoding used in the request. `ServletRequest` is actually a Java interface, not a class. Because you don't have to create the `request` object, however, it doesn't really matter whether it's an interface or a class. A

`ServletRequest` is typically made available as a parameter to a method, such as `service`.

By the Way

The Request Object Is a `ServletRequest`

The built-in `request` object used by JSPs is actually an instance of `ServletRequest`. In practice, it is usually a subclass of `HttpServletRequest`.

Accessing Request Parameters

Request parameters are values passed to the server two different ways. First, as you have already seen, you can pass parameters in the URL by appending a `?` to the URL, followed by parameters in the form `name=value` separated by `&`. Here's an example URL with parameters:

```
http://localhost:8080/servlet/MyServlet?firstName=Kaitlynn&age=4
```

When the browser uses an HTTP `GET` request to send the server a form, it automatically passes parameters as part of the URL. The browser can also pass parameters as part of the body of the request. To pass parameters in the request body, the browser must do an HTTP `POST`, because the HTTP `GET` request doesn't have a request body, just request headers.

By the Way

Parameters, Any Way You Like Them

There is actually a third way for your JSP or servlet to receive a parameter. When you use the `<jsp:include>` or `<jsp:forward>` tag, you can supply parameters that are added to the set of parameters that the browser passed. You'll learn more about these tags in Hour 10, "Using JSP Standard Actions to Organize Your Web Application."

No matter how the server gets the parameters, you can use the `ServletRequest` object to access them. You can use `getParameter` to retrieve a single parameter (or the first parameter if multiple ones are passed) and `getParameterValues` to retrieve multiple values:

```
public String getParameter(String name)
public String[] getParameterValues(String name)
```

If you request a parameter that doesn't exist, both `getParameter` and `getParameterValues` return `null`. You can find out all the parameter names by calling `getParameterNames`:

```
public java.util.Enumeration getParameterNames()
```

If you want access to the `Map` that contains the names and values of the parameters, you can use

```
public java.util.Map getParameterMap()
```

Accessing Request Attributes

Often, you will need to save information that you want to associate with a page, session, or application. You use an **attribute** to do this. You can store attributes in the `request` object yourself. Typically, you need to store attributes in the `request` object when you want to include or forward to another JSP or servlet. Later in the hour, you'll see how to use session and application-level attributes.

You can use `getAttribute`, `setAttribute`, and `removeAttribute` to retrieve, store, and delete attributes:

```
public Object getAttribute(String name)
public void setAttribute(String name, Object attr)
public void removeAttribute(String name)
```

Almost anything can be stored as an attribute, since `setAttribute` only requires an `Object` for an attribute.

You can get the names of all the attributes stored in the request by calling `getAttributeNames`:

```
public java.util.Enumeration getAttributeNames()
```

Some Attribute Names Are Reserved

Attribute names of the form `java.*`, `javax.*`, and `com.sun.*` are reserved for use by Sun.

Accessing Protocol-Related Information

You occasionally need to get protocol-related information, such as the kind of protocol or the network addresses of the server and the browser. Many Web servers, like Apache, can handle incoming requests for multiple network addresses and ports at one time. A server that can do this is said to be **multihomed.** You can find out which hostname and port received a request by calling getServerName and getServerPort:

```
public String getServerName()
public int getServerPort()
```

As of the Java Servlet 2.4 specification, you can also use the more aptly named getLocalName, getLocalAddr, and getLocalPort:

```
public String getLocalName()
public String getLocalAddr()
public int getLocalPort()
```

You can also retrieve the hostname and IP address and port of the machine that sent the request by calling getRemoteHost, getRemoteAddr, and getRemotePort:

```
public String getRemoteHost()
public String getRemoteAddr()
public Int getRemotePort()
```

Listing 6.1 shows a servlet that displays the address of the client accessing the server.

LISTING 6.1 Source Code for ShowAddressServlet.java

```
package examples;

import javax.servlet.*;
import java.io.*;

public class ShowAddressServlet extends GenericServlet
{
    public void service(ServletRequest request,
        ServletResponse response)
        throws IOException
    {
// Tell the Web server that the response is HTML.
        response.setContentType("text/html");

// Get the PrintWriter for writing out the response
        PrintWriter out = response.getWriter();

// Write the HTML back to the browser.
        out.println("<html>");
        out.println("<body>");

        String clientHost = request.getRemoteHost();
```

LISTING 6.1 Continued

```
        out.println("You are accessing this server from "+
            clientHost);

        out.println("</body>");
        out.println("</html>");
    }
}
```

The `getProtocol` method returns the name and version of the protocol used to make the request:

```
public String getProtocol()
```

The protocol is returned in the form `protocol/version`, such as `http/1.1`. If you are familiar with the CGI protocol, the protocol is in the same form as the `SERVER_PROTOCOL` server variable.

The `getScheme` method is similar to the `getProtocol` method:

```
public String getScheme()
```

Example schemes would be `http`, `https`, and `ftp`.

You can determine whether a secure protocol was used to make the request by calling the `isSecure` method:

```
public boolean isSecure()
```

When your servlet processes requests made via the secure protocol HTTPS (HTTP over SSL), you can access the client's security certificate, if it is available, with the attribute `javax.servlet.request.X509Certificate`. Hour 23, "Security," provides more information about client certificates.

Retrieving Request Data

As you saw in Hour 4, "How the Browser Interacts with the Server," an HTTP `POST` or `PUT` request can send data to the server. Most of the time, the data is a list of form variables. There is no restriction on what kind of data can be sent, however. You can upload an image to a servlet or a JSP if you want. You can find out the size and type of the data that was sent by calling `getContentLength` and `getContentType`:

```
public int getContentLength()
public String getContentType()
```

If the content length is unknown, getContentLength returns -1. If the content type is unknown, getContentType returns null.

If the request contains character data, you can find out the kind of character encoding used to write the request. The getCharacterEncoding method returns the encoding type:

```
public String getCharacterEncoding()
```

If the request doesn't specify a character encoding, getCharacterEncoding returns null.

If you need to override the character encoding, you can use setCharacterEncoding:

```
public void setCharacterEncoding(String env)
throws UnsupportedEncodingException
```

To read the request content, use either getReader or getInputStream:

```
public java.io.BufferedReader getReader()
    throws IOException
public ServletInputStream getInputStream()
    throws IOException
```

When the request contains character data, you should use the BufferedReader to read the data. It performs any necessary character conversions. To read binary data, use getInputStream.

Watch Out!

> **It's One or the Other—Readers or InputStreams**
> You can't use both getReader and getInputStream. If you try to use both methods, the second one throws an IllegalStateException.

Handling Uploaded Files

The ServletInputStream class returned by getInputStream is useful when you want to upload a file to a servlet or a JSP. There are many ways to upload a file, but the easiest way is through a Java client.

Listing 6.2 shows a servlet that receives a file uploaded from a Java client (or any client that can send data via an HTTP POST request).

LISTING 6.2 Source Code for `FileReceiverServlet.java`

```
package examples;
import javax.servlet.*;
import javax.servlet.http.*;

import java.io.*;

/** Receives a file uploaded via a straight HTTP POST request */


public class FileReceiverServlet extends HttpServlet
{
    public void service(HttpServletRequest request,
        HttpServletResponse response)
        throws java.io.IOException, ServletException
    {
// Get the input stream for reading the file.
        InputStream in = request.getInputStream();

// The file is always saved with the same name (just for this demo).
        OutputStream fileOut = new BufferedOutputStream(
            new FileOutputStream("/tmp/uploaded_file"));
// Create a buffer for reading bytes from the input stream.
        byte[] buff = new byte[4096];
        int len;

// Read bytes from the input stream, and write them to the file.
        while ((len = in.read(buff)) > 0)
        {
            fileOut.write(buff, 0, len);
        }
        fileOut.close();

// Send a response back to the client saying the upload was successful.
        response.setContentType("text/plain");
        PrintWriter out = response.getWriter();

        out.println("Upload successful!");
    }
}
```

Did you Know?

Using Other Paths with File I/O and Servlets

In Listing 6.2, the file's path was hard-coded to `/tmp`. If you would like to place the file in the Web application's root directory, you can obtain the path using

```
String path = getServletContext().getRealPath("/");
```

If you want to use a subdirectory such as "data" off of the application root, replace "/" with "/data".

Additionally, some servlet containers make a temporary directory available to your application in this way:

```
File dir = (File)
getServletContext().getAttribute("javax.servlet.context.tempdir");
```

Finally, when opening resource for reading, you can use the preferred method

```
InputStream is = getServletContext().getResourceAsStream("/");
```

The path given to `getResourceAsStream` is relative to the context root. Resources obtained this way are available from any source, including a local or remote file-system, a database, or a war file. We'll discuss this further in a moment.

Watch Out!

Where, Oh Where, Did My File Go?

If you neglect to specify the path for your file when you open it to write, the servlet container will decide where the file is written. Tomcat will write the file in its `bin/` directory.

Listing 6.3 shows the Java client class that performs the upload.

LISTING 6.3 Source Code for `Uploader.java`

```
package examples;

import java.net.*;
import java.io.*;

/** Performs an HTTP POST to upload a file to a servlet */
public class Uploader
{
    public static void main(String[] args)
    {
        if (args.length < 1)
        {
            System.out.println("Please supply the name of the file to upload.");
            System.exit(1);
        }

        try
        {
```

LISTING 6.3 Continued

```
            File inFile = new File(args[0]);

// Open the file to be uploaded.
            InputStream in = new BufferedInputStream(
                new FileInputStream(inFile));

// Create a URL object for the destination servlet.
            URL destination = new URL("http://localhost:8080/servlet/"+
                "examples.FileReceiverServlet");

// Open a connection to the servlet.
            URLConnection conn = destination.openConnection();

// Tell the connection that there is output to be sent.
            conn.setDoOutput(true);

// Tell the receiver that this is a stream of bytes.
            conn.setRequestProperty("Content-type",
                "application/octet-stream");

// Tell the receiver how many bytes there are.
            conn.setRequestProperty("Content-length",
                ""+inFile.length());

            OutputStream out = conn.getOutputStream();

            byte[] buff = new byte[4096];

            int len;

// Copy bytes from the file to the output stream.
            while ((len = in.read(buff)) > 0)
            {
                out.write(buff, 0, len);
            }

            InputStream response = conn.getInputStream();

// Read the response back from the receiver servlet.
            while ((len = response.read(buff)) > 0)
            {
                System.out.write(buff, 0, len);
            }
        }
        catch (Exception exc)
        {
        }
    }
}
```

You don't always have the luxury of writing a Java client to perform the upload. Sometimes you must perform a file upload from an HTML page. Listing 6.4 shows a simple HTML page that enables you to select a file to upload.

LISTING 6.4 **Source Code for** `FileUploader.html`

```
<html>
<body bgcolor="#ffffff">
<h1>File Uploader</h1>
<form action="/servlet/examples.FileReceiverServlet" method="post"
    enctype="multipart/form-data">
Please select a file to upload: <input type="file" name="foo">
<p>
<input type="submit" value="Upload File!">
</form>
</body>
</html>
```

The difficulty with receiving a file uploaded from an HTML form is that the content is of the type `multipart/form-data`. When you upload a file in this format, the content type is usually something like

```
multipart/form-data; boundary=------------------
    --------7d03d0287003dc
```

The actual content starts with an additional header, too:

```
----------------------------7d03d0287003dc
Content-Disposition: form-data; name="foo";
    filename="H:\jspbook\ch13\examples\Uploader.java"
Content-Type: application/octet-stream
```

Because the upload can contain multiple parts, the boundary string is used to separate each part. After the boundary, as shown previously, are several header lines terminated by a blank line. After you read the blank line, the rest of the data is content until you reach another boundary.

Listing 6.5 shows a servlet that can wade through the multipart headers and retrieve an uploaded file.

LISTING 6.5 **Source Code for** `ReceiveUploadServlet.java`

```
package examples;

import javax.servlet.*;
import javax.servlet.http.*;
import java.io.*;

public class ReceiveUploadServlet extends GenericServlet
{
```

LISTING 6.5 Continued

```
    public void service(ServletRequest request,
        ServletResponse response)
        throws IOException
    {
// Get the content type.
        String contentType = request.getContentType();

// Set a default for the boundary string length.
// Find out where the boundary string starts.
        int boundaryIndex = contentType.indexOf("boundary=");

// Get the boundary string.
        String boundary = contentType.substring(boundaryIndex+9);
        int boundaryStrLength = boundary.length();

// Get the input stream to read the uploaded file.
        ServletInputStream servIn = request.getInputStream();

        DataInputStream in = new DataInputStream(servIn);

// Lop off the headers from the content (read until you get a blank line).
        String line;

        while ((line = in.readLine()) != null)
        {
            getServletContext().log("Got line: "+line);
            if (line.trim().length() == 0) break;
        }

        ByteArrayOutputStream byteOut = new ByteArrayOutputStream(
            request.getContentLength());

        byte[] buffer = new byte[4096];
        int len;

// Copy the uploaded file to a byte array.
        while ((len = in.read(buffer)) > 0)
        {
            byteOut.write(buffer, 0, len);
        }

        byte[] outBytes = byteOut.toByteArray();

        FileOutputStream fileOut = new FileOutputStream("/tmp/uploaded_file");

// Write the byte array out to the file, trim off the boundary plus some
// padding surrounding the boundary.
        fileOut.write(outBytes, 0, outBytes.length - boundaryStrLength - 8);
        fileOut.close();

// Tell the Web server that the response is HTML.
response.setContentType("text/html");

// Get the PrintWriter for writing out the response
        PrintWriter out = response.getWriter();
```

LISTING 6.5 Continued

```
// Write the HTML back to the browser.
        out.println("<html>");
        out.println("<body>");

        String clientHost = request.getRemoteHost();

        out.println("File Accepted, thank you.");

        out.println("</body>");
        out.println("</html>");
    }
}
```

You can use this servlet with `FileUploader.html` (Listing 6.4). Just remember to change the form action to point to `examples.ReceiveUploadServlet`. You may need to clear your browser cache to get it to recognize the new version.

Getting Locale Information

When a browser requests a page, it can send a list of locales that it supports. If you are not familiar with the internationalization features of Java, a locale specifies how Java should represent certain data items, such as dates and currencies. You can even determine the client's preferred language in case you want to support multiple languages on your Web site. You will learn more about locales and internationalization in Hour 22, "Internationalization."

The `getLocale` method returns the browser's preferred locale, and `getLocales` returns an enumeration of all the locales the browser says it supports:

```
public java.util.Locale getLocale()
public java.util.Enumeration getLocales()
```

The `HttpServletRequest` Class

The `HttpServletRequest` interfaces add HTTP-specific capabilities to the existing `ServletRequest` interface. If your servlet is an `HttpServlet`, you receive an `HttpServletRequest` object in your servlet's `service` method, or in any of the `doGet`, `doPost`, `doPut`, and other methods. In a JSP, the `request` object is an `HttpServletRequest` object.

Getting Header Values

You sometimes need to examine header values sent in the request. The getHeaderNames method returns an enumeration of all the possible header values:

```
public java.util.Enumeration getHeaderNames()
```

You can retrieve the header objects as strings, using either getHeader for a single value or getHeaders to get all the values for a particular header name:

```
public String getHeader(String name)
public java.util.Enumeration getHeaders(String name)
```

Sometimes a header contains a number or a date. Instead of parsing the value yourself, you can let the request use either getIntHeader or getDateHeader to parse the value:

```
public int getIntHeader(String name)
public long getDateHeader(String name)
```

The value that getDateHeader returns is the number of milliseconds since January 1, 1970. If you need a date object, you can create an instance of date like this:

```
Date d = new Date(getDateHeader("If-Modified-Since"));
```

By the Way

The Unix Epoch

Midnight on January 1, 1970, is known as the UNIX epoch—it's the beginning of time for UNIX systems. There's no special reason for having chosen that date, but all time is measured in seconds relative to it.

The UNIX epoch ends GMT 03:14:07, Tuesday, January 19, 2038, when it will overflow the 32-bit type given it by most systems.

By the Way

In Case of Trouble

If you are having trouble retrieving header values, see the "Q&A" section at the end of this hour.

Getting the HTTP Method

As you have seen, there are several different kinds of HTTP requests. When a browser just requests a page, it uses a GET method. When the browser needs to send form data in the request body instead of the URL, it uses the POST method.

When the browser uploads a file to the server it uses the PUT method. You can find out what method was used to make the request by calling getMethod:

```
public String getMethod()
```

Obtaining Information About the Request URI

Occasionally, you might want to access different portions of the URL used to invoke the servlet. For example, in the last hour, you learned that a servlet's context can be identified by inspecting the URL—the context is added as a prefix. getContextPath returns the portion of the URL that identifies the context of the request.

```
public String getContextPath()
```

In addition to the context, you can get information about the path that follows a servlet mapping, either as requested or as translated to a real path:

```
public java.lang.String getPathInfo()
public java.lang.String getPathTranslated()
```

To get to the portion that directed the container to the servlet, you can use getServletPath:

```
public java.lang.String getServletPath()
```

Finally, to obtain the URI or URL, which includes everything but the query string, you use:

```
public java.lang.String getRequestURI()
public java.lang.StringBuffer getRequestURL()
```

Accessing the Query String

The list of parameters added to the end of a URL is referred to as the **query string**. You can retrieve the query string, just as it was originally sent, by calling getQueryString:

```
public String getQueryString()
```

Don't forget—even if the browser uses the POST method, it can still pass parameters on the query string. The query string doesn't have to be in the name=value format. You can put any string in a request's query string.

Getting Session Information

HTTP is a stateless protocol, which means that the protocol doesn't remember anything about clients or their transactions between requests. HTTP delegates this responsibility to the application. Applications use **sessions** to group related requests together and to associate them with a client. Whenever you use a Web application that is able to recall your interactions, such as displaying items you added to a shopping cart, you can be certain that the application is using sessions.

Sessions are an integral part of servlets and JSPs. In Hours 12 and 13, you will learn how to use sessions in more detail.

The `getSession` method returns the session associated with the client and optionally creates a session if one doesn't already exist:

```
public Session getSession()
public Session getSession(boolean create)
```

If the `create` flag is `true`, `getSession` creates a new session if one doesn't exist. If a session doesn't exist and `create` is `false`, `getSession` returns `null`. Calling `getSession` with no parameter is the same as calling it with a value of `true` for the `create` flag.

Several mechanisms exist that are used to manage sessions. You are probably familiar with cookies, which make it possible to deposit a small amount of information with a client. Cookies can be used to store a session identifier. A session identifier may also be encoded into the request URI. Fortunately, using sessions with JSPs or servlets doesn't require specialized handling by a method.

Although a session identifier is usually stored in a cookie, the servlet API provides a way to keep track of sessions by passing the session ID as a form variable in the URL. You can determine whether the session ID comes from a cookie or from the URL by calling `isRequestedSessionIdFromCookie` or `isRequestedSessionIdFromURL`:

```
public boolean isRequestedSessionIdFromCookie()
public boolean isRequestedSessionIdFromURL()
```

If you need to see whether the session ID is still valid, call `isRequestedSessionIdValid`:

```
public boolean isRequestedSessionIdValid()
```

You can also find out the session ID that the client requested by using `getRequestedSessionId`:

```
public java.lang.String getRequestedSessionId()
```

Retrieving Cookies

Beyond providing support for sessions, cookies can be used to store up to 4KB of data. They are often used to save user preferences.

The `getCookies` method returns an array of cookie objects passed in from the client:

```
public Cookie[] getCookies()
```

Cookies are discussed in detail at the end of this hour.

The `ServletContext` Class

The `ServletContext` object, available to both JSP and servlets via the `getServletContext` method, contains information about the servlet engine and the servlet environment. It provides an application-level view to your component.

Getting the Server Version

There are three methods you can use to get information about the server version and the Servlet API version:

```
public int getMajorVersion()
public int getMinorVersion()
public String getServerInfo()
```

If you are running with version 2.4 of the servlet API, `getMajorVersion` returns `2`, and `getMinorVersion` returns `4`. The `getServerInfo` method returns the name and version of the server separated by slashes. The current version of Tomcat returns the following server version:

```
Apache Tomcat/5.0
```

Getting the Context Name

The name of the context, as defined in the deployment descriptor by the `display-name` element, is obtained by using `getServletContextName`:

```
public String getServletContextName()
```

Initialization Parameters

The ServletContext object contains the same getInitParameterNames and getInitParameter methods that we discussed earlier in the book:

```
public java.util.Enumeration getInitParameterNames()
public String getInitParameter(String name)
```

These methods return information for an entire Web application, not just for a specific servlet.

Saving Application-Wide Objects

All the servlets and JSPs within an application can share objects when they are stored in the ServletContext object. The getAttribute, setAttribute, and removeAttribute methods work just like the ones in the ServletRequest class, except that the objects are visible to the entire application:

```
public Object getAttribute(String name)
public void setAttribute(String name, Object attr)
public void removeAttribute(String name)
```

Just as with the request object, you can get a list of the attribute names available in the ServletContext object by calling getAttributeNames:

```
public java.util.Enumeration getAttributeNames()
```

Logging Messages

One of the difficulties with debugging a server is that you can't easily see what is going on. After all, with a desktop application, you can see a dialog box pop up with an error message. Most developers writing a server application end up writing their own logging routines so they can gain some visibility into what the server is doing. The ServletContext object supplies two logging methods:

```
public void log(String message)
public void log(String message, Throwable throwable)
```

Although these methods are part of the standard Servlet API, the location of the log file varies between servers. When you pass a Throwable object to the log method, the server prints a stack trace to the log file.

By the Way

In Case of Trouble

If you are having trouble logging messages, see the "Q&A" section at the end of this hour.

Calling Other Servlets and JSPs

You use a `RequestDispatcher` object to include or forward to another JSP or servlet. You use the `ServletContext` object to locate the request dispatcher via either the `getRequestDispatcher` or `getNamedDispatcher` methods:

```
public RequestDispatcher getRequestDispatcher(String url)
public RequestDispatcher getNamedDispatcher(String name)
```

The request dispatcher enables you to access any resource on the local server. You aren't restricted to just servlets and JSPs. You can include an HTML file if you want. When you use `getRequestDispatcher`, the URL that you pass to the method must start with a `/`. Most of the time, you can think of the path as being relative to the server root. The `/` is actually relative to the context root in which the servlet or JSP is running.

By the Way

Obtaining a `RequestDispatcher` Using `ServletRequest`

You can also obtain a reference to a `RequestDispatcher` from the `ServletRequest` by a method of the same name. The only difference between the two methods is that the `RequestDispatcher` obtained through a `ServletRequest` can take a parameter that is a path relative to the current servlet.

The `getNamedDispatcher` method lets you refer to a servlet by its name as opposed to the path. The name in this case is the name specified in the `web.xml` file in the application's WAR file. For example, a servlet might be defined using the following tags:

```
<servlet>
    <servlet-name>shopping</servlet-name>
    <servlet-class>examples.cart.ShoppingCartServlet</servlet-class>
</servlet>
```

You can access this servlet with the line:

```
getServletContext().getNamedDispatcher("shopping");
```

One advantage of `getNamedDispatcher` is that it allows you to access servlets that are not directly available to users. When you use `getRequestDispatcher` to access a servlet, the servlet must have a URL mapping configured in the `web.xml` file. When this mapping is present, any browser can access the servlet. The `getNamedDispatcher` method doesn't require a URL mapping, however.

When you need to obtain a resource or obtain a `RequestDispatcher` that belongs to another context, `getContext` retrieves a reference to the context you need:

```
public ServletContext getContext(String uripath)
```

Accessing Application Resources

An application often requires additional resources other than its servlets and JSPs. You might need data files, image files, or sound files. When you install your application, you can copy all the files into one or more directories, or you can package all the necessary files into a WAR file (similar to a JAR file). You can use `getResource` and `getResourceAsStream` to retrieve these resources:

```
public java.net.URL getResource(java.lang.String path)
    throws java.net.MalformedURLException

public java.io.InputStream getResourceAsStream(
    java.lang.String path)
```

Using `getResourcePaths`, you can get a directory-like listing of resources available within a context:

```
public java.util.Set getResourcePaths(java.lang.String path)
```

If you need to access a resource directly, `getRealPath` takes a path that is appropriate to the context and returns an absolute file path that is appropriate to the server's file-system.

```
public String getRealPath(String path)
```

The `ServletResponse` Class

When a servlet needs to send data back to the browser, it uses the `ServletResponse` object. Using this object, you can get an output stream for sending data back, set the content type and length, and set the character encoding if you need to send back character data.

Setting the Content Type and Length

You can set the content type and length by calling `setContentType` and `setContentLength`:

```
public void setContentType(String contentType)
public void setContentLength(int contentLength)
```

When you set the content type, you can also set the character encoding. For example, you could set the content type to `text/html; charset=ISO-8859-4`.

Opening an Output Stream

There are two methods for obtaining an output stream:

```
public ServletOutputStream getOutputStream()
    throws IOException

public PrintWriter getWriter() throws IOException
```

When you need to send character data back to the browser, you should use the `getWriter` method. If you need to send binary data, use `getOutputStream`.

Setting Locale-Specific Information

When you send a response back to the browser, you might want to target it to a specific locale, which implies a specific language and possibly country. For example, if you need to write out a date or a currency value, you want to write it in a format that the end user understands. The `ServletRequest` object tells you which locales the browser supports. When you send a request, you can set a locale in the output stream. The locale can imply a particular character encoding and can even change the character encoding based on the content type. To set the locale for the response, call `setLocale`:

```
public void setLocale(Locale aLocale)
```

You can get the locale and character encoding for the response by calling `getLocale` and `getCharacterEncoding`:

```
public Locale getLocale()
public String getCharacterEncoding()
```

> **Internet Clients—Parlez-vous français?**
> The ServletRequest method also contains getLocale and getCharacterEncoding methods, indicating the locale and character encoding of the incoming request.

By the Way

We'll discuss internationalization in additional detail in Hour 22.

Response Buffering

Most of the time, a servlet or JSP response is buffered. You can control the amount of memory used for buffering and also clear out the buffer if you need to. Use `getBufferSize` and `setBufferSize` to control the amount of buffering:

```
public int getBufferSize()
public void setBufferSize(int bufferSize)
```

If you want to change the buffer size, you should do it before you try to send any data back to the browser. After you send data back, or at least write it to the buffer, you can't change the buffer size. If you want to send the current buffer contents back to the browser immediately, call `flushBuffer`:

```
public void flushBuffer() throws IOException
```

If you want to clear the contents of the buffer, call `reset`:

```
public void reset()
```

For those occasions where you need to reset the buffer contents without affecting the headers or status code, you use `resetBuffer`:

```
public void resetBuffer()
```

After the response status and headers have been sent back to the browser, the response is said to be "committed." After it is committed, you can't change any header values, which you can normally set in the `HttpServletResponse` object. You can find out whether the response has been committed by calling `isCommitted`:

```
public boolean isCommitted()
```

The `HttpServletResponse` Class

The `HttpServletResponse` object allows you to set various HTTP-related options in the response to the browser. It is a subclass of `ServletResponse`, so it contains all the methods you need to send an HTTP response.

Setting Header Variables

Many of the options you have already encountered, such as content type and content length, are stored in the HTTP header. For header variables that don't have a corresponding `ServletResponse` method, use the `setHeader`, `setIntHeader`, or `setDateHeader` methods:

```
public void setHeader(String header, String value)
public void setIntHeader(String header, int value)
public void setDateHeader(String header, Date value)
```

The HTTP header can contain multiple values for the same header name. When you need to store multiple header values, use `addHeader`, `addIntHeader`, or `addDateHeader`:

```
public void addHeader(String header, String value)
public void addIntHeader(String header, int value)
public void addDateHeader(String header, Date value)
```

The `containsHeader` method returns `true` if a header value has already been set:

```
public boolean containsHeader(String header)
```

Redirecting the Browser

When you need to tell the browser to access a different page, use the `sendRedirect` method:

```
public void sendRedirect(String redirectURL)
```

By the Way

Which Way Did My Request Go?

A redirect is useful when you need to send the browser to a different server. A `forward` is much more efficient than a redirect because the redirect must first go back to the browser, which must then request the redirected page. If you are redirecting to a page in the same server, try doing a `forward` rather than a redirect.

Returning Status

Unless you need to send a status other than `SC_OK` (HTTP response code 200) indicating a normal response, you don't need to change the status code of the response. If you need to send an abnormal response code, however, you can call `setStatus` or `setError`:

```
public void setStatus(int statusCode)
public void setError(int statusCode)
public void setError(int statusCode, String errorMessage)
    throws IOException
```

Encoding URLs

When you want to send a URL to the browser, either as a link in a Web page or as a request to redirect, you should call either `encodeURL` or `encodeRedirectURL`:

```
public String encodeURL(String url)
public String encodeRedirectURL(String url)
```

The main purpose for the encoding is to handle cases when you need to store data in a session but the browser doesn't allow cookies. If the browser doesn't allow cookies, the encode routines append a session ID parameter to the URL. If the browser supports cookies, the encode routines return the URL unchanged.

Sending Cookies

When you need to send a cookie back to the browser, use the `addCookie` method:

```
public void addCookie(Cookie cookie)
```

After it receives them, the browser saves cookies until they expire. You don't need to keep sending the same cookies back to the browser unless their data values change.

The `ServletInputStream` Class

When the browser does a `POST` or a `PUT` request, a servlet or JSP can use `ServletInputStream` to read the request body. If the posted data contains form variables, you don't need to use the input stream because the Servlet API automatically reads the variables.

The `ServletInputStream` class is a subclass of `InputStream` and adds only one extra method. The `readLine` method reads a line of data into the byte buffer:

```
public int readLine(byte[] buffer, int offset, int length)
```

Did you Know?

Use a Reader to Input Character Data

If you are reading character data, you should be using a `BufferedReader` rather than the `ServletInputStream` because the reader performs character conversions properly.

The `ServletOutputStream` Class

The `ServletOutputStream` class is a subclass of the `OutputStream` class and adds the `print` and `println` methods normally found in the `PrintStream` class:

```
public void print(boolean b)
public void print(char c)
public void print(double d)
public void print(float f)
public void print(int i)
public void print(long l)
public void print(String s)
public void println()
public void println(boolean b)
public void println(char c)
public void println(double d)
public void println(float f)
public void println(int i)
public void println(long l)
public void println(String s)
```

Did you Know?

Use a Writer to Output Character Data

You are better off using `PrintWriter` rather than `ServletOutputStream` because `PrintWriter` performs the character conversions correctly.

The `HttpSession` Class

The `HttpSession` stores information between browser requests. In addition to storing and retrieving objects, you can control when the session is created and how long the session stays active after there has been no activity.

Storing and Retrieving Objects

You can store and retrieve objects in the session that will be available the next time the browser sends a request. Use the `getAttribute`, `setAttribute`, and `removeAttribute` methods to store and retrieve the objects:

```
public Object getAttribute(String name)
public void setAttribute(String name, Object value)
public void removeAttribute(String name)
```

You can get a list of available objects by calling `getAttributeNames`:

```
public Enumeration getAttributeNames()
```

Did you Know?

> **Same Method Names, Different Classes**
> In case you haven't noticed, the classes that allow you to store objects with application, session, request, and page scope (`ServletContext`, `HttpSession`, `ServletRequest`, and `PageContext`) all use the same methods to get, store, and remove attributes.

To make it easier to get to the servlet context that this session is associated with, `HttpSession` provides the method `getServletContext`:

```
public javax.servlet.ServletContext getServletContext()
```

Controlling Session Termination

One of the difficulties in dealing with sessions is that the server never knows for sure that the session has ended unless you create some sort of logout mechanism. Because the server and the browser spend most of their time disconnected from each other, the server has no way to know that the user has closed the browser window and is now deeply involved in a game of EverQuest.

Putting a logout mechanism into your Web pages is a great idea if your Web site has the notion of login and logout. When the user logs out, you just invalidate the session by calling the `invalidate` method:

```
public void invalidate()
```

Even with a logout mechanism, though, you can't be sure that the user will be kind enough to actually log out before shutting down the browser. Whether or not you have a logout mechanism, you can force sessions to terminate after a specified period of inactivity. Typical servlet and JSP engines set the timeout at 30 minutes to begin with. You can usually change the default timeout for all sessions with the server's administration tools, or you can query and change the session timeout by calling `getMaxInactiveInterval` and `setMaxInactiveInterval`:

```
public int getMaxInactiveInterval()
public void setMaxInactiveInterval(int interval)
```

Getting Session Status

There are a few aspects of the session that you might be interested in. First, you can get the unique identifier of the session by calling `getId`:

```
public String getId()
```

This identifier is unique across all the sessions within your servlet engine, but not necessarily unique if you are running multiple servlet engines. If you are using only a single servlet engine, you can pass this identifier to other parts of your application (CORBA services, Enterprise JavaBeans) to serve as a unique identifier for any session-oriented data stored elsewhere.

If you use the session ID in other parts of your application, you are limiting yourself to using only a single servlet engine. To allow for the possibility of multiple servlet and JSP engines passing session identifiers to other portions of your application, consider putting some unique prefix in front of the session ID before you pass it to another module. For example, you might have an "Internet customer" JSP engine with a consumer-friendly interface. You might also have an "Internal-only" servlet engine that handles internal company data. If both of these engines need to access the same service and pass session IDs, you might append "Net" before the Internet customer session IDs and "Int" before the internal customer session IDs.

The `isNew` method tells you whether a session has just been created:

```
public boolean isNew()
```

If a session is new, none of the session information has been sent to the client browser. Remember, the only part of the session that is sent to the browser is the session ID, which may be stored in a cookie.

You can find out when a session was created by calling `getCreationTime`:

```
public long getCreationTime()
```

The time value returned by `getCreationTime` is the number of milliseconds since January 1, 1970. You can create a date object from the creation time by passing the time value to the `Date` constructor like this:

```
Date creationTime = new Date(session.getCreationTime());
```

The `getLastAccessedTime` method returns the most recent time that a client browser with this session accessed the server:

```
public long getLastAccessedTime()
```

As with the creation time, the last access time value is the number of milliseconds since January 1, 1970; you can create a `Date` object from this time value by passing the value to the `Date` constructor. The last access time is the value the servlet engine uses to determine when a session has timed out.

Accessing Session Variables Does Not Reset the Session Timer

Accessing session variables does not change the last access time. The only thing that updates the time is an incoming request from a browser. In other words, you cannot prevent a servlet from timing out by accessing a session variable.

The `Cookie` Class

A cookie is a value stored on the browser and sent from the browser to the server whenever the browser requests a page. Cookies usually store information such as usernames or session IDs. The session ID of the `HttpSession` is sent to the browser as a cookie.

Not Everybody Likes Cookies

Most browsers allow the user to disable cookies. If your application requires cookies, make sure you warn your users.

Creating a New Cookie

When you create a new cookie, you must give the cookie a name and provide an initial value. After the cookie has been created, the value can change, but the name must remain the same. The constructor for the `Cookie` class takes the name and value as arguments:

```
public Cookie(String name, String value)
```

The `getName` and `getValue` methods return the name and value of an existing cookie:

```
public String getName()
public String getValue()
```

Naming Your Cookies

A cookie's name can contain only printable ASCII characters and cannot contain commas, spaces, or semicolons. A cookie name cannot begin with $.

You can also change the cookie's value by calling `setValue`:

```
public void setValue(String newValue)
```

By the Way

The Contents of Cookies

There are a number of restrictions on the format of cookie values. A cookie value cannot contain spaces, parentheses, brackets, commas, double-quotes, semicolons, at-signs, or several other characters. If you need to store anything other than characters or numbers in a cookie value, consider using an encoding scheme such as base64.

By the Way

In Case of Trouble

If you are having trouble storing or retrieving cookies, see the "Q&A" section at the end of this hour.

Setting the Domain and Path

A browser doesn't send all its cookies to a server whenever it makes a request. Instead, each cookie is tagged with a domain and path. The browser sends only those cookies that match the server's domain and path. For example, if the browser is accessing `http://examples.wutka.com/examples/DemoServlet` and it has a cookie with a domain of `.wutka.com` and a path of `/examples`, it sends that cookie to the server. If it has a cookie with a domain of `.wutka.com` and a path of `/other`, it does not send the cookie because the paths don't match. If it has a cookie with a domain of `hackingjava.wutka.com` and a path of `/examples`, it does not send the cookie because the domains don't match. Even alternate host names for the same host are different when it comes to processing cookies. For example, if I access a URL with `http://localhost` and then later hit the same server with `http://flamingo.wutka.com`, any cookies stored by localhost are unavailable from the flamingo URL even though they are the same host.

By default, a cookie's domain is the server that sent the cookie to begin with. If you have a large environment with multiple servers handling requests, make sure you set only the domain on your cookies so that the client will return cookies to all the servers that can process a request.

You can query and set the domain with `getDomain` and `setDomain`:

```
public String getDomain()
public void setDomain(String newDomain)
```

You can query and set the path with `getPath` and `setPath`:

```
public String getPath()
public void setPath(String newPath)
```

If you want a cookie to match any possible path, use `/` for the path.

Cookie Aging

Nobody likes to eat stale cookies, not even a browser. When you send a cookie to the browser, you can give it an expire time. After the expire time has elapsed, the browser gets rid of the cookie. The `getMaxAge` and `setMaxAge` methods enable you to query and set the expire time for a cookie:

```
public int getMaxAge()
public void setMaxAge(int maxAge)
```

When you set the maximum age of a cookie, you are telling the browser how many seconds it should keep the cookie. If the browser should hold on to the cookie for an hour, you need to set the maximum age to 3600 seconds. If the age is a positive number, the browser saves the cookie so it will be available even if the user shuts the browser down and starts it up again. If the age is a negative number, the browser holds on to the cookie only as long as the browser is running. When the user shuts the browser down, all cookies with a negative age value disappear. If you set the maximum age to 0, the cookie is immediately removed. If you have stored a cookie on the browser in the past and you want to delete it, the proper way to delete it is to set the age to 0.

Secure Cookies

Sometimes a cookie holds sensitive data. When you need to store sensitive data in a cookie and want to ensure that the cookie is sent to the browser only when the connection is secure, you can mark the cookie as secure by calling `setSecure`:

```
public void setSecure(secureFlag)
```

If a cookie's `secureFlag` is `true`, the browser sends the cookie to the server only if it's using a secure protocol such as HTTPS (SSL). You can query the secure flag by calling `getSecure`:

```
public boolean getSecure()
```

Watch Out!

Cookies Are Not Secure

Resist the temptation to store dangerous information such as credit card numbers in a cookie. Even though the cookie might be sent over only a secure protocol, the cookie might be stored on the user's hard disk. Many people would be unhappy to find their credit card numbers stored on a hard disk. Worse, if the user is on a network and the browser saves the cookie to a network drive, someone snooping the network could see the cookie. In other words, the cookie might still be visible over an insecure network.

Cookie Protocol Versions

The cookie protocol was originally developed by Netscape and then copied by other browser vendors as the use of cookies became more widespread. Since that time, the IETF (the Internet standards body) has created a standard cookie protocol. You can find the standard cookie protocol online at `www.ietf.org/rfc/rfc2109.txt`.

By the Way

More About Internet Standards

Internet standards are defined by the IETF in the form of Request For Comment documents. You will often see "RFC *xxxx*" (where "*xxxx*" is the number of the RFC) in reference to an Internet standard. There are several online sites that let you search by RFC number or by keywords.

One of the problems with standards that are developed by a committee is that it takes some time for them to be adopted, if they are adopted at all. The officially blessed RFC 2109 cookie protocol adds some additional features that are not yet supported on many browsers. You can get and set the protocol version that your cookie requires by calling `getVersion` and `setVersion`:

```
public int getVersion()
public void setVersion(int version)
```

The original Netscape cookie protocol has a version number of 0, whereas RFC 2109 has a version number of 1. Unless you have special circumstances in which you know that all the browsers using your system will support RFC 2109, you should stick to version 0 until most of the browser population supports RFC 2109.

Cookie Comments

One of the features added in RFC 2109 is a comment describing the purpose of the cookie. Many browsers have the capability to prompt the user when a server tries to save a cookie. You can use the comment to give the user a clue as to what is being saved in the cookie so the user can decide whether to accept it. Obviously, this is on the honor system. You could easily tell the user that the cookie contains a simple session ID although it actually contains his or her name, address, and credit card number.

Because the comment field was added in RFC 2109, it is not available in version 0 cookies and is probably not supported by a large number of browsers yet.

Use the `getComment` and `setComment` methods to query and change the cookie's comment:

```
public String getComment()
public void setComment(String comment)
```

Summary

In one of the longer hours of the book, you've just learned about most of the objects and methods needed to work effectively with servlets. Because JavaServer Pages ultimately become servlets, you also know how to work with objects that are important to JSPs. You studied the details of the perennial request and response objects, `ServletRequest`, `HttpServletRequest`, `ServletResponse`, and `HttpServletResponse`. You saw how to use the `ServletInputStream` and `ServletOutputStream` classes to read from and write to buffers that contain client data, and how to manage those buffers.

An important application-level class is `ServletContext`. It provides access to information about the servlet container, initialization parameters, system-wide logging, and application resources such as images. In addition, you can forward or redirect pages using a `RequestDispatcher`.

Sessions are used to group related requests and are often tracked by using cookies. `HttpSession` is a class used to create and manage sessions.

Storing attributes that can be associated with a request, context, or session is important. Each of the respective classes has the methods `setAttribute`, `getAttribute`, and `removeAttribute` so that you can store, retrieve, and delete associated data.

Cookies can also be used to store information other than session IDs. The `Cookie` class allows you to perform all of the functions related to creating and managing cookies, including setting and changing values or causing a cookie to expire.

Q&A

Q. ***Why do some header values show up on only one kind of browser?***

A. There are standard header names, but a browser isn't required to send any header values. Some browser implementations just send more information than others.

Q. ***Why can't I access a particular header value?***

A. You probably misspelled the name of the header value. The `HttpServletRequest` class is very forgiving when it comes to capitalization, but it does require you to spell the header name correctly. Also, make sure you use hyphens and not underscores for header values, as in `content-type` and `content-length`.

Q. ***Where are my log messages going?***

A. Each JSP and servlet engine stores its log messages in different places. Tomcat places logs in the `logs/` subdirectory of the installation directory. For other servers, consult the documentation for your server.

Q. ***Why aren't my log messages showing up in the log file?***

A. Occasionally, a server might delay logging, either intentionally or unintentionally. This is purely an implementation-specific detail and not related at all to the JSP or servlet specifications. Sometimes you can force the server to write to the log by shutting it down gracefully.

Q. ***I stored a cookie on the browser; why can't I see it?***

A. First check to make sure you spelled the cookie name correctly. Next make sure the browser has cookies enabled. Also, if you specified a root path for the cookie, make sure that the JSP or servlet reading the cookie is in that path. Remember, too, that if you don't give the cookie a specific expiration time, the cookie vanishes when the user shuts the browser down.

Workshop

The Workshop is designed to help you review what you have learned and help you to further increase your understanding of the material covered in this hour.

Quiz

1. How do you get to the raw content of a request?
2. When is the content of a response buffer sent to a client?
3. What are a few common methods used to identify sessions?

Answers

1. You can get the body of a request by using the `getReader` or `getInputStream` methods of a request object. There's no way provided by the servlet request objects to obtain the raw HTTP request. Fortunately, you will never need to access this information directly in a Web application, since `ServletRequest` and `HttpServletRequest` make the parsed information easily available.
2. A number of activities can cause the content of a buffer to be sent. In most cases, the `service` method ends or the amount of content specified by `setContentLength` has been written to the buffer. The container will also send the content when the buffer is filled or when the method `flushBuffer` is called. Finally, the content of a buffer will be sent if the `sendError` or `sendRedirect` methods of the response object are invoked.
3. Sessions are commonly identified through the use of cookies or by adding a session ID to the URL. However, containers are free to implement other methods as well. For example, when using SSL as part of HTTPS, a container can use the session information provided by SSL.

Activities

1. Write a servlet that displays all of the information about an `HttpServletRequest`.
2. Create a simple servlet that receives a username from a form, stores the name in a context attribute and forwards to another servlet that displays the name.
3. Create a simple servlet that stores a username as part of a cookie. Write a companion servlet that displays the username retrieved from the cookie.

HOUR 7

Servlet Filters

What You'll Learn in This Hour:

- What the basic methods of a `Filter` are
- How to configure a filter into a container
- How to write a simple `Filter`

Although JSPs and servlets are fairly powerful, there are times when you need to augment their capabilities. For example, you may want to compress the output of a JSP or servlet if the browser supports compression. Or you may be interested in encrypting or filtering content.

Servlet filters enable you to intercept incoming requests, possibly modifying the request parameters before invoking other filters or the desired JSP or servlet. After the JSP or servlet executes, the filter can modify the response parameters before returning the response to the browser. Filters can also modify headers.

In addition to all of the capabilities mentioned above, filters can be applied collectively to resources, making them a versatile instrument for factoring out functionality that may be reusable. Filters can also be used to extend the capabilities of a request or response object by using the Decorator pattern.

The Filter Interface

The `Filter` interface defines the methods that any servlet filter must implement, just as the `Servlet` interface defines methods that any servlet must implement. The interface defines three methods:

```
public void init(FilterConfig config)
```

```
public void destroy()
```

```
public void doFilter(ServletRequest request,
   ServletResponse response, FilterChain chain)
   throws ServletException, IOException
```

The init Method

Whenever the servlet container activates a filter, the container invokes the filter's init method, similar to the way the container invokes a servlet's init method. The FilterConfig object allows the filter to access its configuration items (configured by <init-param> tags in the web.xml file) as well as the ServletContext object.

The destroy Method

When the servlet container deactivates a filter, the container invokes the filter's destroy method, allowing the filter to perform any necessary cleanup. If a filter doesn't need to perform any cleanup, this method can be empty.

The doFilter Method

The doFilter method is the heart of the Filter interface. If a servlet or JSP is filtered, the servlet container invokes the filter's doFilter method rather than the servlet's service method. When the filter is ready for the servlet's service method to execute, the filter calls the doFilter method in the FilterChain object. The FilterChain object may refer to another filter (filters may be chained together) or it may refer to the actual servlet.

After the FilterChain's doFilter method returns, the filter may perform any additional processing on the response object.

Filter Lifecycle

The filter lifecycle is very similar to the servlet lifecycle. The servlet container creates an instance of a filter (usually one instance of a particular filter per container, just as with servlets). Before invoking the filter's doFilter method for the first time, the servlet container initializes the filter by calling the init method. Because usually only one instance of a particular filter is in the servlet container, the servlet container may invoke the doFilter method many times simultaneously, so you must be careful to ensure that the doFilter method is thread-safe. If the servlet container needs to remove the filter from service for some reason, it invokes the filter's destroy method first, allowing the filter to perform any necessary cleanup.

Filter Configuration

Like servlets, you must configure filters in the Web application's `web.xml` file. The configuration of a filter looks almost identical to that of a servlet. You first define a filter, giving it a name and specifying the name of the class that implements the filter. For example,

```
<filter>
   <filter-name>Example Filter</filter-name>
   <filter-class>examples.ExampleFilter</filter-class>
</filter>
```

Next, you specify the various URL mappings that define when the filter is invoked. You can make a filter apply to all resources in the application with a URL of `/*` or you can apply it to only specific resources. For example,

```
<filter-mapping>
<filter-name>Example Filter</filter-name>
<servlet-name>FilterMe.jsp</servlet-name>
</filter-mapping>
```

In this case the filter applies only to a JSP named `FilterMe.jsp`.

By the Way

Naming JSPs as Servlets

Remember that it's possible to name JavaServer Pages just like you would a servlet. If you don't recall how to do this, return to the "JSP Initialization" section of Hour 5, "JSP and Servlet Lifecycles," for a moment.

When you want to apply a filter to several resources, you use the `url-pattern` element instead of a `servlet-name` element, as shown:

```
<filter-mapping>
   <filter-name>Example Filter</filter-name>
   <url-pattern>/myContext/*</url-pattern>
</filter-mapping>
```

In this case the filter is applied to all resources available within the `myContext`.

By defining more than one filter in the deployment descriptor, filters can be chained to each other. In other words, when the first filter calls `FilterChain`'s `doFilter` method, control will be passed to the next filter.

To determine which filter is next, a container will first test the request URI against filter URL patterns to determine which filter belongs to the set that will be applied to a resource. Once the set is determined, filters are applied in the order they appear in the deployment descriptor. Then, any resource specific filters defined by servlet-name elements will follow.

In version 2.3 of the Java Servlet specification, a filter could only apply to a resource requested by a client. The filter wouldn't apply to servlets invoked via the request dispatcher (that is, by forwarding or including). Version 2.4 of the specification allows you to specify that a filter can apply to forwards, includes, requests, or error pages via the error page mechanism. You simply add one or more <dispatcher> tags to the filter-mapping. The values of the <dispatcher> tags may be FORWARD, INCLUDE, REQUEST, or ERROR. For example, to configure a filter to be invoked via a request from a client or an include using a RequestDispatcher, but not a forward, use the following declaration:

```
<filter-mapping>
   <filter-name>Example Filter</filter-name>
   <url-pattern>/FilterMe.jsp</url-mapping>
   <dispatcher>REQUEST</dispatcher>
   <dispatcher>INCLUDE</dispatcher>
</filter-mapping>
```

By the Way

Using Filters to Program Without Linking Binaries

You may have realized that filters allow you to program without linking binaries. The *flow* is specified at deployment. This loose coupling is one of the benefits of filters.

The <filter> and <filter-mapping> elements must appear before any <servlet> and <servlet-mapping> elements.

Using FilterConfig

A FilterConfig object is passed as a parameter in the init method of a Filter. FilterConfig provides methods to discover a filter's name, retrieve initialization parameters, and access the servlet context:

```
public java.lang.String getFilterName()
public java.lang.String getInitParameter(java.lang.String name)
public java.util.Enumeration getInitParameterNames()
public ServletContext getServletContext()
```

Initialization parameters are added to the deployment descriptor by adding init-params elements as children to a filter element.

Request and Response Wrappers

When a filter invokes the doFilter method in the FilterChain object, it must pass in a request and response. The request and response don't necessarily need to be the same request and response that were originally passed to the filter. For example, if you want to supply an alternate output stream to a servlet, you need to supply a response object whose getOutputStream method returns the alternate output stream.

The problem with supplying an alternate request or response object is that there are so many methods in each of these objects that it becomes cumbersome to implement your own. One of the common design patterns (the Decorator pattern) for a situation like this is to create a wrapper class. The wrapper keeps a reference to the real object (the original request or response, in this case) and implements the same methods as the real object. In most cases, the wrapper's methods just invoke the methods in the real object. In a few cases, however, the wrapper has its own implementation (its own getOutputStream, for example), or may even supplement functionality with additional methods.

Creating wrapper classes is a little less cumbersome than writing your own classes from scratch, but it still involves creating a large number of methods yourself. Fortunately, the servlet API provides prebuilt wrappers for the request and response objects. You simply subclass these classes and override the particular methods in which you are interested.

The ServletRequestWrapper class wraps a ServletRequest object, just as the HttpServletRequestWrapper wraps an HttpServletRequest object. In both cases, the constructor for the wrapper class takes the real request object as a parameter. Similarly, the ServletResponseWrapper class wraps a ServletResponse, and the HttpServletResponseWrapper wraps an HttpServletResponse.

An Example Filter—JSP/Servlet Timings

In a production system, you often need to know how well your application is responding. If the system is running slowly, you should find out about it before you get calls from irate users. Some of the statistics you might find useful include the following:

- **The number of pending requests.** If this number continues to grow, there may be an infinite loop somewhere, or at least very slow responses.
- **The total number of requests.** Lets you gauge how often people access various parts of your site.

- **The last execution time**. Lets you know how long a particular JSP or servlet took to run.
- **A weighted average of execution times**. Gives you an idea how long a particular JSP/servlet has been taking to run recently.
- **A full average of execution times**. Gives you an idea of how long a particular JSP or servlet usually runs.

Listing 7.1 shows a class that keeps track of the various execution statistics for a single JSP or servlet. The formula for the weighted average uses a simple weighting process to give you an average over the last 20 times.

LISTING 7.1 Source Code for `Times.java`

```
package examples.filter;

public class Times
{
    public String timerName;
    public long totalTime;
    public long weightedAverage;
    public long lastRunTime;
    public long numAccesses;
    public int numPending;

    public static final long NUM_WEIGHTS = 20;

    public Times(String aTimerName)
    {
        timerName = aTimerName;
    }

    public void addTime(long time)
    {
        numAccesses++;
        lastRunTime = time;
        totalTime += time;
        long weight = NUM_WEIGHTS;

        if (numAccesses < NUM_WEIGHTS) weight = numAccesses;

        if (weight > 0)
        {
            weightedAverage = (weightedAverage * (weight-1) +
                    time) / weight;
        }
    }

    public synchronized void begin()
    {
        numPending++;
    }
```

LISTING 7.1 Continued

```
    public synchronized void end()
    {
        numPending--;
    }

    public String getTimerName() { return timerName; }
    public long getTotalTime() { return totalTime; }
    public long getWeightedAverage() { return weightedAverage; }
    public long getNumAccesses() { return numAccesses; }
    public long getNumPending() { return numPending; }

    /** Return average time converted into seconds */
    public double getAverageTimeSec() {
        return ((double) totalTime) / (1000.0 * (double) numAccesses); }

    /** Return weighted average in seconds */
    public double getWeightedAverageSec() {
        return ((double) weightedAverage) / 1000.0;
    }
}
```

Listing 7.2 shows the timing filter that actually gathers the statistics for each JSP and servlet. For each different JSP or servlet, it creates an instance of a `Times` object. Then, for each execution of that JSP or servlet, it adds the execution time to the `Times` object. The class also includes a static method that returns the times for all JSPs and servlets, so you can display them in a JSP.

LISTING 7.2 Source Code for `TimingFilter.java`

```
package examples.filter;

import javax.servlet.Filter;
import javax.servlet.FilterConfig;
import javax.servlet.FilterChain;
import javax.servlet.ServletRequest;
import javax.servlet.ServletResponse;
import javax.servlet.ServletException;
import javax.servlet.http.HttpServletRequest;
import java.util.HashMap;
import java.util.ArrayList;
import java.util.Iterator;

public class TimingFilter implements Filter
{
    // The table of time values for each JSP/Servlet
    public static HashMap times = new HashMap();

    public TimingFilter()
    {
    }
```

LISTING 7.2 Continued

```
    public void init(FilterConfig filterConfig)
    {
    }

    public void destroy()
    {
    }

    public void doFilter(ServletRequest request,
            ServletResponse response, FilterChain chain)
        throws java.io.IOException, ServletException
    {
        // If this isn't an HTTP request, don't bother timing it.
        if (!(request instanceof HttpServletRequest))
        {
            chain.doFilter(request,response);
            return;
        }

        HttpServletRequest httpRequest = (HttpServletRequest) request;

        // Get the pathname of the requested JSP/servlet.
        String uri = httpRequest.getRequestURI();

        // See whether there is an existing time value for this object.
        Times time = (Times) times.get(uri);

        // If not, create a new one.
        if (time == null)
        {
            time = new Times(uri);
            times.put(uri, time);
        }

        time.begin(); // Tells the time object this is a pending request

        // Note the start time.
        long startTime = System.currentTimeMillis();

        // Invoke the JSP/servlet or other chained filter objects.
        chain.doFilter(request, response);

        // Note the finish time.
        long endTime = System.currentTimeMillis();

        // Tell the time object that the pending request has completed.
        time.end();

        // Add the execution time to the time object.
        time.addTime(endTime-startTime);
    }

    /** Returns an array of all the time values known by this filter */
    public static Times[] getTimes()
    {
```

LISTING 7.2 Continued

```
        ArrayList timeArray = new ArrayList();

        for (Iterator iter=times.keySet().iterator(); iter.hasNext();)
        {
            timeArray.add(times.get(iter.next()));
        }

        return (Times[]) timeArray.toArray(
                new Times[timeArray.size()]);
    }
}
```

Examining Listing 7.2, you can see all of the required elements. It implements the interface `Filter`, by providing methods for `init`, `doFilter`, and `destroy`. All of the work is performed in `doFilter`, so `init` and `destroy` are empty. The filter first checks to make sure that the request is an `HttpServletRequest`. If the request is not an `HttpServletRequest`, the filter ignores the request and passes the request undisturbed to the next filter or its target resource. Otherwise, a reference to the request is saved locally and then used to get the URI of the requested resource. Because filters work with all kinds of `ServletRequests`, it was necessary to down-cast to an `HttpServletRequest` to use the method `getRequestURI`. The URI is used as a unique key to store the instance of `Time` used to keep the usage statistics for the resource.

The start time of the invocation is recorded and a call is made to `doFilter`. Upon the completion of `doFilter`, the request has been processed by all downstream filters and the JSP or servlet. The filter then performs post-processing by recording the end time and execution duration. The example highlights the opportunity to do work throughout the lifecycle of a request.

Finally, Listing 7.3 shows a JSP that displays the execution statistics gathered by the `TimingFilter`.

LISTING 7.3 Source Code for `ShowTimes.jsp`

```
<%@page import="examples.filter.*, java.text.*, java.util.*" %>
<html>
<body>
<h1>Current JSP/Servlet Times</h1>
<table border="4">
<tr>
<th>URL</th><th>Total Requests</th><th># Pending</th>
<th>Weighted Average Time (mSec.)</th><th>Average Time</th>
</tr>
```

LISTING 7.3 Continued

```
<%
    Times[] times = TimingFilter.getTimes();
    DecimalFormat formatter = new DecimalFormat("00.00");

    for ( int i = 0; i < times.length ; ++i ) {
       out.println("<tr>");
       out.println("<td>" + times[i].timerName + "</td>");
       out.println("<td>" + times[i].numAccesses + "</td>");
       out.println("<td>" + times[i].numPending + "</td>");
       out.println("<td>" + formatter.format(times[i].weightedAverage) + "</td>");
       out.println("<td>" + formatter.format(times[i].totalTime) + "</td>");
       out.println("</tr>");
        }

%>
</table>
</body>
</html>
```

Listing 7.4 shows the deployment descriptor for the application.

LISTING 7.4 Source Code for web.xml

```
<?xml version="1.0" encoding="ISO-8859-1"?>
<web-app xmlns="http://java.sun.com/xml/ns/j2ee"
    xmlns:xsi="http://www.w3.org/2001/XMLSchema-instance"
    xsi:schemaLocation="http://java.sun.com/xml/ns/j2ee
    http://java.sun.com/xml/ns/j2ee/web-app_2_4.xsd"
    version="2.4">
    <display-name>Show Times</display-name>
    <description>An application to demonstrate the use of a filter
    </description>

<filter>
   <filter-name>Timing Filter</filter-name>
   <filter-class>examples.filter.TimingFilter</filter-class>
</filter>

<filter-mapping>
   <filter-name>Timing Filter</filter-name>
   <url-pattern>/*</url-pattern>
</filter-mapping>

</web-app>
```

This deployment descriptor will apply the timing filter to all resources in the current context. As mentioned earlier, by changing the `filter-mapping` you can limit filters to specific resources.

Did you Know?

Repeating Elements

You can repeat `filter-mapping` elements to apply filters to groups of resources.

Figure 7.1 shows the output of `ShowTimes.jsp`.

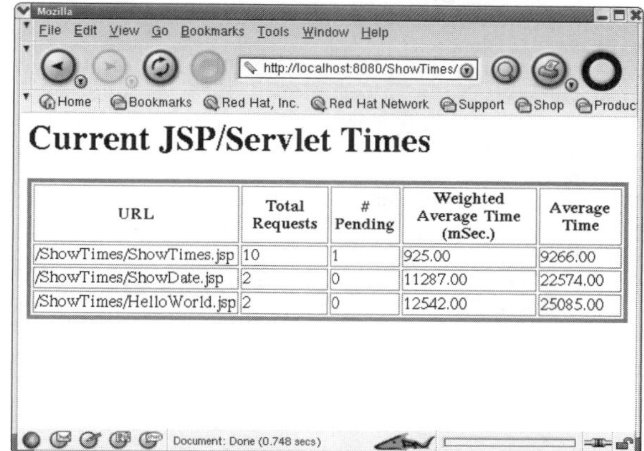

Current JSP/Servlet Times

URL	Total Requests	# Pending	Weighted Average Time (mSec.)	Average Time
/ShowTimes/ShowTimes.jsp	10	1	925.00	9266.00
/ShowTimes/ShowDate.jsp	2	0	11287.00	22574.00
/ShowTimes/HelloWorld.jsp	2	0	12542.00	25085.00

FIGURE 7.1
The `ShowTimes` JSP shows various execution statistics.

Figure 7.1 shows the times from several simple JSPs. You don't need to do anything special in a JSP to support ShowTimes. Just include the JSPs in the same Web application as ShowTimes. In this case, the example was packaged with a few JSPs from earlier chapters.

An Example Filter—Session Logging

Another useful application of filtering is the logging of incoming requests for later playback. You may occasionally want to take a snapshot of what users are doing on your system so you can simulate actual user activity for load testing and capacity planning.

The recording process is very simple. For each different session, you generate a unique filename and store that filename in the session. (If a session doesn't contain a filename, you know that you are starting a new recording.)

For each incoming request, write out the request parameters to the session recording, along with the name of the JSP or servlet. When the session is invalidated, either due to a timeout or being explicitly invalidated, the recording is closed out.

Listing 7.5 shows the session recording filter.

LISTING 7.5 Source Code for `SessionRecorder.java`

```
package examples.filter;

import javax.servlet.Filter;
import javax.servlet.FilterConfig;
import javax.servlet.FilterChain;
import javax.servlet.ServletRequest;
import javax.servlet.ServletResponse;
import javax.servlet.ServletException;
import javax.servlet.http.HttpServletRequest;
import javax.servlet.http.HttpServletResponse;
import javax.servlet.http.HttpSession;
import javax.servlet.http.HttpSessionBindingListener;
import javax.servlet.http.HttpSessionBindingEvent;
import java.util.HashMap;
import java.util.ArrayList;
import java.util.Iterator;
import java.util.Enumeration;
import java.io.PrintWriter;
import java.io.FileWriter;
import java.io.BufferedWriter;

public class SessionRecorder implements Filter
{
    public static final String RECORDING_FILE = "RECORDING_FILE";

    public static HashMap times = new HashMap();
    public static int recordingId;
    public static String recordingPrefix;
    public FilterConfig config;

    public SessionRecorder()
    {
    }

    public void init(FilterConfig filterConfig)
    {
        // Grab the destination of the recording files from
        // the filter configuration. The prefix should contain
        // a directory name and the beginning of a filename.
        // The rest of the filename will be a sequence number
        // and ".xml".
        recordingPrefix = filterConfig.getInitParameter("prefix");
        config = filterConfig;
    }

    public void destroy()
    {
    }
```

LISTING 7.5 Continued

```
    public void doFilter(ServletRequest request,
            ServletResponse response, FilterChain chain)
        throws java.io.IOException, ServletException
    {
        // Ignore non-http requests.
        if (!(request instanceof HttpServletRequest))
        {
            chain.doFilter(request,response);
            return;
        }

        HttpServletRequest httpRequest = (HttpServletRequest) request;
        request.getSession();

        // Execute the JSP/servlet or chained filter.
        chain.doFilter(request, response);

        // Write the request out to the recording file.
        recordRequest((HttpServletRequest) request,
                (HttpServletResponse) response);
    }

    public synchronized static int getNextRecordingId()
    {
        return recordingId++;
    }

    public String generateRecordingFilename()
    {
        return recordingPrefix+getNextRecordingId()+".xml";
    }

    public PrintWriter openRecordingFile(String filename)
    {
        try
        {
            PrintWriter out = new PrintWriter(new BufferedWriter(
                        new FileWriter(filename, true)));
            return out;
        }
        catch (Exception exc)
        {
            config.getServletContext()
                        .log("Error opening recording file: ", exc);
            return null;
        }
    }

    public void recordRequest(HttpServletRequest request,
            HttpServletResponse response)
    {
        HttpSession session = request.getSession();
```

LISTING 7.5 Continued

```
        // Get the recording file name.
        RecordingFile recordingFile =
            (RecordingFile) session.getAttribute(RECORDING_FILE);

        // If there is no recording file, create a new one.
        if (recordingFile == null)
        {
            recordingFile = new RecordingFile(generateRecordingFilename());
            session.setAttribute(RECORDING_FILE, recordingFile);
            initializeRecordingFile(recordingFile.filename);
        }

        // Write the request parameters and URI to the file.
        try
        {
            PrintWriter out = openRecordingFile(recordingFile.filename);
            if (out == null) return;

            out.println("<request>");
            out.print("<uri>");
            out.print(request.getRequestURI());
            out.println("</uri>");
            Enumeration e = request.getParameterNames();
            while (e.hasMoreElements())
            {
                String paramName = (String) e.nextElement();
                String[] values = request.getParameterValues(paramName);
                for (int i=0; i < values.length; i++)
                {
                    out.print("<param><name>");
                    out.print(paramName);
                    out.print("</name><value>");
                    out.print(values[i]);
                    out.println("</value></param>");
                }
            }
            out.println("</request>");
            out.close();
        }
        catch (Exception exc)
        {
            config.getServletContext()
                        .log("Error appending to recording file: ", exc);
        }
    }

    public void initializeRecordingFile(String filename)
    {
        try
        {
            PrintWriter out = openRecordingFile(filename);
            if (out == null) return;
            out.println("<?xml version=\"1.0\"?>");
```

LISTING 7.5 Continued

```
            out.println("<session>");
            out.close();
        }
        catch (Exception exc)
        {
            config.getServletContext()
                        .log("Error initializing recording file: ", exc);
        }
    }

    public void finishRecordingFile(String filename)
    {
        try
        {
            PrintWriter out = openRecordingFile(filename);
            if (out == null) return;
            out.println("</session>");
            out.close();
        }
        catch (Exception exc)
        {
            config.getServletContext()
                        .log("Error finishing recording file: ", exc);
        }
    }

    class RecordingFile implements HttpSessionBindingListener
    {
        public String filename;

        public RecordingFile(String aFilename)
        {
            filename = aFilename;
        }

        public void valueBound(HttpSessionBindingEvent event)
        {
        }

        public void valueUnbound(HttpSessionBindingEvent event)
        {
            // When the session terminates, this method is invoked.
            // Close out the recording file by writing the closing tag.
            finishRecordingFile(filename);
        }
    }
}
```

The deployment descriptor for this application is shown in Listing 7.6.

LISTING 7.6 Source Code for `web.xml`

```
<?xml version="1.0" encoding="ISO-8859-1"?>
<web-app xmlns="http://java.sun.com/xml/ns/j2ee"
    xmlns:xsi="http://www.w3.org/2001/XMLSchema-instance"
    xsi:schemaLocation="http://java.sun.com/xml/ns/j2ee
    http://java.sun.com/xml/ns/j2ee/web-app_2_4.xsd"
    version="2.4">
    <display-name>Show Times</display-name>
    <description>An application to demonstrate the use of a filter
    </description>

    <filter>
       <filter-name>Session Recorder</filter-name>
       <filter-class>examples.filter.SessionRecorder</filter-class>
       <init-param>
           <param-name>prefix</param-name>
           <param-value>/tmp/sessions</param-value>
       </init-param>
    </filter>

    <filter-mapping>
       <filter-name>Session Recorder</filter-name>
       <url-pattern>/*</url-pattern>
    </filter-mapping>

</web-app>
```

Remember to change the `<init-param>` of the session recorder filter to a directory suitable to your configuration.

Listing 7.7 shows the recording of a request to a simple JSP.

LISTING 7.7 Example Recorded Session

```
<?xml version="1.0"?>
<session>
<request>
<uri>/sessionrecorder/postit.jsp</uri>
<param><name>age</name><value>10</value></param>
<param><name>age</name><value>7</value></param>
<param><name>name</name><value>Samantha</value></param>
<param><name>name</name><value>Kaitlynn</value></param>
</request>
</session>
```

Information like this can be very useful in debugging applications or for security purposes. In addition, with a complementary application that enables you to "play-back" the session, you can perform automated regression or load testing.

Summary

Filters are very powerful. They can manipulate requests prior to being handled by servlets or JSPs or perform post-processing on a response before returning it to a client. This makes them ideal for content filtering, authentication, and data manipulation. Implementing a filter is often as simple as writing methods to initialize and deconstruct a filter, and writing the `doFilter` method, which does most of the work.

Filters also give you flexibility of design. Functionality that is common to many application resources can be factored out, making it possible to build cleaner, more maintainable Web applications. `TimingFilter` and `SessionRecorder` are examples of how logging can be performed for many resources using only a single filter.

You may also decide to use filters to remove code that might ordinarily be part of a JavaServer Page—so that you have improved separation between business logic and presentation. And you can extend objects to provide more specialized interfaces, such as presenting a DOM interface to a servlet that expects XML documents.

Q&A

Q. ***I can't seem to get my filter to work. What is the matter?***

A. If your filters aren't working, it is usually one of two reasons. First, the container is having difficulty loading and initializing it. Check the server's logs to see if your filter is throwing an exception when the server instantiates or initializes it. Tomcat's log file is found at `logs/Catalina.out`. Otherwise, you might have made an error in the deployment descriptor. Look at the `url-pattern` element to make certain that it matches the URI of the resource you are trying to apply the filter to. Other configuration errors will likely result in entries in the log files. Also, make sure you are using a servlet container that supports filters. Tomcat did not support filters until version 4.

Workshop

The Workshop is designed to help you review what you have learned and help you to further increase your understanding of the material covered in this hour.

Quiz

1. Does a filter need to be thread-safe?
2. What is the purpose of the wrapper classes?

Answers

1. A filter may need to be thread-safe. A container creates only one instance of a filter to service resources and will reuse that filter for many requests. Filters should be designed to handle concurrent requests.
2. Wrapper classes can save you time by providing a prebuilt class that implements the appropriate interfaces so that you can adapt a request to a servlet. The four wrapper classes are `ServletRequestWrapper`, `ServletResponseWrapper`, `HttpServletRequestWrapper`, and `HttpServletResponseWrapper`.

Activity

Using the `sendRedirect` method in an `HttpServletResponse` object, write a filter that redirects requests for a page at a URL to another location.

HOUR 8

Core JavaServer Page Components

What You'll Learn in This Hour:

- The implicit objects available within a JSP
- The `JspWriter` class
- The `PageContext` class
- The `JSPEngineInfo` class

By now, you have a good understanding of the basics of JavaServer Pages and a better understanding of servlets. You're ready to begin an in-depth look at JavaServer Pages.

Built-in JSP Objects

JSPs create a simplified layer on top of the servlet API. Aside from making it easy to produce HTML output, the JavaServer Pages API makes it easy to access information provided by objects that represent a request, response, or session. You access these objects through **implicit**, or **built-in**, **objects**.

The built-in objects and their associated implementation classes are shown in Table 8.1.

TABLE 8.1 Built-in JSP Objects and Their Implementation Classes

JSP Object	Implementation Class
`request`	`HttpServletRequest`
`response`	`HttpServletResponse`

TABLE 8.1 Continued

JSP Object	Implementation Class
`out`	`JspWriter`
`session`	`HttpSession`
`application`	`ServletContext`
`pageContext`	`PageContext`
`config`	`ServletConfig`
`page`	`Object`
`exception`	`Throwable`

These objects are implicitly created at the beginning of a page when your JSP is invoked, and they directly reference objects in the underlying servlet. They are always available to scriptlets and expressions. As such, you use them the same way you would if you were writing a servlet. From earlier reading, you should already be familiar with the operation of many of these objects.

The `request` Object

The `request` object represents the current request from the browser and is a subclass of the `ServletRequest` class. For most current implementations of JSP, the `request` object is an instance of `HttpServletRequest`. If your JSP engine supports protocols other than HTTP, you might find that your `request` object is an instance of some other protocol-specific subclass of `ServletRequest`.

The `response` Object

Like the `request` object, the `response` object is usually a subclass of the HTTP-specific version of `ServletResponse`. In other words, it is usually an instance of `HttpServletResponse`. Again, if you have a JSP engine that is centered on a protocol other than HTTP, the `response` object might be an instance of a different class.

The `out` Object

The `out` object is responsible for writing responses back to the browser and is an instance of the `JspWriter` class. You will learn more about the `JspWriter` class later in this chapter.

The `session` Object

The `session` object is an instance of `HttpSession`. Because there is an obvious dependence on HTTP, this object is available only if your JSPs use HTTP.

The `application` Object

The `application` object is an instance of the `ServletContext` object. The names "application" and "ServletContext" don't seem very similar, but if you recall what the `ServletContext` class does, you'll see that it manages data at the application level.

The `pageContext` Object

The `pageContext` object is an instance of the `PageContext` class. Many of the items available through built-in variables are also available through the `pageContext` object. You will learn more about the `pageContext` object later in this chapter.

The `config` Object

The `config` object gives you access to configuration information for your JSP and is an instance of the `ServletConfig` class.

The `page` Object

The `page` object is rather peculiar because it is a reference to the current JSP. In other words, it's like an alias for the `this` keyword in Java. Although most JSPs are currently written in Java, the JSP architecture is designed to allow scripting in languages other than Java. These other languages also need to support the built-in objects, such as `request`, `response`, and `out`. In those languages, there might not be a `this` keyword, so the `page` object provides a reference to the current page instead.

The `exception` Object

When you create an error page to deal with exceptions that occur during normal JSP processing, you might need access to the exception that caused the error page to be invoked. You can access that exception through the `exception` object.

The JspWriter Class

The JspWriter class acts like the PrintWriter class most of the time, except that it is specially tailored to deal with the buffering you need to do in a JSP. If you look at the PrintWriter class, none of the print or println methods throw an IOException. On the other hand, the JspWriter versions of print and println can and will throw an IOException if the buffer fills up and is not automatically flushed.

In addition to the print and println methods, the JspWriter class gives you access to information about buffering. Using this information, you can flush the buffer if necessary or determine how much more you can write to the buffer before it needs to be flushed.

By the Way

If in Doubt, Use Default Buffering

Don't worry if you don't understand buffering, or if it seems overly complicated. If you use the default settings, you don't have to worry about it at all.

Sending Output Data

Most of the time, you aren't explicitly sending output in your JSP. In other words, you aren't calling the out.print or out.println methods directly. Instead, you put the text that you want to display directly into the JSP. If you look at the servlet generated from your JSP source file, however, you see that the JSP compiler took that text and converted it into an out.print or out.println statement.

Occasionally, you'll need to write to the output stream from within your JSP. For example, you might have a huge block of Java code that loops through some data to extract items that you want to display. Rather than closing the scriptlet and using a JSP expression to display the data, you are much better off calling out.print or out.println.

The print and println methods available in the JspWriter class are

```
public void print(boolean b) throws IOException
public void print(char c) throws IOException
public void print(char[] s) throws IOexception
public void print(double d) throws IOException
public void print(float f) throws IOException
public void print(int i) throws IOException
public void print(long l) throws IOException
public void print(Object obj) throws IOException
public void print(String s) throws IOException
public void println()throws IOException
```

```
public void println(boolean b) throws IOException
public void println(char c) throws IOException
public void println(char[] x) throws IOException
public void println(double d) throws IOException
public void println(float f) throws IOException
public void println(int i) throws IOException
public void println(long l) throws IOException
public void println(Object obj) throws IOException
public void println(String s) throws IOException
```

Also, instead of calling `out.println()` to print a blank line, you can call `out.newLine()`.

Because the `JspWriter` is a subclass of the `Writer` class, you can also use the `write` method to write out a string, a single character, or an array of characters:

```
public void write(String str)
public void write(String str, int offset, int length)
public void write(int singleCharacter)
public void write(char[] charArray)
public void write(char[] charArray, int offset, int length)
```

Buffer Control

Automatic buffer flushing can be turned off if you want to have more control over when information is sent. It's a simple matter of telling a page that you'll be managing the buffering. You'll learn the details in the next chapter.

If you turn off automatic buffer flushing, the most important method to you, aside from `print` and `println`, is the `flush` method:

```
public void flush()
```

If you have a chain of writers set up (that is, if the output of the `JspWriter` is going to another writer) the `flush` method flushes all the writers along the output chain. In other words, calling `flush` ensures that the current contents of the buffer get sent back to the browser, even if they need to go through another writer first.

Rather than flush the buffer, you might need to clear it out, erasing its current contents. The `clear` or `clearBuffer` methods empty out the buffer's contents:

```
public void clear() throws IOException
public void clearBuffer() throws IOException
```

It might seem strange to have two methods that appear to do the same thing. The `clear` method, though, throws an `IOException` if the buffer has been flushed before. The idea is that when you clear the buffer, the chances are good that you meant to clear out the entire page. If the buffer has been flushed, you aren't clearing out the entire page because some of it has already been sent back to the browser. When that happens, you want the system to let you know that it can't do what you want.

If you want to clear the current contents of the buffer, and you don't care whether the buffer has been flushed before, use the `clearBuffer` method.

The `getBufferSize` method returns the buffer's size in bytes, and the `getRemaining` method returns the number of bytes left in the buffer:

```
public int getBufferSize()
public int getRemaining()
```

If buffering is turned off, the `getBufferSize` method returns `0`.

The `isAutoFlush` method returns `true` if the system is handling the automatic flushing of the buffer:

```
public boolean isAutoFlush()
```

By the Way

In Case of Trouble

If you are having trouble getting the buffering to work correctly, see the "Q&A" section at the end of this hour.

Using a `PrintWriter`

Sometimes, you need a real `PrintWriter` object rather than `JspWriter`. For example, the `printStackTrace` method in the `Throwable` class can print a stack trace to a `PrintStream` or a `PrintWriter`. Unfortunately, `JspWriter` is neither of these. You can, however, create a new `PrintWriter` on top of a `Writer` object. Thus, if you absolutely need a `PrintWriter`, just create one around the `JspWriter`. Listing 8.1 shows a JSP that uses the `printStackTrace` method to print a stack trace.

LISTING 8.1 Source Code for `PrintException.jsp`

```
<%@ page language="java" import="java.io.*" %>

<html>
<body bgcolor="#ffffff">
<pre>
<%
    try
    {
        throw new RuntimeException("Print me, please");
```

LISTING 8.1 Continued

```
    }
    catch (RuntimeException exc)
    {
        PrintWriter pw = new PrintWriter(out);

        exc.printStackTrace(pw);
    }
%>
</pre>
</body>
</html>
```

Figure 8.1 shows the output from the `PrintException` JavaServer Page.

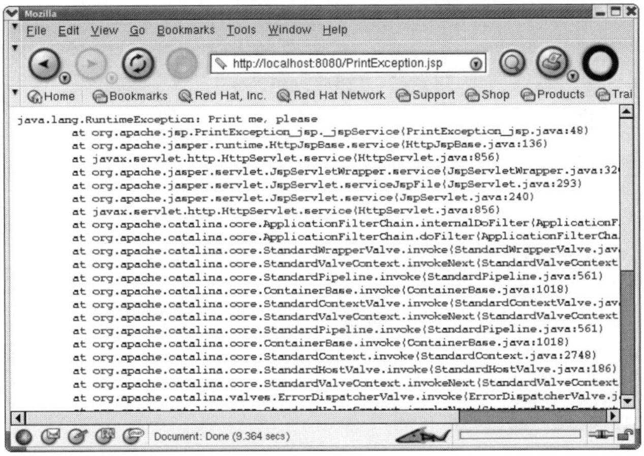

FIGURE 8.1
You can create a `PrintWriter` to print a stack trace to the browser.

Working with the `pageContext` Object

The `pageContext` object acts as a central repository for information that a JSP might need to obtain. A `pageContext` is associated with the "execution" of a page, which means that it is created at the beginning of the servlet that implements a JSP and is destroyed at the end. Typically, the system initializes the built-in variables by calling a method within the `pageContext` object. For example, if your JSP uses the `session` object, the generated servlet usually contains a line such as this:

```
HttpSession session = pageContext.getSession();
```

All of the implicit objects are available through the `pageContext`.

\ addition to providing access to built-in objects, the pageContext object has the pability to scan for attributes and attribute names among all the possible scopes (page, request, session, and application).

Finally, the pageContext object contains convenience methods that make it easy to include or forward to another servlet or JSP.

By the Way

Using PageContext Enhances Portability

The PageContext class was created to enhance portability between JSP environments, including an environment based upon servlets. That's why the implicit objects are obtained using the pageContext object as outlined previously. As a JSP developer, you will most often use pageContext to store or retrieve attributes or for forwarding to or including JSP pages.

Accessing the Implicit Objects

The objects associated with built-in variables (request, response, out, session, and so on) are available from the pageContext object.

The implicit objects are initialized from the following methods in pageContext:

```
public ServletRequest getRequest()
public ServletResponse getResponse()
public JspWriter getOut()
public HttpSession getSession()
public ServletContext getServletContext()
public ServletConfig getServletConfig()
public Object getPage()
public Throwable getException()
```

Accessing Attributes from the PageContext Class

The PageContext class performs double duty when it comes to storing and retrieving attributes. First, you can store attributes in an instance of a PageContext explicitly. These attributes have a page scope, meaning that the attributes are only available for use within the lifecycle of a page. Every instance of every JSP page has its own separate PageContext for storing attributes. Also, any JavaBeans you create with a page scope are stored as attributes in PageContext as well.

The methods for storing, retrieving, and removing attributes in PageContext are similar to their counterparts in ServletRequest, HttpSession, and ServletContext:

```
public Object getAttribute(String name)
public void setAttribute(String name, Object ob)
public void removeAttribute(String name)
```

The most interesting aspect of PageContext is that it gives you access to attributes in any scope by adding an extra parameter to getAttribute, setAttribute, and removeAttribute:

```
Public Object getAttribute(String name, int scope)
Public void setAttribute(String name, Object object,
    int scope)
public void removeAttribute(String name, int scope)
```

By the Way

JSP 2.0: More Than Just Features

The JSP 2.0 specification has brought more than just great new JSP features. It's also decoupling JSPs from servlets. JSPs are capable of standing on their own, and the authors of the specification can see that future JSP containers may elect to work with JSPs in their own environment. Consequently, there are some design changes. For example, PageContext now extends JspContext—a new class that abstracts information that is not specific to servlets. It supports SimpleTags, which you'll learn about in Hour 16, "Extending JSP with New Tags." Along with other methods, JspContext also provides the methods for working with attributes we just covered.

The scope values are defined by the PageContext constants PAGE_SCOPE, REQUEST_SCOPE, SESSION_SCOPE, and APPLICATION_SCOPE. For example, to retrieve an object from a session, you can make the following call:

```
Object ob = pageContext.getAttribute("myObject",
    PageContext.SESSION_SCOPE);
```

You can locate all the attribute names in a given scope by calling getAttributeNamesInScope:

```
public Enumeration getAttributeNamesInScope(int scope)
```

You can search through all the scopes for a particular object by calling findAttribute:

```
public Object findAttribute(String name)
```

The pageContext object first searches within the page scope, then the request scope, the session scope, and finally the application scope. The search stops at the first scope in which it finds a match. If you have an attribute named myObject stored in the request object and also in the application object, findAttribute("myObject") returns the object stored in the request object.

The getAttributesScope method returns the scope in which it finds a particular name:

```
public int getAttributesScope(String name)
```

For example, if findAttribute finds myObject in the request object, getAttributeScope returns PageContext.REQUEST_SCOPE.

Listing 8.2 shows a JSP that dumps out all the objects it can see in the various scopes.

LISTING 8.2 Source Code for DumpAttributes.jsp

```
<%@ page import="java.util.*" %>
<html>
<body>
This page has access to the following attributes:
<pre>
<%

// Create an array of the possible scopes.
    int scopes[] = new int[] {
        PageContext.PAGE_SCOPE,
        PageContext.REQUEST_SCOPE,
        PageContext.SESSION_SCOPE,
        PageContext.APPLICATION_SCOPE };

// Create names for each possible scope.
    String scopeNames[] = new String[] {
        "Page", "Request", "Session", "Application"
    };

// Loop through the possible scopes.
    for (int i=0; i < scopes.length; i++)
    {
        out.println("In the "+scopeNames[i]+" scope:");

// Get all the attribute names for the current scope.
Enumeration e = pageContext.getAttributeNamesInScope(scopes[i]);

        while (e.hasMoreElements())
        {
// Get the attribute name.
            Object nameOb = e.nextElement();
```

LISTING 8.2 Continued

```
// The name should always be a string, but just in case someone put
// some bad data somewhere, you won't get a class cast exception this way.
            if (nameOb instanceof String)
            {
// Print out the attribute name and its value.
                String name = (String) nameOb;

                out.print(name+": ");
                out.println(pageContext.getAttribute(name, scopes[i]));
            }
            else
            {
                out.println("Oops, the attribute name isn't a string! It's "+
                    nameOb.getClass().getName());
            }
        }
        out.println();
    }
%>
</pre>
</body>
</html>
```

Figure 8.2 shows the output from the `DumpAttributes` JSP.

FIGURE 8.2 The `getAttributeNamesInScope` method is useful for exploring the various scope objects.

Forwarding and Including

Often, when designing a Web application, you will want a Web resource, such as a JSP, to interact with other resources. You may want to create a page that is an aggregation of pages that include a banner, menu, main section, and footer. Or you may want to continue on to another page after making a decision based upon a request parameter.

Normally you use the `<jsp:include>` and `<jsp:forward>` tags to include or forward to other pages. You will learn about these shortly. You have already learned how to handle the case when a resource has moved and you want to redirect the client to the new location by using the `sendRedirect` method of `HttpServletResponse`.

If you want to do an include or forward in a scriptlet, you can use `ServletContext.getRequestDispatcher` to get the request dispatcher for the page you want to include or forward to. The request dispatcher is a little messy, however. First, you must get the dispatcher for the page you want to call and then invoke either the `include` or the `forward` method in the dispatcher.

The `PageContext` class gives you a useful shortcut for `forward` and `include`. You can just call `forward` or `include` and pass the name of the page you are including or are forwarding to:

```
public void forward(String url)
    throws IOException, ServletException
public void include(String url)
    throws IOException, ServletException
```

You can prevent the content of the buffer from being flushed prior to processing the include by using

```
public void include(String url, boolean flush)
    throws IOException, ServletException
```

and setting the `flush` parameter to `false`.

By the Way

In Case of Trouble

If you are having trouble forwarding or including, see the "Q&A" section at the end of this hour.

The `JspEngineInfo` Class

Occasionally you might want to obtain information about the current version of the JSP engine. You might even have code that adapts itself to various versions of the JSP specification. For example, you might create a JSP that takes full advantage of the features of JSP version 2.0 and another page that runs under JSP 1.2 but doesn't do everything the 2.0 page does. By examining the current version of the JSP engine, you can decide which page to call.

The `JspEngineInfo` class defines just one method, which returns a string containing the current version number of the JSP engine. The version number is a series of numbers separated by periods, such as 2.0 or 1.2.3.4.5. The `getSpecificationVersion` method returns the current version number:

```
public String getSpecificationVersion()
```

You must take a roundabout path to get to the `JspEngineInfo` object. You must get the object from a `JspFactory` object. The `JspFactory` class is used internally by the JSP engine and by the generated servlets. Typically a single `JspFactory`, which is called the **default factory**, is used by all the JSPs. To get the default factory, just call `getDefaultFactory`:

```
JspFactory defaultFactory = JspFactory.getDefaultFactory();
```

After you have the `JspFactory`, you can call `getEngineInfo` to retrieve the `JspEngineInfo` object:

```
JspEngineInfo engineInfo = defaultFactory.getEngineInfo();
```

Listing 8.3 shows a JSP that prints out the version of the JSP specification that the current JSP engine supports.

LISTING 8.3 Source Code for `PrintEngineInfo.jsp`

```
<html>
<body>
The current JSP Engine is:
<%= JspFactory.getDefaultFactory().getEngineInfo().
    getSpecificationVersion() %>
</body>
</html>
```

Figure 8.3 shows the output from `PrintEngineInfo.jsp`.

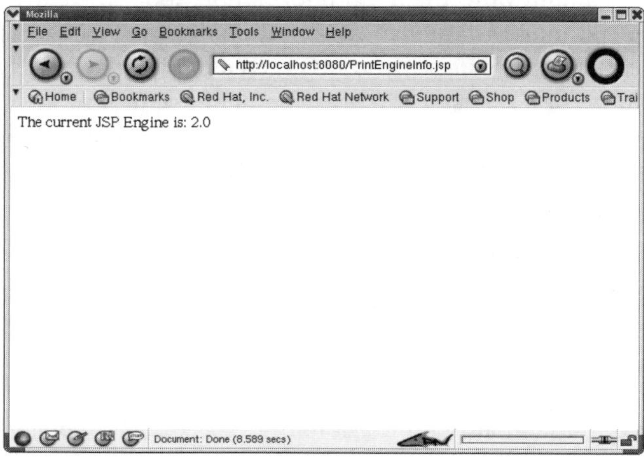

FIGURE 8.3 You can get the supported JSP version number from the JSP engine.

By the Way

You Can Use `JspFactory`

Section JSP.12.1.3 of the Proposed Final Draft (PFD) 3 for JSP 2.0, which describes `JspFactory`, might be somewhat confusing. `JspFactory` is used by containers to obtain an implementation of a `PageContext`. As shown in the example, you can also use it to obtain information about the JSP engine, such as the version of specification the engine supports.

The end of the description for `JspFactory` warns that "`JspFactory` objects should not be used by JSP page authors." It is illegal for anyone other than the container to use `setDefaultFactory`. Page authors should also use the implicit objects provided by the container instead of using methods from `JspFactory` to attempt to manage them. The only method you might use is `getEngineInfo`, when it's necessary to make adjustments to the behavior of your application based on the JSP specification version the engine supports. For most cases, the need to do this is rare. You should carefully consider your design if you need to know the version of JSP specification to run your application.

Summary

Several implicit objects are available for you to use in your JSPs. These objects make it convenient to access important objects you may need to interact with in scriptlets and expressions. They include the `request` and `response`, `session` and `application`, `exception`, and several other useful objects. Among the ones that you will use most frequently are `out` and `pageContext`. In addition to providing a way to write to the output stream, you learned that `out`, an instance of `JspWriter`, has a number of methods used to manage buffering. You can let the system manage the buffer automatically, or you can do it yourself. The `pageContext` provides a single object that is used most frequently for storing and retrieving objects in any scope. It also has convenient methods to forward the current request to or include other Web resources. If it's important to know what version of container you are running in, then you can use the `JspEngineInfo` class to determine that.

Q&A

Q. ***I cleared the buffer, so why do I still see part of the old page?***

A. The buffer was probably already flushed. You might need to increase the size of the output buffer, or if you really don't know how big to make it, set `autoFlush` to `false`. Be careful, though. You need to flush the buffer yourself if you set `autoFlush` to `false`.

Q. ***I turned off*** `autoFlush`***, so why do I still see part of the old page?***

A. You probably included this page from another one. Whenever you include another page at runtime by using the `include` method of `pageContext`, the JSP engine automatically flushes the buffer for the including page. If you want to prevent this from happening, set the `flush` parameter of the `include` method to false.

Q. ***Why do I get an error when I try to forward to another page or include another page?***

A. The first thing to check is that you entered the correct filename and that you are using a relative path. If you just enter a filename with no directory names, that file should be in the same directory as the JSP that is including it or forwarding to it. Assuming that the filename is correct, the other thing to check is that the target page compiles correctly on its own. If you forward to or include a bad page, you'll get an error. Try accessing the page manually and see whether there is an error.

Q. ***When I include or forward to another page, why do I get an exception referring to the buffer?***

A. When you forward to another page, the JSP engine attempts to clear the output buffer. If the buffer has already been committed, you'll get an error. When you include another page, the JSP engine automatically flushes the output buffer. So if you include another page and then try to forward, you're almost assured of getting an error. You need to rethink your design to avoid these situations.

Workshop

The Workshop is designed to help you review what you have learned, and help you to further increase your understanding of the material covered in this chapter.

Quiz

1. Which implicit object can be used to get request parameters?
2. Which built-in objects are specific to JSPs?
3. How do you save and retrieve an object for use during the lifecycle of a request?

Answers

1. The `request` object is an instance of `HttpServletRequest`, which provides methods such as `getParameter` that can be used to obtain parameter values. Remember that most of the implicit objects are instances of classes that implement a core Java technology or the servlet API.
2. `page`, `pageContext`, and `out` are all instances of classes that are unique to JSPs—they are not defined in the servlet API. As a developer, you will need to be aware of the differences between `out`, which is a `JspWriter`, and the `Printwriter` returned by the `getWriter` method of a `ServletResponse`. In essence, you will need to remember that several methods of the `JspWriter` throw exceptions. Similar methods in a `PrintWriter` do not. In addition, a `JspWriter` may provide additional flexibility because of extended buffer control. For example, in spite of the fact that template text may have been buffered to output, you can often still set HTTP header information, because a response has not yet been sent.
3. You can use the `pageContext` implicit object. The method `setAttribute` with a scope parameter of `PageContext.REQUEST_SCOPE` will store an object so that it can be accessed by any resource servicing a request. The corresponding method `getAttribute` with the same scope parameter or `findAttribute` is used to retrieve the object.

Activity

Write a JSP that stores objects in each of the scopes. Cause the JSP you have written to also forward to `DumpAttributes.jsp` and verify that the objects you saved are in the proper scope.

HOUR 9

JSP Directives

What You'll Learn in This Hour:

- How directives influence the operation of a JSP or the way a container interacts with it
- Write JSPs in languages other than Java
- Specify an error page that should be displayed in the event of an error
- How directives allow you to compose JSPs that are made up of several components

Often, you'll want to guide the JSP container by providing information that will help the container work with your JSP. For example, if you use Java packages that aren't standard, you'll need to tell the container where to find those packages. JSP directives instruct a container how to do many things related to the construction and operation of your Java Server Pages.

An Overview of JSP Directives

The JavaServer Pages specification contains four different types of tags that start with the characters `<%`. The plain `<%` tag begins a block of Java code. The `<%!` tag begins a declaration of class attributes or methods. The `<%=` tag inserts the result of a Java expression in the output. The final `<%` tag is the directive tag, which is `<%@`. There are currently three directives in the JSP specification:

- `page`
- `include`
- `taglib`

The page directive is a catchall for various page options that don't really warrant their own directives. The include directive enables you to include other files at compile time as opposed to runtime. The taglib enables you to include an external library of custom JSP tags so you can expand the core set of tags recognized by JSP. The taglib directives will be covered in more detail in Hour 16, "Extending JSP with New Tags."

The page Directive

The page directive has a number of options that bear no relation to each other except that they apply to the page. The options are of the form *name=value* and are separated by spaces. The following is an example page directive:

```
<%@ page info="My first JSP Page" %>
```

In this example, the page directive has an attribute-value pair that specifies a string that describes the page.

You can have multiple page directives—in fact, it's common to have several—but you can't have two page directives with the same option in the same page. This rule has two exceptions: the import option and the pageEncoding option. The import option, which enables you to specify Java classes to import, can appear as many times as necessary. The pageEncoding option can appear once in each file, even if the files are combined to produce a single JSP.

You can also combine several options within the same page directive, but again only import may appear more than once.

By the Way

In Case of Trouble

If you are having trouble putting a page directive in your JSP, see the "Q&A" section at the end of this hour.

The contentType Option

The contentType option allows you to specify the kind of data that you are returning to the browser. The default content type is text/html, which is the standard content type for HTML pages. If you want to write out XML from your JSP, use the following page directive:

```
<%@ page contentType="text/xml" %>
```

You can also specify the character encoding for the response. For example, if you wanted to specify that the resulting page that is returned to the browser uses ISO Latin 1, you would use the following page directive:

```
<%@ page contentType="text/html:charset=ISO-8859-1" %>
```

The `pageEncoding` Option

If you need to use a different character encoding for your JSP page, you specify the encoding using the `pageEncoding` attribute. For standard syntax JSP pages, the default encoding is ISO-8859-1.

The `language` Option

The `language` option enables you to specify the language you want to use for scripting in your JSP. For example, because you usually use Java as the scripting language, your `language` option looks like this:

```
<%@ page language="java" %>
```

The JavaServer Pages environment was designed to support scripting languages other than Java. You can, for example, use JavaScript as the scripting language if you have a JSP engine, such as Resin, that supports it. In that case, the `language` option on the page would be

```
<%@ page language="javascript" %>
```

Listing 9.1 shows the familiar "Hello World!" JSP with JavaScript, rather than Java, being used as the scripting language. The example works with the Resin JSP engine.

LISTING 9.1 Source Code for `JSHello.jsp`

```
<%@ page language="javascript" %>
<html>
<body>
<%
    var helloStr = 'Hello World!';
%>
<h1><%=helloStr%></h1>
</body>
</html>
```

However, in JSP 2.0, only the value `java` is defined and required.

The `isELIgnored` Option

JavaServer Pages 2.0 arrives with an Expression Language (EL) that makes it possible to construct dynamic pages without scripting elements. We'll spend time discussing this in Hour 15, "The JSP Expression Language." For now, you need to know that the `isELIgnored` option gives you the ability to disable the evaluation of EL expressions.

The `import` Option

Of all the options for the `page` directive, the `import` option is the one you use the most. You can't use the `import` keyword within scriptlets or declarations to import Java packages. Instead, you must use the `import` option in the `page` directive. The value for the `import` option is the name of the package you want to import. For example, to import `java.sql.*`, use the following `page` directive:

```
<%@ page import="java.sql.*" %>
```

By default, a container automatically imports `java.lang.*`, `javax.servlet.*`, `javax.servlet.jsp.*`, and `javax.servlet.http.*`.

You can have multiple `page` directives, so one way to import multiple packages is to have multiple `page` directives:

```
<%@ page import="java.sql.*" %>
<%@ page import="java.util.*" %>
```

Because you can also have multiple `import` attributes in a single `page` directive, you can import multiple packages by using multiple attributes:

```
<%@ page import="java.sql.*" import="java.util.*" %>
```

The easiest and most compact method of importing multiple packages, however, is to list them all in one `import` option, separated by commas:

```
<%@ page import="java.sql.*,java.util.*" %>
```

The JSP compiler reads through the entire JSP file before it generates a servlet, so if you put `import` statements later in the code, they still appear at the beginning of the generated servlet where they belong. For example, the JSP shown in Listing 9.2 compiles cleanly and runs even though the `import` statement is in the middle of the page.

LISTING 9.2 Source Code for `TestImport.jsp`

```
<HTML>
<BODY>
<PRE>
<%
    out.println("Hello!");
%>
<%@ page import="java.sql.*,java.util.*,java.math.*" %>
</PRE>
</BODY>
</HTML>
```

You may wonder why the JSP compiler doesn't require you to put the `import` statements at the top the way you would in a Java source file. When you include additional code at compile time (using another JSP directive that you will see later in this hour), that code appears later in a file, and it may contain `import` statements. For example, suppose you have one version of a class or function that stores information to a text file and another version that stores data in a database. You can include either one of these at compile time. Rather than importing `java.sql.*` in your main JSP, you can let the included file import whatever packages it needs, knowing that the JSP compiler will handle it properly.

The `info` Option

The `info` option lets you provide a description of the servlet. For example, you may want to indicate what kind of function the JSP performs:

```
<%@ page info="JSP that receives new customer orders" %>
```

You can access the value of this attribute through the pages implementation of `Servlet.getServletInfo()`.

The `session` Option

The `session` option tells the JSP compiler whether you want to use sessions:

```
<%@ page session="true" %>
```

The default value is `true`, indicating that you want to use sessions. This option makes the `session` implicit variable available for your use. If you absolutely can't use sessions in your application, set the session value to `false`.

Frequently, the only reason to turn sessions off is to help in error checking. If you haven't enabled sessions, the JSP compiler will tell you whether you accidentally tried to use the session variable.

Did you Know?

Bug Catcher

It's far better to catch bugs at compile time than it is to catch them at runtime. The `session` option is a specialized tool to help you locate a specific error at compile time.

If you try to store an object in a session and you have turned sessions off for the page, you might get a compile error or a runtime error, depending on your JSP engine. For example, Listing 9.3 shows a simple JSP whose only goal is to challenge the `session` option to see whether it really has turned off sessions.

LISTING 9.3 Source Code for `UseSession.jsp`

```
<%@ page session="false" %>
<jsp:useBean id="item" class="usingjsp.cart.Item" scope="session"/>
<html>
<body>
</body>
</html>
```

Figure 9.1 shows the response from the Jakarta Tomcat JSP engine, which compiles fine but generates a runtime error when you try to use the session object.

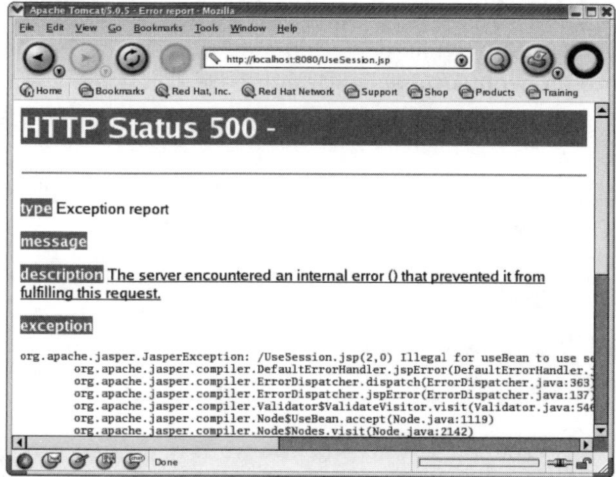

FIGURE 9.1
Some JSP engines give you a runtime error if you try to use a session with sessions disabled.

The `buffer` and `autoFlush` Options

The `buffer` and `autoFlush` options let you control your JSP's buffering. To turn the buffering off completely, set the `buffer` option to none:

```
<%@ page buffer="none" %>
```

You can also specify the size of the buffer in kilobytes. For example, to set the buffer size to 16KB, you can use either of the following two `page` directives:

```
<%@ page buffer="16" %>
<%@ page buffer="16kb" %>
```

The default buffer size may be no less than 8KB, according to the JSP specification.

Did you Know?

Buffer Size May Change

The buffer size you specify with the `buffer` option sets only the minimum size for the buffer. The JSP engine may choose a larger buffer size than you requested, but it can never be smaller.

The `autoFlush` option controls whether the buffer is automatically flushed when it fills. The default value is `true`, meaning the buffer is automatically flushed when it is full. If you turn off `autoFlush` and the buffer fills up, the JSP engine throws a runtime exception when you try to write more data to the buffer.

Sometimes you might want such detailed control over the buffer, but, in general, you should leave this option alone.

The `isThreadSafe` Option

The `isThreadSafe` option marks a page as being thread-safe. By default, all JSPs are considered thread-safe. If you set the `isThreadSafe` option to `false`, the JSP engine makes sure that only one thread at a time is executing your JSP. The following `page` directive sets the `isThreadSafe` option to false:

```
<%@ page isThreadSafe="false" %>
```

Watch Out!

`isThreadSafe` Isn't Safe

The Servlet 2.4 specification deprecates the interface `SingleThreadModel`, which is a common mechanism for JSP containers to implement `isThreadSafe`. To be certain that a generated servlet does not contain this deprecated code, don't use `isThreadSafe`.

isThreadSafe is a misleading name for this option. It is possible for you to encounter threading issues even if you mark the page as not being thread-safe. For instance, multiple threads can still access any objects that are shared in the session object or the application object. You must make sure that you synchronize access to any shared resources when you label the JSP as not being thread-safe.

The errorPage Option

The errorPage option tells the JSP engine which page to display if there is an error while the current page runs. For example, suppose you want to call handleError.jsp if the current page encounters an error. You would use the following page directive:

```
<%@ page errorPage="handleError.jsp" %>
```

Watch Out!

Flushing May Cause Additional Errors

Be careful with error pages when you include other pages. When you include another page and specify flush="true", the output buffer is automatically flushed. Some JSP engines try to clear the buffer when they call an error page and throw an exception if the buffer has already been flushed. Your best bet is to do the operations that are likely to throw an exception before you get to the included files.

By the Way

In Case of Trouble

If you are having trouble specifying an error page in your JSP, see the “Q&A,” section at the end of this hour.

The isErrorPage Option

The isErrorPage option indicates that the current JSP can be used as the error page for another JSP. For example, the handleError.jsp sets the isErrorPage option to true because it is supposed to handle errors:

```
<%@ page isErrorPage="true" %>
```

By setting the isErrorPage to true, you tell the JSP compiler to create an implicit exception object that contains the Throwable object that caused the error page to be invoked.

Listing 9.4 shows an error page that prints the message from the exception that caused the error page to be invoked.

LISTING 9.4 Source Code for `ErrorPage.jsp`

```
<%@ page isErrorPage="true" %>
<html>
<body>
<h1>Error</h1>
An error occurred while processing your request.
<p>
The error message is: <%= exception.getMessage() %>.
</body>
</html>
```

Listing 9.5 shows a page that intentionally throws an exception just to invoke the error page shown in Listing 9.5.

LISTING 9.5 Source Code for `ThrowException.jsp`

```
<%@ page errorPage="ErrorPage.jsp" %>
<html>
<body>
You shouldn't see this because I plan
to throw an exception in just a second.
<%
    if (true) throw new RuntimeException("Sorry about that, Chief!");
%>
</body>
</html>
```

Figure 9.2 shows the results of the error page. Notice that none of the text from the original page shows up on the error page.

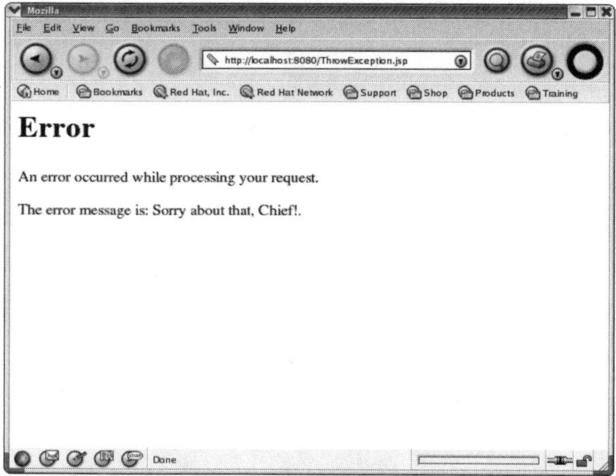

FIGURE 9.2 The JSP engine clears the output buffer, if possible, before displaying an error page.

The `extends` Option

The `extends` option enables you to specify the superclass for your JSP. Most of the time, you should stick to the superclass that the JSP compiler chooses. If you find that you want to create your own superclass, first ask yourself why you need to.

If, for example, you find several utility routines that your JSPs need to call, consider implementing those routines as static methods in some utility class.

Many times, the superclass for your JSP has been optimized to give you the best performance. If you decide to create your own superclass, you may be throwing away some of the benefits of the JSP engine that you are using.

If you choose to implement your own superclass, there are a few things you need to be aware of. A JSP's superclass must implement the `JspPage` interface. If your JavaServer Pages use HTTP, as most currently do, the superclass must implement `HttpJspPage`, which extends `JspPage`.

Because the `JspPage` interface extends the `Servlet` interface, a JSP's superclass must also implement all the methods in the `Servlet` interface. These include the `init`, `service`, and `destroy` methods. Also, you must declare the `Servlet` interface methods in your class as final, meaning the JSP can't override them.

Typically, your superclass will extend HttpServlet, which does most of the work for you. From there, you only need to add two methods:

```
public void jspInit()
public void jspDestroy()
```

You must call jspInit from within your superclass's init method and jspDestroy from its destroy method. Finally, the service method must invoke the _jspService method in the JSP. The _jspService method is already defined in the HttpJspPage interface and is declared in the following way:

```
public void _jspService(HttpServletRequest request,
    pttpServletResponse response)
    throws ServletException, IOException
```

Listing 9.6 shows an example servlet that may be used as the superclass for a JSP.

LISTING 9.6 Source Code for JSPSuperclass.java

```
package usingjsp;

import javax.servlet.*;
import javax.servlet.http.*;
import javax.servlet.jsp.*;

/** An example superclass for a JavaServer Page */

public abstract class JSPSuperclass extends HttpServlet
    implements HttpJspPage
{
// init must be declared as final for this to be a superclass for a JSP.
    public final void init(ServletConfig config)
        throws ServletException
    {
// Let the superclass do its initialization.
        super.init(config);

// Initialize the JSP
        jspInit();
    }

// destroy must be declared as final for this to be a superclass for a JSP.
    public final void destroy()
    {
        super.destroy();

        jspDestroy();
    }

// getServletConfig must be declared as final for this to
// be a superclass for a JSP.
    public final ServletConfig getServletConfig()
    {
```

LISTING 9.6 Continued

```
        return super.getServletConfig();
    }

// service must be declared as final for this to be a superclass for a JSP.
    public final void service(ServletRequest request,
        ServletResponse response)
        throws ServletException, java.io.IOException
    {
        super.service(request, response);
    }

    public final void service(HttpServletRequest request,
        HttpServletResponse response)
        throws ServletException, java.io.IOException
    {
// DEMO ALERT! Put a dummy data item in here to show
// how the subclassing works.
request.setAttribute("Demo", "Hello from your superclass");

// Now call the _jspService method to run the JSP.
        _jspService(request, response);
    }

// Provide a dummy jspInit method.
    public void jspInit()
    {
    }

// Provide a dummy jspDestroy method.
    public void jspDestroy()
    {
    }
// The _jspService method is implemented by the servlet generated
// from the JSP page source.
    public abstract void _jspService(HttpServletRequest request,
        HttpServletResponse response)
        throws ServletException, java.io.IOException;
}
```

Listing 9.7 shows a JSP that extends the example superclass.

LISTING 9.7 Source Code for `TestSubclassing.jsp`

```
<%@ page extends="usingjsp.JSPSuperclass"%>
<html>
<body>
I am a subclass of a custom servlet. My parent class
left me a message. Here it is:
<%= request.getAttribute("Demo") %>
</body>
</html>
```

By the Way

In Case of Trouble

If you are having trouble specifying a superclass in your JSP, see the "Q&A" section at the end of this hour.

The `include` Directive

Many programmers who come from the C and C++ worlds are disappointed with the lack of an `include` keyword in Java. The `include` directive in JSP performs the same service that the C `include` keyword does: It includes a file at compile time as opposed to runtime.

The nice thing about including a file at compile time is that it requires less overhead than a file included at runtime. The included file doesn't need to be a servlet or JSP, either. When the JSP compiler sees an `include` directive, it reads the included file as if it were part of the JSP that's being compiled.

You might have a standard HTML header that you want to put on all your files. For example, to include a file named `header.html`, your `include` directive would look like this:

```
<%@ include file="header.html" %>
```

The filename in the `include` directive is actually a relative URL. If you just specify a filename with no associated path, the JSP compiler assumes that the file is in the same directory as your JSP, as in the example with `header.html`.

The `taglib` Directive

The JavaServer Pages API has an extension mechanism known as a **tag library**. You can create custom JSP tags that look like HTML or XML tags. By segregating more of your Java code into custom tags, you reduce the amount of Java code that appears in the JSP. This topic is important enough to give it its own hour. You'll read about it in Hour 16.

The `taglib` directive loads a tag library for use in the JSP. When you load a tag library, you must specify the URI of the tag library and the prefix for the tags, like this:

```
<%@ taglib uri="http://usingjsp.wutka.com/taglib/testlib"
   prefix="testing" %>
```

When you use a custom tag, it is typically of the form <*prefix:tagname*>. The prefix is the same as the prefix you specify in the taglib directive, and the tagname is the name of a tag implemented in the tag library.

For example, suppose the testlib tag library contains a tag called checkmate. If you wanted to use the checkmate tag with a prefix of testing, your tag would be <testing:checkmate>.

Summary

Directives instruct the container on how to work with JSPs. The page directive affects the construction and operation of JSPs. It includes options that are attribute-value pairs that define attributes or behavior for a JSP. Generally, there are many page directives. However, each option usually appears only once per page. The import attribute is notable in that it may appear as many times as necessary.

The include directive permits the JSP author to compose JSPs from several files.

Finally, the taglib directive declares that a JSP is using a library of custom tags. It defines the location of the tag library and the prefix that is used within a JSP to uniquely identify tags that are associated with the library.

Q&A

Q. ***Why do I get compile errors on the line with my*** `page` ***directive?***

A. The most likely cause of this problem is that you put a space between the `<%` and the `@`. The `<%@` tag used for JSP directives is not the same as the `<%` tag. When you put a space in there, the JSP compiler thinks you want the `<%` tag, and the `@` symbol becomes part of the Java code within the `<%` tag.

Q. ***Why doesn't my import work?***

A. Did you remember the `.*` at the end? Programmers often mean to import `java.util.*` or `java.sql.*` and forget the `.*` at the end. Make sure you don't put a ";" after the import as you do in a normal java class.

Q. ***Why do I get an exception when I go to an error page?***

A. You probably have already committed the output buffer (sent it to the browser). When you go to an error page, the JSP engine attempts to clear the output buffer so that the error page doesn't contain a mixture of the original page and the error page. This problem occurs most often when you have included another page or forwarded to another page. If you must include or forward, try moving the code that throws the exception as close to the top of the page as you can so you handle any exceptions before you commit the buffer.

Q. ***Why do I see part of the original page before the error page?***

A. You have most likely already committed the output buffer, but your JSP engine doesn't throw an exception when you try to hit the error page. Some JSP engines will not let you forward to the error page after output has been sent to the browser. Others don't care, but you see part of the original page. Again, try to do things that can throw an exception as early as possible.

Q. ***I specified an alternate superclass; why won't my JSP compile?***

A. Are you sure that the superclass is in the classpath? Usually you just put the superclass in the `WEB-INF/classes` directory of your Web application.

Q. ***My JSP compiles; why do I get a runtime error when the page executes?***

A. Make sure your superclass is really a servlet and that it implements the `HttpJspPage` interface. Depending on the JSP engine, the JSP might compile even if the class doesn't implement `HttpJspPage`, but when the JSP engine goes to load the JSP's servlet, it sees that the superclass isn't a JSP servlet because it doesn't implement `HttpJspPage`.

Workshop

The Workshop is designed to help you review what you have learned, and help you to further increase your understanding of the material covered in this hour.

Quiz

1. Which packages are imported by default?
2. What are the three ways that you can structure `page` directives to import several packages?
3. Which implicit objects depend on `page` directives to make them available for use?

Answers

1. A JSP container automatically imports `java.lang.*`, `javax.servlet.*`, `javax.servlet.jsp.*`, and `javax.servlet.http.*`. If you require packages other than these, you'll need to explicitly import them using one or more page directives.
2. `page` directives that import packages can have the following forms:
   - ```
     <%@ page import="java.sql.*" %>
     <%@ page import="java.util.*" %>
     ```
   - `<%@ page import="java.sql.*" import="java.util.*" %>`
   - `<%@ page import="java.sql.*,java.util.*" %>`

   The particular form that you use will depend on personal preference, but the first form is usually best. For additional help with style choices in JSPs, see `http://developer.java.sun.com/developer/technicalArticles/javaserverpages/code_convention/`.
3. The implicit object `exception` is available only when you declare that `isErrorPage=true`. The implicit object session is available when `session=true`—however, by default session is true.

Activity

Write a JSP that outputs a large amount of text and another that acts as an error page. Turn `autoFlush` off and change the values for the buffer size until you get an exception. Turn `autoFlush` back on. Observe the behavior and explain it.
     ```

HOUR 10

Using JSP Standard Actions to Organize Your Web Application

What You'll Learn in This Hour:

- How to include Web resources in JSPs or servlets
- How to forward clients to other pages
- How to build reusable elements using the `include` mechanisms
- How to use applets within your Web applications

All of the programmable elements that you have worked with so far have been in the form of source files that are compiled into classes (for servlets) or in the form of JSP declarations, scriptlets, or expressions. JavaServer Pages add JSP actions to the elements you can use to produce dynamic pages.

JSP actions are represented by tags that, when placed in JavaServer Pages, cause some programmatic behavior to occur. The actions available as part of the core JSP specification are known as **standard actions**. By convention, they're prefixed with `jsp`. For example, the `<jsp:include>` tag that we'll discuss in a moment allows you to include one JSP inside another. In Hour 16, "Extending JSP with New Tags," you'll learn how to create your own custom actions. Then, in Hour 17 you'll be introduced to the Standard Tag Library, a collection of very useful tag extensions.

Many of the examples you have seen so far are difficult to read because they shift frequently between Java and HTML. In fact, one of the biggest complaints about JSP is that the pages end up looking very messy and become very difficult to maintain. In this hour you will see how to organize your JavaServer Pages and servlets to make them much easier to read and maintain.

Including Other Files

Using tags to perform functions can make your JSPs more readable, since they are used in a manner that is similar to other tags on the page. As you'll see in later hours, they significantly reduce the number of transitions between Java code and other elements of the JSP. In many cases, they can replace all of the scriptlets and expressions you might have used to construct a page. In addition, some of the standard tags can help you structure your applications to make them even easier to work with.

Splitting your code is one of the first techniques you can use to organize your code. Many sites have a consistent header on every page. You can put the header into a separate file and include it in every page. When you need to change the header, you need to change only one file.

Within a JavaServer Page, you can choose to include another file at page compile time or at runtime. The advantage of including a file at compilation time is performance. At runtime, the JSP engine doesn't need to do any work because the file has already been included. Unfortunately, with servlets, you can only include files at runtime. After all, you are the one who compiles the servlet. How could the container include something at runtime?

To include another file at compile time, use the `include` directive, like this:

```
<%@ include file="includedFileName" flush="true"%>
```

By the Way

The Path to an Included File Is Relative

The path for the included file is relative to the path of the original JSP. That is, if the included file is in the same directory as the including file, you don't need to specify a directory name.

Listing 10.1 shows a JSP file that includes another file. Because the file is included at compile time, you can look at the generated servlet and see that the included code is there.

LISTING 10.1 Source Code for `CrazyWorld.jsp`

```
<html>
<body>
<%@ include file="Header.html" %>
<p>
Welcome to <i>It's a Crazy World</i>
<p>
</body>
</html>
```

By putting all your header code in a single file, you can make sure that all your pages have an identical header. When you change the header, you need to change only one file.

Listing 10.2 shows the `Header.html` file included by `CrazyWorld.jsp`.

LISTING 10.2 Source Code for `Header.html`

```
<table bgcolor="#0000ff">
<tr><td><img src="face.jpg" align=left></td>
<td><h1><font color="#ffff00">It's a Crazy World</font></h1></td>
<td><img src="face.jpg" align="right"></td></tr>
</table>
```

Figure 10.1 shows `CrazyWorld.jsp` as it appears in a browser. The image and header come from `Header.html`, whereas the welcome message comes from `CrazyWorld.jsp` itself.

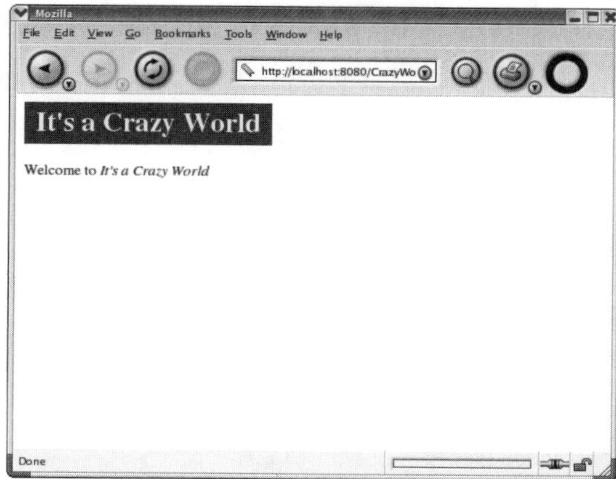

FIGURE 10.1 You can include header information at compile time by using `<%@ include %>`.

When you include a file with the `include` directive, the JSP compiler processes the included file as if it were part of the JSP. You can use any JSP directives within the included file and can even include another file. Any variables and methods defined in the main JSP are available to included files.

Watch Out!

> **Has It Changed? Your Container Might Not Know.**
>
> The JSP specification does not provide a standard way for a JSP engine to learn that an included file has changed. Tomcat can detect whether an included file is changed. If you are using another engine, you should determine if that engine does also.

Although there is a potential speed gain in including files at compile time, you give up a lot of flexibility. When you include files at runtime, you are able to freely mix servlets and JavaServer Pages.

By the Way

Having Trouble with the Example?

If you are having trouble including a file at compile time, see the “Q&A” section at the end of this hour.

Including Files in a JSP at Runtime

When you want to include a servlet or another JSP into your JSP, use the `<jsp:include>` directive, like this:

```
<jsp:include page="includedFileName" flush="true"/>
```

The `flush` attribute indicates whether the output buffer should be flushed before the file is included. The default value for this attribute is `false`.

Listing 10.3 shows a menu JavaServer Page that displays a tab-style menu, highlighting a specific menu item according to a parameter that is passed to it.

LISTING 10.3 Source Code for `Menu.jspf`

```
<%
// See which menu item should be highlighted.
    String highlighted = request.getParameter("highlighted");

// Set the names for the individual menu items.

    String welcome = "welcome.jpg";
    if (highlighted.equalsIgnoreCase("welcome"))
        welcome = "welcomeS.jpg";

    String products = "products.jpg";
    if (highlighted.equalsIgnoreCase("products"))
        products = "productsS.jpg";

    String services = "services.jpg";
    if (highlighted.equalsIgnoreCase("services"))
        services = "servicesS.jpg";

    String support = "support.jpg";
    if (highlighted.equalsIgnoreCase("support"))
        support = "supportS.jpg";

    String aboutUs = "aboutUs.jpg";
    if (highlighted.equalsIgnoreCase("aboutUs"))
        aboutUs = "aboutUsS.jpg";
%>
```

LISTING 10.3 Continued

```
<table cellpadding="0" cellspacing="0">
<tr>
<td><a href="welcome.jsp"><img src="<%=welcome%>" border="0"></a></td>
<td><a href="products.jsp"><img src="<%=products%>" border="0"></a></td>
<td><a href="services.jsp"><img src="<%=services%>" border="0"></a></td>
<td><a href="support.jsp"><img src="<%=support%>" border="0"></a></td>
<td><a href="aboutUs.jsp"><img src="<%=aboutUs%>" border="0"></a></td></tr>
</table>
```

Because Listing 10.3 is intended to be used within other JSPs, it's given a different extension—`jspf`, which originally stood for **JSP fragment**. Although the specification does not require you to use this extension, it does recommend its use. In spite of the extension origin, the specification calls these types of files JSP **segments** to avoid confusion between them and a new type of fragment that you'll learn about in Hour 16, "Extending JSP with New Tags."

Listing 10.4 shows a JSP that uses the `<jsp:include>` tag to include the `Menu.jsp`.

LISTING 10.4 Source Code for `support.jsp`

```
<html>
<body bgcolor="#ffffff">
<%@ include file="Header2.html"%>

<jsp:include page="Menu.jspf" flush="true">
    <jsp:param name="highlighted" value="support"/>
</jsp:include>
<p>
<h1>Frequently Asked Questions</h1>
<p>
<i>What in the world is a Zither?</i>
<br>
A zither is a stringed instrument that has between 30 and 40 strings.
<p>
<i>How do you expect to earn money if all you sell is zithers?</i>
<br>
We don't. This business is a tax write-off for our highly successful
Amalgamated Golf Tees, Inc.

</body>
</html>
```

By the Way

Some Notes About Some "Advanced Features" of Listing 10.4

Listing 10.4 uses the `<jsp:param>` tag (discussed later in this hour) to tell the `Menu.jsp` file which item to highlight. It also uses an `include` directive to include a standard header.

Figure 10.2 shows the output of `support.jsp`. The menu items are generated by the `Menu.jsp` file.

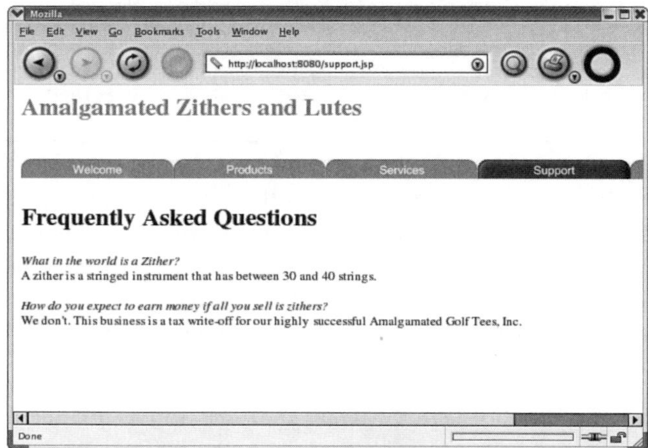

FIGURE 10.2 You can use the `<jsp:include>` tag to implement a menu.

There are a few restrictions imposed on files when they are included at runtime. These restrictions are not imposed on files that are included at compile time. An included file cannot change any header information sent back to the browser. For example, you cannot set any cookie information from within an included file.

By the Way

Having Trouble with the Example?

If you are having trouble including a file at runtime, see the "Q&A" section at the end of this hour.

Passing Parameters to an Included File

Included files can access all the information in the `request` object, so they have access to any form variables passed from the browser. In addition, you can pass parameters to the included file by using the `<jsp:param>` directive:

```
<jsp:include page="someIncludedPage" flush="true">
    <jsp:param name="myParamName" value="paramData"/>
</jsp:include>
```

By the Way

Directives and End Tags

The <jsp:include> tag follows the XML standard of ending a tag with /> when there is no closing tag. When you include a file and don't pass any parameters, end the <jsp:include> tag with />. When you pass parameters with <jsp:param>, you include a closing </jsp:include> tag. Notice, too, that the <jsp:param> tag closes with a />.

The included file uses `request.getParameter` and `request.getParameterValues` to fetch the parameters just as if the parameters were passed from the browser as form variables. Values from <jsp:param> take precedence over parameters already in the request. In other words, if you use `getParameter` to retrieve the parameter value, you get the value specified in <jsp:param>. If you use `getParameterValues`, you get both the value specified by <jsp:param> and the value passed from the browser.

By the Way

Visibility of Parameters

The parameters added with the <jsp:param> tag are visible to the included page only. They are not visible to the original page (that is, they don't affect the original set of parameters).

Listing 10.5 shows a page that passes a parameter to an included page.

LISTING 10.5 Source Code for `MainForm.jsp`

```
<html>
<body bgcolor="#ffffff">
<jsp:include page="IncludedForm.jspf" flush="true">
    <jsp:param name="myVar" value="I was passed from main"/>
</jsp:include>
</body>
</html>
```

Listing 10.6 shows the included page that uses `getParameter` and `getParameterValues` to print out the values for `myVar`.

LISTING 10.6 Source Code for `IncludedForm.jspf`

```
<pre>
<%
    String myVar = request.getParameter("myVar");
    String myVars[] = request.getParameterValues("myVar");

    out.println("myVar = "+ myVar);
    out.println("The values for myVar are:");
    for (int i=0; i < myVars.length; i++)
    {
        out.println(myVars[i]);
    }
%>
</pre>
```

Notice that the included form doesn't contain `<html>` or `<body>` tags. The form always assumes that it has been included from another page and that the surrounding page contains those tags. Figure 10.3 shows the output from `MainForm.jsp`. The original value for `MainForm.jsp` is passed as part of the URL, as you can see in the address line on the browser.

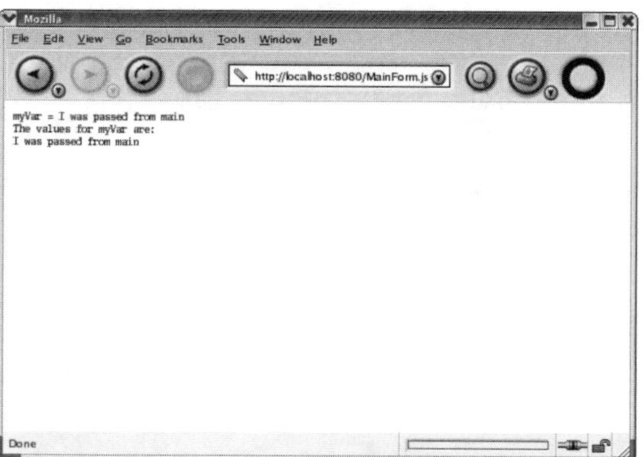

FIGURE 10.3 Included pages usually assume that they are included and don't contain `<html>` or `<body>` tags.

Including Files from a Servlet

The servlet API has a peculiar way to include files. Although you might expect either the `request` or `response` objects to provide a method to include a file, it's not that simple. To include another servlet, JSP, or text file, you must obtain a request dispatcher for the resource you want to include.

Fortunately, you can obtain a request dispatcher quite easily. The fastest way to get a request dispatcher is to call `request.getRequestDispatcher` and pass it through the URL of the resource you want to include, like this:

```
RequestDispatcher d =
        request.getRequestDispatcher("destinationURL"");
d.include(request, response);
```

Listing 10.7 shows a servlet that includes the `IncludedForm.jsp` from Listing 10.6.

LISTING 10.7 Source Code for `MainFormServlet.java`

```
package examples;

import javax.servlet.*;
import java.io.*;

public class MainFormServlet extends GenericServlet
{
    public void service(ServletRequest request,
        ServletResponse response)
        throws IOException, ServletException
    {
// Tell the web server that the response is HTML.
        response.setContentType("text/html");

// Get the PrintWriter for writing out the response.
        PrintWriter out = response.getWriter();

// Write the HTML back to the browser.
        out.println("<html>");
        out.println("<body>");

// Get the request dispatcher for the JSP to include.
        RequestDispatcher dispatcher =
            request.getRequestDispatcher(
                "/IncludedForm.jspf");

        dispatcher.include(request, response);

        out.println("</body>");
        out.println("</html>");
    }
}
```

By the Way

GenericServlet or HttpServlet?

Developers will often extend `HttpServlet` in most servlets they write. In this example, it extends `GenericServlet` because it only requires the `service` method. You can use either `HttpServlet` or `GenericServlet`.

The output from the included resource is written to the stream of the `response` object passed to it through the `include` method.

Listing 10.7 uses the full pathname for the included JSP. The servlet is not in the same directory as the JSP it is including. The `getRequestDispatcher` method takes a relative URL, so if you include another servlet that is in the same directory as your servlet, you don't have to specify the full pathname.

Watch Out!

Don't Forget the Parameters

If you run this example, don't forget to provide parameters to the servlet. The URL for this example will look something like this:

```
http://localhost:8080/servlet/examples.MainFormServlet?myVar=aVar
```

In the last example, the JSP provided the parameters within the main JSP.

Did you Know?

Passing Parameters to an Included Resource

To pass parameters to a resource you are including, add the parameters to the URL when you call `getRequestDispatcher`—for example, `getRequestDispatcher ("MyForm.jsp?param1=avalue")`.

Forwarding to Another Page

In addition to including another page, you can transfer to another page without returning to the original. This technique is called **forwarding**. When you forward the request on to another page (or servlet), the forwarding page is no longer involved in handling the request. You typically would use forwarding to handle an error, or if you need several different response pages that depend on the data in the request. In the latter case, a JSP or a servlet looks at the incoming request, decides which response page to use, and forwards the request on to the proper response page.

Forwarding to Another Page from a JSP

The JSP syntax for forwarding is very similar to the syntax for including. You use the `<jsp:forward>` tag like this:

```
<jsp:forward page="destinationPage"/>
```

When you forward to another page or servlet, your original page is replaced with the new page. That is, any output you might have sent is cleared.

Forwarding and Buffering

If you get an `IllegalStateException` when forwarding to another page, you might not be buffering the page. Make sure you turn the buffering on using the page directive.

Listing 10.8 shows a very simple JSP that forwards itself to another page.

LISTING 10.8 Source Code for `MainForwarder.jsp`

```
<html>
<body>

You should never see me because my output is erased before forwarding.

<jsp:forward page="ForwardedPage.jsp"/>
</body>
</html>
```

As you can see in Figure 10.4, the text in the `MainForwarder.jsp` file doesn't show in the browser because it is erased before the `ForwardedPage.jsp` page executes.

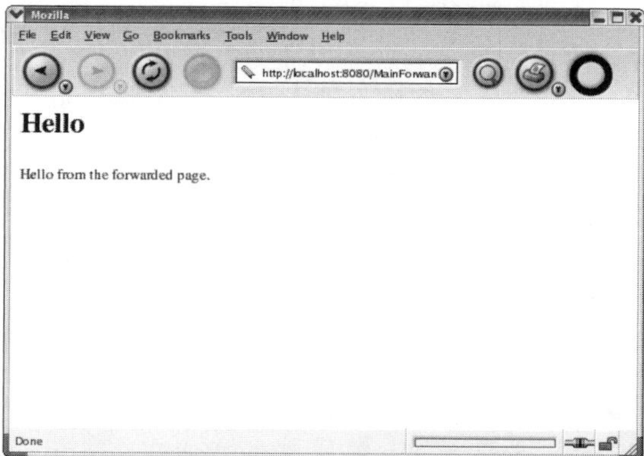

FIGURE 10.4
When a JSP forwards to another JSP, the output from the original JSP is lost.

Forwarding to Another Page from a Servlet

Just as the syntax for forwarding from a JSP is similar to the syntax for including, the syntax for forwarding from a servlet is also very similar to the syntax for including. You again use the `RequestDispatcher` object, only this time, instead of calling its `include` method, you call its `forward` method:

```
RequestDispatcher d =
        request.getRequestDispatcher("destinationURL");
d.forward(request, response);
```

Listing 10.9 shows an example servlet that forwards to the same `ForwardedPage.jsp` page used by the JSP in Listing 10.8. Again, the output from the servlet is erased before the forwarded page runs.

LISTING 10.9 Source Code for `ForwarderServlet.java`

```
package examples;

import javax.servlet.*;
import java.io.*;

public class ForwarderServlet extends GenericServlet
{
    public void service(ServletRequest request,
        ServletResponse response)
        throws IOException, ServletException
    {
// Tell the web server that the response is HTML.
        response.setContentType("text/html");

// Get the PrintWriter for writing out the response.
        PrintWriter out = response.getWriter();

// Write the HTML back to the browser.
        out.println("<html>");
        out.println("<body>");

        out.println("You should never see this");
        out.println("because my output buffer gets erased");

// Get the request dispatcher for the JSP to include.
        RequestDispatcher dispatcher =
            request.getRequestDispatcher(
                "/ForwardedPage.jsp");

        dispatcher.forward(request, response);

        out.println("</body>");
        out.println("</html>");
    }
}
```

Passing Parameters to the Forwarded Page

As you might have already guessed, you pass parameters to a forwarded page in exactly the same way as you would to an included page. From a JavaServer Page, you use the `<jsp:param>` tag, and from a servlet, you add the parameters to the end of the URL when you call `getRequestDispatcher`.

Passing Java Objects Between JSPs and Servlets

Although it is often convenient to just pass parameter strings between servlets and JSPs, you can't always fit everything you want into a string. If your servlet pulls some information from a database and you want to pass all that information to a JSP, you certainly don't want to convert all the information into strings. You are much better off just passing the Java objects containing the information.

In Hour 6, "Looking Under the Hood—Core Servlet Components," you saw that you can store Java objects in a session by calling `getAttribute` and `setAttribute`. You can use the session to pass data to an included page or to a forwarded servlet, but you don't really want that data hanging around in the session after you are done with it. You also don't want to add housekeeping code to the included page to clean up the variables stored in the session.

Luckily, there is a better solution. You can store Java objects in the `request` object using `getAttribute`, `setAttribute`, and `removeAttribute`, just as you can with a `session` object. The methods are identical to those in the `session` object, except that they can't throw `IllegalStateException`:

```
public void setAttribute(String name, Object value)
public Object getAttribute(String name)
public void removeAttribute(String name, Object value)
```

Because the `request` object exists only as long as the request is being processed, you don't have to worry about performing any cleanup. When you finish handling the request and have sent a response back to the browser, the `request` object disappears. The next time a request comes in, there is a new `request` object.

Making Your Application More Modular

Maintaining a JSP-based application can be a lot of work when the JavaServer Pages aren't well organized. Over time, they tend to grow and end up with an ugly mixture of HTML and Java code that can be almost unreadable. In most cases, you can reorganize the pages and make use of the `<jsp:include>` tag to split your page into manageable segments.

A Reusable HTML Table Module

One of the really handy things you can do with the `<jsp:include>` tag is create reusable modules. How many times have you had to take an array or a vector of objects and display them in an HTML table? Depending on the kind of applications you have done, you may have had to do this many times.

You can make a servlet or a JSP that takes an array or a vector of data and displays the data in a table. Then, every time you need to show a table, you can call the servlet. Listing 10.10 shows a servlet that uses the Reflection API to fetch data from either an array or a vector of objects and then displays the data in a table. It uses `request.getAttribute` to get the array/vector but uses `request.getParameter` to retrieve any other options.

LISTING 10.10 Source Code for `TableServlet.java`

```
package examples;

import javax.servlet.*;
import java.io.*;
import java.util.*;
import java.lang.reflect.*;

/** This class uses the Reflection API to fetch data from an array or
 *  a vector and put it in a table. */

public class TableServlet extends GenericServlet
{
    public static final Class[] NO_PARAMS = new Class[0];

    public void service(ServletRequest request, ServletResponse response)
        throws IOException, ServletException
    {

// First, get the parameters for the TABLE, TR, TD, and TH options.
        String tableOptions = request.getParameter("tableOptions");
        if (tableOptions == null) tableOptions = "";

        String trOptions = request.getParameter("trOptions");
        if (trOptions == null) trOptions = "";
```

LISTING 10.10 Continued

```
        String tdOptions = request.getParameter("tdOptions");
        if (tdOptions == null) tdOptions = "";

        String thOptions = request.getParameter("thOptions");
        if (thOptions == null) thOptions = "";

// Now, get the name of the object that contains the data to display.
        String data = request.getParameter("data");

        if (data == null)
        {
            getServletContext().log("No data available");
            throw new ServletException(
                "No data parameter available");
        }

// Get the actual data object.
        Object dataOb = request.getAttribute(data);
        if (dataOb == null)
        {
            getServletContext().log("No data object found");
            throw new ServletException(
                "Can't locate the data object named "+
                data);
        }

// Get the list of method/field names to display in each column.
        String[] columns = request.getParameterValues("column");

// Get the types of each column field.
        String[] columnType = request.getParameterValues("columnType");

// Get the headers for each column
        String[] columnHeaders = request.getParameterValues(
            "columnHeader");

// Create a table of column names and Fields/Methods for fetching data.
        Hashtable columnAccessors =
            getAccessors(dataOb, columns);

// First print the table header.
        PrintWriter out = response.getWriter();
        out.println("<table "+ tableOptions+">");

// If there are any headers, print them out.
        if (columnHeaders != null)
        {
            out.println("<tr "+trOptions+">");
            for (int i=0; i < columnHeaders.length; i++)
            {
                out.print("<th "+thOptions+">");
                out.println(columnHeaders[i]);
                out.println("</th>");
```

LISTING 10.10 Continued

```
            }
            out.println("</tr>");
        }

// If the object is a vector, loop through the elements.
        if (dataOb instanceof Vector)
        {
            Vector v = (Vector) dataOb;

            Enumeration e = v.elements();

            while (e.hasMoreElements())
            {
// For each row, print out the <tr> tag plus any options.
                out.println("<tr "+trOptions+">");

// Print out the column values for the row.
                printRow(out, e.nextElement(),
                    columns, columnType,
                    columnAccessors, tdOptions);
                out.println("</tr>");
            }
        }
// If the object is an array, loop through the objects.
        else if (dataOb instanceof Object[])
        {
            Object[] obs = (Object[]) dataOb;

            for (int i=0; i < obs.length; i++)
            {
// For each row, print out the <tr> tag plus any options.
                out.println("<tr "+trOptions+">");

// Print out the column values for the row.
                printRow(out, obs[i],
                    columns, columnType,
                    columnAccessors, tdOptions);
                out.println("</tr>");
            }
        }
        out.println("</table>");
    }

    protected void printRow(PrintWriter out, Object ob,
        String[] columns, String[] columnTypes,
        Hashtable columnAccessors, String tdOptions)
        throws ServletException
    {

// Loop through all the column names.
        for (int i=0; i < columns.length; i++)
        {
// Get the value for this column out of the object.
            Object value = getColumnValue(ob, columns[i],
                columnAccessors);
```

LISTING 10.10 Continued

```
// Print the <td> tag.
            out.print("<td "+tdOptions+">");

// If the column type is data, just print the data.
            if (columnTypes[i].equalsIgnoreCase("data"))
            {
                out.print(value);
            }
// If the column type is "image", print out an <img> tag.
            else if (columnTypes[i].equalsIgnoreCase("image"))
            {
                out.print("<img src=\""+value+"\">");
            }
            out.print("</td>");
        }
    }

/**Use either a Field or a Method object to fetch a value from an object.*/
    protected Object getColumnValue(Object ob, String columnName,
        Hashtable columnAccessors)
        throws ServletException
    {
// Get the object used to fetch this column's value.
        Object accessor = columnAccessors.get(columnName);

// If the column is a field...
        if (accessor instanceof Field)
        {
// ... use the field's get method to fetch the value.
            try
            {
                Field f = (Field) accessor;

                return f.get(ob);
            }
// Log and then return the IllegalAccessException.
            catch (IllegalAccessException exc)
            {
                getServletContext().log(
                    "Error getting column "+
                    columnName, exc);
                throw new ServletException(
                    "Illegal access exception for column "+
                    columnName);
            }
        }
// If the column is a Method...
        else if (accessor instanceof Method)
        {
// ... invoke the method.
            try
            {
                Method m = (Method) accessor;
```

LISTING 10.10 Continued

```
// The NO_PARAMS value is an empty array of Class defined at the top
// of this class.
                return m.invoke(ob, NO_PARAMS);
            }
// Log and then return any exceptions that come up while invoking the method.
            catch (IllegalAccessException exc)
            {
                getServletContext().log(
                    "Error getting column "+
                    columnName, exc);
                throw new ServletException(
                    "Illegal access exception for column "+
                    columnName);
            }
            catch (InvocationTargetException exc)
            {
                getServletContext().log(
                    "Error getting column "+
                    columnName, exc);
                throw new ServletException(
                    "Invocation target exception "+
                    "for column "+columnName);
            }
        }
// If the column is neither a Field nor a Method, return null. You should
// never get to this point.
        return null;
    }

/** Creates a table mapping column name to Field/Method */
    protected Hashtable getAccessors(Object ob, String[] columns)
        throws ServletException
    {
        Hashtable result = new Hashtable();

// First, get the Class for the kind of object being displayed.
        Class obClass = null;

        if (ob instanceof Object[])
        {
// If the objects are in an array, get the first object in the array.
            Object[] obs = (Object[]) ob;
// If there are no objects, don't bother filling the table
// because it won't be needed.
            if (obs.length == 0) return result;

            obClass = obs[0].getClass();
        }
        else if (ob instanceof Vector)
        {
// If the objects are in a vector, get the first element of the vector.
            Vector v = (Vector) ob;
```

LISTING 10.10 Continued

```
// If there are no objects, don't bother filling the table
// because it won't be needed.
            if (v.size() == 0) return result;

            obClass = v.elementAt(0).getClass();
        }

// For each column, look for a field and then a method with the column name.
        for (int i=0; i < columns.length; i++)
        {
// First see whether there is a field that matches the column name.
            try
            {
                Field f = obClass.getField(columns[i]);
// If so, put it in the table and go to the next column name.
                result.put(columns[i], f);
                continue;
            }
            catch (Exception ignore)
            {
            }

// Now see whether there is a method that matches this column name.
            try
            {
// The NO_PARAMS value is an empty array of Class defined at the top
// of this class.
                Method m = obClass.getMethod(columns[i],
                    NO_PARAMS);
// If so, put it in the table.
                result.put(columns[i], m);
            }
            catch (Exception exc)
            {
                getServletContext().log(
                    "Exception location field "+
                    columns[i], exc);
                throw new ServletException(
                    "Can't locate field/method for "+
                    columns[i]);
            }
        }

        return result;
    }
}
```

Although the `TableServlet` servlet is pretty large compared with the amount of code needed to write out a single table, it begins to pay off as you start using it in several JSPs. Listing 10.11 shows a JavaServer Page that invokes `TableServlet`.

LISTING 10.11 Source Code for `ShowTable.jsp`

```
<html>
<body>

<%
// Initialize an array with some data to display.

    Person[] people = new Person[]
        { new Person("Samantha Tippin", 9, "770-123-4567"),
          new Person("Kaitlyn Tippin", 6, "770-123-4567"),
          new Person("Edward Alexander", 3, "No phone"),
          new Person("Star Alexander", 12, "Phone off hook"),
          new Person("Norton Alexander", 12, "No phone")
        };

// Stick the array in the request where the servlet can get to it.
    request.setAttribute("people", people);
%>
<%-- Invoke the Table servlet, tell it the name of the attribute
     where the data is stored (data=people), set the border size to 4
     on the <table> tag, and describe each column to display --%>

<jsp:include page="/TableServlet" flush="true">
    <jsp:param name="data" value="people"/>

    <jsp:param name="tableOptions" value="BORDER=4"/>

    <jsp:param name="column" value="name"/>
    <jsp:param name="columnType" value="data"/>
    <jsp:param name="columnHeader" value="Name"/>

    <jsp:param name="column" value="age"/>
    <jsp:param name="columnType" value="data"/>
    <jsp:param name="columnHeader" value="Age"/>

    <jsp:param name="column" value="getPhoneNumber"/>
    <jsp:param name="columnType" value="data"/>
    <jsp:param name="columnHeader" value="Phone #"/>
</jsp:include>
</body>
</html>
<%!
// Define a class to contain information. This would normally not
// be defined within a JSP.
    public class Person
    {
        public String name;
        public int age;
        protected String phoneNumber;
```

LISTING 10.11 Source Code for `ShowTable.jsp`

```
        public Person(String aName, int anAge,
            String aPhoneNumber)
        {
            name = aName;
            age = anAge;
            phoneNumber = aPhoneNumber;
        }

// Just to show that methods work as well as fields, allow the
// phone number to be accessed only via a method call.
        public String getPhoneNumber()
        {
            return phoneNumber;
        }
    }
%>
```

Figure 10.5 shows the output from `ShowTable.jsp`.

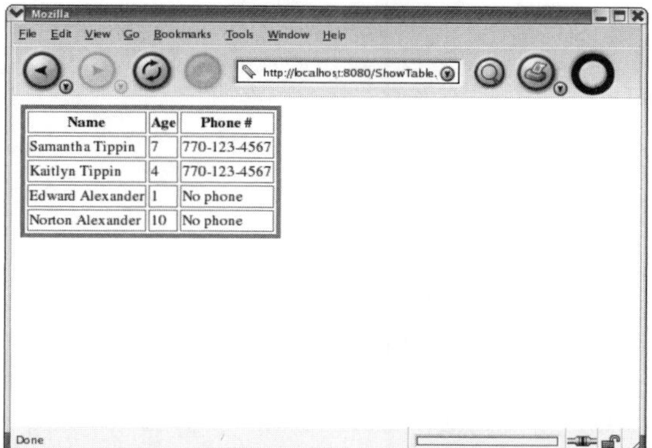

Name	Age	Phone #
Samantha Tippin	7	770-123-4567
Kaitlyn Tippin	4	770-123-4567
Edward Alexander	1	No phone
Norton Alexander	10	No phone

FIGURE 10.5
You can create a reusable servlet to generate HTML elements such as tables.

Using an Applet in Your Form

Applets are used to provide a rich user experience through a Web browser by allowing the user to interact with a GUI. Applets also make it possible to reorganize your application by encapsulating the presentation and performing validation of user input. They are often used to do client-side processing.

You can easily find dozens of Java books that tell you how to create an applet and put it in an HTML page. You may be familiar with the `<applet>` tag. The problem with the `<applet>` tag is that you don't have any control over the Java Virtual Machine that runs the applet. It's possible that the browser has a feature-incompatible virtual machine, or it may not have one installed at all.

Sun's solution to this issue is a part of the standard JRE (Java Runtime Environment) called the Java Plug-In. The `<embed>` tag in Netscape Navigator and the `<object>` tag in Internet Explorer let you force the browser to run your applet with Sun's VM. Better yet, you can use the most recent version of the VM, in case you need some of the newer features.

The JSP environment provides a special tag for embedding an applet in a Web page. The tag automatically detects the browser type and inserts the appropriate HTML tag (either `<embed>` or `<object>`) in the output. The JSP tag is called `<jsp:plugin>`. Listing 10.12 shows an example usage of `<jsp:plugin>`.

LISTING 10.12 Source Code for ShowApplet.jsp

```
<html>
<body>
Here is the applet:
<br>

<jsp:plugin type="applet" code="examples.SwingApplet" codebase="."
    width="500" height="400">
    <jsp:fallback>
        <p>Unable to use Java Plugin</p>
    </jsp:fallback>
</jsp:plugin>

</body>
</html>
```

The text inside the `<jsp:fallback>` tag is displayed when the browser can't run the Java Plug-In, either because the browser isn't capable or there are problems loading it. If you need to pass parameters to the applet, you can use the `<jsp:params>` tag, which encodes a number of `<jsp:param>` tags. For example:

```
<jsp:params>
    <jsp:param name="myParam1" value="param1Value"/>
    <jsp:param name="myParam1" value="param1Value"/>
</jsp:params>
```

The `<jsp:params>` tag should be enclosed within the `<jsp:plugin>` in the same way that `<jsp:fallback>` is enclosed in Listing 10.12.

Listing 10.13 shows the generated HTML code when the `ShowParams.jsp` applet is run from within Internet Explorer.

LISTING 10.13 `ShowApplet.jsp` **Generated HTML for Internet Explorer**

```
<html>
<body>
Here is the applet:
<br>

<object classid=clsid:8AD9C840-044E-11D1-B3E9-00805F499D93 width="500"
height="400" codebase="http://java.sun.com/products/plugin/1.2.2/jinstall-1_2_2-
win.cab#Version=1,2,2,0">
<param name="java_code" value="examples.SwingApplet">
<param name="java_codebase" value=".">
<param name="type" value="application/x-java-applet;">
<comment>
<embed type="application/x-java-applet;" width="500" height="400"
pluginspage="http://java.sun.com/products/plugin/"
java_code="examples.SwingApplet" java_codebase="."/>
<noembed>

        <p>Unable to use Java Plugin</p>

</noembed>
</comment>
</object>


</body>
</html>
```

The `<jsp:plugin>` tag accepts most of the common `<applet>` attributes, such as `code`, `codebase`, `archive`, `width`, and `height`.

Summary

Partitioning can help you build Web applications that are easier to work with. By factoring out common functionality and putting it in JSPs or JSP segments, you can often simplify the code and create reusable elements. The JSP standard action `<jsp:include>` allows you to include other resources into JSPs. Standard actions can also be used to forward to other JSPs by using `<jsp:forward>`. You can pass parameters to pages you are including or forwarding to by using the `<jsp:param>` standard action. Servlets use a `RequestDispatcher` to include or forward to resources.

If the information you want to pass between pages is complex, you can create an object to hold the information. Objects can be passed between JSPs or servlets using the `request` object to store them.

There are also standard actions for using applets in a JSP. These actions isolate you from the browser-specific details of how to embed an applet in HTML.

Q&A

Q. ***Why won't my included file show up?***

A. If you entered the correct filename and the JSP engine didn't report an error while including the file, chances are that the place where you included the file causes it to not show up. For example, if you include some tags within the `<head>` tag, they probably won't show up. Likewise, if you include the file within an HTML comment, it won't show up. View Source from your browser and see what's being sent from your JSP. Most browsers let you right-click the page and select a View Source option. Some browsers also have a View Source option on the main menu.

Q. ***Why doesn't my JSP recompile when I change the contents of the included file?***

A. The JSP specification doesn't require JSP engines to check included files to see whether they have changed. Yours probably doesn't.

Q. ***Why do I get an HTTP Error 500 when I try to access a JSP with an included file?***

A. Most likely, the included file has some error that prevents it from being compiled. Check the log files of your JSP engine to see what the error is, or just try to access the included file directly. By accessing it directly, you should see any errors on your screen.

Workshop

The Workshop is designed to help you review what you have learned and help you further increase your understanding of the material covered in this hour.

Quiz

1. What are some of the effects of including a resource at compile time or run time?
2. What is jspf?
3. What class is used by servlets to include or forward to a resource?
4. If you want the client of a page to see the output of a resource that forwards to another, what can you do?

Answers

1. Resources that are included at compile time produce a compound resource that is used at runtime. The one becomes a part of the other. There may be a performance advantage since the runtime component is "prepared beforehand." Resources that are included at compile time cause the result of their evaluation at runtime to become a part of the output of the other. The most important effect of this is that the resources included at runtime are more limited—for example, they cannot set headers. However, this combination is often more flexible, since the included file can also be determine at runtime. Beyond simply selecting the resource at runtime, you can also mix servlets and JSPs.

2. `jspf` is an extension used with jsp segments, which are syntactically the same as a JSP, but are designed for inclusion as a type of component.

3. A `RequestDispatcher` is used for both operations. You use its `include` and `forward` methods.

4. Recall that forwarding to another resource causes the output buffer to be cleared. In most cases, this is desireable. If you want the client to see the output of the first page, flush the buffer prior to forwarding.

Activities

1. Write a JSP that includes another JSP at runtime. Pass a dynamic parameter such as the current time between the two. Display the parameter in the included page. Do this once using scriptlets or declarations and the other time without.

2. Repeat the previous exercise, substituting a servlet for the first JSP.

HOUR 11

Debugging and Error Handling

What You'll Learn in This Hour:

- The differences between translation and runtime errors
- How to effectively use logging
- The use of debuggers with servlets and JSPs
- How to use your own error pages

Sooner or later, one of your servlets or JSPs will not work as expected. Actually, if you've been following along in the book and done any experimenting at all, you've already begun bug squashing and your initiation as a Web developer is complete. Debugging software is part of the life of a developer. When you think about it, as you become more experienced, you only move from bugs that are easier to solve to those that are more difficult, but at least you can take this as a sign that you're making progress as a developer.

Why Debugging Is Tough

Web applications tend to be difficult to debug because they are often made up of cooperating elements that run on different hosts. To add to the diversity, a single component may be an aggregation of programming languages or technologies. For example, you have already constructed applications made up of HTML and scriptlets that run on a server and interact with Web browsers. Problems might appear at the server or browser or as a result of errors in the HTML or Java.

In the case of JSPs, you've seen that there's a considerable amount of behind-the-scenes work done by the underlying container in translating the JSP source to a servlet. Problems arise, particularly when using scriptlets, when the JSP developer does not understand the supporting objects and execution environment. In addition, debugging JSPs usually means working with the implementing servlets.

Server-side programs tend to have more threading problems and more database-locking problems because they usually perform multiple services simultaneously. One person running an application is unlikely to try to edit the same record in two different windows, but two people might try to use the same server to edit the same record.

Finally, Web applications are dependent upon other software to provide a workable environment and for resource management. Problems can arise because of configuration errors or because containers or application servers cache executables.

Compile Versus Runtime Errors

Problems with JavaServer Pages can appear during compilation or runtime. Because you compile your own servlets, servlet problems appear only at runtime. You may recall from Hour 5, "JSP and Servlet Lifecycles," that a JSP goes through translation and execution phases. During translation, a container inspects and validates a JSP and then locates or creates an implementation. In most containers, this produces a Java source file and its corresponding servlet class. In most cases, a JSP is compiled when it is first invoked. However, a container can compile a JSP when it is deployed, or it can be compiled as part of a build process using `Ant` and the Tomcat precompiler, `jspc`.

Let's look at two of the most common problems that occur during translation. Figure 11.1 shows the result of misspelling the `page` directive.

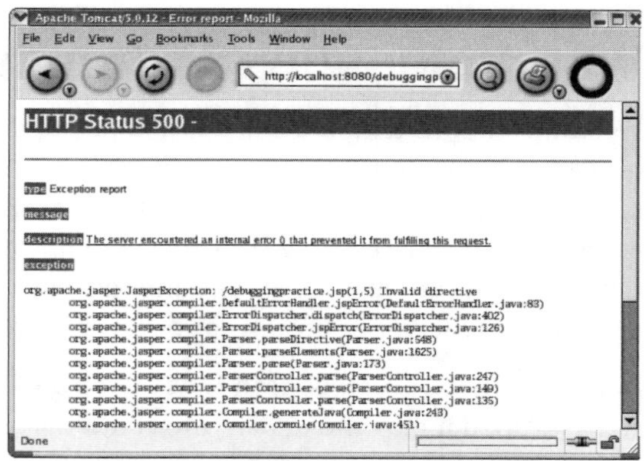

FIGURE 11.1
This easy-to-understand error results from misspelling a directive.

If you look at the exception produced, the problem is easily identified by the phrase "Invalid Directive." The container even provides the line and column numbers (in parentheses following the name of the JSP file) where it believes the problem occurred.

To illustrate an error that occurs while generating the servlet class, the second example attempts to invoke a method from an object that does not exist. Figure 11.2 presents the error page.

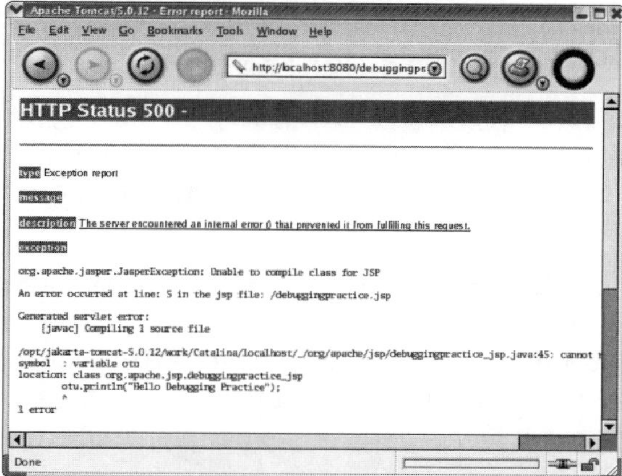

FIGURE 11.2
This results from an error produced during compilation.

Once again, the report is very informative. In most cases, Tomcat is good at identifying the problem or at least putting you pretty close to it.

Unfortunately, troubleshooting runtime errors is almost always more difficult. Here, servlets and JSPs begin to look alike from a debugging perspective. Runtime errors are usually the result of programming mistakes. If you're lucky, you'll get an exception that will help you. In other cases, you'll stare at a blank screen or ponder some peculiar behavior. For these, you have to roll up your sleeves and go to work.

Using Log Files to Debug an Application

At one time, there were no symbolic debuggers. You couldn't bring up the source code and step through one line at a time, printing out variable values as the program changed them. The only thing you could do was write out debugging statements to indicate what the program was doing.

Logging, or writing program state information during execution, is still one of the most common ways to debug a program. Debuggers, although very useful, often interfere with the debugging process in a number of ways. It is not uncommon for a program to run fine under a debugger and crash without the debugger.

Logging lets you display information at different points in the program without interfering too much with the overall running of the program. Obviously, if you spend too much time writing to log files, your program will slow down, but overall, logging is an excellent way to locate bugs.

Using `System.out` and `System.err`

In a stand-alone Java program, you frequently write debugging information to `System.out` and `System.err`. When you call the `printStackTrace` method in a `Throwable`, for example, the stack trace goes to `System.err` unless you specify otherwise.

Because servlets and JSPs run inside a servlet/JSP engine, messages you write to `System.out` and `System.err` don't necessarily appear on your screen. Exactly where the messages appear depends on the servlet/JSP engine. For Tomcat, writing to either results in messages in `catalina.out` in the `logs/` subdirectory of Tomcat's home. Not all servlet and JSP engines support the use of `System.out` and `System.err`.

Using the Servlet-Logging API

Recognizing that not all servlet engines can support `System.out` and `System.err` for logging, Sun added a pair of standard `log` methods in the `ServletContext` object. Using these methods, you can write log messages to a log that your application server maintains. For Tomcat, it's also located in the `logs/` subdirectory and is usually named `localhost_log.date.txt` where `date` identifies the date for the entries contained within the file.

Accessing the `log` Methods

If your servlet is a subclass of `GenericServlet` or `HttpServlet`, as most are, the `log` methods are available as methods in the servlet itself. Also, remember that you can access the `ServletContext` object through the `application` implicit variable in a JSP.

The log methods in ServletContext are

```
public void log(String message)
public void log(String message, Throwable throwable)
```

The second variation of the log method lets you print the stack trace from an exception along with your message.

Disabling JIT During Debugging

Using a Just-in-Time (JIT) compiler keeps the `printStackTrace` method from determining the exact line number where an exception occurred. You can turn off the JIT with `-Djava.compiler=none` under Java 1.2 (and higher). Java 1.4 also supports the `-Xint` option (interpreted-only), which is the equivalent of `-nojit` or `-Djava.compiler=none`.

Using Log4J for Detailed Logging

For some time, Web developers using Tomcat have been using a capable logging package called Log4J. Log4J makes it possible to define logging categories, manage log destinations, and control the formatting of your messages. Log4J is available at `http://jakarta.apache.org/log4j/docs/index.html`.

Log4J defines these core components: **`Loggers`**, **`Appenders`**, and **`Layouts`**.

`Loggers` are responsible for outputting messages to destinations, or `Appenders`. When you create a Logger, you give it a name and a **Level**. `Levels` define the informational type of the messages and are organized hierarchically. The following are the predefined levels (in order):

- `DEBUG`—The most fine-grained informational level, used to provide detailed information used to debug applications
- `INFO`—Used to announce the progress of an application
- `WARN`—Indicates a potentially harmful situation
- `ERROR`—Designates a situation that is the result of an error that may allow the application to continue running
- `FATAL`—Indicates that the application has had a serious fault that will likely lead to its termination

Log4J also defines these levels:

- ALL—Show all informational messages
- OFF—Do not show any informational messages

Loggers use levels to decide whether to output messages. For example, if a logger is created with an assigned level of DEBUG, it will produce entries for every informational level. On the other hand, if a logger is assigned a level of ERROR, it will log only messages that are of type ERROR or FATAL. The Logger class has methods that correspond to each of the levels. Each of the methods has a signature that looks like this:

```
void debug(Object message)
void debug(Object message, Throwable t)
```

The methods take an object that is rendered into a string and an optional Throwable that can be used to provide additional diagnostic information. In addition to the debug, info, warn, error, and fatal methods, the Logger class also has a generic method, log, which can be used to create logs at various levels. The log method is intended for use by wrapper methods, but can be useful if you need to produce different types of logs in one place at run time.

Appenders represent the strategy for outputting log statements. For our purpose, an appender is responsible for deciding whether a message should be output based on its level and for managing the log destination. Log4J provides appenders for writing to the console, files, and databases. There are also appenders that e-mail events and write to remote log servers. Log4J can output to multiple appenders.

Cutting Logs Down to Size

Log4J provides a GUI log viewer that is very useful. It allows you to examine logs on remote machines and to filter them. Look at the Log4J documentation for information about how to use Chainsaw.

As you would expect, Layouts define the format of the log output. SimpleLayout provides a log level and message, HTMLLayout outputs events in an HTML table, and PatternLayout allows you to specify the format using a pattern.

You can define components or configure Log4J programmatically or through the use of a `properties` file. Listing 11.1 is an example of a simple `log4j.properties` file:

LISTING 11.1 Source Code for `log4j.properties`

```
log4j.category.examples.logger=DEBUG, file

log4j.appender.file=org.apache.log4j.RollingFileAppender
log4j.appender.file.File=<TOMCAT_HOME>/webapps/logs/log.txt

log4j.appender.file.layout=org.apache.log4j.SimpleLayout
```

On the first line, we've defined a logger whose name is `examples.logger`, which logs events of `DEBUG` level or greater and whose appender is named `file`. The second and third lines of the example define the appender to be a `RollingFileAppender` whose output is a file in the `webapps/logs/` subdirectory of the Tomcat installation. Don't forget to replace `<TOMCAT_HOME>` with the actual name of the directory Tomcat is installed in. A `RollingFileAppender` will back up log files when they reach a predetermined size. The last line sets the format of the output to `SimpleLayout`.

To use Log4J with Tomcat, you need to copy `log4j.jar` to `/common/lib/` in the Tomcat installation directory. Then, it's only a matter of including the functionality in your Web applications.

Listing 11.2 is an example of a servlet that uses Log4J to log an informational message.

LISTING 11.2 Source Code for `Log4JServlet`

```
package examples;

import javax.servlet.*;
import javax.servlet.http.*;
import java.io.*;
import java.util.*;

import org.apache.log4j.*;

public class Log4JServlet extends HttpServlet {

   public void doGet(HttpServletRequest request, HttpServletResponse response)
        throws ServletException, IOException {

      Logger logger = Logger.getLogger("examples.logger");
      logger.info("In the doGet method of Log4JServlet!");

      PrintWriter out = response.getWriter();
      out.println("<html>");
```

LISTING 11.2 Continued

```
        out.println("<head><title>A Servlet That uses Log4J</title></head>");
        out.println("<body>");
        out.println("<p>We've just logged an event!</p>");
        out.println("</body></html>");
    }
}
```

The `log4j.properties` for this Web application should be placed in the `WEB-INF/classes` subdirectory of the application. By doing this, you can configure each application independently of one another.

The resulting log file contains the event

```
INFO - In the doGet method of Log4JServlet!
```

By using scriptlets, you can add Log4J to your JSPs as well. Better yet, beginning in Hour 16, you'll learn enough about custom tags to be able to use the Log Tag Library in your JavaServer Pages. Visit `http://jakarta.apache.org/taglibs/doc/log-doc/intro.html` for additional information about the Log Tag Library.

By the Way

Logging in Java 1.4

Beginning with Java 1.4, there's an in-house logging facility. It's not nearly as feature-packed, but it's a standard part of the Java distribution. If you don't need extra features, such as a very flexible `PatternLayout`, you can use the standard logging facilities. Because of some recent changes to Log4J, the code you use to obtain a logger and log events is similar.

Logging to a File

When all else fails, you can always open up a file and write log messages to it. If you close the file after writing, remember to make sure you open it again with the `append` option set to `true`. That is, make sure you don't overwrite the existing file; otherwise, you'll lose the previous log message every time you write a new one.

Using Exceptions to Trace Execution

Sometimes when you're debugging, you want to find out what routine called a particular method. You could throw an exception, but you don't want to stop executing the method; you just want to write a log message indicating who called the method. For instance, one class might be calling a method with bad values and you want to locate the offending class.

You can throw an exception and catch it immediately to get an instant snapshot of the current thread's call stack, like this:

```
try
{
    throw new Exception("dummy");
}
catch (Exception exc)
{
    System.out.println("This method was called from:");
    exc.printStackTrace(System.out);
}
```

This technique isn't the prettiest thing in the world, and it isn't very fast, but sometimes it's the only choice you have.

Using a Debugger

When you're working with a program that isn't behaving properly, you need to examine the state of the program while it is running. If it's not too complicated, it's possible to dump the state using any of the methods discussed earlier. However, if the state is complex or if you need to monitor changes in state or watch events that initiate transitions, a debugger is often the only way to do it.

There are many different kinds of debuggers for Java. The JDK comes with a command-line debugger called `jdb`. Many people find `jdb` painful to use because it isn't a graphical debugger, as you would find in an Interactive Development Environment.

Many times, however, you're working on a server in which you might not have access to a graphical environment anyway. When you have a lot of machines stored away in a machine room somewhere and you can't use the X Window system because of firewall restrictions, you might need to resort to using Telnet to access the machines. If you're using Telnet, `jdb` is probably your best bet.

Did you Know?

Use VNC for Remote Access

If you can't use the X Window system because of firewall restrictions, you might try Virtual Network Computing (VNC) from `http://www.realvnc.com/`. VNC often lets you go through firewalls that don't allow X traffic. It can also let you access a Windows machine the same way PCAnywhere does.

In general, there are two ways to debug a Java program: Start the program from a debugger, or run the Java program with remote debugging enabled and attach a debugger to the program. The advantage of remote debugging is that you don't need to figure out what class to run at startup. You let the server go through its normal startup and then attach the debugger and start running. However, it's also generally more complicated and error-prone.

Debugging a Servlet with Tomcat Using `jdb`

The jdb debugger enables you to step through code one line at a time and also display the value of variables. To debug a Java program, use the `jdb` command just as you would use the `java` command. For example, to debug a class called `HelloWorld`, type

```
jdb HelloWorld
```

Here, jdb is being used to debug a program locally. You can debug servlets running under the control of Tomcat the same way. Tomcat normally requires a number of options for the `java` command, so you might think that it would be difficult to start Tomcat under jdb. Fortunately, the `catalina` script (`catalina.bat` on Windows, `catalina.sh` on Unix/Linux) can start Tomcat under jdb automatically. To start Tomcat under jdb on Windows, type

```
catalina debug
```

To start Tomcat under `jdb` on Unix/Linux, type

```
catalina.sh debug
```

Did you Know?

`startup.sh` or `catalina.sh`?

You may be in the habit of using `startup.sh` or `startup.bat` to run Tomcat. These scripts are wrappers for `catalina.sh`. You can use `catalina.sh` directly as we suggested for debugging. However, it may be necessary for you to run `setclasspath.sh` or `setclasspath.bat` first. These scripts require that `JAVA_HOME` is set to the home directory of your JDK installation and `BASEDIR` is set to the base (or home) directory of Tomcat.

To debug a servlet like `HelloWorldServlet`, just tell `jdb` to `stop` in the servlet's `doGet` method, like this:

```
stop in examples.HelloWorldServlet.doGet
```

Did you Know?

Setting Breakpoints on Overloaded Methods

If you want to set a breakpoint on a method that is overloaded, you'll also need to provide the method's arguments to `jdb`. If you don't know whether a method is overloaded, you can issue the command `methods classname` to get a list.

Then, in order to start Tomcat, simply issue the command

```
run
```

When you access the servlet, the debugger notifies you that a thread has reached the breakpoint, as you can see in Figure 11.3.

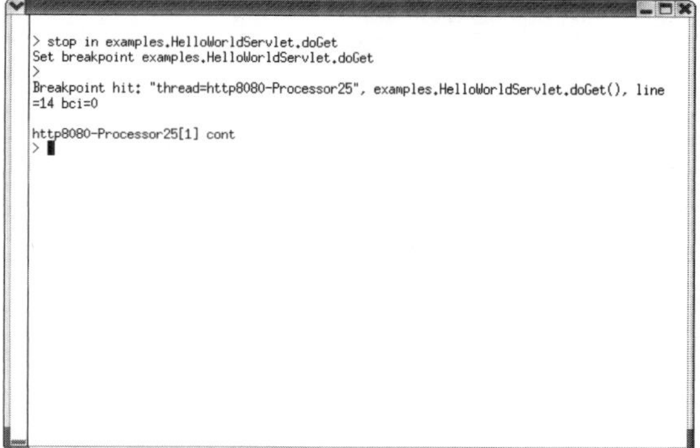

FIGURE 11.3
The debugger tells you when a thread hits a breakpoint.

You can use the `list` command to see the current line in the source code, but first you must tell `jdb` where to find the source code. Give `jdb` the path to your source code, like this:

```
use /home/tyjsp20/
```

Most Java debuggers expect the source code to have the same directory structure as the classes. For example, because `HelloWorldServlet` is in a package named `examples`, `jdb` looks for `HelloWorldServlet.java` in `/home/tyjsp20/examples/`. Notice that it appends the package structure to the path you provided earlier. Setting up the proper directories is the biggest hurdle new developers must face when learning to debug with tools.

After you have the source path set up, if you type `list`, you should see something like the screen shown in Figure 11.4.

```
> stop in examples.HelloWorldServlet.doGet
Set breakpoint examples.HelloWorldServlet.doGet
>
Breakpoint hit: "thread=http8080-Processor25", examples.HelloWorldServlet.doGet(), line
=14 bci=0

http8080-Processor25[1] cont
>
Breakpoint hit: "thread=http8080-Processor24", examples.HelloWorldServlet.doGet(), line=14
 bci=0

http8080-Processor24[1] use /home/tyjsp20
http8080-Processor24[1] list
10                          HttpServletResponse response)
11              throws IOException
12          {
13     // Tell the Web server that the response is HTML
14 =>           response.setContentType("text/html");
15
16     // Get the PrintWriter for writing out the response
17              PrintWriter out = response.getWriter();
18
19     // Write the HTML back to the browser
http8080-Processor24[1] cont
>
```

FIGURE 11.4
The Java Debugger can show you the source code that is executing.

The Java Debugger has many commands and includes some online help, which you can get by typing `help` or just `?`. Use the `cont` command to send control back to the program you're debugging and `quit` to exit.

By attaching to a server, you can use `jdb` to debug remotely. If you're working in a distributed environment, where Tomcat is hosted on a machine other than your workstation, you can start Tomcat on the server using the command

```
catalina.sh jpda start
```

This causes Tomcat to run in a JVM that supports debugging using the Java Platform Debugging Architecture (JPDA), which is what makes it possible to debug over-the-wire.

Then, at your workstation, you simply issue the command

```
jdb -connect com.sun.jdi.SocketAttach:hostname=HOSTNAME,port=8000
```

Be certain to replace `HOSTNAME` with the actual name of the server running Tomcat. You'll see the same prompt you saw before and can debug in the same way. The only difference is that you will not need to issue the command `run`, since Tomcat will already be running.

Any debugger that supports JPDA should be able to debug servlets running inside Tomcat.

Using a Graphical Debugger with Tomcat

Several excellent Integrated Development Environments (IDE) and stand-alone debuggers exist that can help you debug problems efficiently. Here is a list of a few of them that are freely available:

- Netbeans—A superb open-source IDE that has built-in support for developing JSPs and servlets. (`http://www.netbeans.org`)
- Eclipse—Another great open-source IDE that is feature-rich. By design, you'll need to add plug-ins to get functionality to support JSPs and servlets, but there are a few good ones out there. (`http://www.eclipse.org`)
- Communiqué JSP Debugger—A free debugger that can currently do source-level JSP debugging. (`http://www.day.com/content/en/product/productline/unify/ide/dnlogin.html`)
- JSwat—An open-source debugger that is quite capable and easy to use. (`http://www.bluemarsh.com/java/jswat/`)

Although the debuggers vary in the set of features they provide and in the way you use them, there are some common elements when it comes to working with servlets and JSPs.

Generally, debugging begins by identifying or creating a project or session through which you identify the location of the source files and classes. Most of these tools integrate nicely with Tomcat when the tool and Tomcat are hosted on the same machine. They are often able to start and stop Tomcat and may also be able to deploy (or redeploy) Web applications or components. With JDK 1.4, some of the tools are even able to "hot-swap" classes, allowing you to change your source, back up to a point prior to your changes, and start debugging again.

All of the debuggers are JPDA compatible. Like `jdb`, you simply need to start Tomcat with JPDA enabled and tell the debugger the address of the machine that is hosting Tomcat. As you saw earlier, you only need to provide a path to the source code for the debugger to provide you with a listing.

Figure 11.5 shows a debugging session in Netbeans.

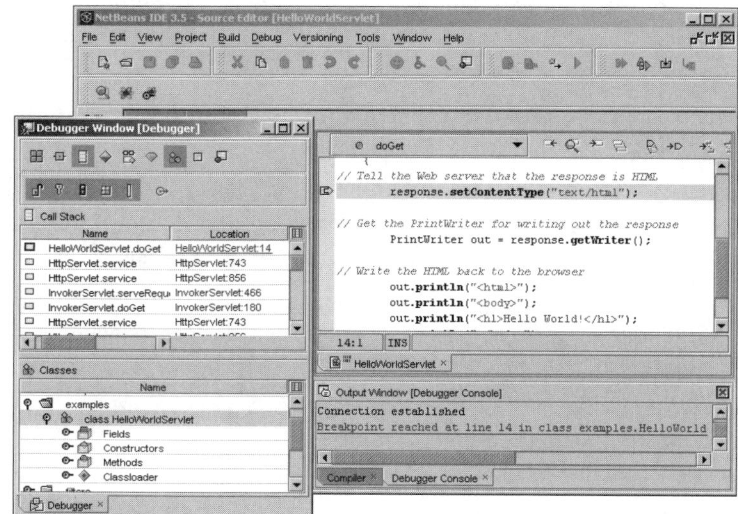

FIGURE 11.5
The Netbeans Debugger presents a global view of the application.

You can see that there's quite a bit of information that Netbeans provides. It will give you a view into the source code and identify the particular line that is currently executing. It also traces the flow of methods and shows you variables that are in scope. Like jdb, you can insert breakpoints and manage the execution state. If you have an environment that can support them, GUI debuggers are often easier to use and can give you a snapshot that is very useful while troubleshooting an application.

Debugging a JavaServer Page with Tomcat

Because JavaServer Pages eventually become servlets, you can debug a JSP by following the same procedure you use to debug servlets—with a few extra steps.

When Tomcat translates a JSP into a servlet, it puts the generated servlet code and classes into the work directory underneath the main Tomcat directory. This is where you need to look for a JSP's servlet. If you take a minute to look at this directory in your Tomcat installation, you'll see that there's a `Catalina/localhost/` subdirectory under the `work/` directory. Then, you may have noticed that there are directories for each application context. One, the root context, is identified by a simple underscore (_). Following the directory that corresponds to the application context in which you are debugging, you'll find the familiar hierarchy of directories used with packages. The default package for JSPs is `org.apache.jsp`, so the full path to the code and classes for a simple JSP is

```
<TOMACT_HOME>/work/Catalina/localhost/_/org/apache/jsp
```

By the Way

Debugging and Tomcat 5

Tomcat has a JSP compiler and execution servlet whose configuration determines the work directory, whether the source files are saved, and whether debugging information is produced. Look in the global `web.xml` for details. If you're not using Tomcat, you may need to alter your server's configuration to be able to debug JSPs.

Also, Tomcat 5 has made significant strides to make it easier to debug JSPs, such as implementing the simple directory structure mentioned earlier. Earlier versions used to mangle the names.

Having located the source file, you need to let your debugger know where it is. When the debugger is integrated with Tomcat, it often already knows this. In some cases, particularly when doing remote debugging, the source file is synchronized to a local directory. Developers can also mount directories for local use.

Although it's nice to be able to get under the hood, it probably seems like a little much to expect JSP developers to be experts at debugging servlets. After all, JSPs are supposed to make Web application development easier, right?

Several IDEs make it possible to locally debug JSPs using only JSP source files. Figure 11.6 shows another debugging session using Netbeans—this time directly debugging a JavaServer Page.

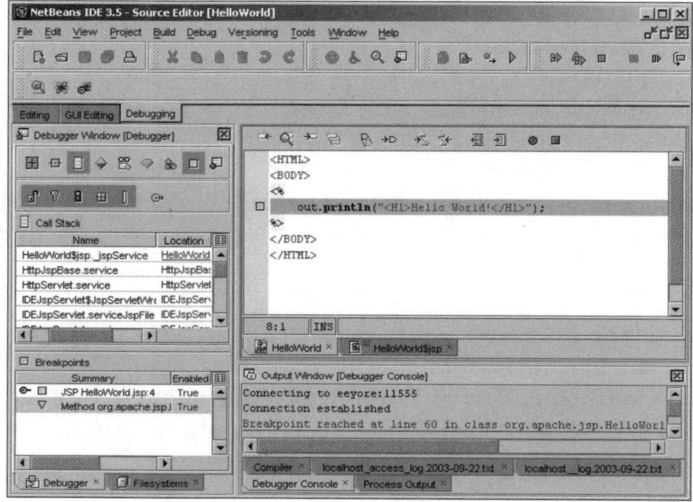

FIGURE 11.6
The Netbeans Debugger can also debug JSPs directly.

Most debuggers that can do this use proprietary methods. The JSP 2.0 specification introduces standardized support for debugging in other languages, including JSP itself.

Error Handling

You usually won't be able to find all the errors in your Web application no matter how much debugging you do. Eventually, an error is going to crop up somewhere. In a servlet, you can put a try-catch block around your code to make sure the servlet doesn't throw an exception but goes to an error-handling page instead.

Specifying an Error Page for a JSP

For a JavaServer Page, you might be able to insert a try-catch block, but there's a better solution. You can specify an error page for each JSP. Whenever the page throws an exception, the JSP engine automatically invokes the error page. The error page can then log the exception (which is passed via the `exception` built-in variable) and display some sort of response to the user.

To set up an error page, use the `<%@ page errorPage="xxx" %>` directive. For example, Listing 11.3 shows a JavaServer Page that intentionally throws an exception.

LISTING 11.3 Source Code for ThrowError.jsp

```
<%@ page errorPage="ShowError.jsp" %>
<html>
<body>
<h1> Hello World!</h1>
</body>
</html>

<%
// Throw an exception to invoke the error page
// Do a stupid expression to keep the compiler
// from generating "Statement Not Reached" errors
    int x = 1;
    if (x == 1)
    {
        throw new RuntimeException("Oh no!!!");
    }
%>
```

Listing 11.4 shows the error page that was specified in Listing 11.3. Notice that the error-handling page includes the directive `<%@ page isErrorPage="true" %>`. This directive causes the JSP compiler to generate the `exception` instance variable.

LISTING 11.4 Source Code for ShowError.jsp

```
<%@ page isErrorPage="true" %>
<html>
<body bgcolor="#ffffff">
<h1>Error</h1>
Sorry, an error occurred.
<p>
Here is the stack trace:
<p>
<pre>
<% exception.printStackTrace(new PrintWriter(out)); %>
</pre>
</body>
</html>
```

Did you Know?

Error Pages and Output

When the JSP engine calls an error page, it is essentially doing the same thing as a JSP forward. If you have already flushed the output buffer, the JSP engine might not be able to display the error page, or the user might see the first part of the original output followed by the error page. Try to do the things that are likely to cause an exception first; that way, the exceptions can be handled before any output is returned.

Specifying Error Handlers for Web Server Errors

Some errors that occur in an application can't be detected from a JSP or servlet. For instance, if you have a typo in one of your HTML hyperlinks, the Web server generates an HTTP 404 error. Because no servlet or JSP is involved when the 404 error occurs, there is normally no way to know about the error until the user calls up on the phone asking about it.

Fortunately, the servlet API specification provides a hook that enables you to specify an error handler for a specific Web server error or Java exception. The only difficulty you'll have in setting up these error handlers is that you must put them in a deployment descriptor, which is a file describing the contents of a Web application. Appendix B, "Packaging a Web Application," tells you everything you need to know about setting up a deployment descriptor and deploying a Web application on a server.

To add a handler for the 404 error, you just add the following information to the deployment descriptor:

```
<error-page>
    <error-code>404</error-code>
    <location>My404Handler.html</location>
</error-page>
```

Instead of a numeric error code, you can also specify a Java exception type for the error page. For example, whenever a `java.lang.NullPointerException` occurs in a JSP or servlet, you can invoke a special handler by adding the following information to the deployment descriptor:

```
<error-page>
    <exception-type>java.lang.NullPointerException</exception-type>
    <location>NullPointerHandler.jsp</location>
</error-page>
```

The location for an error page might be an HTML page, a JSP, a servlet, or some other kind of Web resource.

Summary

Even though debugging can be tough, there are a number of techniques you can use to help you knock out the pests. Logging is a simple task that often produces the information you need without too much complexity. With Log4J or the Java 1.4 Logging APIs, you can produce software that gives you the right amount of information for different events without too much effort. For situations that require a closer look, debuggers are useful. Although they're more difficult to set up, particularly when working in distributed environments, they provide a perspective on the application that is difficult to get anywhere else.

Finally, well-designed applications will use error pages to handle unexpected exceptions in your JSPs or to inform users in a friendly way about content or server errors.

Q&A

Q. ***Why are exceptions getting by my catch block even when I'm catching*** `Exception`***?***

A. In some fairly rare cases, you might be getting an error instead of an exception. The `Error` and `Exception` classes are both subclasses of `Throwable`. If you catch `Throwable`, you will definitely catch any possible exception or error.

Q. ***Where are my log messages going?***

A. The location of the servlet and JSP log files is implementation-dependent. You should consult the document for the JSP/servlet engine.

Q. ***Where are my*** `System.out` ***and*** `System.err` ***messages going?***

A. Like the log files, the location for `System.out` and `System.err` messages is implementation-dependent. You should consult the documentation for your servlet engine.

Q. ***Why don't my messages show up in the log file?***

A. Although there are rare cases where the JSP/servlet engine delays writing output messages, most of the time you don't see the messages because you aren't really writing them. Exceptions are usually the root cause of these problems. You might want to try catching `Exception` to make sure there aren't unexpected exceptions, and in some cases you might even want to catch `Throwable`.

Q. ***Why doesn't the*** `jre` ***command recognize the*** `-debug` ***option?***

A. You must use the `java` command for debugging. The `jre` command is intended as a production-level VM and doesn't include some of the extra baggage of the `java` command. Recent versions of Java don't even include the `jre` command anymore.

Workshop

The Workshop is designed to help you review what you have learned and help you further increase your understanding of the material covered in this hour.

Quiz

1. How do you obtain access to the `log` method?
2. What are some of the advantages of using a formal logging environment such as Log4J?
3. When setting up a debugger to debug an application, what's the most likely reason you can't see the source code for the application?

Answers

1. The `log`method is available as part of the `GenericServlet` and `HttpServlet` classes. It's also available as a method of the `ServletContext` object available through the `application` implicit variable.
2. There are several advantages. Some of them are that you can easily standardize the format, associate additional meaning to a log through the use of a level, and take advantage of the flexibility of the software to produce logs at different destinations.
3. The source code must be placed in a directory structure that is the same as the corresponding class files. Most developers make the mistake of pointing directly to the source files, instead of pointing to the directory that is the root for the source files. For example, if you're debugging an application that is packaged in `com.cde.abc`, the source files must be in `com/cde/abc` and the debugger needs to be set up to look for the source files in the directory containing the subdirectory `com`.

Activities

1. Modify the Log4J example to use Chainsaw.
2. Use jdb to run a simple application. Set a breakpoint, examine the source and a variable, and resume the application so that it runs to completion.
3. Select an IDE, perform the tasks of the last activity using the debugging portion of the IDE.

HOUR 12

Saving Data Between Requests

What You'll Learn in This Hour:

- How to securely store data in hidden form variables
- What sessions are and how they can be used to store information about a client
- How to store information that can be used by the entire application

Web programmers often need to keep track of data between user requests. For example, you'll often need to remember who the client is so that you can personalize the content or services.

Storing Data in Hidden Form Variables

Given what you already know about JSP, servlets, and HTML forms, you already have the ability to keep track of data between requests. You can store user data in hidden form variables.

Although not the most elegant solution, many applications use form variables to store user data. The idea is that every time the user submits a form, the form contains some hidden variables that provide information about the user. These variables might be a login ID and password or the user's name. The big hassle with using form variables is that all your forms must preserve these hidden variables and continue to pass them around.

The best way to illustrate this technique is with an example. Listing 12.1 shows a login form that calls a JSP to handle the login.

LISTING 12.1 Source Code for `Login.html`

```
<html>
<body bgcolor="#ffffff">
<H1>Login</H1>
Please log in

<form action="Login.jsp" method="POST">

<table>
<tr><td>User Name:<td><input type="text" name="username">
<tr><td>Password:<td><input type="password" name="password">
</table>
<p>
<input type="submit" value="Login!">
</form>
</body>
</html>
```

The goal of this example is to preserve the username across multiple pages. The `Login.jsp` page will have the username because it's passed as a form variable from `Login.html`. Listing 12.2 shows `Login.jsp`. Notice that it inserts the username as a hidden form variable.

LISTING 12.2 Source Code for `Login.jsp`

```
<html>
<body bgcolor="#ffffff">

<%
// Get the login information.
    String userName = request.getParameter("username");
    String password = request.getParameter("password");

%>
Welcome, <%=userName%>!
<form action=" ColorServlet" method="POST">

<%-- Save the username in a hidden form variable. --%>
<input type="hidden" name="username" value="<%=userName%>">

<p>
Please enter your favorite color:
<select name="color">
    <option value="blue" SELECTED>Blue</option>
    <option value="red">Red</option>
    <option value="green">Green</option>
    <option value="yellow">Yellow</option>
    <option value="mauve">Mauve</option>
```

LISTING 12.2 Continued

```
</select>
<p>
<input type="submit" value="Choose color!">
</form>
</body>
</html>
```

Figure 12.1 shows the output from `Login.jsp`.

FIGURE 12.1 A page can contain hidden form variables that the user can't see.

The third part of this example is a servlet that receives the hidden form variable along with the user's color choice. Listing 12.3 shows the servlet.

LISTING 12.3 Source Code for `ColorServlet.java`

```
package examples;

import javax.servlet.*;
import javax.servlet.http.*;
import java.io.*;

public class ColorServlet extends HttpServlet
{
    public void doPost(HttpServletRequest request,
        HttpServletResponse response)
        throws IOException
    {
// Tell the Web server that the response is HTML.
        response.setContentType("text/html");

// Get the PrintWriter for writing out the response.
        PrintWriter out = response.getWriter();
```

LISTING 12.3 Continued

```
// Fetch the username and color parameters.
        String userName = request.getParameter("username");
        String color = request.getParameter("color");

// Write the HTML back to the browser.
        out.println("<html>");
        out.println("<body bgcolor=\"#ffffff\">");
        out.println("Well, I see that "+userName+
            "'s favorite color is "+color+".");
        out.println("</body>");
        out.println("</html>");
    }
}
```

Watch Out!

Trying Out These Examples

You'll need to create a deployment descriptor to try these examples out. If you need to review this topic, you learned how to do this in Hour 2, "JavaServer Pages Behind the Scenes."

Security Concerns with Hidden Variables

One of the reasons you don't see hidden variables used very often in commercial Web sites, especially e-commerce sites, is that they are inherently insecure. Suppose `Login.jsp` actually verified the username and password. You would then assume that the username passed to `ColorServlet` is valid. But there is nothing to stop someone from inserting a bogus username and even a bizarre color by passing it in the URL for the servlet. Figure 12.2 shows an example of how the system can be tricked by inserting a phony username and color into the URL.

FIGURE 12.2 A malicious user can send phony values for hidden form variables.

Changing a username is bad enough, but imagine what could happen if someone did this with a bank account or credit card number! Certainly this technique needs some work. You might get clever and choose a variable name that is far less obvious than `username`. Suppose, for example, that you changed the name of the hidden variable to `xpq7564HHgk`. Surely no one would guess the variable name! Unfortunately, all someone needs to do is ask the browser to display the source for the page, as shown in Figure 12.3.

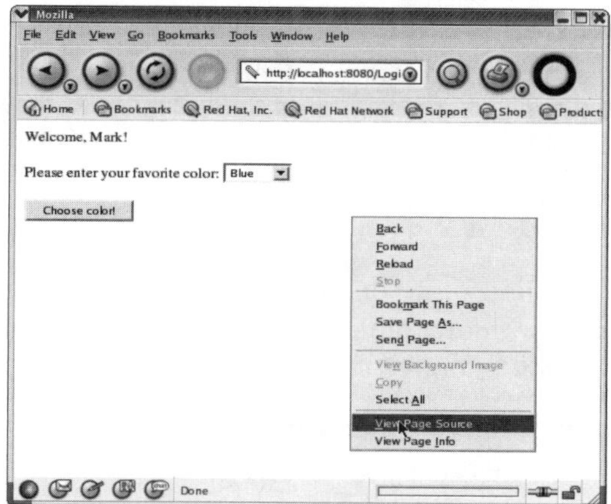

FIGURE 12.3
Because a user can view the source to a page, you can't safely hide anything in the page.

Another big concern with hidden form variables is that the user might accidentally bookmark the secure information. When you use an HTTP `GET` method (by setting `method="get"` in your `<form>` tag) to submit a form, the form variables all appear in the URL and will be part of a bookmark if the user bookmarks the page. Even hidden form variables show up in the URL.

Most of these concerns can be eliminated by using an HTTP `POST` instead of `GET`. You'll recall that a `POST` embeds variables in the body rather than in the URL. If you use hidden form variables, even storing a single value, make sure you use an HTTP `POST` to help secure your application.

The hidden form variable approach seems to work fairly well except for one thing: the hidden variable itself. First of all, putting the hidden variable in every form is a hassle. Second, it requires the application to use only forms for accessing server-side pages. This presents quite a few problems. For example, if you use a hyperlink, there are no form variables to pass. You must either rewrite your hyperlinks to include all of the information that is included in your form or find a better alternative. That alternative is the `session` object.

Storing Data in a session Object

When dealing with HTTP, there is no permanent connection between a browser and a Web server. When the browser needs a page from the Web server, it opens a connection, retrieves the page, and then closes the connection. After that, the Web server has no idea what is happening on the browser. The browser could crash, or the entire client computer could be turned off, and the Web server would be oblivious.

By the Way

HTTP Persistent Connections

Because opening and closing connection is time-consuming, HTTP 1.1 provides a mechanism to keep a connection open during the exchange of requests and responses between a client and server. A **persistent connection** can remain open until either the client or server decides to close the connection. However, HTTP remains stateless as far as the application is concerned.

Furthermore, when another connection is made, the Web server does not associate the new connection with any other that has been made in the past. In other words, HTTP is not session-oriented.

Sessions allow an application to remember something about a client that persists between connections. In the first part of this hour, we saved information that we did not want to forget by passing it back and forth between the client and application. In this way, we created a primitive session.

Servlets and JSPs do have a notion of a session. Instead of playing toss with variables, servlets and JSPs can store information on the server using a single key that the client remembers. Servlets and JSPs use an `HttpSession` object to accomplish this.

Using the session Object in a JSP

JavaServer Pages have several built-in objects. You have already seen two of them: `request` and `out`. The next important one is called `session`, and it's an instance of `HttpSession`. The three methods that you use the most in the `session` object are `getAttribute`, `setAttribute`, and `removeAttribute`. The declarations for these methods are

```
public void setAttribute(String name, Object value)
    throws IllegalStateException
public Object getAttribute(String name)
    throws IllegalStateException
public void removeAttribute(String name)
    throws IllegalStateException
```

These methods act much like the `get` and `put` methods in the `Hashtable` class. That is, `setAttribute` associates a name with a value, and `getAttribute` returns the value associated with a name or returns `null` if there is no value associated. For example, to store some data in a session, you would type the following:

```
session.setAttribute("someKey", "here is my data");
```

To retrieve the data back out of the session, you would type this:

```
String myData = (String) session.getAttribute("someKey");
```

An `IllegalStateException` is thrown when you try to get or set an attribute on an invalid session. A session becomes invalid either when you call its `invalidate` method or after the session has timed out. The servlet engine keeps track of how long it has been since a session has been accessed; after a certain period of inactivity, the session is marked as invalid. You can configure the amount of time it takes to time out a session, either on a per-session basis or for all sessions.

By the Way

Specifying the Session Timeout Duration

The Servlet API specifies a way for you to control the timeout period on a per-session basis. Most servlet engines also provide a way for you to specify a default timeout length, but the Servlet API does not require them to.

Listing 12.4 shows the `Login.jsp` page modified to support the `session` object. Notice that it no longer needs to use hidden form variables.

LISTING 12.4 Source Code for `Login2.jsp`

```
<%@ page language="java" import="java.util.*" %>


<html>
<body bgcolor="#ffffff">

<%
// Get the login information.
    String userName = request.getParameter("username");
    String password = request.getParameter("password");

// Store the username in the session.
session.setAttribute("username", userName);
%>
Welcome, <%=userName%>!
<form action="ColorServlet2" method="POST">
```

LISTING 12.4 Continued

```
<p>
Please enter your favorite color:
<select name="color">
    <option value="blue" SELECTED>Blue</option>
    <option value="red">Red</option>
    <option value="green">Green</option>
    <option value="yellow">Yellow</option>
    <option value="mauve">Mauve</option>
</select>
<p>
<input type="submit" value="Choose color!">
</form>
</body>
</html>
```

By the Way

Having Trouble with the Example?

If you are having trouble storing or retrieving your session information, see the "Q&A" section at the end of this hour.

Using the `session` Object in a Servlet

You have probably guessed this already, but the `session` object you use in a servlet is identical to the one you use in a JSP. The only difference is that it isn't already conveniently sitting around in a variable named `session`. Instead, you must get the `session` object from the `request` object.

By the Way

JSPs Automatically Obtain a Session

JavaServer Pages also get the `session` object from the `request` object. The only reason you don't notice is that the JSP compiler automatically generates code to fetch the `session` object and put it in a variable named `session`.

To get the `session` object from the `request` object, just call the `getSession` method:

```
HttpSession session = request.getSession();
```

Inside a servlet, you use the same `getAttribute` and `setAttribute` methods to update session variables as you do in a JSP. After all, the `session` object is an instance of `HttpSession` in both a servlet and a JSP.

Obtain a Session Before Starting Your Response

Because the servlet engine needs to send a session cookie back to the browser, make sure that you get the `session` object before you start sending a response back to the browser. Cookies must be sent back in the header portion of the response. In a JSP, the `session` object is usually available immediately. You really need to worry about this only inside a servlet.

Watch Out!

Listing 12.5 shows the necessary modifications to `ColorServlet` to make it use `HttpSession` rather than form variables.

LISTING 12.5 Source Code for `ColorServlet2.java`

```
package examples;

import javax.servlet.*;
import javax.servlet.http.*;
import java.io.*;
import java.util.*;

public class ColorServlet2 extends HttpServlet
{
    public void doPost(HttpServletRequest request,
        HttpServletResponse response)
        throws IOException
    {
// Tell the Web server that the response is HTML.
        response.setContentType("text/html");

// Get the PrintWriter for writing out the response.
        PrintWriter out = response.getWriter();

// Fetch the color parameter.
        String color = request.getParameter("color");

// Get the username from the session.
        HttpSession session = request.getSession();

        String userName = (String) session.getAttribute("username");
```

LISTING 12.5 Continued

```
// Write the HTML back to the browser.
        out.println("<html>");
        out.println("<body bgcolor=\"#ffffff\">");
        out.println("Well, I see that "+userName+
            "'s favorite color is "+color+".");
        out.println("</body>");
        out.println("</html>");
    }
}
```

By the Way

HttpSessions Work Only in HttpServlets

Because the `HttpSession` object relies specifically on features of HTTP, you can use it only in servlets that are subclasses of `HttpServlet`.

How Sessions Work

Now that you see that servlets and JSPs can support sessions, you can take a step back and look at how the sessions work. When the servlet engine creates a session, it sends a session identifier (also referred to as a session key) back to the browser in the form of a cookie. A cookie is just a piece of information that the browser sends back to the server whenever it asks the server for a page.

Usually, for a session, the cookie disappears when the Web browser is shut down. As you will see in Hour 13, "More About Saving Data," a browser can save cookies to disk, so when the browser starts up again it still knows about the cookies it had when it shut down. Because sessions are typically short-lived, and because shutting the browser down is an action that warrants the termination of a session, the session cookie is usually not saved to disk. Remember, the server has no idea when the Web browser shuts down. Figure 12.4 illustrates the interaction between the browser and the servlet engine as it relates to cookies and sessions.

Watch Out!

These Examples Require Cookies

You must enable cookies in your browser for these examples to work.

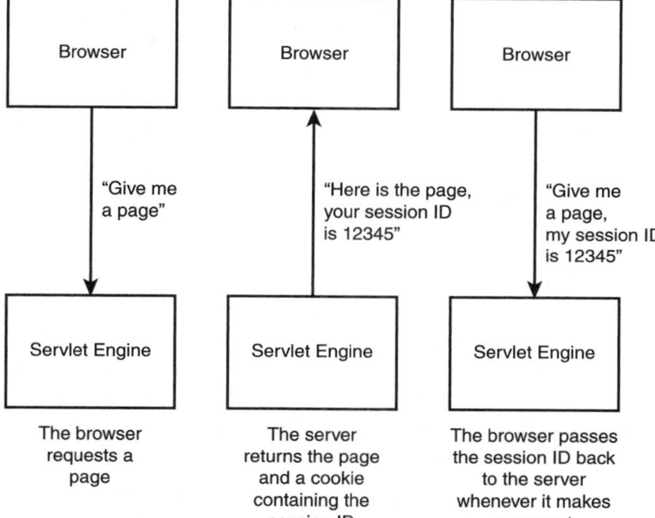
Browser
Browser
Browser
"Give me a page"
"Here is the page, your session ID is 12345"
"Give me a page, my session ID is 12345"
Servlet Engine
Servlet Engine
Servlet Engine
The browser requests a page
The server returns the page and a cookie containing the session ID
The browser passes the session ID back to the server whenever it makes a request

FIGURE 12.4
The server sends the session identifier in a cookie, which the browser passes back.

When the browser asks the server for a page, the server looks at the session cookie and then finds the session corresponding to that session identifier.

Occasionally, the servlet engine looks through its sessions and gets rid of those that haven't been accessed in a long time. If it didn't do this, eventually the servlet engine would be wasting a lot of memory by holding on to sessions that could never be accessed again because the cookies associated with those sessions are long gone. (People do shut down their browsers eventually, and that kills the session cookies.)

Forcing a New Session

When you call the `getSession` method to retrieve the current session, the `request` object automatically creates a session if one doesn't already exist. In some JSP implementations, the session is created automatically even if you never use it. Most of the time, you don't really care when the session has been created. Other times, however, you need to explicitly reset the existing session and start over.

Suppose, for example, that you have implemented an online shopping site. A user logs on, visits a few pages, and selects several items to buy. You store these items in the user's session as she travels from page to page. Now, suppose the user decides that she doesn't want any of those items, and rather than go through the trouble of removing them from her shopping cart, she decides to just log in to your site again.

If a user comes back into your login page, you probably want to start her over with a clean slate. Although you can design a site that is smart enough to figure out what the user was last doing and send her back to where she left off, most people assume that when they come in through the "front door" they are starting over.

Did you Know?

Security and Sessions

There's a good reason to start a session over when entering through the login page. A user might walk away from the computer while at the login screen, thinking his order is now gone. Imagine his surprise if another user could walk up to the computer, log in, and have access to his order, complete with his credit card number. For this reason, you should either clear the session or associate it with a user.

The `getSession` method in the `request` object enables you to control the creation of new sessions. When you ask for a session, you can ask that the request object not create a new session if one doesn't already exist. The following segment of code automatically invalidates the previous session and then creates a new one:

```
// Get the old session, but don't create a session if
// one didn't already exist (passing true would allow
// creation of a new one).
    HttpSession oldSess = request.getSession(false);

// If there was an old session, invalidate it.
    if (oldSess != null)
    {
        oldSess.invalidate();
    }

// Now create a fresh new session.
    HttpSession session = request.getSession(true);
```

This code works for both JSP and servlets, except that you shouldn't re-declare a session for a JSP. Instead, the last line should just read

```
    session = request.getSession(true);
```

Handling Session Termination

A session can be terminated in two ways: You force the termination by calling the `invalidate` method on the session, or the servlet engine times the session out. Depending on the kind of data you store in the session, you might need to perform some kind of cleanup of the session data. For example, you might have a database connection stored in the session. Although Java's garbage collector eventually eliminates these resources, you shouldn't keep them open any longer than you need to.

A `session` object has a callback mechanism to notify an object when it has been associated with a session and when it is no longer associated with a session. That is, when you call `session.setAttribute("someName", someObject)`, the `session` object can notify the object that it is being associated with a session. When the session terminates, the `session` object can also notify the object that it is no longer associated with the session.

This notification is on an object-by-object basis. Although it might seem strange at first, the notification technique is actually very flexible. You can write objects that are session-aware and can perform their own cleanup. If you are using standard objects, such as a JDBC `Connection` object, you can create a special session cleanup object that releases your database connection.

The `HttpSessionBindingListener` Interface

The `HttpSessionBindingListener` interface defines notification methods that the `session` object uses to notify objects when they are added to or removed from a session. There are two methods in the interface:

```
public void valueBound(HttpSessionBindingEvent event);
public void valueUnbound(HttpSessionBindingEvent event);
```

As you might have guessed, `valueBound` is called when an object is added to a session; `valueUnbound` is called when the object is removed from a session. Listing 12.6 shows an example class that listens for `valueBound` and `valueUnbound` messages and counts the number of sessions that are bound to each instance of the class.

LISTING 12.6 Source Code for `BindListener.java`

```
package examples;

import javax.servlet.http.*;

/** Counts the number of sessions that are bound to this object. */

public class BindListener implements HttpSessionBindingListener
```

LISTING 12.6 Continued

```
{
// The current session count
    protected int numSessions;

    public BindListener()
    {
        numSessions = 0;
    }

// Every time this object is added to a session,
// valueBound is called.
    public synchronized void valueBound(HttpSessionBindingEvent event)
    {
        numSessions++;
    }

// Every time this object is removed from a session,
// valueUnbound is called.
    public synchronized void valueUnbound(HttpSessionBindingEvent event)
    {
        numSessions--;
    }

// Returns the current number of bound sessions
    public int getNumSessions()
    {
        return numSessions;
    }
}
```

To test the `BindListener` class, you need to observe what happens when you access it from multiple sessions and also see what happens when you invalidate a session that contains a `BindListener` object. You should expect to see the session count go up whenever the object is added to a session, and you should see the count go down when the object is removed from a session or when the session it belongs to is invalidated.

Listing 12.7 shows a test harness JSP that exercises the `BindListener` class. By selecting various hyperlinks, you can remove the `BindListener` object from the session or invalidate the session.

LISTING 12.7 Source Code for `BindTest.jsp`

```
<%@ page language="java" import="examples.BindListener" %>

<html>
<body bgcolor="#ffffff">
```

LISTING 12.7 Continued

```
<%-- Set up a static BindListener shared by all instances of this JSP.

     There is probably only one instance, but just in case the server creates

     multiple instances, this page can handle it. --%>
<%!
    protected static BindListener listener = new BindListener();
%>

<%

    BindListener l = null;

// Allow the browser to pass a "removeListener" parameter to remove
// a listener from the session.

    if (request.getParameter("removeListener") != null)
    {
        session.removeAttribute("listener");
    }

// Allow the browser to pass a resetSession parameter to clear out
// the session.
    else if (request.getParameter("resetSession") != null)
    {
// See whether there is already a session.
        HttpSession oldSession = request.getSession(false);

// If there is already a session, invalidate it.
        if (oldSession != null)
        {
            l = (BindListener)
                oldSession.getAttribute("listener");
            oldSession.invalidate();

// Tell the user that the session was reset and show that the
// bind counts have been updated. Make sure that there was a
// listener on the old session, too.

            if (l != null)
            {
%>
Your current session was reset. The listener now has <%=l.getNumSessions()%>
active sessions.<p>
<%
            } else {
%>
Your old session didn't have a listener.<p>
<%
            }
```

LISTING 12.7 Continued

```
            l = null;
        }
    }
    else
    {
// See if the listener is already in the session.
         l = (BindListener)
            session.getAttribute("listener");

// If not, add the global copy of the listener to the session.
        if (l == null)
        {
// Put the global listener variable into the session.
            session.setAttribute("listener", listener);
            l = listener;
        }
    }
%>
<%
    if (l != null)
    {
%>
You have a listener bound to your session.
<%
    } else {
%>
You do not have a listener bound to your session.
<%
    }
%>
There are currently <%=listener.getNumSessions()%> sessions holding onto the
bind listener.
<p>
<table>
<tr>
<td>
<A href="BindTest.jsp">Refresh Form</A>
<td>
<A href="BindTest.jsp?removeListener">Remove Listener</A>
<td>
<A href="BindTest.jsp?resetSession">Reset Session</A>
</table>
</body>
</html>
```

Figure 12.5 shows several browser sessions running `BindTest.jsp`.

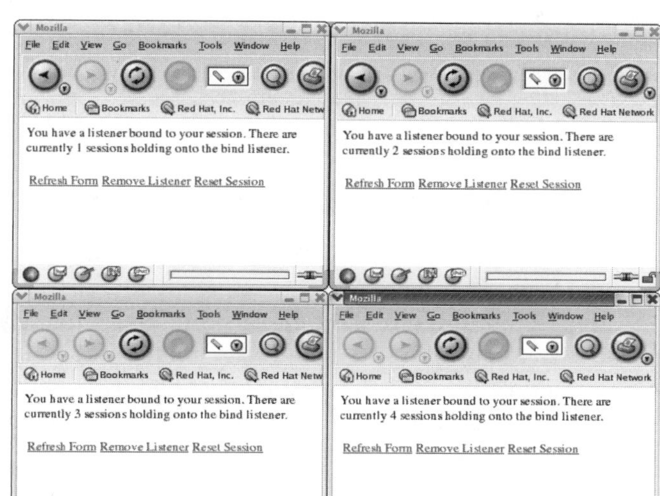

FIGURE 12.5
The `BindListener` object keeps track of how many sessions it belongs to.

The `HttpSessionListener` and `HttpSessionActivationListener` Interfaces

Because sessions are not permanent, it's useful to know when a session is about to go away. Conversely, it's also helpful to know when they are created. Objects that are associated with sessions can receive notification of lifecycle events so that they can respond appropriately. For example, if an object provided a session specific access to a file, you would want to make sure that the file was opened on session creation and was flushed and closed when the session ended.

Objects that want to know when a session is created or destroyed can implement the `HttpSessionListener` interface. It consists of only two methods:

```
public void sessionCreated(HttpSessionEvent se)
public void sessionDestroyed(HttpSessionEvent se)
```

Unlike an object that implements the `HttpSessionBindingListener` interface, you must configure the class to receive events in the deployment descriptor for the Web application. In addition to creating and destroying sessions, some containers may also **passivate** and **activate** sessions. A container that passivates a session puts it away momentarily. Sometime later, the session may be returned to service, or activated. Containers may do this to persist or migrate sessions, so that requests can be handled by several Java Virtual Machines (JVMs). By implementing the `HttpSessionActivationListener` interface, objects can receive notification of passivation or activation.

```
public void sessionDidActivate(HttpSessionEvent se)
public void sessionWillPassivate(HttpSessionEvent se)
```

Handling Sessions Without Cookies

Normally, JSP and servlet sessions rely on HTTP's cookie mechanism to preserve the session identifier between requests. Cookies are really nice for doing things such as helping to maintain sessions or online ordering. Unfortunately, cookies have also been abused. Many Web sites store personal information in cookies, and many Web users don't like their personal information being sent to another Web server without their knowledge. To put it simply, cookie abuse has given cookies a bad name.

Many users now disable cookies within their browsers. You might think that with cookies disabled, the only way to keep track of session information would be the hidden field technique discussed at the beginning of this hour. Fortunately, there is another solution.

Every session has an ID that uniquely identifies it. The Servlet API provides a way for you to insert a session ID into a URL. The idea is that for every URL in your Web application that refers to a servlet or a JSP, you insert the session ID as a parameter to that servlet or JSP. Because the session ID is normally stored in a cookie, you need to pass the session ID as a parameter only when cookies are disabled.

If You Use Cookies, Tell Your Users

Many Web sites that do session-oriented work require users to enable cookies. Although it's nice to be able to support sessions without cookies, users generally find them acceptable for applications such as online shopping. If you decide to require cookies, you might need to put a note on your Web site explaining the necessity of cookies.

The `HttpServletResponse` object (the `response` object in a JSP) contains two methods to help you pass the session ID around to different pages:

```
public String encodeURL(String url);
public String encodeRedirectURL(String url);
```

If you need to do session tracking, but the browser doesn't support cookies, encodeURL and encodeRedirectURL return a modified URL containing the session ID as a parameter for that URL. If the browser supports cookies, the URL is returned unmodified. Listing 12.8 shows a JSP that presents a form, handles the submission of the form, and puts the form results into a session. It calls encodeURL and encodeRedirectURL to make sure that sessions are supported even with cookies turned off.

LISTING 12.8 Source Code for RewriteDemo.jsp

```
<html>
<body>

<h1>URL Rewriting Demo</h1>

<%-- See if the session already contains the name.
    If so, say "Hello" to the user --%>

<%
    String name = (String) session.getAttribute("name");

    if (name != null)
    {
// This user already has a session; show the name and show the list of
// items entered.

        out.println("Hello, "+name+"!");
%>
        <A href="<%=response.encodeURL("RewriteDemo2.jsp")%>">
            Click here to continue</A>
<%

    }
// If name is passed in as a parameter, it must be as a response to
// the form input. Put the name in the session and redirect the browser
// to the second page.
    else if (request.getParameter("name") != null)
    {
        session.setAttribute("name",
            request.getParameter("name"));
        response.sendRedirect(response.encodeRedirectURL(
            "RewriteDemo2.jsp"));
    }
    else
    {
%>
```

LISTING 12.8 Continued

```
<form action="<%=response.encodeURL("RewriteDemo.jsp")%>">
Please enter your name: <input type=text name="name">
<p>
<input type="submit" value="Login!">
</form>
<%
    }
%>

</body>
</html>
```

Listing 12.9 shows `RewriteDemo2.jsp`.

LISTING 12.9 Source Code for `RewriteDemo2.jsp`

```
<html>
<body>
<H1>Hello <%=session.getAttribute("name")%>!</H1>
<p>
See, I still remembered your name.
</body>
<html>
```

Figure 12.6 shows the results of running `RewriteDemo2.jsp`, to which `RewriteDemo.jsp` redirects the user.

FIGURE 12.6 The session ID can be embedded in a URL.

By the Way

Having Trouble with the Example?

If you are having trouble with URL rewriting, see the "Q&A" section at the end of this hour.

Unfortunately, to make full use of URL rewriting, you must pass all your pages through the URL rewriting process. In other words, if you have a static HTML page that needs session information and that has links to JSPs or servlets, you must turn this static HTML page into a JSP that uses `encodeURL` to rewrite the `HREF` values for all the hyperlinks. So, in your HTML file where you have a line such as

```
<a href="CallMe.jsp">
```

the JSP file would read

```
<a href="<%=response.encodeURL("CallMe.jsp")%>">
```

You also need to change the `action` attributes in each of your `<form>` tags. A `<form>` tag with an action of `"HandleForm.jsp"` appears in the JSP like this:

```
<form action="<%=response.encodeURL("HandleForm.jsp")%>">
```

Did you Know?

Minimize Rewriting

Modifying your Web site to rewrite all your forms and hyperlinks is a difficult task. Try to design your site so that you can minimize the amount of rewriting necessary.

Storing Application-Wide Data

The `HttpSession` class stores data items on a per-user basis. Sometimes, however, you have data that you need to share between various servlets and JSPs that doesn't need to be stored for each user. For example, if you are writing a database application, you might need to share a database connection. From a JSP, you can store data in the `application` object. The methods for storing data in the `application` object are identical to the ones for the `session` object:

```
public void setAttribute(String name, Object value)
public Object getAttribute(String name)
public void removeAttribute(String name)
```

From a JSP, if you want to store information in the `application` object under the name "myInformation," you make a call such as this:

```
application.setAttribute("myInformation", "Here is the info");
```

To get the information back out of the `application` object, you call `getAttribute`:

```
String theInfo = (String) application.getAttribute("myInformation");
```

The application object is really an object that implements the ServletContext interface. The servlet context is also available from within the servlet. If your servlet is a subclass of GenericServlet or HttpServlet, as most are, you can call the getServletContext method:

```
ServletContext context = getServletContext();
context.setAttribute("myInformation", "Here is the info");
```

Remember that your servlet doesn't have to be a subclass of GenericServlet or HttpServlet. You can choose to write your own class that implements the Servlet interface. If you need to get hold of the servlet context in these cases, the context is contained in the ServletConfig object that is passed to your servlet's init method. You can always call getServletConfig().getServletContext() to get the servlet context.

Why You Need the application Object

From all appearances, the application object seems like overkill. What is the difference between storing something in the application object and storing it in a static variable somewhere?

The servlet engine knows to what application a particular JSP or servlet belongs. You can, for example, have a set of JSPs deployed in a server under an application called QA and an identical set of JSPs under an application called Beta. These two applications, although running in the same server and the same JVM, would have different application objects (that is, different ServletContext objects).

Now you can see how the application object differs from a static variable. If you tried to store a data item in a static variable, you would circumvent the notion of separate applications. There is only one copy of a static variable within a single JVM. You can't say that the QA application gets its own copy of a static variable and the Beta application gets another unless you are somehow able to run each application in a separate virtual machine. Because you can't count on a servlet engine to support multiple JVMs, you shouldn't rely on static variables for application-level data sharing.

You have also seen in previous hours that you can store application configuration information in the application object that is available to all JSPs and servlets in the Web application. This configuration information comes from the web.xml file that you create when you package your application in a WAR file.

Summary

Saving information between requests is extremely useful. You can personalize content or simply maintain the state of an application by being able to associate related transactions to a session. You can persist information by handing it back and forth using forms and hidden variables. However, it can be difficult to develop complex applications this way. JSPs and servlets make using sessions practically effortless. In JSPs, information that pertains to a session can be stored in the implicit `session` object. If you're using servlets, you can obtain an `HttpSession` through the `HttpServletRequest` object. Objects can implement interfaces such as `HttpSessionBindingListener` so that they can know when they are added to or removed from a session, or when a session is created or destroyed.

Although sessions usually use cookies to save a session key on the client, it's possible to still use sessions even if a client does not permit cookies. In this case, it's necessary to encode URLs so that the session key becomes a part of the URL. The JSP's implicit `request` object provides the `encodeURL` method to do this. Besides storing data on a per-client basis, you can also store data at an application scope.

Q&A

Q. ***I stored data in a session; why can't I find it in the session object?***

A. There are many possible reasons for this. The most common problem is that you mistyped the name of the item you wanted to retrieve. You might have stored it as `name` and you are trying to retrieve it as `Name`. If possible, create a Java class that contains a number of `public static final` string constants defining the names of the items you want to store in the session, and use these constants instead of hard-coding strings into the servlets and JSPs. Another possibility for this problem is that the browser has cookies disabled. Make sure you have cookies enabled or that you use URL rewriting to pass the session ID along.

Q. ***Why do I get a compile error when I retrieve an item from a session?***

A. The `session.getAttribute` method returns items of type `Object`. Even if you store a `String` object or another type, the return value is always `Object`. You must cast the result to the appropriate type when you retrieve it from the session.

Q. ***I turned off cookies in Internet Explorer; why don't I see the session ID when I use URL rewriting?***

A. Make sure you have turned off cookies for the security zone you are using. If you are accessing your local machine, you need to change the security setting for the Local Intranet zone, at least if you use `http://localhost` as the first part of your URL. Internet Explorer does not always notice that a URL is really part of the local intranet, however. It may consider `http://localhost` as being in the local domain, and think that `http://zinger.wutka.com` is in the Internet zone, even though it is the same machine as `localhost`. Try setting the security for the Internet and Local Intranet zones to be High.

Q. ***Why does the browser seem to lose the session ID when I navigate through my site using URL rewriting?***

A. The problem is most likely the presence of an HTML page somewhere along the way. For URL rewriting to work, you must rewrite the URL for every link the browser might access. You must convert any static HTML pages into JSPs, changing the hyperlinks so that they use the URL rewriting routines.

Workshop

The Workshop is designed to help you review what you have learned, and help you to further increase your understanding of the material covered in this hour.

Quiz

1. What methods of the JSP implicit object `session` are used to store, retrieve, and delete objects in a session?
2. What do you have to do so that you can use sessions in a JSP?
3. What causes a session to expire?
4. When a session expires, how can I release resources that are associated with it?

Answers

1. `setAttribute`, `getAttribute`, and `removeAttribute` are the methods used. Methods of the same name are used with the `application` object to store attributes that have application scope.
2. A JSP that participates in sessions must use a Page Directive Attribute `session` whose value is `true`.
3. Sessions expire because they are invalidated by a container or by an application. Sessions are often invalidated by a container after a specific amount of time or when the container discovers that a user has done something to invalidate a session, such as close their browser.
4. Objects that need to know when a session they are attached to expires can implement the `HttpSessionListener` interface and make the appropriate changes to the application deployment descriptor.

Activities

1. Write a JSP that asks a user for their name and a favorite activity. Store the information in an object that is attached to a session. Create another JSP that allows the user to review and change the stored information.
2. Modify the application you wrote above to provide the option to "publish" their information to the application scope. Add another JSP that shows all of the information for every user who has published their data.

HOUR 13

More About Saving Data

What You'll Learn in This Hour:

- How to use sessions
- How to build a shopping cart that demonstrates the use of Data objects, servlets, and JSPs
- How to use cookies to store data

Using Sessions to Save Data in a Shopping Cart Application

Although there are many uses for the session object, one of the most common uses is to store items for online shopping. When you shop online, you usually browse around the Web site, occasionally clicking an "Add to Shopping Cart" button to signal that you want to buy something. When you are done, you click "Check Out" and fill out your billing information.

The `session` object is a logical place to keep shopping cart data. You can, of course, keep the data on the client's browser, but it can get pretty cumbersome trying to keep up with the shopping cart on the client when the user goes from page to page.

You can also store the shopping cart in a database and just keep enough data in the session to make it possible to retrieve the shopping cart out of the database. If the database is fast enough and you have so many sessions active at one time that you can't keep all the data in memory, the database might be a better solution. For most applications, however, the session is the ideal place.

Designing the Shopping Cart

When designing applications, it's often best to focus on the model portion of the application first. In other words, create Java classes that implement the behavior of the shopping cart. These classes should have no relationship to servlets or JSPs. You should be able to use them in an entirely different kind of application if you want to.

By the Way

Model-View-Controller

You've probably heard of Model-View-Controller (MVC). It's an architectural pattern that is successful in achieving design and runtime flexibility. Using MVC often leads to more reusable and maintainable code. In short, the **model** represents some kind of data and the behavior necessary to work with it. A **view** presents a model to a user. And a **controller** defines how a view responds to user input. This example uses MVC. You'll spend more time with MVC in Hour 20, "Building Web Applications with JavaServer Pages and Servlets."

First, ask yourself, "What should I be able to do to a shopping cart?" For a shopping cart, you want to add items, remove items, list items, and purchase items contained in the cart. Next, ask yourself "What exactly is an item?" That's a good question. An item should have a description, a price, a quantity, and some kind of product code that you would use for your ordering system. Also, to purchase a product, the user must supply billing and shipping information. You should have one or more classes that represent this information.

Creating the Data Objects

To kick things off, Listing 13.1 shows the `Item` object that will be stored in the shopping cart. For good measure, it has `get` and `set` methods and implements the `Serializable` interface, so it is fairly well behaved as a bean.

LISTING 13.1 Source Code for `Item.java`

```
package examples.cart;

public class Item implements java.io.Serializable
{
    public String productCode;
    public String description;
    public double price;
    public int quantity;

    public Item()
    {
    }
```

LISTING 13.1 Continued

```
    public Item(String aProductCode, String aDescription,
        double aPrice, int aQuantity)
    {
        productCode = aProductCode;
        description = aDescription;
        price = aPrice;
        quantity = aQuantity;
    }

// Make get/set methods so the attributes will appear
// as bean attributes.

    public String getProductCode() { return productCode; }
    public void setProductCode(String aProductCode) {
        productCode = aProductCode; }

    public String getDescription() { return description; }
    public void setDescription(String aDescription) {
        description = aDescription; }

    public double getPrice() { return price; }
    public void setPrice(double aPrice) { price = aPrice; }

    public int getQuantity() { return quantity; }
    public void setQuantity(int aQuantity) { quantity = aQuantity; }
}
```

The next step is to create a class to hold the billing information. Because this is just an example, the billing is limited to credit card orders. All you need for a credit card order is the name of the person on the card, the card number, the type of card, and the expiration date. Listing 13.2 shows the `Billing` class.

LISTING 13.2 Source Code for `Billing.java`

```
package examples.cart;

public class Billing implements java.io.Serializable
{
    public String nameOnCard;
    public String creditCardType;
    public String creditCardNumber;
    public String creditCardExpiration;

    public Billing()
    {
    }

    public String getNameOnCard() { return nameOnCard; }
    public void setNameOnCard(String aName) { nameOnCard = aName; }
```

LISTING 13.2 Continued

```
    public String getCreditCardType() { return creditCardType; }
    public void setCreditCardType(String aCreditCardType)
        { creditCardType = aCreditCardType; }

    public String getCreditCardNumber() { return creditCardNumber; }
    public void setCreditCardNumber(String aCreditCardNumber)
        { creditCardNumber = aCreditCardNumber; }

    public String getCreditCardExpiration()
        { return creditCardExpiration; }
    public void setCreditCardExpiration(String aCreditCardExpiration)
        { creditCardExpiration = aCreditCardExpiration; }
}
```

The shopping cart needs one more data object. You have the items; you have the billing information; now you just need to know where to ship the item. Listing 13.3 shows the `Shipping` class. Like the other two classes, the `Shipping` class has the `get` and `set` methods to make various bean tools happy.

LISTING 13.3 Source Code for `Shipping.java`

```
package examples.cart;

public class Shipping implements java.io.Serializable
{
    public String name;
    public String address1;
    public String address2;
    public String city;
    public String state;
    public String country;
    public String postalCode;
    public String email;

    public Shipping()
    {
    }

    public String getName() { return name; }
    public void setName(String aName) { name = aName; }

    public String getAddress1() { return address1; }
    public void setAddress1(String anAddress1)
        { address1 = anAddress1; }

    public String getAddress2() { return address2; }
    public void setAddress2(String anAddress2)
        { address2 = anAddress2; }

    public String getCity() { return city; }
    public void setCity(String aCity) { city = aCity; }
```

LISTING 13.3 Continued

```
    public String getState() { return state; }
    public void setState(String aState) { state = aState; }

    public String getCountry() { return country; }
    public void setCountry(String aCountry) { country = aCountry; }

    public String getPostalCode() { return postalCode; }
    public void setPostalCode(String aPostalCode)
        { postalCode = aPostalCode; }

    public String getEmail() { return email; }
    public void setEmail(String anEmail) { email = anEmail; }
}
```

Creating the Shopping Cart Class

Now, all that is left is the shopping cart itself. For the purposes of this example, the shopping cart doesn't do much with the order. Normally, you would insert the order in a database or send it to an application server. But the important thing as it relates to JSPs and servlets is that you can order some items and submit the order. To keep track of the order, you really don't need anything more than a vector of items. The billing and shipping information gets passed to the shopping cart when the order is finally completed. Listing 13.4 shows the source for the `ShoppingCart` class.

LISTING 13.4 Source Code for `ShoppingCart.java`

```
package examples.cart;

import java.util.*;
import java.io.*;

public class ShoppingCart implements java.io.Serializable
{
// The shopping cart items are stored in a Vector.
    protected Vector items;

    public ShoppingCart()
    {
        items = new Vector();
    }

/** Returns a Vector containing the items in the cart. The Vector
 *  returned is a clone, so modifying the vector won't affect the
 *  contents of the cart.
 */
    public Vector getItems()
    {
        return (Vector) items.clone();
    }
```

LISTING 13.4 Continued

```
    public void addItem(Item newItem)
    {
        items.addElement(newItem);
    }

    public void removeItem(int itemIndex)
    {
        items.removeElementAt(itemIndex);
    }

// Warning! This order number is reset every time the server is
// restarted. This technique of generating an order number is
// just for demonstration.
    protected static int nextOrderNumber = 1;

// Submit the order and return a confirmation number.
    public String completeOrder(Shipping shipping, Billing billing)
        throws ShoppingCartException
    {
// You would normally insert the order into a database or send
// it to an application server. For the sake of simplicity
// this shopping cart just writes the order to a file.
        try
        {
            int orderNumber = 0;

// Make sure no other threads can be generating an order number.
            synchronized (this)
            {
                orderNumber = nextOrderNumber;
                nextOrderNumber = nextOrderNumber + 1;
            }
            PrintWriter out = new PrintWriter(
                new FileOutputStream("order"+orderNumber));

// Print the shipping info.
            out.println(shipping.nameOnCard);
            out.println(shipping.address1);
            if (shipping.address2 != null)
            {
                out.println(shipping.address2);
            }
            out.print(shipping.city);
            if (shipping.state != null)
            {
                out.print(", "+shipping.state);
            }
            if (shipping.postalCode != null)
            {
                out.print(" "+shipping.postalCode);
            }
            out.println(" "+shipping.country);
            out.println(shipping.email);
```

LISTING 13.4 Continued

```
// Print the billing info.
            out.println(billing.name);
            out.println(billing.creditCardType);
            out.println(billing.creditCardNumber);
            out.println(billing.creditCardExpiration);

// Print out the items.
            Enumeration e = items.elements();
            while (e.hasMoreElements())
            {
                Item item = (Item) e.nextElement();

                out.println(item.productCode+","+
                    item.quantity);
            }
            out.close();

// Return a confirmation number (the order number as a string in this case).
            return ""+orderNumber;
        }
        catch (Exception exc)
        {
            throw new ShoppingCartException(
                "Error saving order: "+exc.toString());
        }
    }
}
```

The `ShoppingCartException` used by the `ShoppingCart` class is just a subclass of `java.lang.Exception` and doesn't add any additional capabilities. It does help you organize your error handling, however, because you can catch `ShoppingCartException` rather than the more generic `Exception`. Listing 13.5 shows the `ShoppingCartException` class.

LISTING 13.5 Source Code for `ShoppingCartException.java`

```
package examples.cart;

public class ShoppingCartException extends Exception
{
    public ShoppingCartException()
    {
    }

    public ShoppingCartException(String message)
    {
        super(message);
    }
}
```

Displaying the Contents of the Shopping Cart

So far, you have a lot of shopping cart code and not a single JSP or servlet. Like any technology, you should use Java's Web technologies where they are applicable. In this case, you are much better off with a shopping cart that doesn't care whether it's on the Web. If you end up making some sort of standalone kiosk application where someone can walk up, select some items, and immediately make a purchase, you could still use the `ShoppingCart` class even though the application would not be Web-based.

Now it's time to put the shopping cart out on the Web by putting servlets and JSPs on top of it. When it comes to displaying a shopping cart's contents, you might need to show the contents at different times. For example, the user might click a Display Shopping Cart button and see just the shopping cart's contents. Later, when the user clicks the Check Out button to make a purchase, you need to display the shopping cart again, but this time with other information on the page as well.

Because you need to display the shopping cart in different pages, it makes sense to create a separate JSP to display the shopping cart. The trick is, this JSP is not a complete Web page in itself. That is, it does not contain the `<html>` or `<body>` tags. Instead, it contains just the HTML tags necessary to display the shopping cart. That way, you can include it in other pages. Listing 13.6 shows the code for `DisplayShoppingCart.jsp`.

LISTING 13.6 Source Code for `DisplayShoppingCart.jsp`

```
<%@ page language="java" import="examples.cart.*,java.util.*,java.text.*" %>

<%-- Show the header with the shopping cart image --%>
<table border="0">
<tr><td><img src="cart4.png"><td><h1>Shopping Cart</h1>
</table>

<%
// Get the current shopping cart from the user's session.
    ShoppingCart cart = (ShoppingCart) session.getAttribute("ShoppingCart");

// If the user doesn't have a shopping cart yet, create one.
    if (cart == null)
    {
        cart = new ShoppingCart();
        session.setAttribute("ShoppingCart", cart);
    }

// Get the items from the cart.
    Vector items = cart.getItems();
```

LISTING 13.6 Continued

```
// If there are no items, tell the user that the cart is empty.
    if (items.size() == 0)
    {
        out.println("<h3>Your shopping cart is empty.</h3>");
    }
    else
    {
%>
<%-- Display the header for the shopping cart table --%>
<br>
<table border=4>
<tr><th>Description</th><th>Quantity</th><th>Price</th></tr>
<%

        int numItems = items.size();

// Get a formatter to write out currency values.
        NumberFormat currency = NumberFormat.getCurrencyInstance();

        for (int i=0; i < numItems; i++)
        {
            Item item = (Item) items.elementAt(i);

// Print the table row for the item.
            out.print("<tr><td>");
            out.print(item.description);
            out.print("</td><td>");
            out.print(item.quantity);
            out.print("</td><td>");
            out.print(currency.format(item.price));

// Print out a link that allows the user to delete an item from the cart.
            out.println("</td><td>"+
                "<a href=\"/shoppingcart/RemoveItemServlet?item="+
                i+"\">Remove</a></td></tr>");
        }
    }
%>
</table>
```

Figure 13.1 shows the shopping cart as it looks after you have added some items.

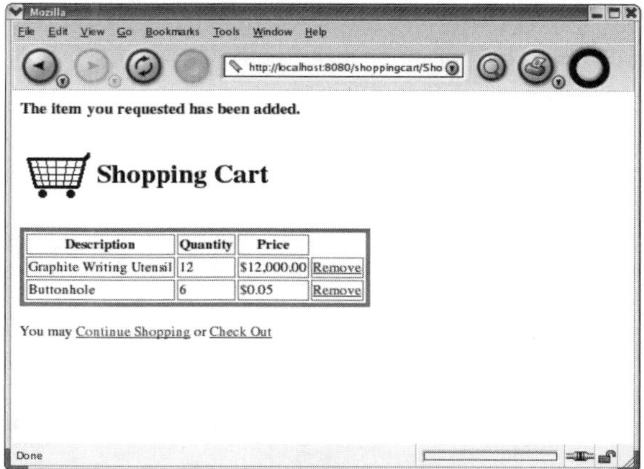

FIGURE 13.1
Many pages can use the same shopping cart display.

Adding and Removing Items

Adding and removing shopping cart items are tasks that are nicely suited for servlets. We'll reserve functions that interface with the user for JSPs and use servlets for functions such as this.

The `addItem` method in the `ShoppingCart` class seems simple enough. You just need to create an `Item` object to add. There are three basic approaches to creating the `Item` object:

- The client browser can send all the information necessary to create the item. This implies that you must pass all the necessary information to the client, even if it won't be needed.
- You can create the `Item` object ahead of time and store it in memory on the server in the session or application objects. When the user orders the item, you pull it out of the session or application object and put it in the shopping cart.
- You retrieve the `Item` information from an application server or a database. You need only enough information to uniquely identify the item you want to add.

Each of these approaches has advantages and disadvantages, and you might find yourself using different approaches for different types of systems. Although the `Item` class in this example contains only four data elements, the `Item` class for your real-world application might contain far more data elements. A complex item structure really requires the item information to stay somewhere on the server, either in the session object or in a database.

You might be wondering why you would create an `Item` object ahead of time and store it in memory. If you think about the way you shop for things online, you usually look at a page of items, each of which can be added to your shopping cart. The chances are good that the code that generated that page of items had to work with a bunch of `Item` objects. That is, when you generate the page from which you can order, you probably need the `Item` object anyway. Why not just store it in the `application` object or the session and bring it back out when the user orders it?

Users May Need Their Own Objects

Watch Out!

If you allow the user to modify the contents of an `Item` object, such as changing the quantity or color, you must have a separate copy of the item for each user. If all the users share the same object, then when one user changes the quantity, it changes for everyone.

If you can store the objects in the application object, you save a lot of memory. If you store the objects in the session, you end up saving many copies of the same object. With specialized items, however, it might be better to save the objects in the server. For example, if your pricing structure varies depending on the user, it might be better to keep track of items on a per-session basis. If you have several kinds of pricing, you can store one copy of an item for each price. The item may have other attributes that change depending on the user as well.

Passing the `Item` Object from the Browser

If your item is small enough that all its data can be passed easily from the browser, that's probably your best solution. After all, you won't have to worry about cleaning up the session when the user has finished placing the order.

Cleaning up After a Session Terminates

Did you Know?

Remember, cleaning up after a session terminates is not a big deal. You just have to create objects that recognize when they have been unbound from a session and clean themselves up. You learned how to do this in the last hour.

Listing 13.7 shows a JSP that generates a page of items that are available to be ordered. Notice that the `Add to Shopping Cart` links each have all the information for the item embedded in their URLs. When the user clicks on a link, all the data elements for an item are passed to the server.

LISTING 13.7 Source Code for ShowProductCatalog.jsp

```
<%@ page language="java" import="examples.cart.*,java.net.*,java.text.*" %>
<html>
<body bgcolor="#ffffff">

<%
// Initialize the array of available products.
    Item[] catalog = new Item[] {
        new Item("X-1", "Jet Plane", 2999999.95, 1),
        new Item("GWU-123876345-27B/6",
            "Graphite Writing Utensil", 12000.00, 12),
        new Item("BCT-12", "Bionic Cat Tongue", 3700.00, 1),
        new Item("EZ-1", "Professional Electronic Zither",
            699.95, 1),
        new Item("PF-101", "Pink Flamingo", 12.00, 1),
        new Item("LOD-7", "Lump Of Dirt (Medium)", 1.00, 1)
    };

%>

<a href="/shoppingcart/ViewShoppingCart.jsp">View Shopping Cart</a>
<p>
<h1>Available Products</h1>
<table border="1">
<tr><th>Description</th><th>Quantity</th><th>Price</th></tr>
<%

// Get a currency formatter for showing the price.
    NumberFormat currency = NumberFormat.getCurrencyInstance();

    for (int i=0; i < catalog.length; i++)
    {
        Item item = catalog[i];

// Create the URL for adding the item to the shopping cart.
        String addItemURL =
            "/shoppingcart/AddToShoppingCartServlet?"+
            "productCode="+URLEncoder.encode(item.getProductCode())+
            "&description="+URLEncoder.encode(item.getDescription())+
            "&quantity="+URLEncoder.encode(""+item.getQuantity())+
            "&price="+URLEncoder.encode(""+item.getPrice());
%>
<tr><td><%=item.getDescription()%></td><td><%=item.getQuantity()%>
    </td><td><%=item.getPrice()%></td>
<td><a href="<%=addItemURL%>">Add to Shopping Cart</a></td></tr>
<%
    }
```

LISTING 13.7 Source Code for `ShowProductCatalog.jsp`

```
%>
</table>
</body>
</html>
```

Figure 13.2 shows the product catalog as displayed by `ShowProductCatalog.jsp`.

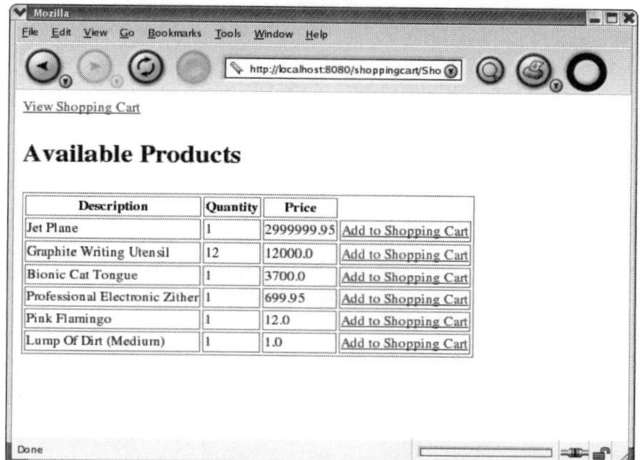

FIGURE 13.2 A catalog display contains links to add items to the shopping cart.

Listing 13.8 shows the `AddToShoppingCartServlet` class that takes the items from the product catalog and adds them to the shopping cart.

LISTING 13.8 Source Code for `AddToShoppingCartServlet.java`

```
package examples.cart;

import javax.servlet.*;
import javax.servlet.http.*;
import java.io.*;

public class AddToShoppingCartServlet extends HttpServlet
{
    public void service(HttpServletRequest request,
        HttpServletResponse response)
        throws IOException, ServletException
    {

// First get the item values from the request.
        String productCode = request.getParameter("productCode");
        String description = request.getParameter("description");
        int quantity = Integer.parseInt(
            request.getParameter("quantity"));
        double price = Double.parseDouble(
            request.getParameter("price"));
```

LISTING 13.8 Continued

```
// Now create an item to add to the cart.
        Item item = new Item(productCode, description, price, quantity);

        HttpSession session = request.getSession();

// Get the cart.
        ShoppingCart cart = (ShoppingCart) session.
            getAttribute("ShoppingCart");

// If there is no shopping cart, create one.
        if (cart == null)
        {
            cart = new ShoppingCart();

            session.setAttribute("ShoppingCart", cart);
        }

        cart.addItem(item);

// Now display the cart and allow the user to check out or order more items.
        response.sendRedirect(response.encodeRedirectURL(
            "/shoppingcart/ShowCartAfterAdd.jsp"));
    }
}
```

Keeping Items in Memory

If your shopping cart items are fairly complex, you are usually better off keeping them on the server and passing only a unique identifier for each item back to the client. For example, suppose you offer an item called "Pale Blue Japanese Guitar" with a product code of PBJG-1. When the user clicks the `Add to Shopping Cart` link to buy the guitar, the browser just sends the product code PBJG-1 to the server. The server looks up the product code and retrieves the object associated with that code.

Listing 13.9 shows a product catalog class that allows you to look up objects by product code, and also get a list of the available products. You might not want to display all the products on one page, so the product catalog enables you to display a certain number of objects at a time, starting at a particular position in the list.

LISTING 13.9 Source Code for `ProductCatalog.java`

```
package examples.cart;

import java.util.Vector;

public class ProductCatalog
{
    protected Item[] items;
```

LISTING 13.9 Continued

```
    public ProductCatalog()
    {

// Set up an array of items that represents the catalog.

        items = new Item[] {
            new Item("PBJG-1", "Pale Blue Japanese Guitar",
                700.00, 1),
            new Item("PBJZ-1", "Pale Blue Japanese Zither",
                1400.00, 1),
            new Item("PBJS-1", "Peanut Butter & Jelly Sandwich",
                1.00, 1),
            new Item("GCX", "Garlic Clove", 0.40, 1),
            new Item("XC", "Xenophobic Cat", 72.00, 1),
            new Item("BH", "Buttonhole", 0.05, 6),
            new Item("K9", "Dog", 100.00, 1),
            new Item("ATL", "Atlanta Airport", 9000000.00, 1),
            new Item("TEG", "Sheep", 75.00, 1),
            new Item("UPC", "Universal Price Code", 1.00, 1),
            new Item("ALL", "The Universe", 0.01, 1),
            new Item("ZYZZYVAS", "The last word in Scrabble",
                74.00, 1),
            new Item("SAM", "Urchin (aged for 7 years)", 0.0, 1),
            new Item("KATY", "Urchin (aged for 4 years)", 0.0, 1),
            new Item("FR44", "Flamingo Relish (tastes like chicken)",
                2.00, 1),
            new Item("PF44", "Pickled Flamingo (tastes like chicken)",
                2.00, 1),
            new Item("LF44", "Pink Lawn Flamingo (tasteless)",
                12.00, 1)
        };
    }

/** returns an array containing all the items in the catalog */
    public Item[] getItems()
    {
        return getItems(0, items.length);
    }

/** returns an array containing a subset of items from the catalog */
    public Item[] getItems(int startingLocation, int numItems)
    {
// If the number of items to be returned is larger than the number
// in the catalog, adjust the number to be returned.
        if (numItems > items.length)
        {
            numItems = items.length;
        }

// If by returning numItems items you would run out of items (if there
// are 5 items, you ask for 3, but give a starting location of 4),
```

LISTING 13.9 Continued

```
// adjust the starting location backward to ensure that the proper
// number of items is returned.
        if (startingLocation+numItems >= items.length)
        {
            startingLocation = items.length - numItems;
        }

// Create an array for the returned items.
        Item[] returnItems = new Item[numItems];

// Copy the items from the catalog into the return array.
        System.arraycopy(items, startingLocation,
            returnItems, 0, numItems);

        return returnItems;
    }

/** Returns true if there are items at a particular starting location.
    This is helpful in determining whether a page should show a "Next"
    button to see the next page of catalog items.
*/
    public boolean itemsAvailable(int startingLocation)
    {
        if (startingLocation >= items.length) return false;
        return true;
    }

/** Searches for an item by product code and returns it. If there is
    no such item, this method returns null.  */
    public Item findItemByProductCode(String productCode)
    {
// Linear searches aren't a good idea for big arrays, but this
// one is small.
        for (int i=0; i < items.length; i++)
        {
            if (items[i].getProductCode().equals(
                productCode))
            {
                return items[i];
            }
        }

        return null;
    }
}
```

Listing 13.10 shows a JSP that displays the contents of the product catalog, allowing the user to add items to the shopping cart. The user can also view successive pages of the catalog by clicking the Next button.

LISTING 13.10 Source Code for `ShowProductCatalog2.jsp`

```
<%@ page language="java" import="examples.cart.*,java.net.*,java.text.*" %>

<%!
// Declare a constant for the number of items to show on a page.
    public static final int ITEMS_PER_PAGE = 5;
%>

<html>
<body bgcolor="#ffffff">

<a href="/shoppingcart/ViewShoppingCart.jsp">View Shopping Cart</a>
<p>
<h1>Available Products</h1>
<table border="1">
<tr><th>Description<th>Quantity<th>Price
<%

// Get the shared product catalog.
    ProductCatalog catalog = (ProductCatalog) application.getAttribute(
        "ProductCatalog");

// If the shared product catalog hasn't been created yet, create it.
    if (catalog == null)
    {

// Not that it matters because it would be okay for two threads to initialize
// the product catalog, but synchronize this anyway to make sure only one
// thread stores the catalog. Any other JSP or servlet that needs to store
// the product catalog in the application object must also synchronize
// on application.

        synchronized (application)
        {
            catalog = new ProductCatalog();
            application.setAttribute("ProductCatalog", catalog);
        }
    }

// Get the next starting position for displaying catalog items.
    String startingPositionStr = (String) request.
        getParameter("StartingPosition");

    int startingPosition = 0;

// If there is a starting position parameter, parse it as an integer.
    if (startingPositionStr != null)
    {
        try
        {
```

LISTING 13.10 Continued

```
// If there's an error parsing the number, the starting position will
// just remain 0.
                startingPosition = Integer.parseInt(startingPositionStr);
            }
            catch (Exception ignore)
            {
            }
        }

// Get ITEMS_PER_PAGE items at a time.
        Item[] items = catalog.getItems(startingPosition, ITEMS_PER_PAGE);

// Get a currency formatter for showing the price.
        NumberFormat currency = NumberFormat.getCurrencyInstance();

        for (int i=0; i < items.length; i++)
        {
            Item item = items[i];

// Create the URL for adding the item to the shopping cart.
            String addItemURL =
                "/shoppingcart/AddToShoppingCartServlet?"+
                "productCode="+URLEncoder.encode(item.getProductCode())+
                "&description="+URLEncoder.encode(item.getDescription())+
                "&quantity="+URLEncoder.encode(""+item.getQuantity())+
                "&price="+URLEncoder.encode(""+item.getPrice());
%>
<tr><td><%=item.getDescription()%></td><td><%=item.getQuantity()%>
    </td><td><%=item.getPrice()%></td>
<td><a href="<%=addItemURL%>">Add to Shopping Cart</a></td></tr>
<%
        }
%>
</table>
<table border="0">
<tr>
<%
        if (startingPosition > 0)
        {
            int prevPosition = startingPosition-ITEMS_PER_PAGE;

// Don't let the starting position go negative.
            if (prevPosition < 0) prevPosition = 0;

// Write out a link to display the previous catalog page.
            out.println("<td><a href=\"/shoppingcart/ShowProductCatalog2.jsp
                ?StartingPosition="+prevPosition+"\">&lt;&lt;Prev</a></td>");
        }
// Compute the next starting position in the catalog.
        int nextPosition = startingPosition+ITEMS_PER_PAGE;

// Make sure that there are still items to display at that starting
// position (that is, make sure nextPosition isn't greater than the total
```

LISTING 13.10 Continued

```
// catalog size).
    if (catalog.itemsAvailable(nextPosition))
    {
// Write out a link to display the next catalog page.
        out.println("<td><a href=\"/shoppingcart/ShowProductCatalog2.jsp
            ?StartingPosition="+nextPosition+"\">Next&gt;&gt;</a></td>");
    }
%>
</tr>
</table>
</body>
</html>
```

Figure 13.3 shows the paged version of the product catalog. The `<<Prev` and `Next>>` links enable you to scroll through the catalog.

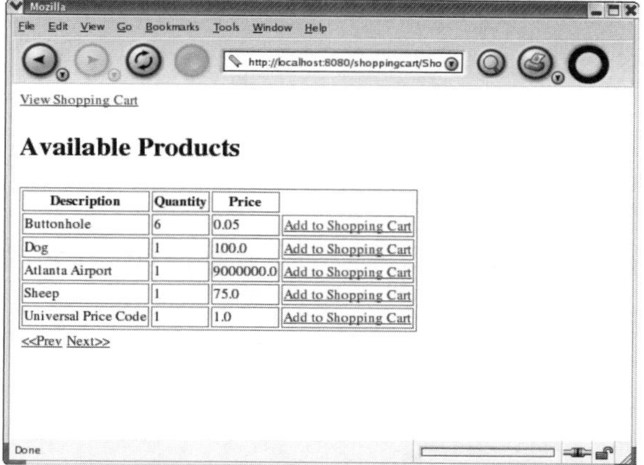

FIGURE 13.3 When you have many products, add links to allow the user to scroll through the catalog.

By the Way

Having Trouble with the Example?

If you are having trouble running the shopping cart examples, see the "Q&A" section at the end of this hour.

Allowing Multiple Quantities

The current shopping cart code isn't very efficient. If you try to order two of the same item, it just keeps two copies of the item in its internal vector. You can enhance the shopping cart to keep track of item quantities. Whenever a user adds an item to the shopping cart, the cart should look through its list of items. When it finds an item that is the same as the one the user is adding, the cart increments the quantity on the item it already has, instead of adding another item to its vector.

Because the `Item` class has a quantity that shows the number of items for one order (12 hot dogs, 6 colas, and so on), you need an order quantity that is the total number of items ordered. Every time you order another pack of 12 hot dogs, you add 12 to the order quantity. Your `Item` class should be something similar to the modified `Item` class shown in Listing 13.11.

LISTING 13.11 Source Code for Modified `Item.java`

```
package examples.cart;
public class Item implements java.io.Serializable
{
    public String productCode;
    public String description;
    public double price;
    public int quantity;
    public int orderQuantity;

    public Item()
    {
    }

    public Item(String aProductCode, String aDescription,
        double aPrice, int aQuantity)
    {
        this(aProductCode, aDescription, aPrice, aQuantity, aQuantity);
    }

    public Item(String aProductCode, String aDescription,
        double aPrice, int aQuantity, int anOrderQuantity)
    {
        productCode = aProductCode;
        description = aDescription;
        price = aPrice;
        quantity = aQuantity;
        orderQuantity = anOrderQuantity;
    }

// Make get/set methods so the attributes will appear
// as bean attributes.

    public String getProductCode() { return productCode; }
    public void setProductCode(String aProductCode) {
        productCode = aProductCode; }

    public String getDescription() { return description; }
    public void setDescription(String aDescription) {
        description = aDescription; }

    public double getPrice() { return price; }
    public void setPrice(double aPrice) { price = aPrice; }
```

LISTING 13.11 Continued

```
    public int getQuantity() { return quantity; }
    public void setQuantity(int aQuantity) { quantity = aQuantity; }

    public int getOrderQuantity() { return orderQuantity; }
    public void setOrderQuantity(int anOrderQuantity)
    {
        orderQuantity = anOrderQuantity;
    }

    public boolean equals(Object ob)
    {
        if (ob == this) return true;
        if (!(ob instanceof Item)) return false;
        if (((Item)ob).getProductCode().equals(getProductCode()))
        {
            return true;
        }
        return false;
    }
}
```

Next, modify the `ShoppingCart` class to update the `orderQuantity` property when you add and remove items. Listing 13.12 shows the modified methods.

LISTING 13.12 Modifications to `ShoppingCart.java` for Multiple Items

```
public synchronized void addItem(Item newItem)
    {
        Enumeration e = items.elements();

// See if there is already an item like this in the cart.
        while (e.hasMoreElements())
        {
            Item currItem = (Item) e.nextElement();

            if (newItem.equals(currItem))
            {
// Update the order quantity on the existing item.
                currItem.orderQuantity = currItem.orderQuantity +
                    newItem.orderQuantity;
                return;
            }
        }

// Didn't find one like this one, so add this one to the cart.
        items.addElement(newItem);
    }

    public synchronized void removeItem(int itemIndex)
    {
        Item item = (Item) items.elementAt(itemIndex);
```

LISTING 13.12 Continued

```
// Remove 1 instance of this item from the quantity (an instance
// is the number of items in the quantity, such as 1 car, 12 hot dogs).
        item.orderQuantity = item.orderQuantity - item.quantity;

// If the order quantity reaches 0, remove this item from the cart.
        if (item.orderQuantity <= 0)
        {
            items.removeElementAt(itemIndex);
        }
    }
```

Also, you must modify the line in `ShoppingCart.java` that writes out the quantity from

```
out.println(item.productCode+","+ item.quantity);
```

to

```
out.println(item.productCode+","+ item.orderQuantity);
```

You must also make one other change. Modify `DisplayShoppingCart.jsp` to show `orderQuantity` rather than `quantity`.

By the Way

The Source Is Available on the CD

The complete sources for the examples in the book are available on the accompanying CD. You're encouraged to try this example out.

Removing Shopping Cart Items

In the example shopping cart class, you remove items based on the item's index in the shopping cart. One of the advantages of using the index is that you don't have to perform any searches. You can just ask the vector to remove the item with the specific index.

The shopping cart display JSP automatically generates the Remove buttons for the items in the cart. Be very careful to ensure that the view of the shopping cart is updated after the user removes an item. When an item is removed from the cart, the indexes on the other items in the cart can change. If the view of the cart isn't updated to match the changed indexes, the user might accidentally delete the wrong item from the cart. Listing 13.13 shows the servlet that performs the removal from the shopping cart.

LISTING 13.13 Source Code for `RemoveItemServlet.java`

```
package examples.cart;

import javax.servlet.*;
import javax.servlet.http.*;
import java.io.*;

public class RemoveItemServlet extends HttpServlet
{
    public void service(HttpServletRequest request,
        HttpServletResponse response)
        throws IOException, ServletException
    {

// Get the index of the item to remove.
        int itemIndex = Integer.parseInt(request.getParameter("item"));

        HttpSession session = request.getSession();

// Get the cart.
        ShoppingCart cart =
            (ShoppingCart) session.getAttribute("ShoppingCart");

// If there is no shopping cart, create one.
        if (cart == null)
        {
            cart = new ShoppingCart();

            session.setAttribute("ShoppingCart", cart);
        }

        cart.removeItem(itemIndex);

// Now display the cart and allow the user to check out or order more items.
        response.sendRedirect(response.encodeRedirectURL(
            "/shoppingcart/ShowCartAfterRemove.jsp"));
    }
}
```

Completing the Order

After the user has selected some items and decides to complete the order, you need to get the user's billing information and shipping address. Listing 13.14 shows the JSP that displays the shopping cart and asks the user for billing and shipping information.

LISTING 13.14 Source Code for `Checkout.jsp`

```
<%@ page language="java" import="examples.cart.*" %>
<html>
<body bgcolor="#ffffff">
<p>
<jsp:include page="DisplayShoppingCart.jsp" flush="true"/>
<p>
<h1>Please enter your shipping information</h1>
<p>
<form action="/shoppingcart/CheckoutServlet" method="post">

<table>
<tr><td>Name:</td><td><input type="text" name="name"></td></tr>
<tr><td>Address:</td><td><input type="text" name="address1"></td>
</tr>
<tr><td></td><td><input type="text" name="address2"></td></tr>
<tr><td>City:</td><td><input type="text" name="city"></td></tr>
    <td>State:</td>
    <td><input type="text" name="state" size=2 maxlength=2></td></tr>
<tr><td>Postal Code (Zip in U.S.):</td>
    <td><input type="text" name="postalCode"></td></tr>
<tr><td>Country:</td><td><input type="text" name="country"></td></tr>
<tr></tr>
<tr><td>Email Address:</td><td><input type="text" name="email">
</td></tr>
</table>
<p>
<h1>Please enter your billing information</h1>
<table>
<tr><td>Name (as it appears on credit card):</td>
    <td><input type="text" name="nameOnCard"></td></tr>
<tr><td>Credit Card:</td>
<td><select name="creditCardType">
    <option value="amex">American Express</option>
    <option value="visa">Visa</option>
    <option value="mc">Mastercard</option>
    <option value="discover">Discover</option>
    <option value="bbbt">Billy Bob's Bank &amp; Trust</option>
    </select></td></tr>
<tr><td>Credit Card Number:</td>
    <td><input type="text" name="creditCardNumber"></td></tr>
<tr><td>Expiration Date:</td>
    <td><input type="text" name="creditCardExpiration"></td></tr>
```

LISTING 13.14 Continued

```
</table>
<p>
<input type="submit" value="Complete Order">
</form>
</body>
</html>
```

Figure 13.4 shows a portion of the checkout page.

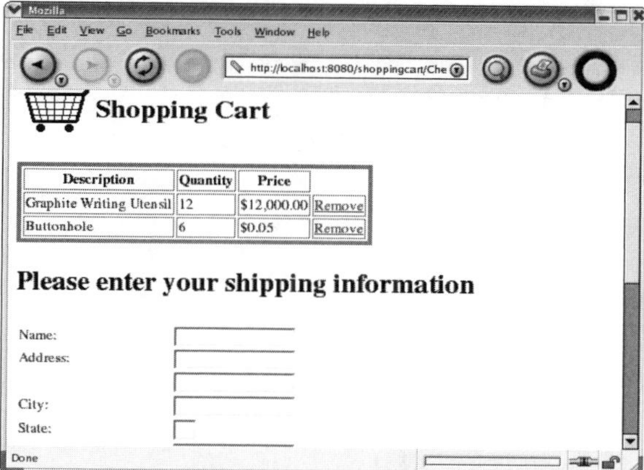

FIGURE 13.4 When checking out, you can show the cart again and then ask for additional information.

Listing 13.15 shows the servlet that takes the billing and shipping information and passes it to the shopping cart to complete the order. After the order has been submitted, the servlet calls a JSP to display the order confirmation.

LISTING 13.15 Source Code for `CheckoutServlet.java`

```
package examples.cart;

import javax.servlet.*;
import javax.servlet.http.*;
import java.io.*;
import java.net.*;

public class CheckoutServlet extends HttpServlet
{
    public void service(HttpServletRequest request,
        HttpServletResponse response)
        throws IOException, ServletException
    {

// First get the shipping values from the request.
        Shipping shipping = new Shipping();
```

LISTING 13.15 Continued

```
        shipping.setName(request.getParameter("name"));
        shipping.setAddress1(request.getParameter("address1"));
        shipping.setAddress2(request.getParameter("address2"));
        shipping.setCity(request.getParameter("city"));
        shipping.setState(request.getParameter("state"));
        shipping.setPostalCode(request.getParameter("postalCode"));
        shipping.setCountry(request.getParameter("country"));
        shipping.setEmail(request.getParameter("email"));

// Next, get the billing values.
        Billing billing = new Billing();

        billing.setNameOnCard(request.getParameter("nameOnCard"));
        billing.setCreditCardType(request.getParameter("creditCardType"));
        billing.setCreditCardNumber(request.getParameter(
            "creditCardNumber"));
        billing.setCreditCardExpiration(request.getParameter(
            "creditCardExpiration"));

        HttpSession session = request.getSession();

// Get the cart.
        ShoppingCart cart =
            (ShoppingCart) session.getAttribute("ShoppingCart");

// If there is no shopping cart, create one (this should really be an error).
        if (cart == null)
        {
            cart = new ShoppingCart();

            session.setAttribute("ShoppingCart", cart);
        }

        try
        {
            String confirmation = cart.completeOrder(shipping, billing);

// Now display the cart and allow the user to check out or order more items.
            response.sendRedirect(response.encodeRedirectURL(
                "/shoppingcart/ShowConfirmation.jsp"+
                "?confirmationNumber="+URLEncoder.encode(confirmation)));
        }
        catch (ShoppingCartException exc)
        {
            PrintWriter out = response.getWriter();

            out.println("<html><body><h1>Error</h1>");
            out.println("The following error occurred while "+
                "processing your order:");
            out.println("<pre>");
            out.println(exc.getMessage());
```

LISTING 13.15 Continued

```
            out.println("</pre>");
            out.println("</body></html>");
            return;
        }
    }
}
```

Listing 13.16 shows the order confirmation page.

LISTING 13.16 Source Code for `ShowConfirmation.jsp`

```
<html>
<body>
<h1>Order Submitted Successfully!</h1>
<p>
Thank you for your order. Your order confirmation number is:
<br>
<pre>
<%=request.getParameter("confirmationNumber")%>
</pre>
<p>
Please use this number when calling to check on your order.
</body>
</html>
```

Storing Data in a Cookie

In the Hour 6, you learned that cookies can be used to store information at the client. As you read through the examples in this hour, you may have even considered the idea of using a cookie to store the items in the shopping cart. Although this is possible, it's generally a better idea to store something that uniquely identifies the user and then use that as a key to find the items and populate a shopping cart.

You should try to avoid sending any sensitive information in a cookie if at all possible. Cookie files on the user's PC usually are not encrypted. Although someone might not be able to retrieve the cookie over the Internet, having unencrypted credit card data in a file on a PC is not very secure.

Using Cookies in Servlets and JSPs

Recall that the `Cookie` class represents a cookie that needs to be stored on a browser or a cookie that has been sent from the browser. When you create a new cookie, you must supply an initial name and value for the cookie. You can change the value and any of the cookie's other attributes after it has been created, but you can't change its name.

The following line of code creates a new cookie:

```
Cookie cook = new Cookie("UserID", "Bob");
```

You can use the `setDomain` and `setPath` methods in the cookie to restrict it to a specific domain and pathname. The following lines of code restrict the cookie to a domain of `".wutka.com"` and a path of `"/examples"`:

```
cook.setDomain(".wutka.com");
cook.setPath("/examples");
```

To store a cookie on the browser, just add the cookie to the response by calling `response.addCookie`:

```
response.addCookie(cook);
```

By the Way

Remember to Set a Cookie First

The cookie is sent back to the browser as part of the response header. If your JSP or servlet is not buffered, you must be very careful to send the cookie back before you write any part of the response. If you call `response.flushBuffer`, you cannot store any cookies after the buffer has been flushed.

By the Way

Having Trouble with the Example?

If you are having trouble storing or retrieving cookies, see the "Q&A" section at the end of this hour.

Listing 13.17 shows a servlet that sends a cookie to the browser.

LISTING 13.17 Source Code for `SaveCookieServlet.java`

```
package examples;

import javax.servlet.*;
import javax.servlet.http.*;
import java.io.*;

public class SaveCookieServlet extends HttpServlet
{
    public void service(HttpServletRequest request,
        HttpServletResponse response)
        throws IOException, ServletException
    {
```

LISTING 13.17 Continued

```
        Cookie cook = new Cookie("examplesinfo", "Hello Cookie!");
        cook.setDomain(".wutka.com");
        cook.setPath("/shoppingcart");

        response.addCookie(cook);

        response.setContentType("text/html");

        PrintWriter out = response.getWriter();
        out.println("<html><body bgcolor=\"#ffffff\">");
        out.println("Your cookie has been saved");
        out.println("</body></html>");
    }
}
```

To retrieve cookie values, use `request.getCookies`:

```
Cookie cookies[] = request.getCookies();
```

Listing 13.18 shows a servlet that retrieves all the cookies that have been sent to it and displays their contents.

LISTING 13.18 Source Code for `DumpCookiesServlet.java`

```
package examples;

import javax.servlet.*;
import javax.servlet.http.*;
import java.io.*;

public class DumpCookiesServlet extends HttpServlet
{
    public void service(HttpServletRequest request,
        HttpServletResponse response)
        throws IOException, ServletException
    {
        Cookie[] cookies = request.getCookies();

        response.setContentType("text/html");

        PrintWriter out = response.getWriter();
        out.println("<html><body bgcolor=\"#ffffff\">");

        out.println("Your browser sent the following cookies:");
        out.println("<pre>");
```

LISTING 13.18 Continued

```
        if (cookies != null)
        {
            for (int i=0; i < cookies.length; i++)
            {
                out.println(cookies[i].getName()+": "+cookies[i].getValue());
            }
        }

        out.println("</pre>");
        out.println("</body></html>");
    }
```

Q&A

Q. ***Why do I get a*** `ClassNotFoundException` ***when I try to use the*** `ShoppingCart` ***class?***

A. The JSP engine probably can't see the class in its classpath. Tomcat uses the system classpath, so if `ShoppingCart.class` is visible somewhere in the system classpath, they should see it.

Q. ***I changed one of the shopping cart classes; why don't any of the servlets or JSPs show the change?***

A. Unless you use the Tomcat Manager, it's possible that the classes are not reloaded automatically. You must restart the JSP/servlet engine to pick up changes in other classes. Tomcat does provide an option to reload servlets without restarting. To do this, you can add the attribute *reloadable=true* to a `Context` component in server.xml. Tomcat will automatically reload classes if a new war file is dropped into the *webapps* directory or in a few other cases. See the Tomcat documentation for details.

Q. ***I stored a cookie on the browser; why can't I see it?***

A. First, check to make sure you spelled the cookie name correctly. Next, make sure the browser has cookies enabled. Also, if you specified a root path for the cookie, make sure that the JSP or servlet reading the cookie is in that path. Remember, too, that if you don't give the cookie a specific expiration time, the cookie will vanish when the user shuts the browser down.

Workshop

The Workshop is designed to help you review what you have learned, and help you to further increase your understanding of the material covered in this hour.

Quiz

1. Why did we use a servlet instead of a JSP to add or remove items from the shopping cart?
2. In this example, the information about items was embedded in the URL used to add them to the shopping cart. How can you simplify the URL?
3. If you attempted to run the cookie example given in this hour, why didn't it work? (Hint: The code is okay.)

Answers

1. By nature, JSPs are oriented to presentation. After all, the majority of their content is markup. On the other hand, servlets are made up of code. Many designers choose to try and place most of the view in JSPs and to use servlets to implement functions involving the model. Adding or removing items from the shopping cart is a function that affects the model.
2. You can give the item an identifier that can be used to lookup information that is needed in other stages of the order. As mentioned in the text, the full description of the item can be stored in the application or session, or in a database.
3. Browsers will only accept cookies for the domain of the resource they requested. This prevents a server in the imacrook.com domain from changing a cookie that belongs to your online banking application. To get the example to work for you, change the cookie's domain.

Activity

1. Modify the shopping cart example to accept an order quantity from the user. Start with ShowProductCatalog2.jsp and use a form.
2. Change ShoppingCart.java so that it's notified when a session is terminated.
3. Modify the shopping cart example to use a cookie to store items that are in the shopping cart. Retrieve the cookie when the user first visits the application and repopulate the cart.

HOUR 14

Interacting with JavaBeans

What You'll Learn in This Hour:

- How to instantiate a JavaBean for use within a JSP
- How to access and set JavaBean properties
- How to use JavaBeans by referring to the interface or superclass of the bean
- How to use JavaBeans in a Web application

When constructing Web applications, you will often find that one of the following is true:

- You want to reuse packages of functionality.
- You want to partition functionality into a freestanding component that your JSP interacts with, so that your JSP is simpler and easier to understand.

To do this, you can create Java classes and use them in your JSP in an expression or scriptlet. However, JSPs also permit you to use JavaBeans, which can be accessed through standard actions.

The `jsp:useBean` Action

JSP scriptlets, expressions, and declarations provide you with a way to access JavaBeans. Pages that use the actions that define these elements, however, tend to look cluttered. You would be better off accessing JavaBean properties in a JSP using actions that look like a few extra actions in a normal HTML page.

The `jsp:useBean` action gives you the ability to create JavaBeans, and the `jsp:getProperty` and `jsp:setProperty` actions allow you to manipulate bean properties. Let's take a moment to examine each of these.

When you want to use a JavaBean within a JSP, use the `jsp:useBean` action to either create a new instance of the bean or to use an existing bean. The idea behind the `jsp:useBean` action and its associates is that you should try to move as much of your application logic as possible out of your JSP so all that remains is code to display the output.

When you encapsulate business objects or business logic into a Java class, you should make that Java class a bean. Many of Sun's Java APIs and tools revolve around the idea that you put your logic into beans and then use tools to help you create applications that use those beans. JSP is one of those tools.

Adding the Bean to the Page

When you add a bean to a JSP, you can either create a new bean or use an existing one. The JSP engine determines whether it needs to create a new bean for you based on the bean's ID.

When you add a bean to a page, you must at least give the bean an ID, which is just a name and the bean's class, like this:

```
<jsp:useBean id="myBean" class="examples.TestBean"/>
```

The JSP engine first searches for an existing bean with the same ID (`myBean` in this case). If it doesn't find an existing bean, the JSP engine creates a new instance of the class you specified. Where the JSP engine looks to find existing beans depends on the bean's scope.

By the Way

Using the useBean ID to Access a JavaBean Instance

The JSP compiler creates a variable with the same name as the ID specified in the `jsp:useBean` element. You can also use this ID in any Java code you put in your JSP. For instance, if you instantiated a bean with an ID of `myBean`, you could write an expression like `<%= myBean.getFirstName() %>`.

One of the other options you can use in the `jsp:useBean` element is scope. The scope determines where the JSP engine stores a created bean and also where it looks to see whether a particular bean ID already exists. A bean can have a scope of `page`, `request`, `session`, or `application`. A bean with a scope of `page` is visible on the current JSP only and disappears when the page finishes executing or forwards itself to another JSP or to a servlet. If you do not specify a scope for a bean, the default scope is `page`.

A bean with `request` scope is visible to other JSPs and servlets and is stored in the `request` object. You can use the bean's ID to get the bean instance out of the request with the `getAttribute` method. For example, suppose you set up the following bean in a JSP:

```
<jsp:useBean id="myBean" scope="request" class="examples.TestBean"/>
```

Now, suppose you want to include a servlet or forward the request on to a servlet, and the servlet needs to access your bean. The servlet would access the bean this way:

```
examples.TestBean theBean = request.getAttribute("myBean");
```

Because the `request` object disappears when the request completes, it should be obvious that a bean stored in the request is no longer visible.

Beans with `session` scope are stored in the `session` object. Suppose you created the following bean:

```
<jsp:useBean id="mySessionBean" scope="session" class="examples.TestBean"/>
```

You could access this bean from a servlet this way:

```
    HttpSession session = request.getSession();
    Examples.TestBean theBean =
          session.getAttribute("mySessionBean");
```

Finally, beans with `application` scope are stored in the `application` object, which is actually a `ServletContext` object. Like anything else stored in the `application` object, a bean with `application` scope is visible to any other JSP or servlet within the same application.

Did you Know?

Servlets Can't Access JSP Page-Scoped Objects

There is no servlet equivalent for accessing a bean stored with page scope because the page scope implies that the bean is visible only within the page. After you leave the page to go to a servlet, you can't access the bean.

By the Way

In Case of Trouble

If you are having trouble locating existing bean objects, see the "Q&A" section at the end of this hour.

Getting Bean Properties

So far, you know how to put a bean on a page. Now you need to do something with it. Obviously, you must put data into the bean, get data out of the bean, or both. Use the `jsp:getProperty` action to get information from a bean. The syntax of `jsp:getProperty` is simple:

```
<jsp:getProperty name="beanId" property="propertyName"/>
```

The `jsp:getProperty` action automatically inserts the property value into the JSP's output. It works like the `<%=` tag in that respect. In fact, for a bean stored in the `request` object, here are two identical ways to display one of the bean's properties:

```
<jsp:getPropery name="myBean" property="firstName"/>

<%= ((examples.TestBean) request.getAttribute("myBean")).
    getFirstName() %>
```

As you can see, the `jsp:getProperty` action takes care of fetching the bean from wherever it is stored, casting it to the appropriate type, and invoking the property's accessor method.

Because the `jsp:useBean` action also creates a variable with the same name as the bean, you could also use the following expression:

```
<%= myBean.getFirstName() %>
```

The main reason you would choose the `jsp:getProperty` action over the `<%=` action is that the `jsp:getProperty` action is language independent. Although the focus of this book is on using Java as the JSP scripting language, the JSP specification allows for other scripting languages, such as JavaScript. Although the expression `<%= myBean.getFirstName() %>` works for JavaScript, it probably wouldn't work for other scripting languages. If you used Smalltalk as a scripting language, the expression would be something like `<%= myBean firstName %>`. You can be sure that `jsp:getProperty` will work no matter which scripting language you are using.

Another reason you would choose to use the former method to access a bean property is because it's similar to the appearance of other tags on the page.

Setting Bean Properties

Obviously, if you can get bean properties from a JSP, you need to set them, too. The `jsp:setProperty` action enables you to set bean properties and provides some useful shortcuts for copying parameter values into a bean.

The basic syntax for setting a bean property is

```
<jsp:setProperty name="beanName" property="propertyName"
    value="propertyValue"/>
```

You can even use the <%= tag inside the `jsp:setProperty` action this way:

```
<jsp:setProperty name="myBean" property="name"
    value="<%=myName%>"/>
```

You can use `jsp:setProperty` to set the value of string properties and certain data types that can be converted from a string. Table 14.1 lists the data types that are automatically converted and the method used to convert them.

TABLE 14.1 Automatic Type Conversions Performed by `jsp:setProperty`

Java Type	Conversion Method
`boolean` or `Boolean`	`Boolean.valueOf`
`byte` or `Byte`	`Byte.valueOf`
`char` or `Character`	`Character.valueOf`
`double` or `Double`	`Double.valueOf`
`float` or `Float`	`Float.valueOf`
`int` or `Integer`	`Integer.valueOf`
`long` or `Long`	`Long.valueOf`

For example, if your bean includes the following `set` method:

```
public void setAge(int age)
```

You can safely set the age this way:

```
<jsp:setProperty name="myBean" property="age" value="35"/>
```

The string `"35"` is automatically converted to an integer when the JSP engine sets the property.

Setting Properties Directly from Parameters

One of the great features of `jsp:setProperty` is that it recognizes the frequent need to copy values out of form variables and into beans. You can automatically copy a parameter into a bean property this way:

```
<jsp:setProperty name="myBean" param="paramName"
    property="propertyName"/>
```

If the property name is the same as the parameter name, you can omit the parameter name:

```
<jsp:setProperty name="myBean" property="propertyName"/>
```

The presence or absence of the `value` keyword in `jsp:setProperty` determines whether the JSP engine uses a specific value or gets the value from a parameter. You can't have both a `value` and a `param` attribute in a single `jsp:setProperty`.

By the Way

Null Parameters and `jsp:setProperty`

If a parameter's value is `null` or if it's an empty string, the `jsp:setProperty` method won't attempt to set the value. Although this behavior is normally good, it could trip you up if you expect to be able to clear out an entry by sending a blank value.

If your property is an indexed property (that is, an array of values), `jsp:setProperty` can handle it as long as it's an array of strings or one of the types previously listed in Table 14.1. To see how this works, imagine you have a class like the one shown in Listing 14.1.

LISTING 14.1 Source Code for `Group.java`

```
package examples;

public class Group implements java.io.Serializable
{
    protected java.util.Vector members;

    public Group()
    {
        members = new java.util.Vector();
    }

    public String getMember(int which)
    {
        return (String) members.elementAt(which);
    }
```

LISTING 14.1 Continued

```
    public void setMember(int which, String member)
    {
        members.setElementAt(member, which);
    }

    public String[] getMembers()
    {
// Convert the members vector into an array of strings.
        String[] memberArray = new String[members.size()];
        members.copyInto(memberArray);

        return memberArray;
    }

    public void setMembers(String[] memberArray)
    {
// If there are no members, just clear out the vector.
        if (memberArray == null)
        {
            members.setSize(0);
            return;
        }
// Copy the contents of the member array into the members vector.
        members.setSize(memberArray.length);
        for (int i=0; i < memberArray.length; i++)
        {
            members.setElementAt(memberArray[i], i);
        }
    }
}
```

The JSP shown in Listing 14.2 copies any `member` parameters it receives into the `Group` object and then displays the contents of the object. Notice how easy it is to copy the values into the bean compared to how difficult it is to get the values out. The `jsp:getProperty` action doesn't handle indexed properties well, so stick to single-value properties when using that action.

LISTING 14.2 Source Code for `ShowGroup.jsp`

```
<html>
<body>

<%-- Create the bean --%>
<jsp:useBean id="group" class="examples.Group"/>

<%-- Copy any member parameters into the bean --%>
<jsp:setProperty name="group" property="members" param="member"/>

<P>
Group members:<br>
```

LISTING 14.2 Continued

```
<%-- Display the contents of the bean --%>
<%
    examples.Group theGroup = (examples.Group) pageContext.
        getAttribute("group");

    String[] members = theGroup.getMembers();

    for (int i=0; i < members.length; i++)
    {
        out.println(members[i]+"<BR>");
    }
%>
</body>
</html>
```

Figure 14.1 shows the `ShowGroup` JSP in action, using values passed directly into the URL. (Look at the address line.)

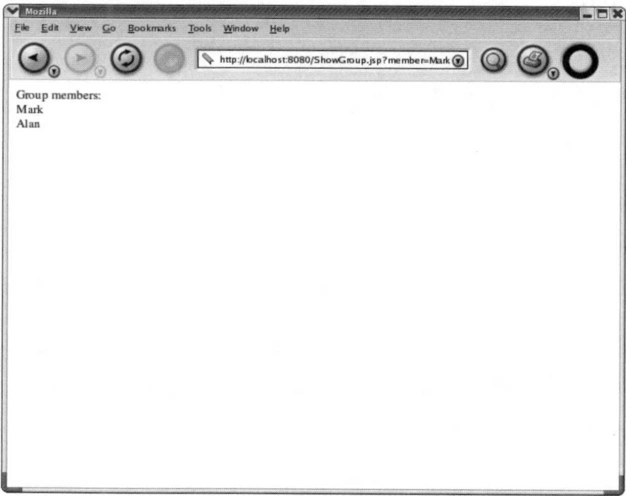

FIGURE 14.1 You can set multi-valued properties easily with `jsp:setProperty`.

In addition to the convenience of setting multiple values, the `jsp:setProperty` action can also scan for matches between property names and parameter names. All you need to do is specify `*` for the parameter name:

```
<jsp:setProperty name="myBean" property="*"/>
```

Listing 14.3 shows a simple test bean with a few properties.

LISTING 14.3 Source Code for `TestBean.java`

```
package examples;

public class TestBean implements java.io.Serializable
{
    protected String firstName;
    protected String lastName;
    protected int age;

    public TestBean() { }

    public String getFirstName() { return firstName; }
    public void setFirstName(String aFirstName)
        { firstName = aFirstName; }

    public String getLastName() { return lastName; }
    public void setLastName(String aLastName)
        { lastName = aLastName; }

    public int getAge() { return age; }
    public void setAge(int anAge) { age = anAge; }
}
```

Listing 14.4 shows a JSP that inserts values into a `TestBean` object and then displays the values again. One of the striking things about this JSP is that it does a fairly good bit of work but doesn't contain any explicit Java code.

LISTING 14.4 Source Code for `ShowTestBean.jsp`

```
<html>
<body>

<%-- Create an instance of the bean --%>
<jsp:useBean id="myBean" class="examples.TestBean"/>

<%-- Copy the parameters into the bean --%>
<jsp:setProperty name="myBean" property="*"/>

The bean values are:<br>
First Name: <jsp:getProperty name="myBean" property="firstName"/><br>
Last Name: <jsp:getProperty name="myBean" property="lastName"/><br>
Age: <jsp:getProperty name="myBean" property="age"/><br>

</body>
</html>
```

Figure 14.2 shows the output of `ShowTestBean.jsp` with parameters passed in directly in the URL.

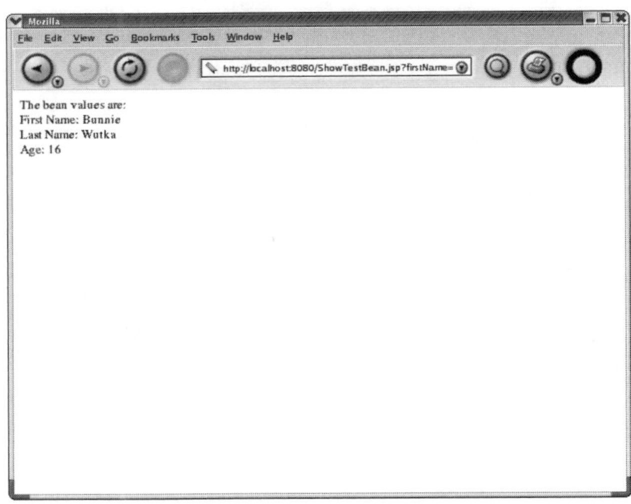

FIGURE 14.2 The `jsp:setProperty` action makes it easy to set several bean properties from `request` parameters.

By the Way

In Case of Trouble

If you are having trouble accessing bean properties, see the "Q&A" section at the end of this hour.

Initializing a New Bean

Frequently, you'll want to set only certain properties on a bean the first time it is created, but after that, you want to leave those properties alone. Rather than putting a `/>` at the end of `jsp:useBean`, you can use a closing `</jsp:useBean>` action and put your initialization tags between the opening and closing tags for `jsp:useBean`. In other words, any code, HTML, or JSP actions that are between the `jsp:useBean` and `</jsp:useBean>` are executed only if the bean is created. If the bean already exists, any content between the opening and closing actions is skipped.

Listing 14.5 shows a variant of the JSP in Listing 14.4. This variant JSP changes the scope of the bean from `page` (the default) to `session` and executes some code when the bean is created.

LISTING 14.5 Source Code for `TestInit.jsp`

```
<html>
<body>

<%-- Create an instance of the bean --%>
<jsp:useBean id="myBean" class="examples.TestBean" scope="session">
    I initialized the bean.<BR>
    <jsp:setProperty name="myBean" property="firstName"
        value="blah"/>
    <% out.println("I ran some Java code during the init, too<P>"); %>
</jsp:useBean>

<%-- Copy the parameters into the bean --%>
<jsp:setProperty name="myBean" property="*"/>

The bean values are:<br>
First Name: <jsp:getProperty name="myBean" property="firstName"/><br>
Last Name: <jsp:getProperty name="myBean" property="lastName"/><br>
Age: <jsp:getProperty name="myBean" property="age"/><br>

</body>
</html>
```

Figure 14.3 shows the output from the `TestInit.jsp` page when it is run for the first time from a browser.

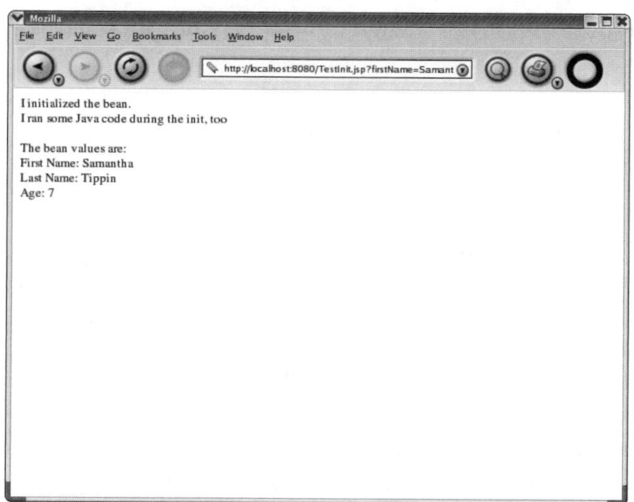

FIGURE 14.3 You can place initialization code between `jsp:useBean` and `</jsp:useBean>`.

Figure 14.4 shows the output from the `TestInit.jsp` page when you click the Refresh button on the browser after seeing the output from Figure 14.3. The initialization code isn't executed because the bean already exists and is stored in the `session` object.

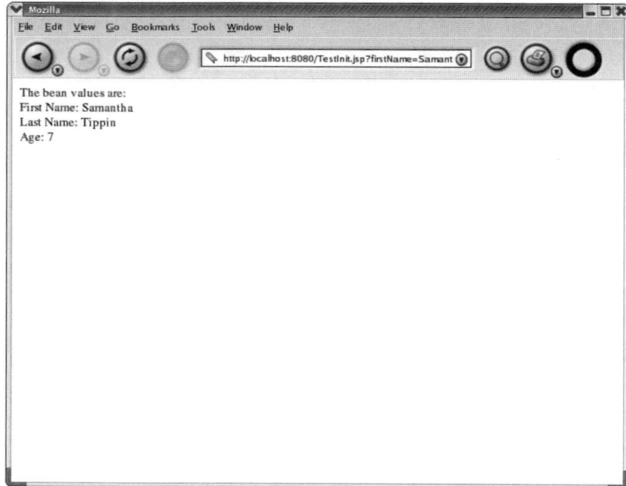

FIGURE 14.4 Initialization code isn't executed if a bean already exists.

The Type of an Existing Bean

When you need to refer to a bean using a superclass or interface, you can use the `type` attribute in the `jsp:useBean` action. For example, suppose you create a `Nameable` interface like the one shown in Listing 14.6, with a `getFirstName` and a `getLastName`.

LISTING 14.6 Source Code for `Nameable.java`

```
package examples;

public interface Nameable
{
    public String getFirstName();
    public String getLastName();
}
```

Objects that implement this interface have first and last names, but may have other attributes that are different. You want to write a JSP that prints out the first name and the last name stored in a bean, but you don't care about the actual class of the bean. All you really care about is that it implements the `Nameable` interface. By specifying `type=examples.Nameable` , you can use any bean that implements `Nameable`. Listing 14.7 shows an example.

LISTING 14.7 Source Code for `ShowNameable.jsp`

```
<html>
<body>

<%-- Locate an instance of the bean and use it as an implementation of Nameable--%>
<jsp:useBean id="myBean" type="examples.Nameable" scope="session"/>

The bean values are:<br>
First Name: <jsp:getProperty name="myBean" property="firstName"/><br>
Last Name: <jsp:getProperty name="myBean" property="lastName"/><br>

</body>
</html>
```

This example will find the object whose `id` is `myBean` in the `session` scope and use it as an implementation of the `Nameable` interface. You can test `ShowNameable.jsp` with `TestNameable.jsp` from Listing 14.8.

LISTING 14.8 Source Code for `TestNameable.jsp`

```
<html>
<body>

<%-- Create an instance of the bean --%>
<jsp:useBean id="myBean" class="examples.TestBean2" scope="session"/>

<%-- Copy the parameters into the bean --%>
<jsp:setProperty name="myBean" property="*"/>

<jsp:forward page="/ShowNameable.jsp"/>

</body>
</html>
```

Notice that Listing 14.7 creates an instance of `TestBean2` using the class attribute, whereas Listing 14.6 declares that the type of the object named `myBean` is

Nameable. The effect is to cast the type of TestBean2 to a Nameable. Of course, TestBean must be an implementation of Nameable, or the container will throw an exception. Similarly, if you're trying to use a class as if it were another type, you can only use the class as if it were one of its ancestors.

By the Way

Classes and Ancestry

Classes group attributes and behavior. Often, there's value in creating a class that encapsulates common behavior and attributes, and in creating specialized classes that derive from it. The derived class is a subclass of the first, which is known as a superclass, parent, or ancestor class. In Java, the latter class extends the former.

Did you Know?

Digging a Little Deeper

Of course, you won't be able to see the results by looking at the page produced by ShowNameable.jsp. It will look the same as if myBean was used directly. To see the effect of using the type attribute, take a moment to look at the code produced by Tomcat. You'll see that the object identified by the id attribute is cast to the type given by the type attribute.

By using both the class and type attributes in a <jsp:useBean> element, you can create a class of one type and use it as another type all in one place. Listing 14.9 shows you how to do this.

LISTING 14.9 An Example of How to Use Class and Type id in <jsp:useBean>

```
<jsp:useBean id="myBean" type="examples.Nameable"
     class="examples.TestBean2" scope="session"/>
```

If you need to create a bean, you must supply a classname. If you try to use the type attribute without a class attribute and the bean does not exist, the bean is null. In other words, the JSP won't try to create a bean.

By the Way

In Case of Trouble

If you make changes to a bean and they don't appear to have any effect, see the "Q&A" section at the end of this hour.

A Bean-Based Web Application

In Hour 13, "More About Saving Data," you learned how to make a shopping cart application by creating several core classes and then using servlets and JSPs to manipulate those core classes. The core shopping cart classes are all implemented as JavaBeans, making them ideal candidates for the `jsp:useBean` action.

Many of the servlets used in Hour 13 become very short JSPs, thanks to the `jsp:useBean` and `jsp:setProperty` actions. Listing 14.10 shows the updated `ShowProductCatalog2.jsp` file.

LISTING 14.10 Source Code for `ShowProductCatalog2.jsp`

```
<%@ page language="java" import="examples.cart.*,java.net.*,java.text.*" %>

<%!
// Declare a constant for the number of items to show on a page.
    public static final int ITEMS_PER_PAGE = 5;
%>

<html>
<body bgcolor="#ffffff">

<a href="ViewShoppingCart.jsp">View Shopping Cart</a>
<p>
<h1>Available Products</h1>
<table border="1">
<tr><th>Description<th>Quantity<th>Price

<%-- Get an instance of the product catalog class --%>
<jsp:useBean id="catalog" class="examples.cart.ProductCatalog"
    scope="application"/>
<%

// Get the next starting position for displaying catalog items.
    String startingPositionStr = (String) request.
        getParameter("StartingPosition");

    int startingPosition = 0;

// If there is a starting position parameter, parse it as an integer.
    if (startingPositionStr != null)
    {
        try
        {
// If there's an error parsing the number, the starting position will
// just remain 0.
            startingPosition = Integer.parseInt(startingPositionStr);
        }
        catch (Exception ignore)
        {
        }
    }
```

LISTING 14.10 Continued

```
// Get ITEMS_PER_PAGE items at a time.
    Item[] items = catalog.getItems(startingPosition, ITEMS_PER_PAGE);

// Get a currency formatter for showing the price.
    NumberFormat currency = NumberFormat.getCurrencyInstance();

    for (int i=0; i < items.length; i++)
    {
        Item item = items[i];

// Create the URL for adding the item to the shopping cart.
        String addItemURL =
            "AddToShoppingCart.jsp?"+
            "productCode="+URLEncoder.encode(item.getProductCode())+
            "&description="+URLEncoder.encode(item.getDescription())+
            "&quantity="+URLEncoder.encode(""+item.getQuantity())+
            "&price="+URLEncoder.encode(""+item.getPrice());
%>
<tr><td><%=item.getDescription()%><td><%=item.getQuantity()%>
    <td><%=item.getPrice()%>
<td><a href="<%=addItemURL%>">Add to Shopping Cart</a>
<%
    }
%>
</table>
<table border="0">
<tr>
<%
    if (startingPosition > 0)
    {
        int prevPosition = startingPosition-ITEMS_PER_PAGE;

// Don't let the starting position go negative.
        if (prevPosition < 0) prevPosition = 0;

// Write out a link to display the previous catalog page.
        out.println("<td><a href=\"ShowProductCatalog2.jsp?StartingPosition="+
            prevPosition+"\">&lt;&lt;Prev</a>");
    }

// Compute the next starting position in the catalog.
    int nextPosition = startingPosition+ITEMS_PER_PAGE;

// Make sure that there are still items to display at that starting
// position (that is, make sure nextPosition isn't greater than the total
// catalog size).
    if (catalog.itemsAvailable(nextPosition))
    {
// Write out a link to display the next catalog page.
        out.println("<td><a href=\"ShowProductCatalog2.jsp?StartingPosition="+
            nextPosition+"\">Next&gt;&gt;</a>");
    }
%>
</table>
</body>
</html>
```

Most of the ShowProductCatalog2.jsp file is identical to the version in Hour 13. The two main differences are the jsp:useBean action that gets the ProductCatalog object and the link to add an item to the shopping cart. Instead of using a servlet to add an item to the cart, the new ShowProductCatalog2.jsp file uses a JSP.

Listing 14.11 shows the AddToShoppingCart.jsp file that adds an item to the cart. This file is significantly smaller and easier to read than its corresponding servlet from Hour 13.

LISTING 14.11 Source Code for AddToShoppingCart.jsp

```
<%-- Get a reference to the shopping cart --%>
<jsp:useBean id="cart" class="examples.cart.ShoppingCart" scope="session"/>

<%-- Create an item object --%>
<jsp:useBean id="item" class="examples.cart.Item" scope="page"/>

<%-- Copy the request parameters into the item --%>
<jsp:setProperty name="item" property="*"/>

<%-- Add the item to the shopping cart --%>
<% cart.addItem(item); %>

<%-- Display the product catalog again --%>
<jsp:forward page="ShowCartAfterAdd.jsp"/>
```

AddToShoppingCart.jsp is much smaller for two reasons. First, the code to get an instance of the shopping cart is reduced to a single line. The servlet must check to see whether the cart already exists and, if not, create it. The jsp:useBean handles that.

Second, the servlet must copy each parameter into the Item object, converting any integer or double quantities as necessary. The jsp:setProperty action copies all the parameters at once, because the parameters conveniently have the same names as their corresponding bean properties.

Likewise, the RemoveItem.jsp file, which replaces the RemoveItemServlet class from Hour 13, is equally small. Listing 14.12 shows RemoveItem.jsp.

LISTING 14.12 Source Code for RemoveItem.jsp

```
<%-- Get the shopping cart --%>
<jsp:useBean id="cart" class="examples.cart.ShoppingCart" scope="session"/>

<%-- Ask the shopping cart to remove the item --%>
<% cart.removeItem(Integer.parseInt(request.getParameter("item"))); %>

<%-- Display the shopping cart --%>
<jsp:forward page="ShowCartAfterRemove.jsp"/>
```

Again, the biggest savings here is the one-line creation/retrieval of the shopping cart.

Listing 14.13 shows the `SubmitOrder.jsp` file that handles the order submission in place of the `CheckoutServlet` from Hour 13.

LISTING 14.13 Source Code for `SubmitOrder.jsp`

```
<%-- Declare a page to receive any errors that occur --%>
<%@ page errorPage="ShoppingCartError.jsp" %>

<%-- Get the shopping cart instance --%>
<jsp:useBean id="cart" class="examples.cart.ShoppingCart" scope="session"/>

<%-- Create an object to hold shipping information --%>
<jsp:useBean id="shipping" class="examples.cart.Shipping" scope="page"/>

<%-- Copy the shipping information into the shipping object --%>
<jsp:setProperty name="shipping" property="*" />

<%-- Create an object to hold billing information --%>
<jsp:useBean id="billing" class="examples.cart.Billing" scope="page"/>

<%-- Copy the billing information into the billing object --%>
<jsp:setProperty name="billing" property="*" />

<html>
<body>
<h1>Thank you for your order.</h1>
<p>
Your order confirmation number is
<%= cart.completeOrder(shipping, billing) %>.
<p>
Please use this number when calling to inquire about your order status.
</body>
</html>
```

Once again, the JSP realizes a huge savings over the servlet by use of the `jsp:useBean` and `jsp:setProperty` actions. The `SubmitOrder.jsp` uses a slightly different philosophy for displaying its results, too. The `CheckoutServlet` class is forwarded to a JSP to display the order confirmation. If it has an error submitting the order, it prints out an error message.

`SubmitOrder.jsp` prints out the order confirmation and uses the `errorPage` option in the `page` directive to specify a page to handle the error. The error-handling page prints out an error message that is only useful for developers. Listing 14.14 shows the error-handling page.

LISTING 14.14 Source Code for `ShoppingCartError.jsp`

```
<%@ page isErrorPage="true" %>
<html>
<body>
<h1>Error</h1>
<p>
Your order could not be processed because of the following error:
<pre>
<%= exception.getMessage() %>
</pre>
We are sorry for the inconvenience.
</body>
</html>
```

Summary

As you can see, JSPs make it easier to take advantage of JavaBeans. In most cases, using JavaBeans with JSPs produces code that is simpler.

To use JavaBeans, you only need to master three standard actions: `jsp:useBean`, `jsp:getProperty`, and `jsp:setProperty`. The `jsp:useBean` action makes a bean available for use in a JSP. The `jsp:getProperty` and `jsp:setProperty` actions allow you to access and set bean properties. JSPs have several shortcut mechanisms so that you can set bean properties with the values of request parameters easily. When we revisited the shopping cart example from Hour 13, we found that we could reduce the amount of code required in the JSPs and even replace the servlets with JSPs that worked with the JavaBeans that implemented the data objects.

Q&A

Q. ***Why is a new object created whenever I call*** `jsp:useBean`***?***

A. You probably forgot to specify a scope for the bean. Remember, the default scope for a bean is `page`, and all beans with `page` scope disappear when the page finishes executing.

Q. ***I changed some bean properties in one page; why don't they show up on my other page?***

A. You might have a scope problem on one of the pages. For example, if you set the properties on a bean with `session` scope and then you try to access the bean on another page, but you give the bean `request` scope on the other page, you have two different beans. The second page looks for the bean in its `request` object and, not finding one there, creates a new instance of the bean, ignoring the one in the session.

Q. ***I checked to see that the scope is correct; why do I still not see the changes?***

A. You should probably check the bean IDs, too. Make sure they are absolutely identical, character for character. A bean ID of `Fred` is different from a bean ID of `fred`.

Q. ***Why don't some of my parameters get copied into properties?***

A. You probably have a spelling difference between the parameter and the bean property name. Remember, unless you have a `BeanInfo` class that says otherwise, your bean property names are going to start with a lowercase letter (except when the first few letters of the property are capitalized). The property name looks capitalized in methods such as `getFirstName` and `setFirstName`, but the property name is still `firstName`. Make sure your parameter name matches the case of the property name.

Q. ***I changed my bean class and recompiled it. Why don't my changes show up?***

A. Many JSP engines don't reload associated classes when they change, only the JSP itself. If you are just testing and don't expect the bean to change in production, or at least not regularly, just restart the JSP engine. If you need to change the bean frequently, you might consider using a JSP engine that automatically reloads associated classes or write a custom class loader.

Q. ***I know my bean class was reloaded; why do I still not see my changes?***

A. Although new instances of the bean will pick up your changes, any existing beans are probably still using the older code. You need to clear the older beans out of whatever scope they belong to. In other words, if you have an old bean in a session, you need to get rid of it.

Workshop

The Workshop is designed to help you review what you have learned, and help you to further increase your understanding of the material covered in this hour.

Quiz

1. If you do not declare the scope of a JavaBean, what scope will it have?
2. How does the `jsp:setProperty` action behave if you do not declare a value attribute?
3. How can you perform initialization of a JavaBean within a JSP?

Answers

1. The default scope for a JavaBean is `page` scope.
2. If you do not declare a `value` attribute, `jsp:setProperty` will assume that there is a request parameter whose name is the same as a declared property. If you have declared a `param` attribute, the value of the `param` attribute will identify the name of the request parameter whose value will be assigned to the property.
3. Instead of using a empty tag (`<jsp:useBean/>`) to declare a JavaBean, you can use a start (`<jsp:useBean>`) and an end (`</jsp:useBean>`) tag to enclose your initialization content. The content can include code or tags that work with the JavaBean you declared.

Activities

1. Write a simple Web application that uses a form to populate a JavaBean in a JSP. Try both the `GET` and `POST` request methods.
2. Create a JSP that uses a JavaBean that implements the `nameable` interface. The JSP should output the first and last name. Create two other JSPs that each forward to this page. For these pages, write separate JavaBeans that implement the `nameable` interface. Make the second JavaBean modify the characters of the first or last name. Invoke each page to demonstrate that the forwarded page is using the different JavaBeans.

HOUR 15

The JSP Expression Language

What You'll Learn in This Hour:

- ▶ What the JSP Expression Language is
- ▶ How to reference variables and literal values
- ▶ How to use various implicit objects
- ▶ How to invoke functions

In the previous hour, you learned about the `<jsp:useBean>` tag. With the power of built-in tags like `<jsp:useBean>` and additional custom tag libraries (which you'll learn about in the next few hours), you can write powerful JSPs that contain no scriptlets—only tags. One of the original limitations of the `<jsp:useBean>` tag and its associated tags is that they could only access simple bean attributes. If the attribute was a collection, you couldn't access individual elements in the collection.

The JSP Expression Language (EL) addresses this limitation by defining an expression syntax that lets you manipulate collections and other complex data structures from within JSP tags. The JavaServer Pages Standard Tag Library (JSTL) also defines a set of operators so you can write simple expressions, and a function syntax so you can invoke utility functions. When coupled with custom tag libraries, the JSP EL becomes a very powerful alternative to scriptlets.

Basic Syntax

Typically, when you specify an attribute value in a JSP tag, you simply use a string. For example,

```
<jsp:setProperty name="order" property="subtotal" value="100"/>
```

JSP EL allows you to specify an expression for any of these attribute values. A JSP EL expression takes the form `${expr}` where *expr* is the expression itself. You might rewrite the previous `<jsp:setProperty>` tag with an expression like

```
<jsp:setProperty name="order" property="subtotal"
    value="${product.price+shipping.price}"/>
```

When the JSP compiler sees the `${}` form in an attribute, it generates code to evaluate the expression. The result of the expression becomes the new attribute value (the expression is evaluated at runtime, of course, not compile time).

You can also use JSP EL expressions within template text for a tag. For example, the `<jsp:text>` tag simply inserts its content within the body of a JSP. The following `<jsp:text>` declaration inserts `<h1>Hello World!</h1>` into the JSP output:

```
<jsp:text>
  <h1>Hello World!</h1>
</jsp:text>
```

You can include a JSP EL expression in the body of a `<jsp:text>` tag (or any other tag) with the same `${}` syntax you use for attributes. For example,

```
<jsp:text>
   Your subtotal is: ${product.price + shipping.price}
</jsp:text>
```

Variables

One of the main features of JSP EL is that it allows you to access JSP variables stored in any of the various scopes (page, request, session, application). By default, the result of an expression like `${product}` is the same as calling `pageContext.findAttribute("product")`. That is, the expression evaluator first looks for the value in the page scope, then the request scope, next the session scope, and finally the application scope, returning the first value found. If `product` exists in both the request scope and the application scope, the value in the request scope is the one used.

Literals and Operators

One of the strengths of JSP EL is that it doesn't just access variable values, it allows you to create expressions—both arithmetic and logical. Within a JSP EL expression, you can use integers, floating point numbers, strings, the built-in constants `true` and `false` for boolean values, and `null`.

One of the tricky parts about using strings is that you need to be careful about your quotation marks. For example, the following expression generates an error:

```
<c:out value="${fn:length("This is a test string")}"/>
```

Although you may not know yet what the `<c:out>` tag or the `fn:length` functions do yet, you might still be able to spot the error. The problem is that JSP compiler sees the quote just after length(as the closing quote for the `value` attribute. It interprets the expression `value="${fn:length("` and then complains about syntax errors in the rest of the expression. There are at least two things you can do to remedy this situation. The first is to use different kinds of quotes around the whole attribute value and for the string within. Either of the two following lines will work and are equivalent:

```
<c:out value='${fn:length("This is a test string")}'/>

<c:out value="${fn:length('This is a test string')}"/>
```

Notice that in each case, single quotes define one string, and double quotes define the other. If you want to stick with the same kind of quotes, you must use a backslash (\) to escape the nested quotes. For example,

```
<c:out value="${fn:length(\"This is a test string\")}"/>
```

If you need to include a backslash within a string, you must escape it as well by using \\. For example,

```
<c:out value="${fn:length(\"The backslash looks like \\.\")}">
```

Access Operators

The most common operators in JSP EL are . and []. These two operators allow you to access various attributes of Java Beans and built-in JSP objects. In Java, the [] operator is only used for referencing array elements. In other languages, however, [] can be used to access dictionary values (the equivalent of a Java Map or Hashtable). Where JSP EL lets you use the expression `table["person"]`, Java requires you to specify `table.get("person")`.

The . operator usually references attributes of a bean or a built-in object. For example, to access the `name` property of a `person` bean, you use the expression `person.name`.

One of the interesting things about the . and [] operators is that they are interchangeable. That is, `person.name` is the same as `person["name"]`. Even if `person` isn't a dictionary type object (Map, Hashtable, and so on), you can still treat it that way.

If you assume that the expression `var.attr` is treated as `var["attr"]`, then you can define the behavior of both these operators in terms of how the [] operator behaves.

The rules for evaluating `var["attr"]` are

- If *var* is `null`, the result of the expression is `null` (without the agony of a `NullPointerException`).
- If *attr* is `null` (which is possible because *attr* can be an expression instead of a constant string), the result is `null`.
- If *var* is a Map, the result is `var.get(attr)`, and is `null` if *var* has no key corresponding to *attr*.
- If *var* is a List or an array, *attr* is evaluated as an integer. If *attr* can't be evaluated as an integer, the result is an error. Otherwise, the result is item in the array or List corresponding to the value of *attr*. That is, if *attr* = 0, the result is the first item in the list or array. If *attr* is outside the bounds of the array or list, the result is `null`.
- If `var` is a JavaBean and `attr` is a readable property of `var`, the result is the value of that property. Otherwise, the result is an error.

In simpler terms, to access an item in a map, use the expression `mapvar[mapkey]`, to access an item in an array or List, use the expression `listvar[index]`; to access a JavaBean property, use the expression `beanvar[propname]`.

Arithmetic Operators

JSP EL supports the common arithmetic operators +, -, *, /, and % just as they are supported in Java. Because JSP EL was designed to be somewhat consistent with both the XPath and ECMAScript languages, you can also use `div` instead of / for division, and `mod` instead of % for modulo (remainder).

Within any arithmetic or logical expression, you can also use parentheses to group items. For example: `${(x + y) * (z - q)}`.

You can also use the unary – operator, which negates a value. That is, you can use the expression -x to represent the negative of the value of `x`.

Relational Operators

JSP EL supports the common relational operators ==, !=, <, >, <=, and >= just as in Java. Again, to maintain consistency with XPath and ECMAScript, JSP EL allows the following alternatives to these operators: `eq`, `ne`, `lt`, `gt`, `le`, and `ge` (for equal, not equal, less-than, greater-than, less-or-equal, and greater-or-equal, respectively).

For example, the expression `${x < 5}` evaluates to `true` if x is less than 5, and `false` otherwise.

Logical Operators

The logical operators && and || perform logical AND and OR operations just as they do in Java expressions. You can also use the operators `and` and `or` instead of && and ||. For example: `${x < 5 && y < 10}`.

You can also use the unary ! operator or `not` to express the logical negative of an expression. That is, if `x` is `true`, then `!x` is `false`, as is `not x`.

The `empty` Operator

The `empty` operator returns `true` if a value is `null` or if it is an empty container, array, or string. A container is empty if it contains no elements. A string or an array is empty if its size is 0. For example: `${empty employees}`.

The Conditional Operator

The conditional operator takes the form *`bool-expr ? true-expr : false-expr`*. The evaluator first evaluates *`bool-expr`*, and if it is `true`, the result of the operator is the value of *`true-expr`*. Otherwise, if *`bool-expr`* is false, the result is *`false-expr`*. Expressed in Java terms, the operator works something like this:

```
if (boolExpr) {
    return trueExpr;
} else {
    return falseExpr;
}
```

For example, suppose you want to calculate an average and you have a variable called `sum` containing the sum of the items, and a `numItems` variable containing the number of items. If `numItems` is 0, computing the average as `sum/numItems` would normally yield an error. If you want the average to be 0 when `numItems` is 0, and `sum/numItems` in all other cases, you can use the following expression:

```
${numItems != 0 ? sum/numItems : 0}
```

Implicit Objects

You should already be familiar with some of the implicit objects available to JSP scriptlets, such as `request`, `response`, and `out`. JSP EL has its own set of implicit objects that allows you to reference commonly -used data items quickly. You can use these objects in an expression as if they were variables.

The `pageContext` Object

The `pageContext` object gives you access to the `pageContext` JSP object. Through the `pageContext` object, you can access the `request` object. For example, to access the incoming query string for a request, you can use the expression:

```
${pageContext.request.queryString}
```

Scope Objects

The `pageScope`, `requestScope`, `sessionScope`, and `applicationScope` variables provide access to variables stored at each scope level. Sometimes, the default search mechanism for locating variables isn't what you need. For example, suppose the variable `product` is located in both the request scope and the application scope. If you use the variable `product` in an expression, the JSP EL evaluator will use the closer scope, which is the request scope. If you need to explicitly access the `product` variable in the application scope, you can access it through the `applicationScope` variable as `applicationScope.product`.

`param` and `paramValues` Objects

The `param` and `paramValues` objects give you access to the parameter values normally available through the `request.getParameter` and `request.getParameterValues` methods. The reason you need a special object to access parameters is that they don't follow the normal JavaBean format for attributes. Both of these methods take a string argument, which is not an allowable form for a bean's `get` method.

For example, to access a parameter named `order`, use the expression `${param.order}` or `${param["order"]}`.

The `param` object returns single string values, whereas the `paramValues` object returns string arrays (if there is only one parameter value, `paramValues` returns an array of length 1).

`header` and `headerValues` Objects

The `header` and `headerValues` objects give you access to the header values normally available through the `request.getHeader` and `request.getHeaders` methods, similar to the way `param` and `paramValues` give you access to parameters. The `header` method returns a single header value, whereas the `headerValues` object returns an array of values.

To access the header value `user-agent`, use the following expression:

```
${header["user-agent"]}
```

The `cookie` Object

The `cookie` object gives you access to the session cookies normally available through the `session.getCookies` method. For example, to access a cookie named `lastOrder`, use this expression:

```
${cookie.lastOrder}
```

Functions

JSP EL allows you to use functions in expressions as well. These functions must be defined in custom tag libraries. As you will see soon, there are a number of handy functions built into the JSTL.

A function has the syntax *`ns:func(param1, param2, ...)`*, where `ns` is the namespace of the function, *`func`* is the name of the function and *`param1`* is the first parameter value. For example, the function `fn:length`, which is part of the JSTL library, returns the length of a string. You can use this function to determine the length of the query string with the following expression:

```
${fn:length(pageContext.request.queryString)}
```

Q&A

Q. ***Why do I need the expression language, isn't Java good enough?***

A. JSP EL provides a more compact syntax than using scriptlets. It is much more convenient to use the ${} syntax and its powerful . and [] operators than it is to use <% %> and the more cumbersome property access methods. Also, JSP EL always works the same way, regardless of the scripting language you use with JSP. Remember, although JSPs are usually written in Java, you can also find JSP containers that support other scripting language. JSP EL remains the same regardless of the scripting language.

Q. ***When do I use . and when do I use []?***

A. Although you can use these operators interchangeably, it is a good idea to use an operator that indicates the kind of data being accessed. For example, if you are accessing a bean property, use the . operator. If you are accessing a map value or an array index, use the [] operator. There are plenty of times when you break this rule, especially in cases where you want a map to look like it is a bean, you want things to make sense to the next person who reads your code. You may know the types of all the variables, but the next person may not.

Workshop

The Workshop is designed to help you review what you have learned, and help you to further increase your understanding of the material covered in this hour.

Quiz

1. Name two ways to represent a string in a JSP EL expression contained with an attribute value.
2. Where does JSP EL look for variables?
3. What's the difference between `order.price` and `order["price"]`?

Answers

1. You can use different quotation marks, such as `value='${fn:length("hello")}'`, or you can use \ to escape the quotes, such as `value="${fn:length(\"hello\")}"`.

2. It looks in the variable scopes, starting at the page scope and proceeding through the request, session, and application scopes, using the first variable it finds

3. There is no difference. The only time there might be a difference is if you are accessing a member of a map with an odd-looking key like "a+b". In this case, the syntax "order.a+b" would be interpreted as "access attribute a of order and then add it to b", instead of "access attribute a+b of order."

Activity

Use a scriptlet to store some values in the request and session scopes, then use the `<jsp:text>` tag to write JSP EL expressions that manipulate those values. Remember that you can use JSP EL expressions within the body text of the `<jsp:text>` tag.

HOUR 16

Extending JSP with New Tags

What You'll Learn in This Hour:

- How to build custom tags using classic tag handlers
- How to create and use tags using `SimpleTag`
- How to use tag files

JSP tag extensions let you create new tags that you can insert directly into a JavaServer Page just as you would the built-in tags you learned about in earlier hours. Through tag extensions, you can define tags that let you insert data into the output stream, include sections of a page only if certain conditions are met, and even modify the contents of the page itself before they are sent back to the browser. They can act like functions, performing actions or modifying variables. Tags allow you to build pages that are consistent in their expression, by eliminating the intermixing of code with elements and template data. They also provide a great way to build reusable elements.

The JSP 2.0 specification includes significant improvements that make it easier to construct and use tag extensions. Where it used to be an advanced subject, it's now something that should be in the toolkit of every JSP developer.

"Hello World" Tag

To create a custom JSP tag, you must first create a Java class that acts as a tag handler. Whenever your custom tag appears in a JavaServer Page, the JSP engine invokes your tag handler. If your custom tag doesn't care about the body text between its opening and closing tags, you can use the simple `TagSupport` class, which implements the `Tag` interface. If you need to access and possibly change the body text within the opening and closing tags, you must subclass the

BodyTagSupport class instead. The BodyTagSupport class implements the BodyTag interface, which allows you to access body text. Tags that implement these interfaces are known as **classic tag handlers**.

Did you Know?

The IterationTag **Interface**

There's another interface you can use to build tags with. It's also a member of the "classic" family of interfaces. If your tag has a body that needs to be evaluated by the container, then you can implement the IterationTag interface. Your tag will not have access to the body but can still examine and affect variables and other contextual information. However, since the BodyTag interface extends the IterationTag interface, most developers use the BodyTag interface by extending the BodyTagSupport class. We won't discuss this interface any further.

For example, suppose you define a custom tag named <mytags:DoSomething> and you use it this way:

```
<mytags:DoSomething>
   Here is some text
</mytags:DoSomething>
```

If your tag handler implements only the Tag interface, it can't see the body text (that is, Here is some text). All it can do is decide whether the client can see the body text or not. However, your custom tag can generate its own output.

Listing 16.1 shows the HelloWorldTagHandler class that inserts the familiar "Hello World!" message into the JSP response. Because it doesn't need to access its body text, it subclasses TagSupport.

LISTING 16.1 Source Code for HelloWorldTag.java

```
package examples.taglibs;
import javax.servlet.jsp.tagext.*;
import javax.servlet.jsp.*;
import java.io.*;

public class HelloWorldTag extends TagSupport
{
    public int doStartTag()
        throws JspException, IOException
    {
        JspWriter out = pageContext.getOut();
        out.println("<h1>Hello World!</h1>");
        return SKIP_BODY;
    }
```

LISTING 16.1 Continued

```
public int doEndTag()
    {
        return EVAL_PAGE;
    }
}
```

The methods doStartTag and doEndTag are invoked by the JSP container at the points in the page where the custom tag starts and ends. Don't worry about the SKIP_BODY and EVAL_PAGE return values just yet. You'll see what they mean shortly.

Listing 16.2 shows a JSP that calls HelloWorldTag via a tag named <mytag:hello>. At this point, you don't know how to relate HelloWorldTag to <mytag:hello>. You will see that in the next section.

LISTING 16.2 Source Code for TestHello.jsp

```
<%@ taglib uri="/hello" prefix="mytag" %>
<html>
<body>
<mytag:hello/>
</body>
</html>
```

Figure 16.1 shows the output from TestHello.jsp.

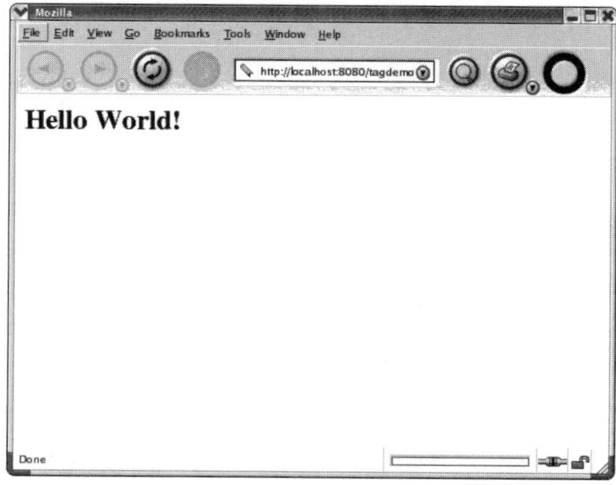

FIGURE 16.1 Custom tags can insert text into the response.

Packaging and Installing a Tag

When you create a custom tag library, you must also create a tag library descriptor (TLD) that describes each tag in your tag library. Listing 16.3 shows the TLD for the `HelloWorldTag` Java class.

LISTING 16.3 Source Code for `hello.tld`

```
<?xml version="1.0" encoding="ISO-8859-1"?>

<taglib xmlns="http://java.sun.com/xml/ns/j2ee"
      xmlns:xsi="http://www.w3.org/2001/XMLSchema-instance"
      xsi:schemaLocation="http://java.sun.com/xml/ns/j2ee/web-jsptaglibrary_2_0.xsd"
      version="2.0">
   <tlib-version>1.0</tlib-version>
   <short-name>hello</short-name>
   <description>
       An example Hello World tag.
   </description>
   <tag>
     <name>hello</name>
     <tag-class>examples.taglibs.HelloWorldTag</tag-class>
     <body-content>empty</body-content>
   </tag>
</taglib>
```

The first few lines of `hello.tld` are pretty standard for an XML file. You must start with the `<?xml?>` tag, of course. The next line specifies the schema and required JSP version. You can usually use this "as is" unless you need to specify additional namespaces or schema locations.

`<taglib>` is the root tag for a TLD and encloses all the other tags. Remember that an XML document has a single root tag that encloses everything else in the document. The next few tags describe the tag library.

The `<tlib-version>` tag describes the version number of the tag library. The `<short-name>` tag gives a short name for the tag library that might be used within a JSP Page Authoring tool. The idea is that you would load various tag libraries and see a list of the available libraries. The short name is the name you would see in the list. The `<description>` tag gives the long description of the tag library.

After the initial information describing the tag library, you can list the tags contained in the library. This tag library contains a single tag with a name of `hello` (as indicated by the `<name>` tag). The tag name, along with the prefix for the tag library, makes up the full tag that you put in the JSP. In other words, you take the tag name hello and combine it with the prefix specified in the JSP (mytag in Listing 16.1) to get the tag's full name, which is <mytag:hello>.

By the Way

Why Tag Names Are Made Up of Two Parts

The reason for splitting the name into two parts is that several people might make a tag named hello in their tag libraries. You need a way to specify which tag you mean, so you must use a prefix to indicate which library you are referring to.

Following <name>, the <tag-class> tag indicates the fully qualified pathname of the class that implements this tag. Finally, the <body-content> tag indicates that this tag will not have a body; in other words, the tag is an empty tag as shown, or there is nothing between the start and end tags.

Now that you have created the TLD file, you must deploy the tag library and test your Web page as a Web application. Create a directory called WEB-INF, and then in the WEB-INF directory create a web.xml that looks like the file in Listing 16.4.

LISTING 16.4 Source Code for web.xml

```
<?xml version="1.0" encoding="ISO-8859-1"?>
<web-app xmlns="http://java.sun.com/xml/ns/j2ee"
    xmlns:xsi="http://www.w3.org/2001/XMLSchema-instance"
    xsi:schemaLocation="http://java.sun.com/xml/ns/j2ee/web-app_2_4.xsd"
    version="2.4">

    <display-name>Tag Demo</display-name>
    <description>An application for testing custom tags</description>
    <taglib>
        <taglib-uri>/hello</taglib-uri>
        <taglib-location>/WEB-INF/tld/hello.tld</taglib-location>
    </taglib>
</web-app>
```

Most of the web.xml file should be familiar from the example in Hour 2, "JavaServer Pages Behind the Scenes," where you packaged a Web application into a WAR file. There are a few tags that you haven't seen before, however. The <taglib> tag defines a tag library that the Web application uses. The <taglib-uri> tag defines the name that a JSP would use as the URI for this tag library. Look back at Listing 16.2 and you can see that TestHello.jsp specifies /hello as the URI for the tag library, which matches what you see in web.xml. The <taglib-location> tag specifies the location of the hello.tld file, which is the file from Listing 16.3. According to the web.xml file, hello.tld should be stored in a directory called tld, which is below the WEB-INF directory.

Now, under the WEB-INF directory, create a classes/examples/taglibs/ directory and copy the HelloWorldTag.class file to that directory. Make sure that TestHello.jsp is in the same directory as the WEB-INF directory. Now create a file called tagdemo.war by going to the directory where WEB-INF and TestHello.jsp are located and entering the following command:

```
jar cvf tagdemo.war WEB-INF TestHello.jsp
```

Now install the WAR file in your Web server. After the file is installed, you should be able to access TestHello.jsp and see the output shown previously in Figure 16.1.

By the Way

Having Trouble with the Example?

If you are having trouble installing your custom tag library, see the "Q&A" section at the end of this hour.

Conditionally Including the Body of a Custom Tag

A tag like the one just demonstrated can be useful in many applications where you want to output "template" text generated within the tag handler or where you want it to perform a function. For example, you could write a tag that outputs the current date and time. Beyond this, custom tags also allow you to interact with the body of a tag.

Earlier in Listing 16.1, you saw that the doStartTag method in the custom tag returns a value of SKIP_BODY and the doEndTag method returns a value of EVAL_PAGE. These values tell the JSP engine how to handle the content between the start and end of the custom tag and also whether to continue evaluating the rest of the page after the custom closing tag. When doStartTag returns SKIP_BODY, it tells the JSP engine to ignore the content between the start and end of the custom tag. If the doStartTag returns EVAL_BODY_INCLUDE, the data between the start and end tags is evaluated and the results are copied to the response.

When doEndTag returns EVAL_PAGE, it tells the JSP engine to continue evaluating the rest of the page. If doEndTag returns SKIP_PAGE, the JSP engine ignores everything else in the JSP after the closing tag and returns the response to the browser.

Because you can control whether the JSP engine includes body text between the start and end of a tag, you can create tags that include text only if certain conditions are met.

Listing 16.5 shows a custom tag that includes its content only when the time of day is between 6 a.m. and 6 p.m.

LISTING 16.5 **Source Code for** `DayTag.java`

```
package examples.taglibs;

import javax.servlet.jsp.tagext.*;
import javax.servlet.jsp.*;
import java.util.*;

public class DayTag extends TagSupport
{
    public int doStartTag()
        throws JspException
    {
// Get the time of day.
        GregorianCalendar currTime = new GregorianCalendar();

// Get the hour of day.
        int hour = currTime.get(Calendar.HOUR_OF_DAY);

// If the time is between 6 a.m. and 6 p.m., tell the JSP engine to
// include the text between the start and end tag.
        if ((hour >= 6) && (hour <= 18))
        {
            return EVAL_BODY_INCLUDE;
        }
        else
        {
// Otherwise, ignore the body text.
            return SKIP_BODY;
        }
    }

    public int doEndTag()
    {
        return EVAL_PAGE;
    }
}
```

To process body content, it is necessary to make a slight change to the TLD. Instead of declaring the body content to be empty, it must now indicate that the body is meaningful. A TLD that works for this example appears in Listing 16.6

LISTING 16.6 **Source Code for** `DayTag.java`

```
<?xml version="1.0" encoding="ISO-8859-1"?>

<taglib xmlns=http://java.sun.com/xml/ns/j2ee
      xmlns:xsi=http://www.w3.org/2001/XMLSchema-instance
      xsi:schemaLocation=http://java.sun.com/xml/ns/j2ee/web-jsptaglibrary_2_0.xsd
      version="2.0">
```

LISTING 16.6 Continued

```
  <tlib-version>1.0</tlib-version>
  <short-name>DayTag</short-name>
  <description>
      A tag to that conditionally includes the body.
  </description>
  <tag>
    <name>DayTag</name>
    <tag-class>examples.taglibs.DayTag</tag-class>
    <body-content>jsp</body-content>
  </tag>
</taglib>
```

You can see that the body-content element has been changed to `jsp`, which causes the container to evaluate the body content as JSP source. You can instruct the container to output the body verbatim by using the value `tagdependant`, or cause the container to treat the body as though it had no scripting elements by declaring the body `scriptless`. Later in the hour, you'll see how to use tags whose bodies are scriptless.

Listing 16.7 is a sample JSP that you can use to exercise this tag.

LISTING 16.7 Source Code for `TestDayTag.jsp`

```
<%@ taglib uri="/daytag" prefix="daytag" %>
<html>
<body>
<daytag:DayTag>
It's between the hours of 6 am and 6 pm!
</daytag:DayTag>
</body>
</html>
```

Processing Body Content with a Custom Tag

Processing body text is a little more involved and requires a specialized tag interface. A tag that processes its body text must implement the `BodyTag` interface and usually extends `BodyTagSupport`.

Because the `BodyTag` interface extends the `Tag` interface, it includes the `doStartTag` and `doEndTag` methods. A tag implementing the `BodyTag` interface might still return `SKIP_BODY` from the `doStartTag` method to indicate that the JSP engine should not evaluate the text between the beginning and end of the tag. A body tag may also return EVAL_BODY_INCLUDE to include its body text or EVAL_BODY_BUFFERED if it wants to examine or manipulate the body content.

Body tags have a complex protocol for operating on body text. If the doStartTag method returns EVAL_BODY_BUFFERED, the JSP engine calls the doInitBody method in the custom tag before it starts evaluating the body text. There is no return value for doInitBody as it is intended for you to perform initialization in this method. After the JSP engine evaluates the body content, it calls doAfterBody in the custom tag. The custom tag can access the current body content by calling getBodyContent until the end of the invocation of doEndTag. If doAfterBody returns EVAL_BODY_AGAIN, the JSP engine reevaluates the current body content and calls doAfterBody again. The JSP engine finally accepts the content after doAfterBody returns SKIP_BODY.

Watch Out!

Avoid Infinite Loops

Make sure you always have a case where your doAfterBody method returns SKIP_BODY. If you return only EVAL_BODY_AGAIN, the JSP engine will get stuck in an infinite loop calling your doAfterBody method over and over.

Let's take a look at a very minimal body tag. Listing 16.8 shows a body tag that prints its body text to the response (in other words, it shows the text between its begin and end tags as if the tags weren't there).

LISTING 16.8 Source Code for TestBodyTag.java

```
package examples.taglibs;

import javax.servlet.jsp.tagext.*;
import javax.servlet.jsp.*;
import java.io.*;

public class TestBodyTag extends BodyTagSupport
{
    public int doStartTag()
        throws JspException
    {
        return EVAL_BODY_BUFFERED;
    }

    public int doEndTag()
    {
        return EVAL_PAGE;
    }

    public void doInitTag()
    {
    }
```

LISTING 16.8 Continued

```
    public int doAfterBody()
        throws JspException
    {
// Get the current body content
        BodyContent body = getBodyContent();

        try
        {
// Ask the body content to write itself out to the response.
            body.writeOut(body.getEnclosingWriter());
        }
        catch (IOException exc)
        {
            throw new JspException(exc.toString());
        }
// Tell the JSP engine that the body content has been evaluated.
        return SKIP_BODY;
    }
}
```

By the Way

Having Trouble with the Example?

If you are having trouble getting a body tag to work, see the "Q&A" section at the end of this hour.

In Listing 16.8, you see that you can write the body content into the response by calling `body.writeOut(body.getEnclosingWriter())`. The `body.writeOut` method writes the contents of the body to any `Writer` object. The `getEnclosingWriter` method returns the writer for the section of the response in which this body tag is contained. You can use `body.getReader` to get a `Reader` object that lets you read the contents of the body, or you can just call `body.getString` to return the body content as a string. In fact, an alternative way to write out the contents of a body is

```
body.getEnclosingWriter().println(body.getString());
```

Usually, you'll use the string representation or `Reader` to inspect or modify the tags content.

Handling Exceptions

If an exception is thrown during the processing of a custom tag, there's a good chance that the container will catch it, leaving you without a way to gracefully recover resources. For example, an exception might be thrown while the container is evaluating the body of your tag. Realizing that you might like additional control, the JSP specification defines an auxiliary interface that can be used to handle thrown exceptions. The `TryCatchFinally` interface provides two methods to help you out. `doCatch` is invoked when the container catches an exception that is thrown during the evaluation of a tag body, or in these methods: `doStartTag`, `doEndTag`, `doInitBody`, and `doAfterBody`. The method `doFinally` is always invoked after `doEndTag` regardless of whether an exception is thrown.

Accessing Tag Attributes

Just like regular tags, custom tags can have attributes. You need to provide `get` and `set` methods for each attribute. Although you enclose each attribute in quotes, you can have numeric attributes in your custom tag. The JSP engine performs the conversion automatically. Listing 16.9 shows a custom tag to display the first and last name of a person. The name displayed can be changed by attributes in the `<name>` tag.

LISTING 16.9 Source Code for `NameTag.java`

```
package examples.taglibs;

import javax.servlet.jsp.tagext.*;
import javax.servlet.jsp.*;
import java.io.*;

public class NameTag extends TagSupport
{
    protected String firstName = "First";
    protected String lastName = "Last";

    public int doStartTag()
        throws JspException
    {
        try
        {
            JspWriter out = pageContext.getOut();
            out.println(firstName + " " + lastName);
        }
        catch (IOException ioExc)
        {
            throw new JspException(ioExc.toString());
        }

        return SKIP_BODY;
    }

    public int doEndTag()
    {
        return EVAL_PAGE;
    }
```

LISTING 16.9 Continued

```
// Get/set methods, just like in a bean

    public String getFirstName() { return firstName; }
    public void setFirstName(String aName) { firstName = aName; }

    public String getLastName() { return lastName; }
    public void setLastName(String aName) { lastName = aName; }

}
```

Now, just putting the attributes in the tag is not enough. You must also configure the attributes in the TLD file. An `<attribute>` tag is used to define each attribute. The only required element within the `<attribute>` tag is a `<name>` tag that defines the name of the attribute. Several optional elements include the following: a `<required>` tag indicating whether the attribute is required; a `<type>` tag that defines the runtime type of the attribute; a `<description>` tag that is used to describe the attribute; and a tag called `<rtexprvalue>`. You might have noticed other JSP examples where a JSP expression (the `<%=` tag) was used to specify the value of a tag attribute. Evaluating custom tags where the attribute value can be generated at runtime is a difficult task for the JSP engine. Rather than allow all attribute expressions to be computed at runtime, the JSP engine wants you to explicitly mark the attributes whose values can be generated at runtime. Set the value of `<rtexprvalue>` to `yes` or `true` if you need the attribute to be evaluated at runtime. The value is `false` by default.

For the `<required>` tag, you can use values of `true` or `false`. The `<required>` tag is `false` by default, meaning that if you don't explicitly say otherwise, an attribute is optional.

A little later in this hour, we'll cover another subelement, the `<fragment>` tag. This element is used with newer constructs of custom tags.

Listing 16.10 shows the TLD file for the `NameTag` class.

LISTING 16.10 Source Code for `name.tld`

```
<?xml version="1.0" encoding="ISO-8859-1"?>

<taglib xmlns="http://java.sun.com/xml/ns/j2ee"
      xmlns:xsi="http://www.w3.org/2001/XMLSchema-instance"
      xsi:schemaLocation="http://java.sun.com/xml/ns/j2ee/web-jsptaglibrary_2_0.xsd"
      version="2.0">
```

LISTING 16.10 Continued

```
    <tlib-version>1.0</tlib-version>
    <short-name>name</short-name>
    <description>
        An example of a tag that uses attributes.
    </description>
    <tag>
      <name>name</name>
      <tag-class>examples.taglibs.NameTag</tag-class>
         <attribute>
             <name>firstName</name>
             <required>no</required>
         </attribute>
         <attribute>
             <name>lastName</name>
             <required>no</required>
         </attribute>
      <body-content>empty</body-content>
    </tag>
</taglib>
```

The `name.tld` file is similar to the other TLD files you have seen, except that this one defines attributes for its tag.

Using Dynamic Attributes

In addition to using attributes that are declared beforehand, custom tags can also make use of attributes whose names are unknown before runtime. Although this might seem strange, it makes it possible to build tags that are flexible and easier to reuse. Tags that support this kind of behavior are known as **dynamic attributes**. They implement the `DynamicAttributes` interface, which consists of only one method:

```
public void setDynamicAttribute(String uri, String localName,
    Object Value ) throws JSPException
```

`setDynamicAttribute` is called when a tag that has declared that it accepts dynamic attributes is passed an attribute that has not been declared in the TLD. You state that a tag can accept dynamic attributes by adding the `<tag>` subelement:

```
<dynamic-attributes>true</dynamic-attributes>
```

The custom tag is responsible for storing the names and values of any dynamic attributes. Listing 16.11 illustrates one way that a tag could save the name and value of an attribute.

LISTING 16.11 Partial Source Code for `dynamic.java`

```
private ArrayList names = new ArrayList();
private ArrayList values = new ArrayList();

public void setDynamicAttribute(String uri,
    String name, Object value ) throws JspException {
    names.add( name );
    values.add( value );
}
```

Adding Scripting Variables

Your custom tags can define scripting variables that are accessible to your JavaServer Pages. Variables can be declared as part of the TLD as illustrated in Listing 16.12.

LISTING 16.12 An Example of How to Declare a Variable in a TLD

```
<tag>
...
<variable>
<name-given>myVariable</name-given>
<variable-class>String</variable-class>
<declare>true</declare>
<scope>AT_END</scope>
<description>An example variable</description>
</variable>
...
</tag>
```

In this example `<name-given>` names the variable and `<variable-class>` identifies the type. When the `<declare>` element's value is true, it indicates that the tag is creating a new variable. Otherwise, it's using an existing variable.

The `<scope>` element defines the lifetime of the variable. A variable is made available for use at different points depending on the declared scope. A scope of `AT_BEGIN` means that the variable comes into existence with the beginning of the tag. A variable whose scope is `AT_END` is available after the end tag. Finally, a variable can have a lifetime for the duration between the start and end tags if its scope is `NESTED`.

You can also comment the variable with the optional <description>.

The tag is responsible for creating and updating an attribute of the same name that is used by the container to set the value of the scripting variable. This is done by simply calling the setAttribute method of pageContext with the name and value of the variable. For example, if you wanted to set the EL variable, var, you would do something like this:

```
pageContext.setAttribute("var", value);
```

The container would take care of creating and updating the EL variable. It will also manage the scope of the variable according to the scope defined.

By the Way

The Difference Between Variables and Attributes

It helps to keep variables and attributes "in their places" as you consider the text. Remember that JSPs have attributes where you can store objects. JSP actions are constructed using XML elements, which also have attributes. In this book we try to distinguish between them by calling them "action element attributes." Variables are programming entities that hold values that may change during execution. Both Java and EL have them. In this hour, we will refer to scripting variables simply as variables and point out when we're talking about other types.

If you want additional flexibility, you can also dynamically name the variable using an action element attribute. Instead of using the <name-given> element in the TLD, you use the <name-from-attribute> element. When you do this, the name of the attribute will be given by the content of the <name-from-attribute> element. For example, if the <tag> element contained a variable declaration that looks like

```
<name-from-attribute>myName</name-from-attribute>
```

and the tag appears in a JSP like

```
<mylib:myTag myName="foo"/>
```

then the attribute would be named foo. The container will use a set method (as explained in the section "Accessing Tag Attributes") to store the value of the action element attribute locally, and the tag will write the attribute using setAttribute and the value of foo for the name. The following example may help clarify things:

```
private String myName;
// set method used by container to store the value of the
// action element attribute, myName
```

```
public void setMyName(String aName) { myName = aName; }
...
// In one of the appropriate tag methods, set an attribute
// in the page context so that the container can create and
// update the EL variable
pageContext.setAttribute(myName, value);
...
```

When defining scripting variables, you can also use the `TagExtraInfo` class. All you need to do is create a special `TagExtraInfo` class that describes the scripting variables your tag might define.

Listing 16.13 shows a subclass of `TagExtraInfo` that defines a scripting variable called `scriptVar`.

LISTING 16.13 Source Code for `ScriptExtraInfo.java`

```
package examples.taglibs;

import javax.servlet.jsp.tagext.*;

public class ScriptExtraInfo extends TagExtraInfo
{
public VariableInfo[] getVariableInfo(TagData data)
    {
        return new VariableInfo[] {
                new VariableInfo("scriptVar", "java.lang.String",
                true, VariableInfo.AT_END) };
    }
}
```

`VariableInfo` is a class that describes a variable. Its constructor's signature includes the name of the variable, its type, whether it is a new variable, and a constant that declares the scope of the variable.

The tag itself doesn't need to know about the extra info class; the container uses it at translation time when it generates the underlying servlet. However, the custom tag needs to put the scripting variables into the page context so that the JavaServer Page can extract the value of each variable and place it in a local Java variable. Listing 16.14 shows a custom tag that puts a value into the page context.

LISTING 16.14 Source Code for `ScriptTag.java`

```
package examples.taglibs;

import javax.servlet.jsp.tagext.*;
import javax.servlet.jsp.*;
import java.io.*;
```

LISTING 16.14 Continued

```
public class ScriptTag extends TagSupport

{
    public int doStartTag()
        throws JspException
    {
        pageContext.setAttribute("scriptVar", "This is the script variable");

        return SKIP_BODY;
    }

    public int doEndTag()
    {
        return EVAL_PAGE;
    }
}
```

Listing 16.15 shows a JavaServer Page that calls the `ScriptTag` custom tag and then accesses `scriptVar` as if it were a local variable.

LISTING 16.15 Source Code for `TestScriptTag.jsp`

```
<%@ taglib uri="/scripttag" prefix="xx" %>
<html>
<body>
<xx:setVar/>
<h1><%= scriptVar %></h1>
</body>
</html>
```

By the Way

Variable Magic?

You might be wondering how a value gets from the page context into a Java variable automatically. It isn't as automatic as you might think. According to the JSP specification, the JSP engine is responsible for getting the value from the page context and copying it to the local variable. If you examine the servlet generated from a JSP that uses a tag-generated scripting variable, you'll see a line that copies the value out of the page context.

To match a `TagExtraInfo` class to its associated tag, you must include a `<teiclass>` element in the Tag Library Descriptor for the custom tag. Listing 16.16 shows the TLD for the `ScriptTag` class.

LISTING 16.16 Source Code for `scripttag.tld`

```
<?xml version="1.0" encoding="ISO-8859-1"?>

<taglib xmlns="http://java.sun.com/xml/ns/j2ee"
      xmlns:xsi="http://www.w3.org/2001/XMLSchema-instance"
      xsi:schemaLocation=
         "http://java.sun.com/xml/ns/j2ee/web-jsptaglibrary_2_0.xsd"
      version="2.0">
   <tlib-version>1.0</tlib-version>
   <short-name>scripttag</short-name>
   <description>
       An example scripting variable tag
   </description>
   <tag>
     <name>setVar</name>
        <tag-class>examples.taglibs.ScriptTag</tag-class>
        <tei-class>examples.taglibs.ScriptExtraInfo</tei-class>
        <body-content>empty</body-content>
   </tag>
</taglib>
```

The choice between using a `TagExtraInfo` class and declaring a variable in the TLD depends on the functionality that you need. Certainly, using `TagExtraInfo` is more work. However, you can dynamically declare the type and scope of the variable as well as the name. If you need this functionality, use `TagExtraInfo`. Otherwise, declaring a variable in the TLD is a better option.

By the Way

Having Trouble with the Example?

If you are having trouble defining scripting variables, see the "Q&A" section at the end of this hour.

The JSP 2.0 `SimpleTag` Interface

If you think there's a lot to remember to develop your own custom tags, you're right. Seizing an opportunity to make the task of developing custom tags easier, the JSP 2.0 specification introduced Simple Tag extensions. Simple Tag extensions provide two new ways to create custom tags:

- Through the use of Java and the `SimpleTag` interface
- By using tag files, which consist of JSP code that can be packaged and used as a custom tag

Watch Out!

Simple Tags, `SimpleTag`, and Simple Tag Extensions

Unfortunately, tags that implement the basic `Tag` interface are known as "Simple Tags." It can be difficult to distinguish between "Simple Tag" and "SimpleTag" and "Simple Tag extensions" unless you take some care, particularly when speaking to somebody or searching the Web.

In this section, we'll discuss the `SimpleTag` interface. Unlike classic tag handlers, `SimpleTag` does not extend `Tag` and thereby avoids the complex invocation protocols. `SimpleTag` declares only one method for handling the tag: `doTag`. Listing 16.17 shows the "Hello World" custom tag rewritten as a `SimpleTag` implementation.

LISTING 16.17 Source Code for `HelloWorldSimpleTag.java`

```
package examples.taglibs;
import javax.servlet.jsp.tagext.*;
import javax.servlet.jsp.*;
import java.io.*;

public class HelloWorldSimpleTag extends SimpleTagSupport
{
    public void doTag()
        throws JspException, IOException
    {
    getJspContext().getOut().write("Hello World");
    }
}
```

`SimpleTagSupport` is a utility class that provides default implementations for the methods of `SimpleTag` and serves as the base class. The method `getJspContext` returns a `JspContext`, which is similar to a `PageContext`. In fact, `JspContext` is the base class for `PageContext`. Its purpose is to abstract all information that isn't specific to servlets, making it possible to use `SimpleTag` outside of the context of a servlet. In this case, we're using the convenience method `getOut` to get to the current `JspWriter` stream.

For this example, the TLD looks the same as it would for a classic tag handler.

JSP Fragments

Working with body content using simple tags requires the use of **JSP fragments**. JSP fragments are exactly what they appear to be—pieces of JSP code. Written using standard JSP syntax, a fragment is translated into an implementation of the interface `JspFragment` for use by tag handlers. A JSP fragment is used to represent the body of a tag for use with a `SimpleTag` handler, or it represents the body of a `<jsp:attribute>` standard action when the attribute's value is declared to be of type `JspFragment`.

The `JspFragment` interface declares only two methods: `invoke` and `getJspContext`. You're already familiar with `getJspContext`. `Invoke` has the method signature

```
public void invoke(java.io.Writer out)
```

`Invoke` causes the fragment to be executed, writing the output produced to the `Writer` passed to it. You can invoke a fragment as many times as needed.

`Invoke` can throw a `SkipPageException`, which signals that the fragment has determined that the remainder of the page doesn't need to be evaluated.

Accessing the Body of a SimpleTag

Now that you understand the role of a JSP fragment, let's take a look at how to access the body of a SimpleTag. Listing 16.18 shows the example from Listing 16.6 rewritten to use a `SimpleTag` implementation.

LISTING 16.18 Source Code for `TestBodySimpleTag.java`

```
package examples.taglibs;
import javax.servlet.jsp.tagext.*;
import javax.servlet.jsp.*;
import java.io.*;

public class TestBodySimpleTag extends SimpleTagSupport
{
    public void doTag()
        throws JspException, IOException
    {
        getJspBody().invoke(null);
    }
}
```

Like the previous example, this example simply writes the body to the output stream. When the `Writer` given to `invoke` is `null`, the output from `invoke` goes to the `JspWriter` associated with the `JspContext` of the tag handler.

SimpleTagSupport provides the convenience method getJspBody to return the JspFragment generated for the body content.

Listing 16.19 demonstrates one way that a SimpleTag can obtain a copy of the body so that it can use or manipulate it.

LISTING 16.19 Source Code for TestBodySimpleTag2.java

```
package examples.taglibs;
import javax.servlet.jsp.tagext.*;
import javax.servlet.jsp.*;
import java.io.*;

public class TestBodySimpleTag2 extends SimpleTagSupport
{
   StringWriter sw = new StringWriter();

   public void doTag()
      throws JspException, IOException
    {
       getJspBody().invoke(sw);
       getJspContex().getOut().write(sw.toString());
    }
}
```

In this case, the output resulting from the invocation is first captured into a StringWriter before being written to the JspWriter associated with the tag.

TLDs for either of these examples vary slightly from the previous tags in that the <body-content> element of <tag> must now contain a value other than empty.

Listing 16.20 shows what the TLD for this tag might look like.

LISTING 16.20 Source Code for TestBodySimpleTag.tld

```
<?xml version="1.0" encoding="ISO-8859-1"?>

<taglib xmlns="http://java.sun.com/xml/ns/j2ee"
      xmlns:xsi="http://www.w3.org/2001/XMLSchema-instance"
      xsi:schemaLocation=
         "http://java.sun.com/xml/ns/j2ee/web-jsptaglibrary_2_0.xsd"
      version="2.0">
   <tlib-version>1.0</tlib-version>
   <short-name>testtag</short-name>
   <description>
       An example of a tag that invokes the body JspFragment
   </description>
   <tag>
     <name>testbody</name>
        <tag-class>examples.taglibs.TestBodySimpleTag </tag-class>
        <body-content>scriptless</body-content>
   </tag>
</taglib>
```

As you can see, the <body-content> value has been set to scriptless, which instructs JspFragment to evaluate the body content upon invocation. As you learned earlier, <body-content> can also be set to tagdependent, which causes JspFragment to produce the body content verbatim. Using scriptless in our example means that EL expressions and child actions will be evaluated to produce the results.

By now, you are probably impressed with the simplicity of tags based on the SimpleTag interface. In fact, you may wonder why you would ever use classic tags again. For most conditions, you'll probably use simple tags. The most notable exception occurs when the body content, or any fragment in general, contains a JSP expression or scriptlet; fragments must contain only template text and JSP action elements. However, with EL and tag extensions, it's not difficult to do this.

Using Attributes and Variables with SimpleTag

There's not much difference between classic and simple tag handlers when working with attributes or variables. The most significant change occurs because attributes may now have values that are JSP fragments. This means that you have to invoke the fragment. The rest of the mechanisms are the same. Like classic tag handlers, simple tag handlers must provide get and set methods for each attribute. The following code excerpt demonstrates how to do this:

```
public class UseAttributeSimpleTag extends SimpleTagSupport
{
   private JspFragment attribute;

   public void doTag()
      throws JspException, IOException
    {
       // Do some stuff  ...
       // Now invoke the fragment
       attribute.invoke( null );
       // Do some more ...
    }

public void setAttribute( JspFragment attribute ) {
      this.attribute = attribute;
    }
}
```

Configuring attributes that are JSP fragments in a TLD is as simple as adding a <fragment> element:

```
...
  <attribute>
     <name>attribute</name>
```

```
    <required>no</required>
    <fragment>true</fragment>
  </attribute
...
```

When you declare that a tag attribute is a fragment type, you are stating that the handler will be responsible for evaluating the attribute. Otherwise, the container will evaluate the attribute prior to passing it to the tag handler. Also, declaring an attribute to be a fragment means that the type of the attribute is fixed at `JspFragment`. It's an error to try and declare the type using a `<type>` element. In addition, `<rtexprvalue>` is also fixed to `true`.

All tags use dynamic attributes the same way, and you will be happy to know that the use of variables with simple tags does not change either.

Tag Files—Tag Extensions Without Java

Tag files make it possible for Web developers to create tag handlers without knowing Java. Tag files are created using JSP syntax and produce a tag handler at translation time. Let's jump right in and create our first tag file, as shown in Listing 16.21.

LISTING 16.21 Source Code for `HelloWorld.tag`

```
Hello World
```

Remarkably, that's all there is to it. The tag must have an extension of `.tag`. The source for a JSP that uses `HelloWorld.tag` is found in Listing 16.22.

LISTING 16.22 Source Code for `HelloWorld.jsp`

```
<%@ taglib prefix="tags" tagdir="/WEB-INF/tags" %>

<tags:HelloWorld />
```

To deploy a tag file, you can place it in one of two locations:

- In a JAR file installed in the `/WEB-INF/lib/` of the Web application. The tag file must be in the `META_INF/tags/` directory or a subdirectory of that directory.
- In the `/WEB-INF/tags/` directory (or a subdirectory of that directory) of the Web application.

If you elect to deploy your tag file (as part of an application or library) in a JAR file, you must create a TLD for it. A new element, `<tag-file>`, describes tags within a tag library. It consists of two subelements, `name` and `path`, which define the name of the tag and location of the tag file. `<tag-file>` is analogous to `<tag>`, and both can be used within the same tag library.

Tag File Directives

Like JSP pages, tag files also have directives. The `taglib` and `include` directives are identical. Tag files have these additional directives:

- `tag`
- `attribute`
- `variable`

The `tag` directive defines the overall tag characteristics. It's similar to the `page` directive. The `attribute` directive is used to declare custom action attributes. Lastly, the `variable` directive defines the variables that are exposed to the calling JSP or tag handler.

By the Way

For Additional Detail on Tag Directives

The current JSP specification provides a complete explanation of tag file directives and the standard actions used with tag files. This portion of the hour will provide you with the information you need to be able to effectively use tags. As an additional reference, you may want to consult the specification.

The `tag` Directive

The `tag` directive describes tag files. Like the `page` directive, there can be more than one `tag` directive in a translation unit, but there can be only one occurrence of any attribute/value, excepting the `import` attribute.

These attributes have the same syntax and semantics of the equivalent attribute in the `page` directive: `language`, `import`, `pageEncoding`, and `isELIgnored`.

The `display-name` attribute is a short name used by tools to identify the tag. It defaults to the name of the tag file, without the `.tag` extension.

The `body-content` and `dynamic-attributes` attributes are analogous to their counterparts in the tag library descriptor for tag extensions and use the same values.

Both small-icon and large-icon are intended to provide the location of an image that represents the tag as an icon in a tool.

A description gives the tag developer an opportunity to provide text that describes the tag. The developer can further document the tag by giving an example of how to use the tag in an example attribute.

The attribute Directive

As mentioned earlier, custom action attributes are declared using the attribute directive. Its own attributes correspond with the subelements of the attribute element in the TLD. Consequently, you're already familiar with them. They are name, required, fragment, rtexprvalue, type, and description.

The variable Directive

Within a tag file, scripting variables that are exposed to calling pages are defined by the variable directive. Like the attribute directive, its attributes mirror the subelements of the variable element in the TLD. They are name-given, name-from-attribute, variable-class, declare, scope, and description. One additional directive attribute, alias, works with name-from-attribute to define a locally scoped member variable in the tag handler that holds the value of the scripting variable. The container will synchronize the member variable with the scripting variable automatically, in much the same way that we did it manually when we discussed variables earlier.

Standard Actions Used with Tag Files

Two additional standard actions are necessary to work with tag files. There has to be a way to work with the body of the tag and another to work with attributes that are JSP fragments. <jsp:doBody> and <jsp:invoke> are standard actions that respectively evaluate the tag body and attributes that are fragments. The actions' syntax and semantics are nearly identical. Both operate on JSP fragments. The only difference appears because <jsp:doBody> does not need to identify the fragment it invokes. As a result, <jsp:invoke> has an additional action element attribute, fragment, which supplies the name of the fragment associated with the action.

The common action element attributes are var, varReader, and scope. var and varReader are used to store the result of the fragment invocation. The value of var is the name of a java.lang.String object, and the value of varReader is the name of a `java.io.Reader` object. These objects will be created by the container in the scope identified by `scope`. The possible values for `scope` are `page`, `request`, `session`, and `application`. The default scope is `page`. `var` and `varReader` cannot be used together. When neither is specified, the result of the invocation goes to the `JspWriter` of the `JspContext` associated with the `JspFragment`.

Using Tag Files

The simple example shown in Listing 16.23 demonstrates how to use tag files with fragment attributes.

LISTING 16.23 Source Code for `showtext.tag`

```
<%@ attribute name="italic" fragment="true" %>
<%@ attribute name="bold" fragment="true" %>
<%@ variable name-given="text" scope="NESTED" %>

<jsp:doBody var="text" />

<table border="0">
   <tr>
     <td>
        <jsp:invoke fragment="italic"/>
     </tdD>
   </tr>
   <tr>
     <td>
        <jsp:invoke fragment="bold"/>
     </td>
   </tr>
</table>
```

Examining `showtext.tag`, you can see that it declares two attributes that are fragments. It also declares a scripting variable, `text`, that becomes visible to the calling page for the time between the start and end tags of the custom tag. It then invokes the standard action `<jsp:doBody>`, saving the result to a page-scoped `String` object named `text`. This object is synchronized by the container with the scripting variable declared earlier. The bulk of the tag is template text to create a simple table. The content of the table detail (TD) elements is the output produced by attributes that are fragments. Listing 16.24 shows showtext.jsp.

LISTING 16.24 Source Code for showtext.jsp

```
<%@ taglib prefix="tags" tagdir="/WEB-INF/tags" %>

<tags:showtext>
    <jsp:attribute name="italic">
       <i>${text}</i>
   </jsp:attribute>

   <jsp:attribute name="bold">
      <b>${text}</b}
   </jsp:attribute>

   <jsp:body>
      Sample Text
   </jsp:body>
</tags:showtext>
```

The first act of showtext.jsp is to declare that it uses the custom tag that was created earlier and to give it a prefix of "tags". It then calls the tag handler, giving it two attributes and a body. Each of the attributes is designed to simply display the value of the text scripting variable in an italicized or bolded font. As you recall from Listing 16.20, the tag handler invokes the body and both attributes to produce the overall output.

Summary

Tag extensions are incredibly helpful to JSP developers. They allow you to create portable and reusable components that naturally fit into the structure of a JSP. In most cases, using tag extensions results in more flexible, easier-to-understand code.

The JSP 2.0 specification has made it much easier to build your own custom tags. While maintaining backward compatibility with JSP 1.2, it introduced the Simple Tag extensions, which greatly simplify the development and deployment of custom tags. The SimpleTag interface and its companion SimpleTagSupport reduce the complexity of writing custom tags in Java. With tag files, Web developers can author tag extensions without knowing Java. Several other useful features make tag extensions very versatile. For example, through dynamic attributes, tags can now work with an unknown number of attributes of varying classes.

Q&A

Q. ***Why do I see my custom tag in the HTML output?***

A. You most likely forgot to put the `taglib` directive at the top of the page. You also might not have remembered to use the prefix you defined in the `taglib` directive, or you mistyped the prefix or the tag name.

Q. ***Why do I get a compile error when I use a custom tag?***

A. Well, the first thing to check is that it's really the tag that's causing the problem. Try removing the tag and see whether that clears up the problem. Next, make sure that you have installed the tag library on the Web server. The class files should be under the `WEB-INF/classes` directory. (`WEB-INF` must be capitalized, so don't count on `web-inf` working the same way.) Also make sure you have a TLD file and that the `web.xml` file in the `WEB-INF` directory has the correct pathname for the TLD.

Q. ***Why do I get a runtime error when I try to set an attribute value?***

A. There is probably some mismatch between the attribute type in the custom tag and the attribute value you are trying to set. For instance, trying to store the string "Fred" into an integer value isn't going to work.

Q. ***I created*** `get` ***and*** `set` ***methods, so why doesn't the JSP engine recognize my attributes?***

A. Don't forget that you must also define the names of the attributes in the TLD file.

Q. ***When I use a body tag, why does the JSP engine stop responding?***

A. You are probably stuck in an infinite loop caused by your `doAfterBody` method returning `EVAL_BODY_AGAIN`, instead of `SKIP_BODY`, over and over.

Q. ***I tried to write out some code in*** `<% %>` ***and reevaluated the body text. Why do the*** `<% %>` ***tags show up in the output?***

A. Remember, the JSP engine parses the body text only one time. It might evaluate custom tags in the body text multiple times, but after the text is parsed, that's it.

Q. ***I rewrote the body text and returned*** `EVAL_BODY_AGAIN`***. Why do I still see the original body text?***

A. Again, the JSP engine parses the body text only once. You will always receive the original body text in `doAfterBody`.

Q. ***I put a value in the page context, so why doesn't the JSP have a variable to hold the value?***

A. You might have forgotten to create the `TagExtraInfo` object, or you forgot to link the `TagExtraInfo` object to the tag class by adding a `<teiclass>` item in the TLD file.

Workshop

The Workshop is designed to help you review what you have learned and help you further increase your understanding of the material covered in this hour.

Quiz

1. What are some of the advantages of using tags?
2. What is the primary difference between SimpleTag and classic tag handlers?
3. What is a JSP fragment?
4. What is a Tag file?

Answers

1. Tags provide a mechanism for creating natural, reusable elements in JSPs. They also allow you to encapsulate functionality, which makes it possible to develop cleaner, more maintainable applications. Tags can also abstract complex operations.
2. A `SimpleTag` has a much simpler invocation protocol with only one method, `doTag()`. Functionally, they're nearly equivalent.
3. A JSP fragment is a segment of JSP code intended for use within a larger component.
4. A Tag file is source file, created using JSP syntax, which is used to produce a tag handler at translation time. It's not necessary to know Java to create a Tag file. Tag files can be deployed by simply copying them to the appropriate location. They have been designed to greatly simplify the creation and deployment of tags.

Activities

1. Write a few tags, using the `SimpleTag` interface, that provide common functions such as outputting the date and time or formatting text. Use them in a JSP.
2. Write a custom tag that interfaces to the shopping cart from Hour 13.

HOUR 17

The JSP Standard Tag Library

What You'll Learn in This Hour:

- How to install and use JSTL
- How to use the Core Tag Library
- How to use the Function Library

One of the goals of tag libraries is to make it easier to create and edit JSPs with automated tools. The presence of Java code within a JSP makes it difficult to parse a JSP, because Java's syntax is considerably more complex than HTML or XML. Because JSP tags use XML's syntax rules, automated XML and HTML editors can process the tags easily.

When you use custom tags, you often find that you still need to insert Java code to display values or execute loops. The Java Standard Tag Library (JSTL) reduces the need for embedded Java code by providing tags that perform many common functions. By using JSTL in conjunction with custom tags, it is possible to write fairly complex JSPs without writing any Java.

JSTL interoperates with JavaBeans defined by the `<jsp:useBean>` tag, as well as any variables defined by custom tags.

Installing and Using JSTL

The Apache Jakarta project includes a good implementation of JSTL (`http://jakarta.apache.org/taglibs/index.html`). Sun's JSTL page (`http://java.sun.com/products/jsp/jstl`) contains a link to the Apache implementation, as well as documentation for JSTL. The Jakarta implementation of JSTL keeps pace with the JSTL standard, so by the time a new version of the JSTL standard comes out, Jakarta already has a working version. The Jakarta JSTL implementation contains a number of JAR files. To include JSTL in your Web application, simply include these files in your WEB-INF/lib directory.

Depending on your version of Java, you may need to install additional JAR files. For example, if you use a JDK older than version 1.3, you may need an XML parser. You can place any additional JAR files in the WEB-INF/lib directory as well.

JSTL consists of four separate tag libraries: Core, XML, SQL, and Fmt (formatting) and a functions library. To use any of these libraries, you must include a taglib directive at the top of each JSP that uses the library.

To use the Core library, use the following directive:

```
<%@ taglib prefix="c" uri="http://java.sun.com/jstl/core" %>
```

The prefix attribute specifies the prefix used in the tag name for a particular library. For example, the Core library includes a tag named out. When combined with a prefix of c, the full tag would be <c:out>. You are free to use any prefix you like, but you must use different prefixes for each of the four standard tag libraries.

To use the XML library, use the directive

```
<%@ taglib prefix="x" uri="http://java.sun.com/jstl/xml" %>
```

To use the SQL library, use the directive

```
<%@ taglib prefix="sql" uri="http://java.sun.com/jstl/sql" %>
```

To use the Fmt library, use the directive

```
<%@ taglib prefix="fmt" uri="http://java.sun.com/jstl/fmt" %>
```

To use the Functions library, use the directive

```
<%@ taglib prefix="fn" uri="http://java.sun.com/jstl/functions" %>
```

You must also put the corresponding .tld file for each tag library in your WEB-INF directory and use the <taglib> in your web.xml file element to include the tag library:

```
<taglib>
    <taglib-uri>http://java.sun.com/jstl/core</taglib-uri>
    <taglib-location>/WEB-INF/tld/core.tld</taglib-location>
</taglib>
```

Core Tag Library

The Core tag library contains tags for getting, setting, and displaying attribute values; executing tags conditionally; and iterating through collections.

General-Purpose Tags

The general-purpose tags let you add and remove variables, display variable values, and enclose a group of tags within a try-catch block.

The <c:out> Tag

The <c:out> tag displays the result of an expression, similar to the way <%= %> works. There are three main differences between <c:out> and <%= %>. First, the <c:out> tag lets you use the simpler "." notation to access properties. To access customer.address.street from <%= %>, the expression would be <%= customer.getAddress().getStreet() %>. The equivalent <c:out> tag is <c:out value="customer.address.street"/>. The second difference is that the <c:out> tag can automatically escape XML tags so they aren't evaluated as actual tags. For example, if you want to display the string <hello> in an XML file, you must either use <hello> or <[CDATA[<hello>]]>. The <c:out> tag includes an attribute called escapeXML, which, if true, automatically escapes the text to prevent it from being evaluated as XML; for example,

```
<c:out value="customer.address.street" escapeXML="true"/>
```

The third difference between <c:out> and <%= %> is the most significant. The <c:out> tag lets you specify a default value to display if the result of the value expression is null. When you use <%= %> to display a null value, it prints out the word null. The <c:out> tag lets you specify a value such as N/A or None or even just a blank to display for null values. You can specify the default value two ways. First, you can use the default attribute, like this:

```
<c:out value="customer.address.street" default="N/A"/>
```

The second option is to specify the default value as the content of the <c:out> tag:

```
<c:out value="customer.address.street">
    No address available
</c:out>
```

The <c:out> tag can be used to display default values for the results from other tag operations. For example, the <fmt:formatDate> tag allows you to store a formatted date in a variable. If the date is null, the value of the variable is null. Although <fmt:formatDate> doesn't have a default attribute, you can use <c:out> to display the formatted date with a default value:

```
<fmt:formatDate var="dateVar" value="${dueDate}/>
<c:out value="${dateVar}" default="No due date specified"/>
```

The <c:set> Tag

The <c:set> attribute lets you create new variables that hold the results of an EL expression. There are two basic variations of <c:set>, each with two ways to specify a value. First, you can set a particular variable with the form

```
<c:set var="variableName" value="expression"/>
```

In this case, the <c:set> tag evaluates the value expression and assigns it to a variable named by the var attribute. The following expression is an example of this:

```
<c:set var="custAddr" value="${customer.address}"/>
```

Rather than using the value attribute, you can also use the body content of the <c:set> tag to specify the value. The interesting thing about specifying a value in the body tag is that you can use other tags, such as <c:out>, in the body; for example,

```
<c:set var="custAddr>
   <c:out value="${customer.address.street}"/><p>
   <c:out value="${customer.address.city}"/>
   <c:out value="${customer.address.state}"/>,
   <c:out value="${customer.address.zip}"/>
</c:set>
```

By default, the scope of a variable in <c:set> is the page scope. You can explicitly specify the scope with the scope attribute. For example, to store the custAddr variable under the session scope, use

```
<c:set var="custAddr" scope="session" value="${customer.address}"/>
```

The <c:set> tag also lets you set individual property values by following this form:

```
<c:set target="bean-or-map-variable" property="propertyName"
    value="expression"/>
```

In this case, the `target` attribute is an expression that must return either a JavaBean or a map. For example, the following code snippet stores a HashMap in the `request` object, then sets a property value in the HashMap by using `<c:set>`:

```
<%
    request.setAttribute("mymap", new java.util.HashMap());
%>
<c:set target="${mymap}" property="myvalue" value="12345"/>
<c:out value="${mymap.myvalue}"/>
```

Again, you can use either the `value` attribute or the body content to set the property's value.

If the `value` expression evaluates to `null` and you use the `var` attribute, the variable is removed from the scope (either the scope specified by the `scope` attribute or the first scope where the variable was found). When you use the `target` or `property` attributes when `value` is null, if the target is a HashMap, the property is removed from the map; and if the target is a JavaBean, the property is set to null.

Also, the `<c:set>` tag performs any necessary type conversions. If a property type is `int` or `double`, for example, the `<c:set>` tag tries to convert a string value to an `int` or a `double`.

Listing 17.1 shows a simple example of `<c:set>` and `<c:out>`.

LISTING 17.1 Source Code for `coutdemo.jsp`

```
<%@ page import="java.util.HashMap" %>
<%@ taglib prefix="c" uri="http://java.sun.com/jstl/core" %>
<html>
<body>
<%
    HashMap person = new HashMap();
    person.put("address", new HashMap());
    request.setAttribute("fred", person);
    ((HashMap) person.get("address")).
        put("street", "123 Blah Blahlevard");
%>
<c:out value="${fred.address.street}"/>
<c:set target="${fred.address}" property="city" value="Blahse"/>
<c:out value="${fred.address.city}"/>
<c:set var="cityName">The city value is
    <c:out value="${fred.address.city}"/>.</c:set>
<p>
CityName=<c:out value="${cityName}"/>
<c:set target="${fred}" property="name" value="Fred Fredrickson"/>
<p><c:out value="${fred.name}"/>
</body>
</html>
```

The <c:remove> Tag

The <c:remove> tag removes a variable from either a specified scope or the first scope where the variable is found (if no scope is specified). For example, to remove the variable custAddr from the session scope, use

```
<c:remove var="custAddr" scope="session"/>
```

The <c:catch> Tag

The <c:catch> tag lets you surround a set of tags by a try-catch block. One of the main reasons for using this tag is that you may evaluate some expressions that result in a NullPointerException. For example, if you have the expression customer.address.street and the address property is null, you will get a NullPointerException; for example,

```
<c:catch>
   <c:out value="${customer.address.street}"/><p>
   <c:out value="${customer.address.city}"/>
   <c:out value="${customer.address.state}"/>,
   <c:out value="${customer.address.zip}"/>
</c:catch>
```

If you need to access the exception itself, you can use the var attribute to specify a variable name to hold the exception. Unlike <c:set> tag, you can't specify a scope for the exception attribute—it always has a scope of page. The following code provides an example:

```
<c:catch var="exc">
   <c:out value="${customer.name.first}"/>
</c:catch>
```

Conditional Tags

The conditional tags make it easy for you to display text under only certain conditions.

The <c:if> Tag

The <c:if> tag evaluates an expression and displays its body content only if the expression evaluates to true. For example, the following displays an address only if customer.address is not null:

```
<c:if test="${customer.address != null}">
   <c:out value="${customer.address.street}"/><p>
</c:if>
```

You can also use the empty operator to test for null:

```
<c:if test="${!empty customer.address">
   <c:out value="${customer.address.street}"/><p>
</c:if>
```

When you use <c:if> to evaluate an expression, you can store the evaluation's result into a variable by using the var attribute (and optionally the scope attribute):

```
<c:if test="${!empty customer.address}" var="custNotNull"
    scope="session">
   <c:out value="${customer.address.street}"/><p>
</c:if>
```

If you don't specify a scope, the default is the page scope. You can use <c:if> to evaluate an expression and set a value without specifying any body content:

```
<c:if test="${!empty customer.address}" var="custNotNull"/>
```

This is equivalent to the following expression:

```
<c:set var="custNotNull" value="${!empty customer.address}"/>
```

The <c:choose> Tag

The <c:choose> tag works like a Java switch statement in that it lets you choose between a number of alternatives. Where the switch statement has case statements, the <c:choose> tag has <c:when> tags. In a switch statement, you can specify a default clause to specify a default action in case none of the cases match. The <c:choose> equivalent of default is <c:otherwise>, for example,

```
<c:choose>
    <c:when test="${emp.salary <= 0}">
        Sorry, no pay for you!
    </c:when>
    <c:when test="${emp.salary < 10000}>
        I'm going to have to ask you to
        come in on Saturday...
    </c:when>
    <c:otherwise>
        Yes sir! Whatever you say, sir!
    </c:otherwise>
</c:when>
```

As you can see, the <c:choose> tag makes up for the lack of a <c:else> in the <c:if> tag. The <c:choose> tag looks for the first <c:when> tag that evaluates to true. Although it is possible for multiple <c:when> clauses to evaluate to true, only the first one that evaluates to true is processed. See the following code as an example:

```
<c:choose>
   <c:when test="${emp.firstName == 'John' &&
      emp.lastName == "Smith"}>
         Hello John!
   </c:when>
   <c:when test="${emp.lastName == "Smith"}">
      Hello, Mr. Smith!
   </c:when>
</c:choose>
```

In this case, for the name John Smith, even though the name matches both <c:when> clauses, the code displays only “Hello John!” but not “Hello, Mr. Smith.”

Iterator Tags

The iterator tags iterate through collections or tokens, or for a fixed number of times. Not only do the tags perform looping functions, but they can also return a loop status variable as well as store the current member of the collection in a variable.

The <c:forEach> Tag

The <c:forEach> tag can iterate for a fixed number of times, similar to a Java for loop, and can also iterate over a collection of items. In both cases, the optional var attribute specifies the variable that holds the current loop variable. When iterating for a fixed number of times, the loop variable is the numeric loop index. When iterating through a collection, the loop variable is the current member of the collection.

To iterate a fixed number of times, specify start and end attributes. You can also specify a step attribute to indicate how much to increment the loop index each time. The default step value is 1. For example, to loop 10 times, use the following:

```
<c:forEach var="i" start="1" end="10">
   Item <c:out value="${i}/><p>
</c:forEach>
```

To iterate through a collection, use the items attribute to specify the collection. The items attribute must be an EL expression that evaluates to an object that implements the Collection interface:

```
<c:forEach var="emp" items="employees">
   Employee: <c:out value="${emp.name}"/>
</c:forEach/>
```

You can also use the start, end, and step attributes in conjunction with collections to iterate through only a specific part of a collection.

The <c:forTokens> Tag

The <c:forTokens> tag takes a string of tokens separated by one or more delimiters and splits them into individual tokens. The items attribute specifies the string to tokenize and the delimiters attribute specifies a list of delimiters (similar to the way java.util.StringTokenizer works). For example:

```
<c:forTokens items="moe,larry,curly" delimiters=","
   var="stooge">
   <c:out value="${stooge}/><p>
</c:forTokens>
```

As with the <c:forEach> tag, you can specify start, end, and step to iterate through only a portion of the tokens.

Loop Status

Both the <c:forEach> and <c:forTokens> tags can provide a loop status variable that lets you examine various aspects of the loop. In both tags, you supply a variable name with the varStatus attribute. The value stored in the varStatus attribute implements the LoopTagStatus interface.

The LoopTagStatus interface provides the methods shown in Table 17.1.

TABLE 17.1 LoopTagStatus **Interface Methods**

Method	Description
Object getCurrent()	Returns the current loop object (the collection member, token, or index (if performing a fixed-length loop).
int getIndex()	Returns the current loop index, starting at 0. Even for a fixed loop, the index is 0 the first time through, regardless of the loop's start value.
int getCount()	Returns the count of the iteration, starting at 1. The count is really just index + 1.
boolean isFirst()	Returns true if this is the first member of the collection, token list, or fixed list of numbers.
boolean isLast()	Returns true if this is the last member of the collection, token list, or fixed list of numbers.
Integer getBegin()	Returns the value specified by the begin attribute.
Integer getEnd()	Returns the value specified by the end attribute.
Integer getStep()	Returns the value specified by the step attribute.

URL-Related Tags

JSTL provides several tags for handling URLs and accessing Web resources. URLs can be difficult to work with when you must worry about URL rewriting (to insert the session ID when the browser doesn't support cookies), URL encoding of parameters, and referencing resources from a separate servlet context within the same servlet container.

The `<c:url>` Tag

The `<c:url>` tag formats a URL into a string and stores it into a variable. The `<c:url>` tag automatically performs URL rewriting when necessary. The `var` attribute specifies the variable that will contain the formatted URL. The optional scope attribute specifies the scope of the variable (page is the default). The value attribute specifies the URL to be formatted:

```
<c:url var="trackURL" value="/tracking.html"/>
```

If the browser doesn't support cookies, the resulting URL will include a parameter containing the session ID. The URL may be a relative URL such as `form.html`, a context-relative URL such as `/welcome.jsp`, or an absolute URL such as `http://www.wutka.com/data.xml` or `ftp://ftp.wutka.com/data.xml`, although, as a security precaution, the URL is only rewritten for relative URLs.

To specify a context-relative URL within a separate servlet context within the same servlet container, specify the other context with the `context` attribute. For example, suppose you have installed a Web application in your servlet container with a context of `"/tracking"`. To access a URL within the `"/tracking"` context, you can use this:

```
<c:url var="trackURL" value="/track.jsp" context="/tracking"/>
```

You can include parameters in the formatted URL by putting `<c:param>` tags inside the `<c:url>` tag. The `<c:param>` tag does any necessary URL encoding. Within a `<c:param>` tag, the `name` attribute indicates the parameter name, and the `value` attribute indicates the parameter value:

```
<c:url value="/track.jsp" var="trackingURL">
   <c:param name="trackingId" value="1234"/>
   <c:param name="reportType" value="summary"/>
</c:url>
```

The <c:import> Tag

The <c:import> tag is similar to the <jsp:import> tag, but it is much more powerful. For example, the <jsp:import> tag usually just imports resources from within the same servlet container. The <c:import> tag can import data from other servers as well as from within the same container. Also, the <jsp:import> tag automatically inserts the imported content directly into the JSP. Although the <c:import> tag can automatically insert content, it can also return the content as either a string or a reader.

The only required attribute in the <c:import> tag is `url`, which specifies the URL to be imported. As with the <c:url> tag, the URL may be a relative URL, a context-relative URL, or an absolute URL.

The advantage of specifying the alternate context instead of just using an absolute URL is that the <c:import> tag can use a `RequestDispatcher` to access the URL rather than using the URL class. The `RequestDispatcher` is more efficient than the URL class because it doesn't go through as many layers of processing.

To retrieve the contents of a URL as a string, use the `var` attribute to specify a variable that will contain the string and, optionally, a scope of `page`, `request`, `session`, or `application` via the `scope` attribute. As usual, the default scope is `page`. If necessary, you can specify a character encoding as well with the `charEncoding` attribute.

The following sequence of tags retrieves the contents of a URL as a string, and then displays the string:

```
<c:import var="data" url="/data.xml"/>
<c:out value="${data}/>
```

The previous two tags are essentially equivalent to the following tag, except that the previous tags leave the contents of the URL in a variable called `data`:

```
<c:import url="/data.xml"/>
```

The `varReader` attribute specifies the name of a variable that will contain a reader that reads the contents of the URL. Again, you can specify a scope with the `scope` attribute and a character encoding with the `charEncoding` attribute:

```
<c:import url="/data.xml" varReader="dataReader" scope="session"/>
```

You can use the <c:param> tag within a <c:import> tag, except in the case where you use the `varReader` tag to obtain a reader. The reason you can't use <c:param> with a reader is that the <c:import> tag creates the reader immediately—that is, before it processes the <c:param> tags. Because the <c:param> tags modify the URL, however, this means that the <c:import> tag needs to access a URL containing the parameters before it actually processes the <c:param> tags.

If you need to pass parameters to a <c:import> tag, use the <c:url> tag to create the URL first:

```
<c:url value="/track.jsp" var="trackingURL">
   <c:param name="trackingId" value="1234"/>
   <c:param name="reportType" value="summary"/>
</c:url>
<c:import url="${trackingURL}"/>
```

The `<c:redirect>` Tag

The `<c:redirect>` tag redirects the browser to an alternate URL. The advantage of using `<c:redirect>` rather than `response.sendRedirect` is that `<c:redirect>` automatically performs URL rewriting, it supports context-relative URLs, and it supports the `<c:param>` tag.

The `url` parameter specifies the URL to redirect to, and the optional `context` attribute specifies a context for a context-relative URL. The following code is an example:

```
<c:redirect url="http://www.wutka.com"/>
```

Functions

Version 2.0 of the JSP specification introduced the notion of functions to the JSP expression language. JSTL includes a number of standard functions, most of which are common string manipulation functions.

The `fn:contains` Function

The `fn:contains` function returns `true` if a string contains a specified substring. The format of the function is

```
fn:contains(string_to_search, string_to_find)
```

For example, `fn:contains("Abracadabra", "brac")` returns `true`, and `fn:contains("Abracadabra", "kazam")` returns `false`. If either argument is `null`, it is treated as an empty string.

The fn:containsIgnoreCase Function

Like the fn:contains function, the fn:containsIgnoreCase function returns true if a string contains a specified substring. The fn:containsIgnoreCase function, however, ignores the case of the strings when performing the search. The format of the function is

```
fn:containsIgnoreCase(string_to_search, string_to_find)
```

For example, fn:containsIgnoreCase("Abracadabra", "BRAC") returns true, and fn:containsIgnoreCase("Abracadabra", "kAzAm") returns false. If either argument is null, it is treated as an empty string.

The fn:endsWith Function

The fn:endsWith function returns true if a string ends with a specified substring. The format of the function is

```
fn:endsWith(string_to_search, string_to_find)
```

For example, fn:endsWith("Abracadabra", "abra") returns true, whereas fn:endsWith("Abracadabra", "Abra") returns false. If either argument is null, it is treated as an empty string.

The fn:escapeXml Function

The fn:escapeXml function returns an XML-safe equivalent of another string. The function performs the same operations as the escapeXml attribute in the <c:out> tag and replaces the characters <, >, &, ' (apostrophe/single quote), and " (double quote) with their XML equivalents (<, >, &, ', and ", respectively). The format of the function is

```
fn:escapeXml(string)
```

For example, fn:escapeXml("<Hello>") returns "<Hello>".

The fn:indexOf Function

The fn:indexOf function returns the first location of a substring within the specified string (similar to the indexOf function in java.lang.String. The format of the function is

```
fn:indexOf(string_to_search, string_to_find)
```

For example, `fn:indexOf("Abracadabra", "brac")` returns `1`, and `fn:contains("Abracadabra", "kazam")` returns `-1`. If either argument is `null`, it is treated as an empty string. Unlike the `indexOf` function in the `String` class, `fn:indexOf` does not let you specify the start location for the search—the function always starts at position 0.

The `fn:join` Function

The `fn:join` function joins each string in an array of strings together into a single string, separated by a given specifier. The format is

```
fn:join(strings[], separator)
```

For example, if the array `stooges` contains "Moe", "Larry", "Curly", and "Shemp", `fn:join(stooges, ";")` returns "Moe;Larry;Curly;Shemp". If the separator is `null` or an empty string, there is no separator. For example, `fn:join(stooges, "")` returns "MoeLarryCurlyShemp".

The `fn:length` Function

The `fn:length` function returns the length of a collection or a string. The format is

```
fn:length(collection_or_string)
```

Invoking `fn:length` on a `null` value results in a length of 0.

The `fn:replace` Function

The `fn:replace` function replaces all occurrences of one substring in a specified string with a replacement string and returns the result. The format is

```
fn:replace(original_string, string_to_find, replacement_string)
```

For example, `fn:replace("Abracadabra", "bra", "ZZZ")` returns "AZZZcadaZZZ". If any of the arguments are `null`, they are treated as empty strings.

The `fn:split` Function

The `fn:split` function splits a string into an array of substrings based on a set of separators. The function works like the `StringTokenizer` class, only it returns an array of token strings rather than an iterator. The format is

```
fn:split(string, token_string)
```

For example, `fn:split("Moe,Larry,Curly", ",")` returns a three-element array containing “Moe”, “Larry”, and “Curly”.

The `fn:startsWith` Function

The `fn:startsWith` function returns `true` if a string starts with a specified substring. The format of the function is

```
fn:startsWith(string_to_search, string_to_find)
```

For example, `fn:startsWith("Abracadabra", "Abra")` returns `true`, and `fn:startsWith ("Abracadabra", "dabra")` returns `false`. If either argument is `null`, it is treated as an empty string.

The `fn:substring` Function

The `fn:substring` function returns the portion of a string from a given starting position up to, but not including, a given ending position. The format is

```
fn:substring(string, starting_pos, ending_pos)
```

For example, `fn:substring("Abracadabra", 2, 5)` returns “rac”. If the end index is less than 0 or greater than the length of the string, it is treated as the length of the string. If the starting position is less than 0, it is treated as 0.

The `fn:substringAfter` Function

The `fn:substringAfter` function searches a string for a specific substring and returns the portion of the string immediately after the substring. The format is

```
fn:substringAfter(string_to_search, string_to_find)
```

For example, `fn:substringAfter("http://www.wutka.com", "http://")` returns “www.wutka.com”.

The `fn:substringBefore` Function

The `fn:substringBefore` function searches a string for a specific substring and returns the portion of the string immediately before the substring. The format is

```
fn:substringBefore(string_to_search, string_to_find)
```

For example, `fn:substringBefore("http://www.wutka.com", ":/")` returns “http”.

The `fn:toLowerCase` Function

The `fn:toLowerCase` function returns the lowercase equivalent of a string. The format is

```
fn:toLowerCase(string)
```

For example, `fn:toLowerCase("AbRaCaDaBrA")` returns "abracadabra".

The `fn:toUpperCase` Function

The `fn:toUpperCase` function returns the uppercase equivalent of a string. The format is

```
fn:toUpperCase(string)
```

For example, `fn:toUpperCase("AbRaCaDaBrA")` returns "ABRACADABRA".

The `fn:trim` Function

The `fn:trim` function removes any leading or trailing whitespace from a string and returns the result. The format is

```
fn:trim(string)
```

For example, `fn:trim("   Hello   ")` returns "Hello".

Q&A

Q. ***Why do the JSTL tags show up in my document?***

A. You probably forgot the `taglib` directive. Without the directive, the JSP engine doesn't recognize the tags as custom tags. Instead, the JSP engine just writes them out as part of the document.

Q. ***Why can't the JSP engine find the JSTL tags?***

A. Make sure that all the required JAR files are in the Web application's `WEB-INF` directory. If you are using Tomcat, you can put them in the `common/lib` directory underneath the main Tomcat directory.

Q. ***I am using Struts and it provides many of the same capabilities as JSTL, which should I use?***

A. There is no reason why you can't use both, but in the interest of code maintenance, if the Struts tags provide all the capabilities you need, stick with them.

Workshop

The Workshop is designed to help you review what you have learned, and help you to further increase your understanding of the material covered in this hour.

Quiz

1. What steps do you need to take before you can use JSTL in a JSP?
2. What JSTL tag would you use to write the value of a variable?
3. How do you find the length of a collection or a string?

Answers

1. Copy the JSTL JAR file(s) to your `WEB-INF/lib` directory, then add a `<taglib>` declaration to your `web.xml` file. Finally, add a `<% taglib %>` declaration to the top of your JSP.
2. The `<c:out>` tag writes out the value of a variable and can also display a default value if the variable is `null`.
3. The JSTL functions library provides a number of utility functions, including `fn:length`, which returns the length of a string or a collection.

Activities

1. Create a JSP that uses the `<c:set>` tag to store several variables in the current request (use "request" as the scope name), and then forwards to a second JSP. In the second JSP, use the `<c:out>` tag to display the variables you stored.
2. Create a JSP that uses `<c:forEach>` and `<c:out>` to display the request header variables. Use the implicit `header` and `headerValues` objects to enumerate through the header names and their values.

HOUR 18

Working with Databases and JSTL Database Actions

What You'll Learn in This Hour:

- The basics of SQL and types of SQL statements
- How to use JDBC from JavaServer Pages and Servlets
- How to use JavaBeans from JavaServer Pages
- How to use the JSTL SQL tag library

This hour briefly introduces the concept of databases, SQL, and JDBC. In no way will this hour make you an expert in SQL or JDBC, but it will point you in the right direction to learn these technologies, if you don't already know them.

The hour will focus on how you can use JDBC from within JavaServer Page. You will learn about scriptlets and JavaBeans as a way to access databases through JDBC. You will dig deep into the use of the JSTL database actions that are part of the JSTL tag libraries that were introduced in the previous hour.

A Brief Overview of Databases

A **database** is a collection of some information that is stored over time in a structured format for retrieval at a later time. This is a vague definition, but by this definition, even a simple file system is an example of a database. This is reasonably accurate.

In practice, a system that allows for the storing of information and some capabilities to manage that data is referred to as a database. Thus, a database can be defined as a system that

- Supports the creation and management of data using some data structure.
- Supports a means of data entry into the data structure.
- Supports a means for searching and retrieving the data.
- Supports the manipulation of the data (editing, deleting, and so on).

What Is SQL?

Structured Query Language, or **SQL**, is the successor of an IBM product called SEQUEL, for Structured English Query Language. SQL is an ANSI (American National Standards Institute) standard computer language that allows developers to access and manipulate a database system. It has been widely adopted as the language of choice to work with all the leading databases such as MS Access, DB2, Informix, MS SQL Server, Oracle, Sybase, and Cloudscape. SQL includes commands to create and manage databases. SQL as a language can be broken into several smaller components as explained in the next sections.

SQL Data Types

SQL supports a variety of different data types that map to the different types of data that can be stored in the database. These include data types such as binary, bit, char, datetime, float, integer, varchar, and several others.

Various Java data types, such as String, Long, Float, byte, short, and so on, are mapped to the SQL data types so that you can move data from SQL queries into Java objects. Every database has a slightly different mapping of Java data structures to SQL data types.

SQL Data Definition Language

The **Data Definition Language**, or **DDL**, is used to create and modify a database. DDL includes commands such as `CREATE`, `ALTER`, and `DROP`. The `CREATE` command is used to create a database and the definition of the tables and columns for each table. The `ALTER` command is used to alter the tables within a database. The `DROP` command is used to delete the database and all its contents.

Some examples of the various DDL commands are

- `CREATE DATABASE` *`databaseName`*

  This creates a database with the given name.

- `CREATE TABLE` *`tableName`* `(` *`columnName dataType`*`,...)`

  This creates a table in the database with the given definition of columns and the data type for each column.

- `ALTER TABLE` *`tableName`* `ADD` *`columnName dataType`*

  This modifies a table definition to add a column.

- `ALTER TABLE` *`tableName`* `DROP` *`columnName`*

  This modifies a table definition to delete a column.

- `DROP DATABASE` *`databaseName`*

  This deletes the database.

- `DROP TABLE` *`tableName`*

  This deletes a particular table from the database.

SQL Data Manipulation Language

The **Data Manipulation Language**, or **DML**, is used to manage the data stored in the database. This includes commands such as `INSERT`, `UPDATE`, and `DELETE`.

The `INSERT` statement is used to insert data into a table, one record at a time. The `UPDATE` command is used to modify the contents of the columns within a single row of a specific database table. The `DELETE` command is used to delete specific rows from a table in the database.

Some examples of DML statements are

- `INSERT INTO` *`tableName`* `(`*`column1`*`,` *`column2`*`,...) VALUES (`*`value1`*`,` *`value2`*`,....)`

  This inserts values into a particular table.

- `UPDATE` *`tableName`* `SET` *`column1`* `= new WHERE` *`column1`* `= old`

  This modifies the value of a column within a table given a specific condition.

- `DELETE FROM` *`tableName`* `WHERE` *`column1`* `= value`

  This deletes a row from a table, given a specific condition

SQL Data Query Language

After you have created the database and added some data to it, you will definitely want the ability to retrieve that data. This is what the Data Query Language allows you to do. It includes the basic `SELECT` command that allows you to select rows from a table in the database. The Data Query Language also includes functionality such as the `WHERE` clause that allows you to specify search criteria to search the data in the database.

Some examples of the Data Query Language are

- `SELECT * FROM` *`tableName`*

  This selects all rows from a table
- `SELECT column1... FROM` *`tableName`* `WHERE` *`column2`* `= value`

  This selects specific columns from a table given a specific condition.
- `SELECT column1... FROM` *`tableName`* `WHERE column1 = value AND column2 =` *`otherValue`*

  This is similar to the previous statement, only with a more complex conditional statement.

By the Way

Learn More About SQL

To learn more about SQL and the syntax and usage of these commands, you can go to `http://www.w3schools.com/sql/default.asp`. You can also read about it in a book such as *Sams Teach Yourself SQL in 24 Hours*, 3rd edition, by Stephens and Plew (ISBN: 0672324423).

Getting Started with Cloudscape

Cloudscape, recently acquired by IBM, is a relational database that supports the SQL standards. This book assumes that you are working with Cloudscape. However, the same concepts described here apply to any relational database available today.

The Cloudscape database also has a JDBC driver. This enables Java applications to use Cloudscape as a data store.

If you don't already have Cloudscape installed, you can download and install a version from the IBM Web site. The Cloudscape site (`http://www.ibm.com/software/data/cloudscape/`) has plenty of documentation that can walk you through this process.

By the Way

Using My SQL

Cloudscape used to be bundled with earlier versions of the JDK. However, it's no longer a part of the release. You'll need to download it if you are using a JDK version greater than 1.4. You can also use a database such as MySQL. Although MySQL is not written in Java like Cloudscape and has fewer features, it's a capable database that is popular, fast and reliable. It also has a footprint that's smaller than Cloudscape. For more information about MySQL, go to `http://www.mysql.com`.

Using Cloudscape's Cview tool, open or create a database and then create a People table to be used with the samples later in this hour. To do this, use the following SQL statement:

```
CREATE TABLE People ( name VARCHAR( 75 ), age TINYINT )
```

From earlier reading, this statement should now look familiar. The only thing that may seem unusual are the data types. In this example, we used a `varchar`, which is used to store strings of varying lengths, and a `tinyint`, which is equivalent to a Java Byte. When declaring the `varchar`, we specified that the maximum size of the string should be 75 characters.

You'll also need to populate the table with some data. Add a few entries using a SQL statement that looks like this:

```
INSERT INTO People( name, age ) VALUES ( 'aName', 'anAge );
```

Simply replace *aName* and *anAge* with the values you want to place in the table. Execute this statement with new values a few times so that you'll have a little bit of data to work with.

Getting Ready to UseCloudscape

The next section describes JDBC, but before getting into the details, you need to know that when using JDBC to connect from a Java application to a database, you require a JDBC Driver. To enable Tomcat to load the Cloudscape-specific JDBC drivers, you need to put the `cloudscape.jar` file in the WEB-INF/lib directory.

What Is JDBC?

Java Database Connectivity (JDBC) is an API that lets you access any tabular data sources from a Java application. These data sources can include SQL-based databases or data stored in spreadsheets or flat files. Most commercial databases, such as the ones listed earlier in this hour, now support JDBC by means of a JDBC driver. A Java application can use different JDBC drivers, all of which expose the same interface to the developers. This enables developers to plug different databases into their Java applications.

JDBC exposes an API that allows developers to connect to a database, execute SQL statements on the database, and manipulate any data that is returned as a result of the execution of a database statement. The JDBC driver manages all of this for a specific database and also supports the pooling of database resources such as the connections.

Using JDBC you can connect to a database. To do this, you would create a new JDBC connection using the following statements:

```
Class.forName("com.ibm.db2j.jdbc.DB2jDriver");
Connection con = DriverManager.getConnection(
    "jdbc:db2j:PeopleDB", username, password);
```

In the first statement, you are loading the appropriate driver class. In the second, you create the connection to the database by passing in the connection URL, which includes the driver name (`db2j`), the database name (`PeopleDB`), and the username and password for the database. The username and password are sometimes optional.

The next step is to create a statement that will contain the SQL that you want to execute on the database. This command looks like

```
Statement stmt = con.createStatement() ;
```

As soon as you have created the statement, you can execute the statement in different ways using appropriate SQL statements. You would create a string with this SQL statement:

```
String sqlString = "some sql code";
```

Now you can execute the SQL statement by using either of the following commands as appropriate:

```
stmt.executeUpdate(sqlString);

ResultSet rs = stmt.executeQuery(sqlString);
```

You would use the executeUpdate database in conjunction with an insert or update SQL statement. You would use the executeQuery statement in conjunction with a select SQL statement.

After using the results of your query, the final step is to release the connection:

```
con.close();
```

By the Way

Learn More About JDBC

To learn more about JDBC and the syntax and usage of the JDBC API, you can go to `http://java.sun.com/j2se/1.4.2/docs/guide/jdbc/index.html`.

Using JDBC from JavaServer Pages and Servlets

JDBC can be used through any piece of Java code, including JavaServer Pages or servlets. The following JSP is an example of using JDBC to access the People table in the database, PeopleDB.

Listing 18.1 shows a JSP that queries a Person table using JDBC.

LISTING 18.1 Source Code for `ShowPeople.jsp`

```
<html>
<head>
<title>JDBC Example for People Table</title>
</head>
<body>
<%@ page language="java" import="java.sql.*, java.io.*" %>
<%
    Connection con = null;
    try
        Class.forName("com.ibm.db2j.jdbc.DB2jDriver");{
        con = DriverManager.getConnection("jdbc:db2j:PeopleDB");
        Statement statement = con.createStatement();
        ResultSet rs = statement.executeQuery("SELECT * FROM People");

%>
        <table border="1"><tr><th>Name</th><th>Age</th>
<%
        while ( rs.next() ) {
            out.println("<tr>\n<td>" + rs.getString("name") + "</td>");
            out.println("<td>" + rs.getByte("age") + "</td>"); + "</td>\n</tr>");
        }
        rs.close();
    } catch (IOException ioe) {
        out.println(ioe.getMessage());
    } catch (SQLException sqle) {
        out.println(sqle.getMessage());
    } catch (Exception e) {
        out.println(e.getMessage());
    } finally {
        try {
            if ( con != null ) {
                con.close();
            }
        } catch (SQLException sqle) {
            out.println(sqle.getMessage());
```

LISTING 18.1 Continued

```
        }
    }
%>
</tr>
</table>
</body>
</html>
```

This simple JSP uses straight JDBC calls to print all the rows in the People table. You will see later in this hour how this lengthy and complicated JDBC code is greatly simplified using the JSTL SQL tag libraries.

Watch Out!

Running the Example

To run this example, you need to tell Cloudscape where to find your database. By default, it looks for database in the "current directory," which is Tomcat's `bin/` directory.

A recommended practice is to put all of your databases in one directory. For example, you may put all of your databases in `c:\Cloudscape_5.1\data`.

By defining the property `db2j.system.home=c:\Cloudscape_5.1\data`, Cloudscape will be able to find your database.

To do this with Tomcat, run the command

```
SET JAVA_OPTS="db2j.system.home=c:\Cloudscape_5.1\data"
```

prior to starting Tomcat.

JSTL SQL Tag Library

The SQL tag library is one of the most powerful tag libraries in JSTL, because it allows you to perform database queries and updates from simple tags. You can use these tags in conjunction with the core tag library to iterate through a resultset and display it.

The `<sql:setDataSource>` Tag

Before you can perform any database operations, you must declare a data source, which is the repository for data that you want to use (specified by the `var` attribute and the optional `scope` attribute). You may optionally declare a scoped variable that will be used to export a reference to the data source. If you don't specify a variable, the data source is stored in a default data source variable. You can specify the scope of the default variable via the `scope` attribute. For example, if you define a data source with a scope of session and don't store it in a variable, the data source will be the default data source for all SQL tag operations for that session but not for other sessions.

There are two ways to specify the data source: You can use either a preconfigured Java Numbering and Directory Interface (JNDI) data source name specified by the dataSource attribute or a JDBC URL and optional driver name, username, and password. The attributes for these are url, driver, user, and password.

After you create the data source, you can perform other database operations.

Did you Know?

Using Data Sources with JNDI

Using JNDI, you can create a data source beforehand and associate it with a name stored in a directory. Data sources are often preconfigured within the application server, when a Web application is deployed. To use a data source with JNDI, you simply look up the name and obtain a reference to the data source. The details of this are beyond the scope of this hour, but it's worth further investigation.

The <sql:query> Tag

The <sql:query> tag executes a query and stores the resulting values in a variable specified by the var attribute and an optional scope attribute. If there is no default data source set, you must specify a data source with the dataSource attribute. The value of the dataSource attribute must be an EL expression that evaluates to a DataSource object. If you have previously stored a data source in a variable, don't forget to surround the variable name with ${}.

The sql attribute specifies the SQL query you want to perform. Instead of the sql attribute, you can specify the query in the body of the <sql:query> tag. You can also specify a maximum number of rows to receive with the maxRows attribute and the first row to return with the startRow attribute.

The <sql:query> parameter can work with parameters. To pass parameters to the query, use the <sql:param> or <sql:dateParam> tags in the body of the <sql:query> tag. You can specify a parameter for the <sql:param> via the value attribute or in the body of the <sql:param> tag. Similarly, you can specify the date value for the <sql:dateParam> in either the value attribute or the body of the tag. You can also specify the kind of date parameter you want: date, time, or timestamp (timestamp is the default).

The result of the query is an object that implements the `Result` interface. The two most important methods in the `Result` interface are `getRows` (which returns an array of `SortedMap` objects where each map represents a row and the keys of the map are the column names) and `getRowsByIndex` (which returns an array or arrays of objects). You can also retrieve an array of column names with `getColumnNames`, the number of rows with `getRowCount`, and an indication of whether the query was limited by a maximum row count with `isLimitedByMaxRows`.

Here is an example.

Listing 18.2 shows a JSP that queries a Person table.

LISTING 18.2 Source Code for `ShowPeopleJSTL.jsp`

```
<%@ taglib prefix="c" uri="http://java.sun.com/jstl/core" %>
<%@ taglib prefix="sql" uri="http://java.sun.com/jstl/sql" %>
<sql:setDataSource driver="com.ibm.db2j.jdbc.DB2jDriver"
    url="jdbc:db2j:PeopleDB" var="ds" />

<sql:query sql="select name, age from People" var="results"
    dataSource="${ds}"/>
<html>
<body>
<table border="4">
<tr><th>Name</th><th>Age</th></tr>
<c:forEach var="row" items="${results.rows}">
    <tr><td><c:out value="${row.name}"/></td>
        <td><c:out value="${row.age}"/></td></tr>
</c:forEach>
</table>
</body>
</html>
```

Compare Listing 18.1 with Listing 18.2. They basically do the same thing—print all rows from the Person table using JDBC and a JSP. The primary difference is that Listing 18.2 shows the use of the JSTL tag libraries. Notice how much simpler and shorter Listing 18.2 is than Listing 18.1.

The `<sql:update>` Tag

The `<sql:update>` tag executes an `INSERT`, `UPDATE`, or `DELETE` statement, optionally returning the number of rows updated in a variable specified by the `var` attribute and optional `scope` attribute. If there is no default data source, you must specify the data source in the `dataSource` attribute. The actual SQL statement is specified either by the `sql` attribute or in the body of the `<sql:update>` tag. As with the <sql:query> tag, you can use the <sql:param> and <sql:dateParam> tags to substitute parameters in the SQL statement.

The <sql:transaction> Tag

Sometimes you need to execute several statements as part of a single database transaction. The <sql:transaction> tag groups any tags in its body content in a single database transaction. If there is no default data source, you must specify the data source in the dataSource attribute and not within any SQL tags contained within the <sql:transaction> tag.

You can also specify the transaction isolation level with the isolation attribute, which must be one of the following: read_committed, read_uncommitted, repeatable_read, or serializable.

Summary

In this hour, you were introduced to a key concept—access to data in a database from a JavaServer Page. In general, it is a bad idea to have database access directly embedded in a JavaServer Page. The use of JavaBeans or JSTL tags is the recommended solution when this sort of data access is needed.

Q&A

Q. ***I can't seem to connect to my database. What am I doing wrong?***

A. There are several things that are often the cause for this. Most frequently, the URL used to obtain the connection is incorrect. Every product seems to have a different format. Check the vendor documentation. The second most frequent error occurs because Tomcat cannot create the driver. Make sure that the Database Management System (DBMS) classes (usually packaged in one or more JAR files) are available to Tomcat. Placing them in the `common/lib` subdirectory will do this. Make sure that you restart Tomcat if it is running, so that it can use the new classes. Finally, the application may not be able to find your database. In the example from this hour, where we used the embedded version of Cloudscape (meaning that Cloudscape was started as part of our application, and not as a separate application instance), it was important to tell Cloudscape how to find the database. Because each product is different, you should consult the product documentation to find out how to do this.

Q. ***Why isn't the JSTL version of the example working?***

A. Make sure that the classes necessary to use JSTL are installed in the appropriate places in Tomcat. It may also be that you have a problem accessing the database. See the previous question for help.

Workshop

The Workshop is designed to help you review what you have learned and help you further increase your understanding of the material covered in this hour.

Quiz

1. What are the different components of SQL?
2. What is the key advantage of using the JSTL tags?
3. How do you pass parameters to the various JSTL SQL tags?

Answers

1. Data Types, Data Definition Language, Data Manipulation Language, and the Data Query Language

2. The JSTL tags are tested and provide documented functionality, without you having to reinvent the wheel.
3. Use the `<sql:param>` tag to pass parameters.

Activities

1. Build a JavaServer Page to add people to the People tables using JDBC.
2. Modify the JavaServer Page to use JSTL tags for the same functionality.

HOUR 19

Creating an XML Application

What You'll Learn in This Hour:

- What XML is and why it is useful
- How to generate XML from a JSP or a servlet
- How to use XSL to transform XML
- How to use JSTL's XML tags

The Extensible Markup Language (XML) represents an important step in data representation. In the past, programs used many different formats for storing data. There have been text files with comma-delimited or pipe-delimited fields, binary files in any number of formats, and even plain ASCII text. Unfortunately, most programs use slightly different ways to store data, even if the overall format is similar. For example, when you save data in comma-separated fields, how do you specify what each field is? You might save the first name followed by the last name. Another developer might save the last name and then the first name. How do you know the format of the file unless someone tells you? You could put a line at the top of the file explaining what each field is, but even that might have different formats.

Another problem you encounter when storing data is that most representations tend to be tabular in nature. That is, when you write data into a file, you typically put all the information for a particular data element on a single line in the file. What happens when the data you want to write is a Java object with many nested data structures? How can you store all those data structures within a single line, especially if you must stick to a prescribed set of fields?

XML solves this problem by defining a standard way to represent data, a standard way to tag the data with its type, and a standard way to describe the overall data structure. (There isn't room to cover XML in its entirety here. You can learn more about XML from *Sams Teach Yourself XML in 21 Days,* 3rd edition, by Steve Holzner,

ISBN: 0672325764.) XML *is* very simple, easy to read, and easy to understand. There are a few things XML *is not*:

- XML is not a replacement for HTML. Although there is an XML-compliant version of HTML, XML does not define how to represent data on a Web browser.
- XML is not a cure for all the data format ills. Various software vendors and the business sector must still agree on a common representation for data. For example, the travel industry needs a standard format to represent a reservation. The banking industry needs a standard format to represent account information.
- XML is not a programming language. XML lets you describe data, but it doesn't let you describe how to process the data.

A "Hello World" XML Page

In a minimal XML page you need two things: a heading identifying the page as an XML page, and a single pair of tags that represents the root of the data. Think of the root tags as being like the `<HTML> </HTML>` tags in an HTML document. They enclose everything else. An XML document must have only one pair of root tags. Everything else in the document must be within those two tags. An XML tag defines an XML "element." The root tags define the "root element" or "document element" of an XML document.

Listing 19.1 shows a "Hello World" XML page.

LISTING 19.1 Source Code for `HelloWorld.xml`

```
<?xml version=_1.0_?>
<greeting>
    Hello World
</greeting>
```

The `<?xml version="1.0"?>` tag must be present in any XML file. The `<greeting>` `</greeting>` tag pair is the root of the document.

Sending XML from a JSP

You can create XML JSPs the same way you create HTML pages. The only difference is that you must set the content type of your page to `text/xml`. To set the content type, use the `<%@page%>` tag, like this:

```
<%@ page contentType="text/xml" %>
```

Listing 19.2 shows the "Hello World" XML page as a JSP.

LISTING 19.2 Source Code for `XMLHelloWorld.jsp`

```
<%@ page contentType="text/xml" %>

<?xml version="1.0"?>
<greeting>
    Hello World!
</greeting>
```

Figure 19.1 shows the `XMLHelloWorld` JSP from Internet Explorer 6. As you can see, Internet Explorer shows you the XML source code.

FIGURE 19.1 Internet Explorer shows you XML source code.

Sending XML from a Servlet

Sending XML from a servlet is just as easy as sending HTML. The only difference is that you must set the content type to `text/xml` as you did with the JSP. Because you always need to set the content type in a servlet (unless you don't send a response at all), sending XML is just as easy as sending HTML.

Listing 19.3 shows a servlet that generates the "Hello World" XML page.

LISTING 19.3 Source Code for `XMLHelloWorldServlet.java`

```
package examples;
import javax.servlet.*;
import javax.servlet.http.*;
import java.io.*;

public class XMLHelloWorldServlet extends HttpServlet
{
    public void service(HttpServletRequest request,
        HttpServletResponse response)
        throws ServletException, IOException
    {
        response.setContentType("text/xml");

        PrintWriter out = response.getWriter();

        out.println("<?xml version=\_1.0\_?>");
        out.println("<greeting>");
        out.println("    Hello World");
        out.println("</greeting>");
    }
}
```

To run XMLHelloWorldServlet, you must create a WAR file containing the servlet and a `WEB-INF/web.xml` file as you have for other servlets. The `WEB-INF/web.xml` file should look like the code in Listing 19.4.

LISTING 19.4 Source Code for `web.xml`

```
<?xml version="1.0" encoding="ISO-8859-1"?>
<web-app xmls="http://javqa.sun.com/xml/ns/j2ee"
xmlns:xsi="http://www.w3.org/2001/XMLSchema-instance"
xsi:schemaLocation="http://java.sun.com/xml/ns/j2ee
http://java.sun.com/xml/ns/j2ee/web-app_2_4.xsd"
version="2.4">
    <servlet>
        <servlet-name>XMLHelloWorldServlet</servlet-name>
        <servlet-class>tyjsp.XMLHelloWorldServlet</servlet-class>
    </servlet>

    <servlet-mapping>
        <servlet-name>XMLHelloWorld</servlet-name>
        <url-pattern>/xmlhello</url-pattern>
    </servlet-mapping>
</web-app>
```

If you deploy XMLHelloWorldServlet on your local machine in a WAR file named `xml.war`, the URL should be `http://localhost/xml/xmlhello`.

A Few Simple Rules for XML

You already know that an XML page must start with the <?xml?> tag and must contain a single root element. A few additional rules dictate how you create an XML page.

First, when you create an XML page, you have the option of specifying a Document Type Definition (DTD) that defines what elements and other components are permitted in the XML page. DTDs let you create standard definitions of XML pages. You can use an XML validator to check an XML page to make sure it conforms to its DTD. Use the <!DOCTYPE> tag to specify the DTD for your page. Listing 19.5 shows an example DTD.

LISTING 19.5 Source Code for `Simple.dtd`

```
<!ELEMENT phone-book (entry*)>

!ELEMENT entry (person? ¦ number*)+>
<!ELEMENT person (first-name? ¦ middle-name? ¦ last-name?)+>
<!ELEMENT first-name (#PCDATA)>
<!ELEMENT middle-name (#PCDATA)>
<!ELEMENT last-name (#PCDATA)>
```

Creating a DTD is more complex than creating an XML page. You should consult the W3C Web site at `http://www.w3c.org` for pointers on how to create a DTD. Listing 19.6 shows an XML page that conforms to the DTD in Listing 19.5.

LISTING 19.6 Source Code for `Simple.xml`

```
<?xml version="1.0"?>
<!DOCTYPE Simple SYSTEM "http://localhost/Simple.dtd">
<person>
<first-name>Samantha</first-name>
   <middle-name>Lauren</middle-name>
    <last-name>Tippin</last-name>
</person>
```

A DTD is optional, of course. You can create an XML page with any set of tags you want. For each opening tag you must have a closing tag. The exception to this rule is that you can end an opening tag with /> to indicate that it doesn't need a closing tag. Remember the <jsp:include/> and <jsp:forward/> tags end with /> and thus take no closing tag. You can't interleave tags, either. In other words, if tag B starts within tag A, then tag B must be closed before tag A closes. The following combination of tags is illegal in XML:

```
<foo>
   <bar>
</foo>
    </bar>
```

Because the <bar> tag starts inside the <foo> tag, it must also close within the <foo> tag.

XML now supports an alternative to DTDs called XMLSchema. An XML schema is similar to a DTD but includes more detail, including specific information about the type of data being stored. More importantly, an XML schema is itself a valid XML document, so it is easy to parse XML schemas.

You can also specify attributes within a tag. Although HTML is lenient about quotes in attributes, XML requires that the value of every attribute be enclosed in quotes. In other words, you might have an HTML tag like this:

```
<img src="katy.jpg" width=140 height=150>
```

A valid XML version of the <IMG> tag would look like this:

```
<img src="katy.jpg" width="140" height="150"/>
```

Notice that the XML version of <IMG> ends with /> because it doesn't need a closing tag.

Why Use XML with JSP and Servlets?

If you are new to the XML world, you are probably wondering why you would care about using XML with servlets and JSPs. After all, you are sending output to a browser and the browser understands HTML, not XML. One thing you often find when you create applications that need to send data to other applications is that there are often firewalls sitting between the applications. This is especially true when one business sends data to another business. You would think that RMI or CORBA would be the technology of choice for exchanging data between businesses, but when it comes to firewalls, many developers take the path of least resistance: HTTP. There are products that allow you to send CORBA over a firewall, and RMI even supports HTTP tunneling, but because most firewalls already support HTTP and HTTPS (HTTP over SSL), you can use the URL and URLConnection classes to communicate with servlets and JSPs with little or no extra work.

When you pass XML data via HTTP, it makes sense to use servlets to handle incoming XML and JSPs to generate outgoing XML. Java has several good XML parsers for handling incoming XML. You might need to perform additional work to copy the XML values into Java classes, however.

Automatically Generated XML

The simple, uniform structure of XML makes it very computer friendly. The nested structure of XML makes it an ideal format for storing complex data structures. In fact, XML makes a nice format for serializing Java objects. There are several different ways to serialize Java objects into XML. Some approaches define an XML DTD that describes a Java object. For example, you might have XML that looks like this:

```
<class>
    <class-name>tyjsp.TestClass</class-name>
    <attribute>
        <attribute-name>myAttribute</attribute-name>
        <attribute-value>Foo</attribute-value>
    </attribute
</class>
```

Although this method is good, it is very Java-centric. XML allows you to describe a huge variety of data structures, so wouldn't it be nice if you could easily map those data structures into Java as well? Conversely, it would be nice to generate XML from these Java classes.

You can use a package called JOX (Java Objects in XML), available at `http://www.wutka.com/jox`, to serialize Java objects into XML. To use JOX, you also need the DTD Parser available from `http://www.wutka.com/dtdparser.html`. Listing 19.7 shows an example JavaBean suitable for serialization.

LISTING 19.7 **Source Code for** `TestBean.java`

```
package com.wutka.jox.test;

import com.wutka.jox.*;
import java.util.*;

public class TestBean implements java.io.Serializable
{
    protected int foo;
    protected String bar;
    protected java.util.Date baz;
    protected Vector thingies;
    protected TestSubbean subbean;
```

LISTING 19.7 Continued

```
    public TestBean()
    {
        bar = "";
        baz = new Date();
        thingies = new Vector();
    }

    public int getFoo() { return foo; }
    public void setFoo(int aFoo) { foo = aFoo; }

    public String getBar() { return bar; }
    public void setBar(String aBar) { bar = aBar; }

    public java.util.Date getBaz() { return baz; }
    public void setBaz(java.util.Date aBaz) { baz = aBaz; }

    public TestSubbean getSub() { return subbean; }
    public void setSub(TestSubbean aSub) { subbean = aSub; }

    public String[] getThingies()
    {
        String[] retThingies = new String[thingies.size()];
        if (thingies.size() > 0) thingies.copyInto(retThingies);

        return retThingies;
    }

    public void setThingies(String[] newThingies)
    {
        thingies = new Vector(newThingies.length);
        for (int i=0; i < newThingies.length; i++)
        {
            thingies.addElement(newThingies[i]);
        }
    }

    public String getThingies(int i)
    {
        return (String) thingies.elementAt(i);
    }

    public void setThingies(int i, String thingy)
    {
        thingies.setElementAt(thingy, i);
    }

    public String toString()
    {
        StringBuffer ret = new StringBuffer(
            "foo="+foo+";bar="+bar+";baz="+baz.toString()+
            ";thingies=");
        for (int i=0; i < thingies.size(); i++)
        {
```

LISTING 19.7 Continued

```
            if (i > 0) ret.append(",");
            ret.append((String) thingies.elementAt(i));
        }

        ret.append(";sub=");
        ret.append(subbean.toString());

        return ret.toString();
    }
}
```

Listing 19.8 shows a servlet that uses the JOX library to display the contents of a bean.

LISTING 19.8 Source Code for `BeanXMLServlet.java`

```
package tyjsp.xml;

import com.wutka.jox.*;
import com.wutka.jox.test.*;
import javax.servlet.*;
import javax.servlet.http.*;
import java.io.*;

public class BeanXMLServlet extends HttpServlet
{
    public void service(HttpServletRequest request,
        HttpServletResponse response)
        throws IOException, ServletException
    {

// Create the bean and populate it.
        TestBean bean = new TestBean();

        bean.setThingies(
            new String[] { "Moe", "Larry", "Curly", "Shemp",
                "Curly Joe" });

        bean.setFoo(5);
        bean.setBar("This is the bar value");
        bean.setBaz(new java.util.Date());

        TestSubbean sub = new TestSubbean();
        sub.setName("Mark");
        sub.setAge(35);

        bean.setSub(sub);

// Set the content type for the response.
        response.setContentType("text/xml");

// Get the Writer for sending the response.
        Writer out = response.getWriter();
```

LISTING 19.8 Continued

```
// Wrap a JOXBeanWriter around the output writer.
        JOXBeanWriter beanOut = new JOXBeanWriter(out);

// Write out the object as XML with a root tag of <MarkTest>.
        beanOut.writeObject("MarkTest", bean);
    }
}
```

Listing 19.9 shows the XML generated by JOX.

LISTING 19.9 Source Code for `TestBean.xml`

```
<?xml version="1.0"?>
<MarkTest>
<thingies>Moe</thingies>
<thingies>Larry</thingies>
<thingies>Curly</thingies>
<thingies>Shemp</thingies>
<thingies>Curly Joe</thingies>
<foo>5</foo>
<baz>5/15/00 5:59 PM</baz>
<bar>This is the bar value</bar>
<sub>
<age>35</age>
<name>Mark</name>
</sub>
</MarkTest>
```

As usual, you need to package TestBean and BeanXMLServlet into a WAR file along with a `WEB-INF/web.xml` file. In addition, you need the copy the `jox.jar` and `dtdparser.jar` files into the `WEB-INF/lib` directory. The `web.xml` file should look something like Listing 19.10.

LISTING 19.10 Source Code for `web.xml`

```
<?xml version="1.0" encoding="ISO-8859-1"?>
<web-app>
    <servlet>
        <servlet-name>BeanXMLServlet</servlet-name>
        <servlet-class>tyjsp.BeanXMLServlet</servlet-class>
    </servlet>

    <servlet-mapping>
        <servlet-name>BeanXMLServlet</servlet-name>
        <url-pattern>/beanxml</url-pattern>
    </servlet-mapping>
</web-app>
```

Parsing XML with SAX and DOM

When you use servlets and JSPs to generate XML for application-to-application communication, the client on the other end must be able to interpret the XML and turn it into useful data structures. More importantly, if a client sends XML to your JSP or servlet, you must be able to parse the XML document. You can use any of several different parsers to turn XML documents into Java data structures.

There are two different approaches for parsing XML: SAX and DOM. **SAX** stands for **Simple API for XML**, and it enables you to handle XML tags in the data as the parser encounters them. In other words, when the parser locates an XML tag, it calls a Java method to handle the tag. It's up to you to decide what to do with it. **DOM**, or **Document Object Model**, isn't strictly an API: It's an object model describing how an XML document is organized. When you use a DOM parser to parse an XML document, the parser reads the entire document and passes you back a `Document` object containing everything that was defined in the XML document.

Each of these approaches has its advantages and disadvantages, and you certainly don't need to choose one over the other. You can use whichever one makes sense for your situation. For example, if you are parsing very large files (in the 10–15MB range and higher), you probably want to use SAX, because a DOM parser first reads the entire file into memory before you can begin processing it. The Java XML API from Sun supports both SAX and DOM.

Using SAX to Parse XML

SAX uses an event-driven model for parsing. The SAX parser reads the XML, and when it finds something interesting, it calls a method in a handler class. The handler class is something that you must write, although there is a skeleton base class that you can start with. SAX will tell you when it finds the beginning of a document, the end of a document, an opening tag, a closing tag, or character data within an element. It will also tell you when it finds an error.

SAX is most useful when you need to read through a very large XML file but you might not need much of the data in the file. If you need to search through a file for a particular tag or data value, SAX is generally much quicker.

Listing 19.11 shows a servlet that reads an XML file sent to it and searches for a particular tag. After it finds the tag, it looks for character data.

LISTING 19.11 Source Code for `SaxParseServlet.java`

```
package examples.xml;

import java.io.*;

import javax.servlet.*;
import javax.servlet.http.*;

import javax.xml.parsers.*;
import org.xml.sax.*;
import org.xml.sax.helpers.DefaultHandler;

public class SaxParseServlet extends HttpServlet
{
    public void doPost(HttpServletRequest request,
        HttpServletResponse response)
        throws ServletException, IOException
    {
        try
        {
// Create a parser factory.
            SAXParserFactory factory = SAXParserFactory.newInstance();

// Ask the parser factory to create a new parser.
            SAXParser parser = factory.newSAXParser();

// This servlet just sends a plain text response.
            response.setContentType("text/plain");

// Create an input source around the request reader; ask the parser
// to parse the input source and invoke methods in the XMLHandler class
// when it finds XML elements.
            parser.parse(new InputSource(request.getReader()),
                new XMLHandler(request, response));
        }
        catch (ParserConfigurationException exc)
        {
            throw new ServletException(exc.toString());
        }
        catch (SAXException exc)
        {
            throw new ServletException(exc.toString());
        }
    }

    class XMLHandler extends DefaultHandler
    {
        protected HttpServletRequest request;
        protected HttpServletResponse response;
```

LISTING 19.11 Continued

```
        protected boolean handlingFirstName;
        protected boolean handlingLastName;
        protected boolean inName;

        protected String firstName;
        protected String lastName;

        public XMLHandler(HttpServletRequest aRequest,
            HttpServletResponse aResponse)
        {
            request = aRequest;
            response = aResponse;

            inName = false;
            handlingFirstName = false;
            handlingLastName = false;
        }

        public void startElement(String uri, String name, String qName,
            Attributes attributes)
        {
// Use qualified name if not namespaceAware.
            if ("".equals(name)) name = qName;
// Look for a <name> element.
            if (name.equals("name"))
            {
                inName = true;
                firstName = null;
                lastName = null;
            }
// If inside a <name> element, look for <first>.
            else if (name.equals("first"))
            {
                if (!inName) return;

                handlingFirstName = true;
            }
// If inside a <name> element, look for <last>.
            else if (name.equals("last"))
            {
                if (!inName) return;

                handlingLastName = true;
            }
        }

        public void characters(char[] chars, int start, int length)
        {
// If these characters are occurring inside a <first> element, save them.
            if (handlingFirstName)
            {
                firstName = new String(chars, start, length);
            }
```

LISTING 19.11 Continued

```
// If these characters are occurring inside a <last> element, save them.
            else if (handlingLastName)
            {
                lastName = new String(chars, start, length);
            }
            else
            {
                return;
            }
        }

        public void endElement(String uri, String name, String qName)
            throws SAXException
        {
// Use qualified name if not namespaceAware.
            if ("".equals(name)) name = qName;

            if (name.equals("name"))
            {
// After the end of the name element, if there's a first and a last name,
// print them separated by a space.
                if ((firstName != null) && (lastName != null))
                {
                    try
                    {
                        PrintWriter out = response.getWriter();

                        out.println(firstName+" "+lastName);
                    }
                    catch (IOException ioExc)
                    {
                        throw new SAXException(ioExc.toString());
                    }
                }
                inName = false;
            }
            else if (name.equals("first"))
            {
                if (!inName) return;
                handlingFirstName = false;
            }
            else if (name.equals("last"))
            {
                if (!inName) return;
                handlingLastName = false;
            }
        }
    }
}
```

Listing 19.12 shows a test client program that sends the XML file to the servlet from Listing 19.11.

LISTING 19.12 Source Code for `XMLTestClient.java`

```
import java.io.*;
import java.net.*;

public class XMLTestClient
{
    public static void main(String[] args)
    {
        try
        {
// args[1] is the name of the file to send.
File f = new File(args[1]);
            int contentLength = (int) f.length();

// args[0] is the URL to send the file to.
            URL url = new URL(args[0]);
            URLConnection conn = url.openConnection();

// Tell the URLConnection that this is an XML file.
            conn.setDoOutput(true);
            conn.setRequestProperty("content-type", "text/xml");
            conn.setRequestProperty("content-length", ""+contentLength);

            FileInputStream in = new FileInputStream(f);

            byte[] buffer = new byte[4096];
            int len;

            OutputStream out = conn.getOutputStream();

// Send the XML file to the servlet.
            while ((len = in.read(buffer)) > 0)
            {
                out.write(buffer, 0, len);
            }

            InputStream resp = conn.getInputStream();

// Read the response back from the servlet.
            while ((len = resp.read(buffer)) > 0)
            {
                System.out.write(buffer, 0, len);
            }
        }
        catch (Exception exc)
        {
            exc.printStackTrace();
        }
    }
}
```

To execute XML test client, make sure you run it in the same directory as `test.xml`. If you have installed the SAX parse servlet in a WAR file called `xml.war` and the servlet URL pattern is saxparse, you would execute XMLTestClient with the following command:

```
java XMLTestClient http://localhost/xml/saxparse test.xml
```

Using DOM to Parse XML

A DOM parser reads an XML file in its entirety before passing any information to you. It uses a set of Java classes to create a representation of the XML contents. An XML file is structured like a tree. The main document tag is the base of the tree, and each nested tag is a branch of the tree. The document model used by a DOM parser is also structured like a tree. You receive a `Document` object, which returns a list of `Node` objects.

The `Node` class is really an interface, not a class. DOM has a number of classes that implement the `Node` interface. The one you deal with most often is the `Element` class, which represents a tag or tag pair from an XML document. You might also find `Comment` nodes, `Text` nodes, `CDATASection` nodes, `Character` nodes, and several others. The `Element` class might contain a list of child nodes representing the tags and data contained between the element's opening and closing tags.

Listing 19.13 shows a servlet that uses a DOM parser to parse through the same file as the servlet in Listing 19.9. You can see how different a DOM parser is from a SAX parser. Although SAX is a bit faster, DOM tends to be a bit easier to use when you need to preserve the document's structure.

LISTING 19.13 Source Code for `DomParseServlet.java`

```
package tyjsp.xml;

import java.io.*;

import javax.servlet.*;
import javax.servlet.http.*;

import javax.xml.parsers.*;
import org.xml.sax.*;
import org.w3c.dom.*;

public class DomParseServlet extends HttpServlet
{
```

LISTING 19.13 Continued

```
    public void doPost(HttpServletRequest request,
        HttpServletResponse response)
        throws ServletException, IOException
    {
        try
        {
// Create a parser factory.
            DocumentBuilderFactory factory = DocumentBuilderFactory.
                newInstance();

// Ask the parser factory to create a new parser.
            DocumentBuilder parser = factory.newDocumentBuilder();

// This servlet just sends a plain text response.
            response.setContentType("text/plain");

            PrintWriter out = response.getWriter();

// Create an input source around the request reader; ask the parser
// to parse the input source.
            Document doc = parser.parse(new InputSource(request.getReader()));

// Get all the Name elements.
            NodeList names = doc.getElementsByTagName("name");

            int numNames = names.getLength();

            for (int i=0; i < numNames; i++)
            {
                Element e = (Element) names.item(i);

                String firstName = null;

// See whether there is a first name.
                NodeList firstNameList = e.getElementsByTagName("first");
                if (firstNameList.getLength() > 0)
                {
                    Element firstNameNode = (Element) firstNameList.item(0);

// Make the really bold assumption that <first> has a child and that
// it is text. You really should check first, though.
                    CharacterData nameText = (CharacterData)
                        firstNameNode.getFirstChild();

                    firstName = nameText.getData();
                }

                String lastName = null;

// See whether there is a last name.
                NodeList lastNameList = e.getElementsByTagName("last");
                if (lastNameList.getLength() > 0)
                {
                    Element lastNameNode = (Element) lastNameList.item(0);
```

LISTING 19.13 Continued

```
// Make the really bold assumption that <last> has a child and that
// it is text. You really should check first, though.
                    CharacterData nameText = (CharacterData)
                        lastNameNode.getFirstChild();

                    lastName = nameText.getData();
                }

                if ((firstName != null) && (lastName != null))
                {
                    out.println(firstName+" "+lastName);
                }
            }
        }
        catch (ParserConfigurationException exc)
        {
            throw new ServletException(exc.toString());
        }
        catch (SAXException exc)
        {
            throw new ServletException(exc.toString());
        }
    }
}
```

Using JOX to Parse XML

The JOX library uses a DOM parser to parse through XML. The main reason to use JOX instead of using DOM directly is that JOX automatically copies values from the XML document into a JavaBean. Also, JOX is geared toward reading and writing files and fits very well within the servlet framework.

Listing 19.14 shows a servlet that uses JOX to read an XML file and copy its values into a JavaBean.

LISTING 19.14 Source Code for `JOXParseServlet.java`

```
package tyjsp.xml;

import java.io.*;

import javax.servlet.*;
import javax.servlet.http.*;

import com.wutka.jox.*;
import com.wutka.jox.test.*;

public class JOXParseServlet extends HttpServlet
{
```

LISTING 19.14 Continued

```
    public void doPost(HttpServletRequest request,
        HttpServletResponse response)
        throws ServletException, IOException
    {
        TestBean newBean = new TestBean();

        JOXBeanReader reader = new JOXBeanReader(request.getReader());

        reader.readObject(newBean);

// This servlet just sends a plain text response.
        response.setContentType("text/plain");

        PrintWriter out = response.getWriter();

        out.println(newBean.toString());
    }
}
```

XML Tag Library

JSTL includes a number of tags for processing and formatting XML. These tags make it much easier to develop XML-based Web applications.

XML Core Tags

The XML core tags focus on three basic capabilities: parsing an XML document, storing value from an XML document into a named variable, and displaying data stored in an XML document.

XPath Expressions in JSTL Tags

Because the JSTL XML tags store parsed XML data in JSP variables, you need a way to extract values out of these variables. You usually use XPath to extract data from XML files (technically, XPath simply specifies where in the document the data is located), but for JSTL you need an easy way to associate an XPath expression with a particular variable. JSTL defines a number of XPath scopes that can be combined with XPath expressions. In a simple case, you can refer to a variable containing a parsed document by using the form `$varname` where *varname* is the name of the variable. For example, if you parse an XML document into a variable named `doc` and you want to refer to an element named `services` directly under the root element named `configuration`, use this XPath expression: `$doc/configuration/services`.

You can also specify a scope in a variable name, like this: `$scopenameScope:varname`. For example, to access a variable called `data` in the session scope, use the expression `$sessionScope:data`.

You can also access form parameters, header values, cookie values, and servlet init parameters with the expressions `$param:paramName`, `$header:headerValueName`, `$cookie:cookieValueName`, and `$initParam:initParamName`. Unlike the scoped variables, which may be any Java type, these four types of values are always strings. Unfortunately, they can't be embedded in the middle of XPath expressions. For example, suppose you want to create an XPath expression that locates all nodes in the variable `doc` whose name matches a form parameter called `which`. You might think that the expression `$doc//$param:which` would work, but it doesn't. Instead, you must use a more verbose form: `$doc//.[name()=$param:which]`. In this longer form, you basically select descendant nodes by using the name function, which returns the node name.

The `<xml:parse>` Tag

The `<xml:parse>` tag parses an XML document from a string variable, from a reader, or from the body of the tag itself. Use the `xml` attribute to specify the location of the parsed XML. The XML can be a string, an EL expression that evaluates to a string, or an EL expression that evaluates to a reader (like the result of `<c:import>`).

If you don't specify an `xml` attribute, then the `<xml:parse>` tag parses its own body content (that is, the XML content should be contained within the `<xml:parse>` tag).

Like other JSTL tags, the `<xml:parse>` tag supports the `var` and `scope` attributes to specify the variable where the parsed document will be stored. The actual type of object stored in the variable is implementation-dependent. It might be a `Document` object, but it might be something else. If you specifically want to parse a document and store it in a DOM `Document` object, use the `varDom` and `scopeDom` attributes, rather than `var` and `scope`.

The `<xml:set>` Tag

The `<xml:set>` tag extracts a value from an XML document and stores the value in a variable. The `select` attribute specifies an XPath expression for the value to be extracted, whereas the `var` and `scope` attributes specify the variable that receives the extracted value.

The <xml:out> Tag

The <xml:out> tag extracts a value from an XML document and writes the value to the JSP's writer (similar to the way that <c:out> displays values). The `select` attribute specifies an XPath expression for the value to be displayed. If the result of an expression contains XML tags and you want to display the tags on a browser, set the `escapeXML` attribute to `true`, which causes characters such as < to be written as <, so that they will be displayed as is by the browser.

Listing 19.15 shows a JSP whose <xml:parse> tag parses its own body content and displays a value selected by a form parameter called `which`.

LISTING 19.15 Source Code for `xml1.jsp`

```
<%@ taglib prefix="xml" uri="http://java.sun.com/jstl/xml" %>
<html>
<body>
<xml:parse var="parsedXML">
<?xml version="1.0"?>
   <doc>
      <message>Hello!</message>
      <thing1>I am thing1</thing1>
      <thing2>I am thing2</thing2>
   </doc>
</xml:parse>
<xml:out select="$parsedXML//.[(name()=$param:which]"/>
</body>
</html>
```

You can run this example by passing form parameters in the URL. For example, with a typical Tomcat installation, the URL would be `http://localhost/tyjsp/ch19/xml1.jsp?what=This+is+a+test.`

XML Flow Tags

The XML flow tags—<xml:if>, <xml:choose>, and <xml:forEach>—work just like their <c:if>, <c:choose>, and <c:forEach> counterparts, except that instead of specifying EL expression values with the `value` tag, you specify them with an XPath expression in the `select` tag.

XML Transform Tags

The <xml:transform> tag applies an XSLT stylesheet to an XML document and stores the results in a variable. The `xml` attribute should contain an EL expression that evaluates to either a string containing the document or a reader that reads the document. If you don't specify the `xml` attribute, the <xml:transform> tag performs the XSLT transform on its own body content. The `xslt` attribute specifies the XSLT stylesheet to apply and must contain an EL expression that evaluates to a string containing the stylesheet, a reader that reads the stylesheet, or an XSLT `Transform` object. The `var` and `scope` attributes specify a variable that will contain the results of the transform, which can then be processed with the other XML tags.

Summary

XML allows you to present data in a structured, human-readable form. To display XML from a JSP or servlet, you must use a content type of `text/xml` instead of `text/html`. Most modern browsers understand XML and can format it with nice colorized tags or apply XSLT transformations to the data.

Java also supports SAX and DOM parsers that allow you to read XML files and process them either tag-by-tag (SAX) or as a whole document (DOM). In order to ease the burden of writing XML code, JSTL provides tags for parsing, displaying, and transforming XML data.

Q&A

Q. *Why doesn't the browser recognize my JSP as an XML file?*

A. You probably forgot to change the content type to `text/xml`.

Q. *Why can't the Java compiler find the XML libraries?*

A. Make sure that both `jaxp.jar` and `parser.jar` are in your classpath.

Q. *My program compiles okay; why does it tell me it can't find the parser library?*

A. You must have both `jaxp.jar` and `parser.jar` in your classpath. The `jaxp.jar` file defines the standard interfaces for SAX and DOM, but it doesn't contain any of the implementation classes. You can compile a program by using only `jaxp.jar`, but when you run the program, you need to include an actual XML parser in the classpath.

Q. *Why do I get a* `ClassNotFoundException` *when I use the JOX library?*

A. JOX also requires the Sun XML libraries, so you must also include `jaxp.jar` and `parser.jar` in your classpath. Make sure that the JOX JAR file is also in your classpath.

Workshop

The Workshop is designed to help you review what you have learned and to help you further increase your understanding of the material covered in this hour.

Quiz

1. What are the two tag forms an XML element may take?
2. How do you tell the browser you are sending it XML?
3. How can you convert XML into HTML?

Answers

1. An XML element may be represented as an opening/closing tag pair like `<page></page>` or by a single tag like `<page/>`.
2. Use the `response.setContentType` method and set the content type to `text/xml`.
3. Create an XSLT stylesheet to convert the various elements in the XML document into the desired HTML equivalents.

Activities

1. Create a simple XSLT stylesheet that converts XML into a simple HTML document. Use a JSTL transform action to display the HTML.

2. Amazon has a Web Services Program available at `http://www.amazon.com/webservices`. Through this program, you can search Amazon and receive an XML response. Create a JSP that displays the results of an Amazon XML search using the JSTL XML tags.

HOUR 20

Building Web Applications with JavaServer Pages and Servlets

What You'll Learn in This Hour:

- Model 1 and Model 2 architectures
- Model-View-Controller
- Writing your own MVC-based application

At this point in the book, you have nearly all of the tools to be able to build great Web applications. You may even have a project or two in mind that you'd like to begin, but you may also have a nagging thought: How do I use all this stuff to build my application? This hour will help you get started.

Web Application Architecture

When considering how to construct an application, you must decide how to divide up responsibilities and how the pieces will interact with one another. In a Web application, that means that you'll assign work to static HTML pages, JSPs, servlets, and other objects. The container and application server will pitch in and take care of some things for you.

You want applications that are useful, easy to construct, and maintainable. Because requirements or uses seem to always change, you're also interested in software that is flexible or extensible.

The trick in building software that does all of this for you is to properly delegate the work to the right components. For example, presenting static content to the client can be accomplished using a plain HTML page or a servlet or JSP. Writing a servlet to do this is more work than you need to do and makes the application complex.

Also, you probably recognize that, in the workplace, employees are often assigned tasks that make the best use of their skills. From a business perspective, it's useful to design software so that the work can be divided into parcels that are completed by employees whose training and talents are appropriate to the tasks. One of the objectives of the JSP and servlet specifications is to make it possible to neatly divide the labor between graphics designers who work on the presentation and programmers who define the behavior of an application.

The specifications for JSPs and servlets have been designed with all of these things in mind. With the release of JSP 2.0, it's even easier to build applications that approach the goals.

The Model 1 and Model 2 Architectures

When JSPs were first introduced, the specifications distinguished the uses of JSPs from servlets by defining two model architectures. Recent specifications have dropped the topic, leaving it (more appropriately) to the J2EE blueprint to define. The models are still useful, so we'll take a few minutes to review them.

Did you Know?

The Parts of the J2EE Standard

A Java 2 Enterprise Edition (J2EE) release is made up of several components. First, there are the constituent specifications, which include the JSP and servlet specifications. Then, there are reference implementations; Tomcat is the reference implementation for the JSP and servlet specifications. Finally, there is a blueprint, which defines the J2EE architecture and provides guidelines for the use of the technologies that compose J2EE. The J2EE blueprint is available online at `http://java.sun.com/blueprints/`.

In the **Model 1** architecture, JSPs accept client requests, decide which actions to take next, and present the results. JSPs work with JavaBeans or other services to affect business objects and generate the content. The important thing to remember about this model is that a JSP always remains in control of the application. Figure 20.1 illustrates a Model 1 architecture.

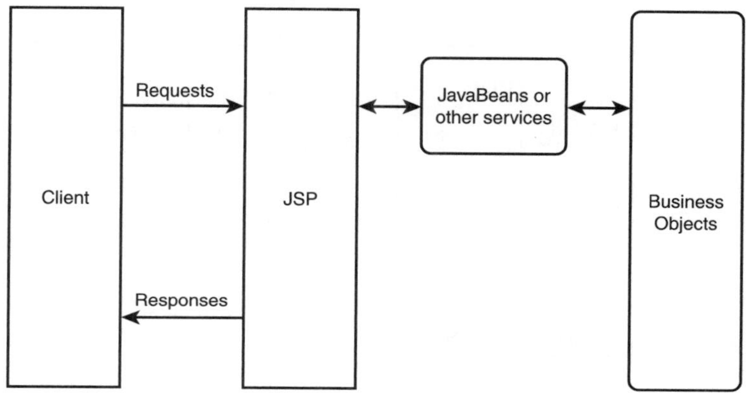

FIGURE 20.1
The structure of a Model 1 architecture is shown here.

Unfortunately, this almost always means that the JSP has a considerable amount of business logic in it, usually in the form of scriptlets littered throughout the page. In most implementations, it's a complex document that rarely meets the objectives presented earlier this hour.

Did you Know?

Consider Your Architectural Requirements

A Model 1 architecture can be successful. You can reduce the complexity by using tags and EL, thereby making it easier to create and maintain. Custom tags can encapsulate most functionality that is sophisticated enough to require Java. You may find that a Model 1 architecture is just right for your needs.

In the **Model 2** architecture, a servlet accepts a client request, handles the processing, and then forwards to a JSP for presentation. In this architecture, the servlet can access the business objects, obtain the information that needs to be displayed, and pass it along to a JSP that is dedicated to presentation. It's quite easy to keep the business logic in the servlet (and Java code for that matter) and use JSPs strictly for presentation. The view of the information will be constructed using directives and standard and custom actions. For the really tough presentation problems, EL is there to help. Figure 20.2 depicts the Model 2 architecture.

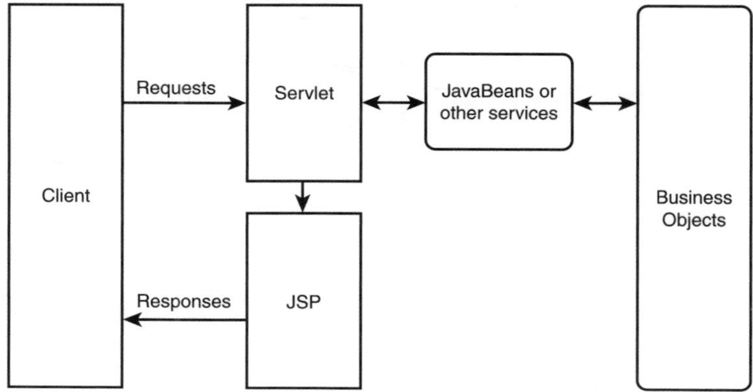

FIGURE 20.2 The structure of a Model 2 architecture is shown here.

Using the Model 2 architecture helps partition functionality and results in reduced coupling between components, making the application flexible and easier to maintain. Let's look at a successful Model 2 architecture in more detail.

Using Model-View-Controller in Your Web Applications

The **Model-View-Controller** (**MVC**) paradigm is a way of dividing an application into three distinct areas:

- The controller, which is really the input that changes the system
- The model, which is the data that describes the system
- The view, which is the display of the data, whether it is graphical, textual, or even just information written out to a file

To put MVC into real-world terms, think of your application as a car. The gas pedal, brake, and steering wheel are **controllers**. They send input signals to the **model**, which is the engine, suspension, transmission, and so on. Your speedometer, tachometer, fuel gauge, and idiot lights are all examples of **views**. They give you some representation of what is happening in the model.

Most developers think of MVC in terms of a graphical user interface, because MVC is used extensively in GUI development. With a little imagination, though, you can extend the MVC paradigm to Web development, in terms of servlets and JSPs. The idea is that you split your application into three sections. A servlet handles any requests from the client and acts as a controller. You put your business logic (the model) in Java classes that are neither servlets nor JavaServer Pages. Finally, you use JavaServer Pages to display the view, which is a representation of the model. This is illustrated in Figure 20.3.

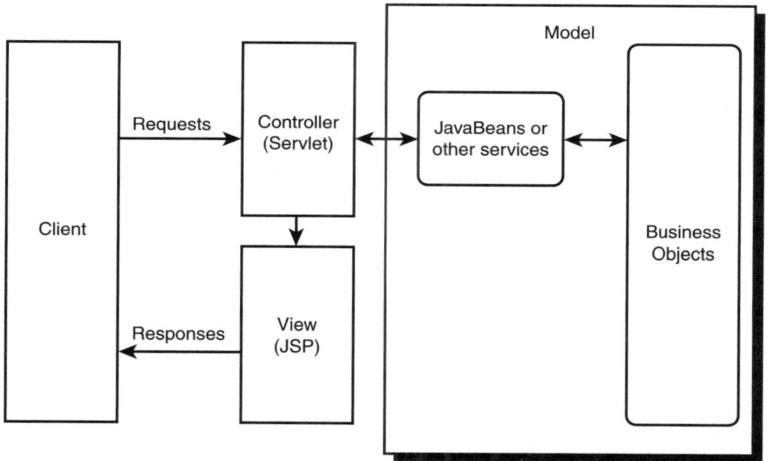

FIGURE 20.3
MVC can be used with servlets and JSPs.

When applying MVC to a Web application, you have to make some concessions toward the way the Web works. When you use MVC in a GUI application, changes to the model can result in immediate feedback to the user.

Because the client and the Web server spend most of their time disconnected from each other, you can't have that kind of dynamic view in a Web application. The important thing is that you concentrate on splitting the model, view, and controller into separate pieces.

How Does Model-View-Controller Help?

Unfortunately, many applications are developed in a piecemeal fashion. Someone comes to a developer and says, "Hey, can you write a JSP to display X on a browser?" A little while later, that person comes back and says, "Great, now can you put X over here, compute Y, and display Z over here?" After a few rounds of this, the JSP might look beautiful to the user, but the source code probably looks hideous to the developer.

The sequence of tasks in the JSP can end up looking something like this:

1. Display some static content using HTML.
2. Go get the user's profile information from the security server.
3. If the user is a manager, go to the part of the JSP that displays the page using the manager's special format.
4. Go get some information from the database.
5. If there's an error in the database, display error information.
6. Display the database information in HTML.

No one ever intends things to be so convoluted; they just get that way sometimes. By applying MVC to this same sequence of events, you get a cleaner picture. The sequence goes something like this:

1. The controller servlet connects to the security server and obtains the user profile.
2. The controller servlet grabs some information from the database and stores it in the `request` object.
3. If there is an error fetching data from the database, the controller servlet forwards to an error JSP.
4. If the user is a manager, the controller servlet forwards to a JSP that displays the manager's view of the data.
5. If the user is not a manager, the controller servlet forwards to the regular display JSP.
6. The display JavaServer Pages grab the information from the `request` object and display it.

An Example Controller

Listing 20.1 shows you an example controller that queries a database and then calls a view JSP to show the results. For the sake of brevity, the code is not as robust as it should be.

LISTING 20.1 Source Code for `ControllerServlet.java`

```
package examples;

import java.io.*;
import java.util.*;
import javax.servlet.*;

public class ControllerServlet extends GenericServlet
{
    private static Person[] people = new Person[]
        { new Person("Samantha Tippin", 9, "770-123-4567"),
          new Person("Kaitlyn Tippin", 6, "770-123-4567"),
          new Person("Edward Alexander", 3, "No phone"),
          new Person("Star Alexander", 3, "Phone off hook"),
          new Person("Norton Alexander", 12, "No phone")
        };

    public synchronized void service(ServletRequest request,
        ServletResponse response)
        throws java.io.IOException, ServletException
    {
// Parse the minimum and maximum ages and go to an error page if they
// are invalid.
        String minimumAgeStr = request.getParameter("minAge");
        int minimumAge = 0;

        try
        {
            minimumAge = Integer.parseInt(minimumAgeStr);
        }
        catch (Exception exc)
        {
            gotoPage("/BadAge.jsp?"+
                "reason=Invalid+minimum+age",
                request, response);
        }

        String maximumAgeStr = request.getParameter("maxAge");
        int maximumAge = 0;

        try
        {
            maximumAge = Integer.parseInt(maximumAgeStr);
        }
```

LISTING 20.1 Continued

```
        catch (Exception exc)
        {
            gotoPage("/BadAge.jsp?"+
                "reason=Invalid+maximum+age",
                request, response);
            return;
        }

// Get all the people matching the criteria.
        Vector v = new Vector();

        for (int i=0; i < people.length; i++) {
            if ((people[i].age >= minimumAge) &&
                (people[i].age <= maximumAge)) {
                v.addElement(people[i]);
            }
        }

// Store the vector of person objects so the JSP can access it.
        request.setAttribute("people", v);

        gotoPage("/ShowPeople.jsp",
            request, response);
        return;
    }

// This method comes in handy as a one-liner for forwarding. It should really
// check to make sure it can get the dispatcher and do something
// predictable if it can't.

    public void gotoPage(String pageName,
        ServletRequest request, ServletResponse response)
        throws IOException, ServletException
    {
        RequestDispatcher d = getServletContext().
            getRequestDispatcher(pageName);

        d.forward(request, response);
    }
}
```

An Example View

The controller does most of the work. The view will just display the results. We'll reuse the `TableServlet` class from Hour 10 to display the names in a table. Listing 20.2 shows the example view.

LISTING 20.2 Source Code for `ShowPeople.jsp`

```
<html>
<body bgcolor="#ffffff">

The following people matched your search criteria:
<P>
<%-- Invoke the Table servlet, tell it the name of the attribute
     where the data is stored (data=people), set the border size to 4
     on the <table> tag, and describe each column to display.

     The "people" attribute was sent from the controller servlet
     and contains a vector of people objects. --%>

<jsp:include page="/TableServlet" flush="true">
    <jsp:param name="data" value="people"/>

    <jsp:param name="tableOptions" value="BORDER=4"/>

    <jsp:param name="column" value="name"/>
    <jsp:param name="columnType" value="data"/>
    <jsp:param name="columnHeader" value="Name"/>

    <jsp:param name="column" value="age"/>
    <jsp:param name="columnType" value="data"/>
    <jsp:param name="columnHeader" value="Age"/>

    <jsp:param name="column" value="phone"/>
    <jsp:param name="columnType" value="data"/>
    <jsp:param name="columnHeader" value="Phone"/>

</jsp:include>
</body>
</html>
```

By the Way

Using Custom Tags in This Example

By now it should be easy for you to imagine the use of custom tags as an alternative way to construct the table.

The front end to this controller-view pairing is a very small HTML page that prompts for the minimum and maximum ages for the query. Listing 20.3 shows the source for the HTML page.

LISTING 20.3 Source Code for `PeopleQuery.html`

```
<html>
<body>

Please enter the minimum and maximum ages to view:
<P>
<form action="/ControllerServlet" method="post">
Minimum Age: <input type="text" name="minAge"><br>
Maximum Age: <input type="text" name="maxAge"><br>
<P>
<input type="submit" value="Perform Query!">
</form>
</body>
</html>
```

Finally, Figure 20.4 shows the output of the `view` class. Most of the view is actually generated by the `TableServlet` class.

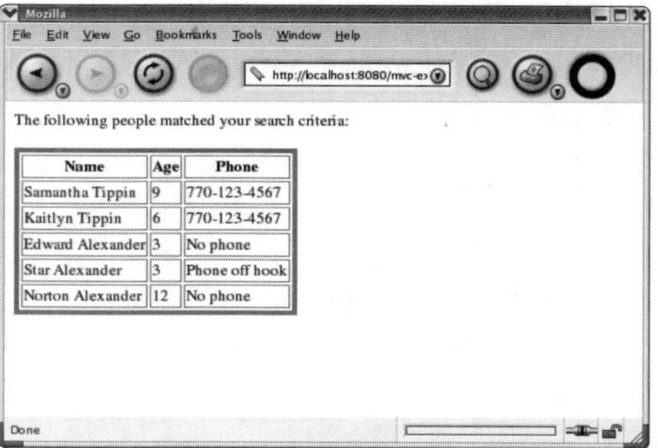

FIGURE 20.4 The View page is responsible for displaying the data retrieved from the model.

Calling Multiple Controllers and Views

One of the things you will notice in the controller servlet is that it has direct knowledge of the JSP that is handling the view—the name of the view that the JSP is coded in. You should strive to break such dependencies whenever you can. What happens if you want to do things exactly the same way in the controller but display a different view of the data?

The controller should be concerned with sending information to the model, and the view should be concerned with displaying the output. The only thing that ties the controller to the view at the moment is the fact that the controller contains the logic to forward the request on to the view. The way to completely separate the controller from the view is with a dispatcher servlet.

A dispatcher performs the crucial transition between the controller and the view. Instead of invoking a controller directly, you call the dispatcher and tell it which controller you want to call and which view to display. That way, the controller doesn't have any specific view hardwired into its code. Likewise, the dispatcher doesn't have a view hardwired in, either.

By the Way

Don't Confuse This Dispatcher with RequestDispatcher

This is not the same dispatcher as the `RequestDispatcher` class that is part of the Servlet API. This section of the book refers to a dispatcher in the generic sense.

You can even have the dispatcher call multiple controllers before invoking a view. That way, you can break your business logic down into finer-grained pieces. When the client sends a request to the server, it may invoke several controllers to update various portions of the model before displaying the view.

Listing 20.4 shows the dispatcher servlet. In this example, you use parameters (form variables) named `controller` to pass the controllers. The pathname for the default view is passed in the `view` parameter, whereas the pathname for the error-handler view is passed in the `errorView` parameter.

LISTING 20.4 Source Code for `DispatcherServlet.java`

```
package examples;

import javax.servlet.*;

public class DispatcherServlet extends GenericServlet
{
```

LISTING 20.4 Continued

```
    public void service(ServletRequest request,
        ServletResponse response)
        throws java.io.IOException, ServletException
    {

// Get the list of controllers to call.
        String[] controllers =
            request.getParameterValues("controller");

// Get the name of the view to call.
        String viewName = request.getParameter("view");

// Get the name of the view to call if there is an error.
        String errorViewName = request.getParameter("errorView");

        try
        {
            for (int i=0; i < controllers.length; i++)
            {
                RequestDispatcher d =
                    getServletContext().
                        getRequestDispatcher(
                            controllers[i]);
                if (d != null)
                {
// Invoke the next controller.
                    d.include(request, response);
                }
                else
                {
                    getServletContext().log(
                        "No controller named " +
                        controllers[i]);
                }
            }

            RequestDispatcher d = getServletContext().
                getRequestDispatcher(viewName);

// The dispatcher includes the other controllers, but it forwards to the view.
            if (d != null)
            {
                d.forward(request, response);
            }
            else
            {
                getServletContext().log(
                    "No view named "+ viewName);
            }
        }
        catch (Exception exc)
        {
// If there is an error, forward to the error view.
```

LISTING 20.4 Continued

```
            request.setAttribute("exception", exc.toString());

            RequestDispatcher d = getServletContext().
                getRequestDispatcher(errorViewName);

            if (d != null)
            {
                d.forward(request, response);
            }
            else
            {
                getServletContext().log(
                    "No errorView named " + errorViewName);
            }
        }
    }
}
```

To use this dispatcher with the `ControllerServlet`, you need to strip a few things out of the controller. You no longer need to include the calls to `gotoPage` because the dispatcher is handling that. Also, rather than have it call the error page, make the controller throw a `ServletException` with the reason for the error. Listing 20.5 gives the source for the modified `ControllerServlet`.

LISTING 20.5 Source Code for `ControllerServlet2.java`

```
package examples;

import java.io.*;
import java.util.*;
import javax.servlet.*;

public class ControllerServlet2 extends GenericServlet
{
    private static Person[] people = new Person[]
    {
        new Person("Samantha Tippin", 9, "770-123-4567"),
            new Person("Kaitlyn Tippin", 6, "770-123-4567"),
            new Person("Edward Alexander", 3, "No phone"),
            new Person("Star Alexander", 3, "Phone off hook"),
            new Person("Norton Alexander", 12, "No phone")
    };


    public synchronized void service(ServletRequest request,
        ServletResponse response)
        throws java.io.IOException, ServletException
    {
        String minimumAgeStr = request.getParameter("minAge");
        int minimumAge = 0;
```

LISTING 20.5 Continued

```
        try
        {
            minimumAge = Integer.parseInt(minimumAgeStr);
        }
        catch (Exception exc)
        {
            throw new ServletException("Invalid minimum age");
        }

        String maximumAgeStr = request.getParameter("maxAge");
        int maximumAge = 0;

        try
        {
            maximumAge = Integer.parseInt(maximumAgeStr);
        }
        catch (Exception exc)
        {
            throw new ServletException("Invalid maximum age");
        }

        // Get all the people matching the criteria
        Vector v = new Vector();

        for (int i=0; i < people.length; i++) {
            if ((people[i].age >= minimumAge) &&
                (people[i].age <= maximumAge)) {
                v.addElement(people[i]);
            }
        }

        // Store the vector of person objects so the JSP can access it
        request.setAttribute("people", v);
    }
}
```

You don't need to change anything in the `ShowPeople.jsp` page to make it work with the dispatcher. The only other thing you need to do is modify the initial HTML form. It now needs to pass parameters to the dispatcher to tell it which controller and view to use. You can insert the information as hidden form variables so that it is automatically passed when the user submits the form. Listing 20.6 shows the modified HTML form.

LISTING 20.6 Source Code for `PeopleQuery2.html`

```
<html>
<body>

Please enter the minimum and maximum ages to view:
<P>
<form action="/DispatcherServlet" method="post">
```

LISTING 20.6 Continued

```
<input type=hidden name="controller"
    value="/ControllerServlet2">
<input type=hidden name="view" value="/ShowPeople.jsp">
<input type=hidden name="errorView"
    value="/ErrorHandler.jsp">

Minimum Age: <input type="text" name="minAge"><br>
Maximum Age: <input type="text" name="maxAge"><br>
<P>
<input type="submit" value="Perform Query!">
</form>
</body>
</html>
```

Summary

Although servlets and JSPs are flexible enough to perform most tasks in a Web application, you'll want to follow some basic guidelines.

Servlets are frequently used to do work that does not directly interact with the end user but rather interacts with server-side components to generate content or perform tasks. On the other hand, JavaServer Pages are most often concerned with presentation. Well-designed JavaServer Pages use programmatic elements to present a response in a useful way to a client.

Architectural patterns such as Model 1 and Model 2 can help you design your application so that it best meets your current and future needs. Model-View-Controller is often used to structure applications so that the application's components have well-defined roles and are able to interact flexibly with their peers. Using MVC, business objects represent the model, servlets act as controllers, and JavaServer Pages provide the views.

Q&A

Q. ***Why don't I see a Web page when I submit a query using*** `PeopleQuery.html`***?***

A. Because `PeopleQuery.html` posts to the controller servlet, it's possible that you have the controller or one of the views set up incorrectly. Since the controller is not a display component, errors that occur there may not be obvious. You'll need to look at the logs to see if there's a problem. Also, check your configuration. In particular, make certain that you have mapped the servlet correctly.

Q. ***I can see part of the Web page, but there are no results. What happened?***

A. The view makes use of a servlet, `TableServlet`, to generate the table portion of the Web page. It's possible that you are passing an incorrect parameter, or that there's a problem with the servlet.

Workshop

The Workshop is designed to help you review what you have learned and help you further increase your understanding of the material covered in this hour.

Quiz

1. What is the essential difference between Model 1 and Model 2 architectures?
2. What's the difference between the `Model`, `View` and `Controller` in MVC?
3. What are some of the benefits of MVC?

Answers

1. In a Model 1 architecture, a JSP is responsible for the control of the application. It also generates the content. In Model 2, these responsibilities are delegated to specialized components.
2. The `Model` represents the attributes and behavior of the application. The `View` represents the presentation of information produced by the application. The Controller defines how the user interface responds to user input. In a typical Web application, the model is represented by business components

such as JavaBeans, Enterprise JavaBeans, or specialized classes. The controller is usually a servlet and the view is constructed using JSPs and occasionally servlets.

3. MVC was designed to provide flexibility. In many cases, the view is the component that is swapped out. For example, using the same underlying model, it's possible to use several views to interact with different clients—or even one client. If you've used Swing, you've seen MVC in action. You can change out the look and feel dynamically.

Activities

1. Write a controller that implements basic security for an application.
2. Extend the application above to handle different classes of users, directing them to pages that are distinct for each type.

HOUR 21

Using Struts and JavaServer Faces

What You'll Learn in This Hour:

- **The basics of Apache Struts**
- **The different components of Struts**
- **The basics of JavaServer Faces**
- **The different components of JavaServer Faces**
- **The relation between Struts and JavaServer Faces**

This hour introduces the Apache Struts Web application framework, which is being adopted very widely as the standard implementation of the Model-View-Controller (MVC) architecture discussed in Hour 20. You will learn about the basic building blocks of Struts and then build a small application that uses this framework.

In the latter part of this hour, you will learn about the JavaServer Faces (JSF) and how JSF and Struts work together. The example used for Struts will be modified to leverage JavaServer Faces.

An Overview of Struts

Struts was originally written by Craig R. McClanahan of Sun Microsystems and was donated to the Apache Software Foundation in May 2000. Like other Apache Jakarta projects, Struts is open source, and developers are encouraged to contribute to its development. To use Struts, all you need to do is make sure that the `struts.jar` file is in your classpath (this will be discussed later in the hour). Struts provides developers with an out-of-the-box implementation of the Model-View-Controller (MVC) design pattern. It provides developers with simplified APIs and a structure that they can use to quickly start programming Web applications using JavaServer Pages and servlets in the MVC paradigm.

Figure 21.1 shows the various components on Struts as they map to the MVC design pattern.

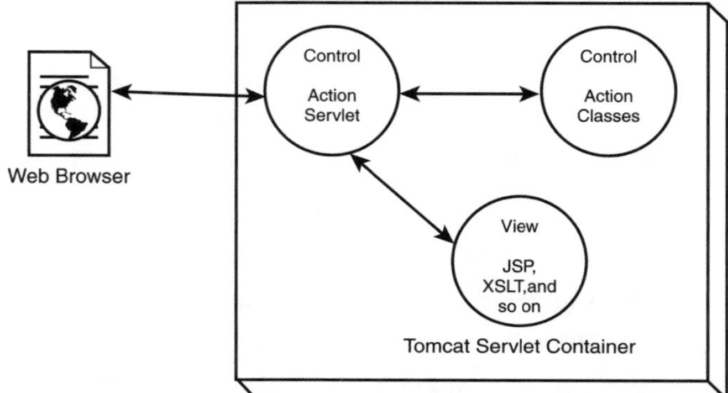

FIGURE 21.1
Struts components map to the MVC architecture.

Struts Model

Action classes in Struts form the "model" in an MVC paradigm. The Controller layer (as discussed in a later section) invokes a particular action class. This action class can use different components such as JavaBeans, Enterprise JavaBeans (EJB), or other Java classes to perform business logic, persistence, and so on. We will look at action classes and the action servlet later in this hour.

The action servlet figures out which action class to call and then invokes the "execute" method on that action class. The example shown in Listing 21.1 shows a simple action class that validates the login information (username and password) for a user.

LISTING 21.1 `LoginUserAction.java`

```
package examples;

import javax.servlet.*;
import javax.servlet.http.HttpServletRequest;
import javax.servlet.http.HttpSession;
import javax.servlet.http.HttpServletResponse;
import org.apache.struts.action.Action;
import org.apache.struts.action.ActionError;
import org.apache.struts.action.ActionErrors;
import org.apache.struts.action.ActionForm;
```

LISTING 21.1 Continued

```
import org.apache.struts.action.ActionForward;
import org.apache.struts.action.ActionMapping;

public class LoginUserAction extends Action {

   public ActionForward execute(ActionMapping theMapping, ActionForm theForm,
                                HttpServletRequest request,
                                HttpServletResponse response)
                  throws ServletException {

        LoginUserForm userForm = (LoginUserForm) theForm;
        User user = User.findUser(userForm.getUsername());
        ActionErrors errors = new ActionErrors();

        if (user == null) {
            errors.add("username",
                       new ActionError("loginform.username.notfound"));
        }
        if (!user.getPassword().equals(userForm.getPassword()) ) {
            errors.add("password",
                       new ActionError("loginform.password.invalid"));
        }
        if (errors.size() > 0) {
            saveErrors(request, errors);
            return theMapping.getInputForward();
        }
        request.getSession().setAttribute("currentUser", user);
        return theMapping.findForward("success");
    }
}
```

Listing 21.2 shows the user class (User) used by the action class (LoginUserAction).

LISTING 21.2 User.java

```
package examples;

public class User {

   private String username = null;
   private String password = null;

   public String getUsername () {
         return this.username;
   }
   public void setUsername(String _username) {
       this.username = _username;
   }

   public String getPassword () {
         return this.password;
   }
```

LISTING 21.2 Continued

```
    public void setPassword(String _password) {
        this.password = _password;
    }

    public static User findUser(String username) {
        User usr = new User();
        usr.setUsername(username);
        usr.setPassword("dummy");
        return usr;
  }
}
```

Struts View

The "view" is generally made up of the JavaServer Pages used to present HTML screens to the client. Other technologies such as XSLT can also form "view" components. In Struts, there is also the concept of an **ActionForm**.

An ActionForm basically models the HTML form on the JavaServer Pages and is used as an intermediary placeholder for transferring data from the "view" to the "model." Every form element on your JavaServer Page should have a corresponding attribute in your ActionForm.

The ActionForm also performs functions such as user input validation. You need to override the "validate" method to add custom validation as shown in Listing 21.3.

The `ActionErrors` object is checked by the controller to see whether there are any errors. If the size of the `ActionErrors` object is greater than 0, then control is redirected to the error page as specified in the `struts_config.xml` file. We will talk about this file in detail later in this hour.

Listing 21.3 shows the ActionForm used for the login page.

LISTING 21.3 `LoginUserForm.java`

```
package examples;

import javax.servlet.http.HttpServletRequest;
import org.apache.struts.action.ActionForm;
import org.apache.struts.action.ActionError;
import org.apache.struts.action.ActionErrors;
import org.apache.struts.action.ActionMapping;

public class LoginUserForm extends ActionForm {
    private String username = null;
```

LISTING 21.3 Continued

```
    private String password = null;

    public String getUsername () {
       return this.username;
    }

    public void setUsername(String _name) {
       this.username = _name;
    }

    public String getPassword () {
        return this.password;
    }

    public void setPassword(String _pass) {
      this.password = _pass;
    }

    public ActionErrors validate(ActionMapping mapping,
                                 HttpServletRequest request)  {
        ActionErrors errors = new ActionErrors();

        if (null == this.username) {
            errors.add("Username",
                       new ActionError("LoginForm.username.required"));
        }
        if (null == this.password) {
            errors.add("Password",
                       new ActionError("LoginForm.password.required"));
        }
        return errors;
    }
}
```

By the Way

DynaForms

There is new concept in Struts called **DynaForms** that saves you from having to create these ActionForms for each JavaServer Page or action. This is still in very early stages and thus we will not be covering it in this book. You should read more about these on the Apache Struts site at `http://jakarta.apache.org/struts`.

Struts also comes with a rich set of tag libraries to provide functionality on the JavaServer Page. Listing 21.4 shows a JavaServer Page that can be used to log in the user. Notice the use of the `struts-html.tld`. This provides Struts-related HTML functionality such as the `html:errors` and the HTML form tags. Struts also offers the following tag libraries:

- HTML, for dealing with HTML components, such as Forms and Textboxes
- Logic, for conditional display and iteration
- Bean, for data access
- Nested, for access to the properties of beans
- Tiles, for layout of pages

Struts has made it very easy to use these tag libraries directly from the Apache site. This will allow you to work with these tag libraries without having to modify your `web.xml` file or copy these tag libraries to your server. To leverage the tag libraries, you can add the following line of code to your JSP:

```
<%@ taglib uri="http://jakarta.apache.org/struts/tags-html"
    prefix="html" %>
```

The other option is to copy the tag libraries to your `WEB-INF` folder and reference the tag libraries in your JavaServer Page as shown in Listing 21.4.

By the Way

Using the JSTL libraries

Except for the Struts HTML and Tiles tag libraries, all the others have been replaced by JSTL. If you are using a Servlet 2.3 container or later, you should use the JSTL libraries instead of the Struts ones.

Listing 21.4 shows the JSP used to get the login information for a user.

LISTING 21.4 loginPage.jsp

```
<%@ page language="java" %>
<%@ taglib uri="/WEB-INF/struts-html.tld" prefix="html" %>

<head>
    <title>Login Page</title>
</head>

<h1>Login Page</h1>
<html:form action="/login">
    <html:errors property="Username"/>
    <BR>
    Username: <html:text property="Username"/>
    <BR>
    <html:errors property="Password"/>
    <BR>
```

LISTING 21.4 Continued

```
    Username: <html:password property="Password"/>
    <BR>
    <html:submit/>
</html:form>
```

Struts Controller

Struts implements the Front Controller design pattern. The controller processes all HTTP requests and determines what to do next. It controls the interaction between the Model and View layers. To do this, it uses a configuration file to store all the mappings for your application. An example of the `struts-config.xml` file is shown in Listing 21.5. This can be used for the login example that we have been building in this hour.

Listing 21.5 shows the `struts-config.xml` file for the login page.

LISTING 21.5 `struts-config.xml`

```
<?xml version="1.0" encoding="ISO-8859-1" ?>

<!DOCTYPE struts-config PUBLIC
          "-//Apache Software Foundation//DTD Struts Configuration 1.1//EN"
          "http://jakarta.apache.org/struts/dtds/struts-config_1_1.dtd">
<struts-config>

  <form-beans>
    <form-bean name="loginUserForm" type="jspbook.LoginUserForm"/>
  </form-beans>

  <action-mappings>
    <action path="/login" name="loginUserForm" scope="request" validate="true"
            type="jspbook.LoginUserAction"
            input="/loginPage.jsp">
       <forward name="success" path="/mainMenu.jsp"/>
    </action>
  </action-mappings>

</struts-config>
```

Form beans define a name that Struts uses to access an ActionForm. Actions define the URL that the action is associated to. They also provide the input, resulting, and error JSPs. Lastly, you specify whether you want to validate this form or not.

The basic code snippets you have seen so far show you all the elements you need to create a simple Struts application. However, you still need to set up your servlet container to work with Struts. You learn how to do this in the next section.

By the Way

Getting the Struts User Guide

The Struts page on the Apache Web site has very extensive documentation and examples that will help you master the more advanced concepts of Struts. Look at the Struts user guide at

`http://jakarta.apache.org/struts/userGuide/index.html`

Setting Up Struts

After you have downloaded Struts, the first thing you need to do is make sure your webapp is set up to use Struts. To do this, you need to make sure the `struts.jar` is in your classpath. Typically, you would copy the `struts.jar` file under your `WEB-INF\lib` directory that will become part of the JAR file you will use to deploy your Web application.

The various other Struts JAR files that start with `common*.jar` should also be copied with the `struts.jar` file. All the Struts properties files will be under the `WEB-INF` directory.

If you have multiple Struts applications, you can copy these JAR files to the `shared\lib` or `common\lib` directories beneath your Tomcat installation home. Doing this allows all your webapps to use the same version of Struts. There are many arguments for and against this approach, but you do not need to worry about these for now.

The Struts download also comes with an empty Struts application called `struts-blank.war`. You can deploy this Web application to the `webapps` directory of Tomcat, and you can use it as a starting point for building a Struts application. Table 21.1 explains the directory structure of a Struts application.

TABLE 21.1 Directory Structure of a Struts Application

File or Directory	Purpose
`META-INF`	Meta information.
`WEB-INF/classes`	You should put all your Java classes here.
`WEB-INF/classes/ApplicationResources.properties`	This file contains all the messages, text, and error messages. Similar concept to internationalization.
`WEB-INF/lib/struts.jar`	This is the Struts library.

TABLE 21.1 Continued

File or Directory	Purpose
`WEB-INF/*.tld`	The Struts tag libraries.
`WEB-INF/struts-config.xml`	Struts configuration file.
`WEB-INF/web.xml`	Standard J2EE Web app configuration file.
index.jsp	Place all your `jsp/html` pages in the root of the Web app directory.

You now know how to create and deploy a simple Struts-based application. Now let's talk about JavaServer Faces (JSF) and how it relates to Struts.

An Overview of JavaServer Faces (JSF)

JavaServer Faces (JSF) is new technology, still in its early specification stages. The brain behind Struts, Craig McClanahan, is specification co-lead for JavaServer Faces (JSR 127). You can get an early reference implementation of this technology from Sun's Web site at

`http://java.sun.com/j2ee/javaserverfaces/`

The JSF technology is targeted at simplifying the development of the user interface or View layer of an MVC application. JavaServer Faces technology includes a collection of APIs that represent various UI components and know how to handle events, perform user input validation, and carry out things such as the state, navigation, and internationalization. JSF also comes with a rich tag library that allows developers to leverage the JSF functionality from a JavaServer Page.

JSF provides a rich set of graphical user interface (GUI) components that use the concept of "renderers" that allow the GUI components to be rendered differently. A UI that is created using JSF runs on the server and renders backs to a target client, which could be a JSP or something else.

Figure 21.2 shows how a JavaServer Faces request works.

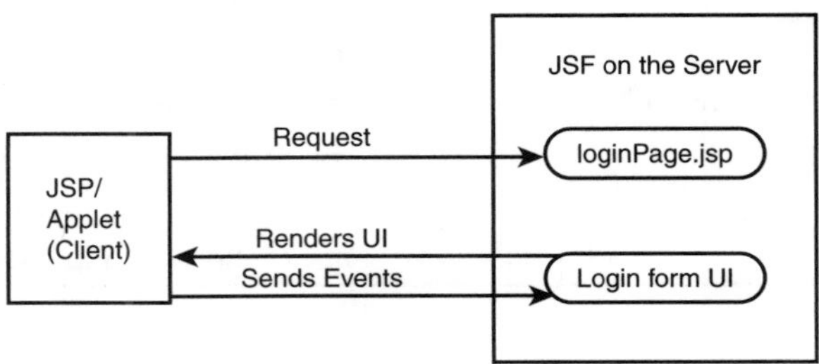

FIGURE 21.2
This illustrates a JSF request cycle.

The easy-to-use JSF API promotes the creation of custom UI components as needed for your application. The tag libraries that come with JSF allow you to render the various GUI components in an HTML format.

JSF replaces several of the Struts tag libraries and provides a cleaner separation and handling of the UI-related tasks and objects. In Struts, you only have the ability to render UI components as HTML. In addition, Struts supports only the basic HTML form components. With JSF, you can design and use a much richer set of UI components and use them uniformly, whether you have a JSP-based client or some other client. You can very easily modify your Struts-based JavaServer Pages to leverage JSF, without any change to the action classes and the rest of the Struts infrastructure.

Struts and JSF Integration

Read the note from Craig McClanahan on what is going on with the Struts and JSF integration project called Struts-Faces at

`http://jakarta.apache.org/struts/proposals/struts-faces.html`

JSF Life Cycle

Before you look at an example, it is important to understand the life cycle of a JSP request. JSF also has the concept of a single servlet that handles all faces requests. A faces request is one that has some faces components. This request is initiated through the submission of a JSF form or a link to an URL with the `/faces` prefix. The `FacesServlet` handles all faces requests. A faces request can return a faces or a non-faces response.

There are six phases in the JSF life cycle:

1. Reconstitute request tree
2. Apply request values
3. Process validations
4. Update model values
5. Invoke application
6. Render response

In the JavaServer Faces Reference Implementation (JSF-RI), each of these phases is supported by a class with the same name. Figure 21.3 shows the JSF life cycle. The dotted lines show alternate flows through the cycle. We will discuss each phase in detail.

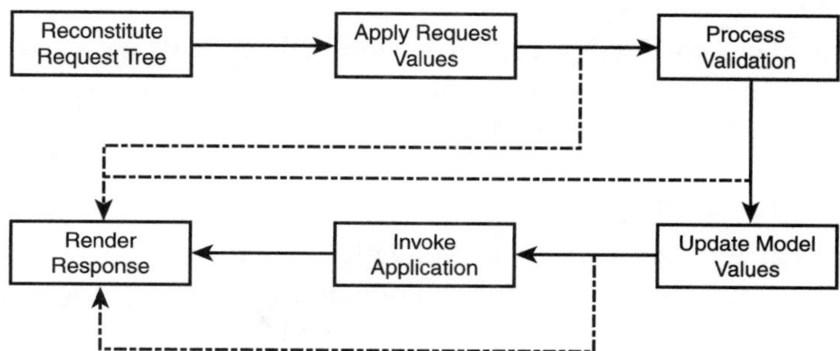

FIGURE 21.3
The JSF life cycle has six phases.

Reconstitute Request Tree

The "reconstitute request tree" phase is initiated when a user clicks a link or a button that has some faces components. During this phase, the JSF needs to do the following:

1. Build the component tree of the JSF pages as shown in Figure 21.4.
2. Set up the event handlers and validators.
3. Save the tree in the FacesContext.

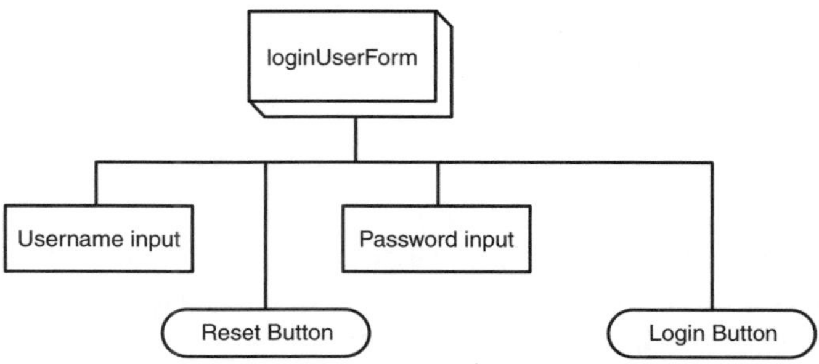

FIGURE 21.4
This shows a JSF component tree.

Apply Request Values

In the "apply request values" phase, each bean updates its value based on the information in the request. Any errors are put into the FacesContext. Events that might occur are sent to the appropriate listeners.

Process Validations

In the "process validations" phase, all validations are executed. Validators perform validations against all the attributes and add any error messages to the FacesContext. If there are error messages, you should jump directly to the "render response" phase.

Update Model Values

At this point, you know you have valid values. Now components having `valueRef` expressions are updated. This is quite similar to the "apply request values" phase.

Invoke Application

All application level events are handled during this phase. JSF executes the action specified in the `actionRef` tags.

Render Response

During this phase, JSF renders the component tree saved in the FacesContext, and this can be in a format such as HTML. This is also cached to improve performance.

JSF UI Components

JSF makes it very easy to create custom UI components. However, out of the box, it has support for the following standard components:

- UICommand—Very similar to an HTML button
- UIForm—Similar to the HTML form tag
- UIGraphic—Similar to the img tag in HTML
- UIInput—Used for user input
- UIOutput—Maps to the output of the table
- UIPanel—Works like the HTML table tag
- UIParameter—Used for parameter passing
- UISelectItem—Maps to a list of items, where you can select one item
- UISelectItems—Maps to a list of items, where you can select multiple items
- UISelectBoolean—Works like a checkbox, to select or deselect
- UISelectMany—Support the selection of multiple items
- UISelectOne—Allows you to select only one item

A Sample JSF Application

Let's modify the sample Struts application to use JavaServer Faces. As we said earlier, you can modify just the JSP and leave the rest of the application almost as is.

Listing 21.6 shows the login JSP that uses JavaServer Faces.

LISTING 21.6 Code for loginPageUsingJSF.jsp

```
<%@ page contentType="text/html; charset=UTF8" %>
<%@ taglib uri="http://java.sun.com/jsf/html" prefix="h" %>
<%@ taglib uri="http://java.sun.com/jsf/core" prefix="f" %>
<%@ taglib uri="http://java.sun.com/jstl/fmt" prefix="fmt" %>

<f:use_faces>
 <h:form id="loginForm" formName="loginForm" >

   <h:input_text id="username" valueRef="User.username">
      <f:validate_required/>
   <h:input_text/>
```

LISTING 21.6 Continued

```
   <h:input_text id="password" valueRef="User.password">
      <f:validate_required/>
   <h:input_text/>

   <h:command_button id="submit" action="success"
     label="Login" commandName="submit" >
       <f:action_listener
         type="jspBook.LoginFormActionListener"/>
   </h:command_button>

  <h:command_button id="reset" action="reset" label="Reset"
     commandName="reset" />
   <h:output_errors/>

 </h:form>
</f:use_faces>
</body>
</html>
```

You will need a `faces-config.xml` file, quite similar to the `struts-config.xml` file that we discussed earlier. Listing 21.7 shows this file.

Listing 21.7 shows the `faces-config.xml` configuration file.

LISTING 21.7 Code for `faces-config.xml`

```
<?xml version="1.0"?>
<!DOCTYPE faces-config PUBLIC
  "-//Sun Microsystems, Inc.//DTD JavaServer Faces Config 1.0//EN"
  "http://java.sun.com/dtd/web-facesconfig_1_0.dtd">
<faces-config>

    <navigation-rule>
        <from-tree-id>/loginPageUsingJSF.jsp</from-tree-id>
        <navigation-case>
          <from-outcome>success</from-outcome>
          <to-tree-id>/mainMenuUsingJSF.jsp</to-tree-id>
        </navigation-case>
    </navigation-rule>

         <managed-bean>
      <managed-bean-name>User</managed-bean-name>
      <managed-bean-class>
        jspBook.User
      </managed-bean-class>
      <managed-bean-scope>session</managed-bean-scope>
    </managed-bean>

</faces-config>
```

You will need to modify your `struts-config.xml` file to leverage JSF. Listing 21.8 shows that change.

LISTING 21.8 Modified `struts-config.xml`

```
<form-bean  name="User"
               type="jspBook.User "/>
<action-mappings>
<action path="/Login"
    type="LoginUserAction"
    name="LoginUserForm"
    scope="request"
    input="/faces/loginPageUsingJSF.jsp">
    <forward name="success" path="/faces/mainMenuUsingJSF.jsp"/>
 </action>
</action-mappings>
```

To enable faces, you will need to modify your `web.xml` file. This is shown in Listing 21.9.

LISTING 21.9 Modified `web.xml`

```
<!-- JavaServer Faces Servlet Configuration -->
<servlet>
<servlet-name>faces</servlet-name>
<servlet-class>javax.faces.webapp.FacesServlet</servlet-class>
<load-on-startup>1</load-on-startup>
</servlet>

<!-- JavaServer Faces Servlet Mapping -->
<servlet-mapping>
  <servlet-name>faces</servlet-name>
  <url-pattern>/faces/*</url-pattern>
</servlet-mapping>
```

Summary

In this hour you have looked at Struts, which is an implementation of the MVC pattern. You have looked at a simple Struts application and seen the different components that make up a Struts application.

This hour concluded with a look at the new JavaServer Faces specification. The sample Struts application created earlier in the hour was modified to leverage JSF specification.

Q&A

Q. ***What is the primary design pattern behind Struts?***

A. Struts is an implementation of the Model-View-Controller design pattern. However, you will see elements of several other design patterns as you use Struts. This includes the Front Controller design pattern.

Q. ***What are the main advantages of JavaServer Faces?***

A. JSF makes it easy to create UIs from a set of predefined components. These components automatically manage their state. JSF also makes it easy for developers to create their own UI components and reuse those components.

Workshop

The Workshop is designed to help you review what you have learned and help you further increase your understanding of the material covered in this hour.

Quiz

1. What Struts components form the controller in an MVC paradigm?
2. Can Struts and JSF be used together?
3. Is JSF a mature technology today?

Answers

1. The action servlet in Struts forms the controller. It uses the `struts-config.xml` file to figure out which view or model component it should invoke.
2. Yes, and with very little modification.
3. JSF is still in its infancy. Visit the Sun site to keep up to date with the status of JSF.

Activities

1. Build a page to edit the user's information using Struts.
2. Modify your user information page to leverage JavaServer Faces.

HOUR 22

Internationalization

What You'll Learn in This Hour

- How to change the page encoding
- How to detect the browser's preferred locale
- How to use locale-based text formatters
- How to use resource bundles in Web pages
- How to use the JSTL format actions

The Internet has had a huge impact on software development. Now developers and users from countries around the world can share information almost instantaneously. Oddly enough, developers rarely consider the fact that the people who use their software might be in another country. At least, this is often the case in the United States.

Java provides reasonable support for internationalization, some of which happens behind the scenes. When a Java program starts, it examines the locale configured in the operating system and sets up a default locale. Several Java classes use the locale for formatting dates and currencies. You can also define sets of resources, called **resource bundles**, which are locale-dependent. By confining your locale-specific data to resource bundles, you can support multiple locales in your programs without hard-coding every possible locale variation.

Setting the Page Encoding

One of the first problems you may encounter in developing an international Web site is that you may need to use a character encoding that is different from the default used by the servlet container. The default character encoding is ISO-8859-1, which is typically used for English and Latin-based languages. If your Web site must support languages that typically require a different encoding (such as Korean, Japanese, Chinese, and so on), you can specify the page encoding with the `pageEncoding` option in the `page` directive. For example, to set the page encoding to `euc-kr` for a Korean-language Web site, use the directive

```
<%@page pageEncoding="euc-kr"%>
```

Detecting the Browser's Preferred Locale

The browser sends a number of header fields in each request indicating certain preferences. One of these preferences is a list of languages that the browser prefers for Web pages. The `ACCEPT-LANGUAGE` header value contains a list of languages that the browser is prepared to handle. Using this header value, you can locate a locale that you are prepared to support and deliver content targeted toward that locale.

For example, suppose you have a Web site that is in both German and English. Although each version contains links to allow you to change languages at any time, you might want to default the user to the language his browser prefers. For example, if you see `de-DE` as the preferred language, you send the user to the German version of the page, and if you see `en-US` or `en-UK`, you send the user to the English version.

Listing 22.1 shows a JSP that detects the preferred language sent by the browser and chooses one of two possible pages.

LISTING 22.1 Source Code for `MyPage.jsp`

```
<%
    String lang = request.getHeader("ACCEPT-LANGUAGE");

    String whatPage = "MyPage_En.html";

    if (lang.startsWith("de"))
    {
        whatPage = "MyPage_De.html";
    }
%><jsp:forward page="<%=whatPage%>"/>
```

By the Way

Don't Expect Immediate Changes

When you change the language setting in Internet Explorer, you must shut down the browser and restart it before the change takes effect.

Figure 22.1 shows the JSP when viewed from a browser with a preferred language setting of English (en/US), and Figure 22.2 shows the JSP viewed from a browser that prefers German (de/DE).

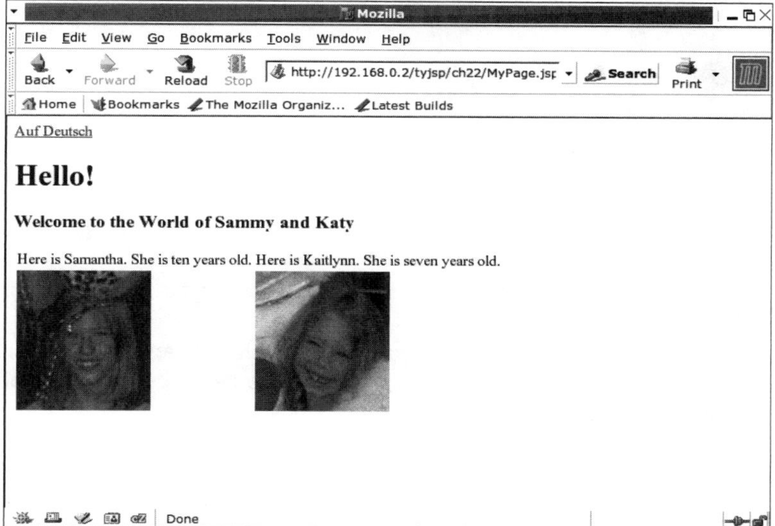

FIGURE 22.1
You can create a multilingual Web site by detecting the preferred language.

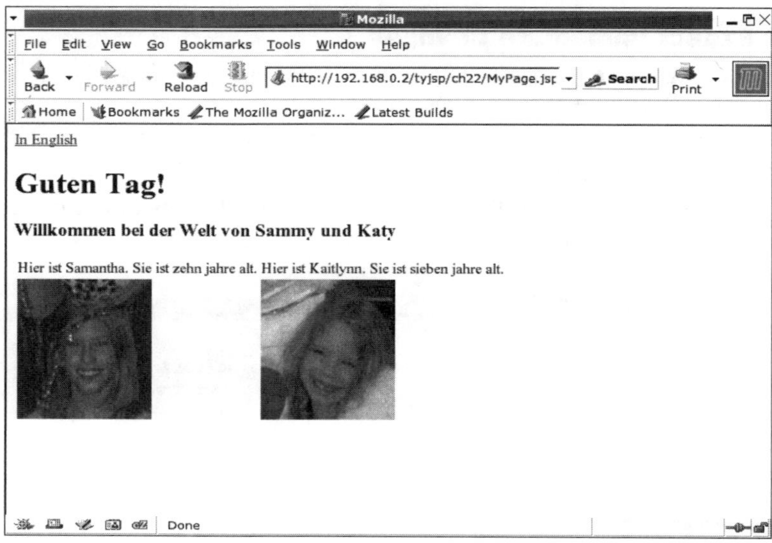

FIGURE 22.2
When you provide alternate language pages, include links to see the other language versions.

Did you Know?

Setting a Preferred Language

Both Netscape and Internet Explorer let you set the preferred language for your browser. These settings allow you to view your alternate language pages without changing the language setting for the entire operating system.

Using Locale-Based Text Formatters

Java relies on the `java.text` and the `java.util` packages for providing locale-based formatting. A locale represents both a language and a country, because two countries might share the same language but still format numbers, dates, and currencies differently. For example, the United States and the United Kingdom share the same language, but they format currencies differently because the United States uses a $ symbol and the UK uses the £ symbol.

In a Java application, you normally rely on the default locale, which the Java Virtual Machine detects by querying the operating system. Because you can assume that users have configured their systems with the locale they prefer, your application can safely rely on the default locale. In a Web application, however, the problem is more complicated. The application is running on a Web server, and the user is using a browser on another computer, possibly halfway around the world. You must create a locale object that conforms to the user's preference.

Creating a Locale Object

To create a locale object, you need at least a language for the locale, and preferably a country as well. There are also variant settings for a locale that are vendor- and browser-specific. If you don't know the country code for a locale, just use a blank string. You can still format dates and numbers without a country, but currencies will not have the correct currency symbol.

By the Way

Online Standards

You can find a list of the standard language codes, as defined by ISO-639, at `http://lcweb.loc.gov/standards/iso639-2/englangn.html`. You can find a list of valid country codes, as defined by ISO-3166, at `http://www.oasis-open.org/cover/country3166.html`.

The following code fragment creates a locale for French but does not specify a country code:

```
Locale french = new Locale("fr", "");
```

This code fragment creates a locale for German with a country code for Austria:

```
Locale germanAustria = new Locale("de", "AT");
```

Watch Out!

Setting the Current Locale

Resist the temptation to use `Locale.setDefault` to set the current locale to be the browser's locale. You don't need to pass the locale to all the formatting routines that way, and for a Web application, you introduce an ugly threading problem. Two servlets might set the default locale at the same time. One servlet might set the locale to U.S. English and another might immediately change it to German for Germany. The servlet that wanted English would suddenly find it was using the German format.

Formatting Dates

You might have used the `SimpleDateFormat` class in the `java.text` package to format dates. Although it might provide an easy way to specify date formats, you lose some of the locale independence when you use it. When you create an instance of `SimpleDateFormat`, you must supply a basic pattern for the date. You might pick a format like `MM/dd/yyyy`, for example. Unfortunately, many countries write dates in the form `dd/MM/yyyy`.

The DateFormat class doesn't give you the leeway that SimpleDateFormat does. The DateFormat class has several factory methods that create a DateFormat object for you. You don't use the constructor. Instead, you call getDateInstance, getDateTimeInstance, or getTimeInstance, depending on whether you want to display dates only, dates and times, or times only.

When you create a DateFormat, you must specify one of four formats: SHORT, MEDIUM, LONG, or FULL. You can also give the locale for the format, and if you omit the locale, you'll get the default locale. For getDateInstance and getTimeInstance, you need to specify only one format. For getDateTimeInstance, you must specify SHORT, MEDIUM, LONG, or FULL for both the date and the time. You might choose to write out the date in long format but the time in full format.

Listing 22.2 shows a JSP that uses the four format options to display the date. The locale is not included in this example, however. You will see how to include it later in this hour.

LISTING 22.2 Source Code for ShowDates.jsp

```
<%@ page language="java" import="java.text.*,java.util.*" %>
<%

    DateFormat dtShort = DateFormat.getDateTimeInstance(
        DateFormat.SHORT, DateFormat.SHORT);

    DateFormat dtMedium = DateFormat.getDateTimeInstance(
        DateFormat.MEDIUM, DateFormat.MEDIUM);

    DateFormat dtLong = DateFormat.getDateTimeInstance(
        DateFormat.LONG, DateFormat.LONG);

    DateFormat dtFull = DateFormat.getDateTimeInstance(
        DateFormat.FULL, DateFormat.FULL);
%>
<html>
<body>
A short date/time looks like: <%=dtShort.format(new Date())%><p>
A medium date/time looks like: <%=dtMedium.format(new Date())%><p>
A long date/time looks like: <%=dtLong.format(new Date())%><p>
A full date/time looks like: <%=dtFull.format(new Date())%><p>
</body>
</html>
```

Figure 22.3 shows the output of the ShowDates JSP.

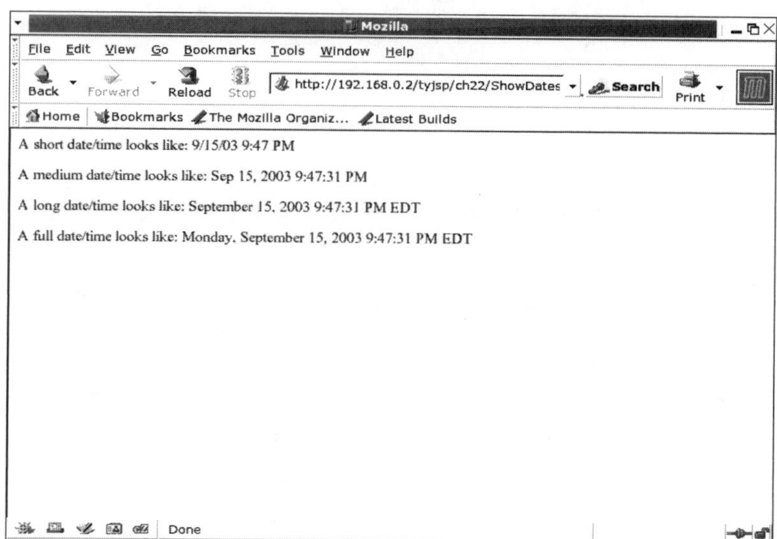

FIGURE 22.3
You can choose between four basic styles of date and time.

Formatting Currency

Formatting currency values is much more involved than formatting dates and times. It's not that there's anything difficult about formatting a currency value; the problem is that you can rarely just switch from one currency to another without performing some sort of conversion. The NumberFormat class formats a specific value such as 12.34 into dollars as $12.34 or into Deutschmarks as 12,34DM, but 12,34DM is not the same amount of money as $12.34. Java does not provide any way to convert from one currency to another.

When you think about it, it's almost impossible to make a standard API for converting currencies because currencies are traded at various rates. Imagine trying to make an API that lets you get the price of a stock or the price of a car. There would be many places to go for the information and many different formats for the data. You have the same problem trying to convert currencies. Perhaps one day all the currency traders will publish rates via a Web service using a standard XML format and you can perform reasonable conversions. Even so, because the rates fluctuate, you must still worry about how stale the information is. The conversion rate for an unstable currency might plummet over the course of a day or two.

By now you see that the capability to display currency values for different locales is not such a useful feature. If you do find that you need to display currency values, you can call `NumberFormat.getCurrencyInstance` and pass it the locale whose currency you want to display:

```
NumberFormat currencyFormat =
    NumberFormat.getCurrencyInstance(someLocale);
```

Getting a Locale for a Browser's Preferred Language

When you examine the `ACCEPT-LANGUAGE` header value, you will find a list of locale codes consisting of a two-letter language code, possibly a country code, and even variant options after the country code. Each locale code is separated by a comma. When you just want the preferred language (the browser sends the locales in order of preference), you need to grab the first one in the list.

Listing 22.3 shows a JavaServer Page that parses the `ACCEPT-LANGUAGE` header value and gets a locale value for the preferred locale.

LISTING 22.3 Source Code for `TestLocale.jsp`

```
<%@ page language="java" import="java.text.*,java.util.*" %>
<%

// Get the default locale in case you can't determine the
// user's locale.
    Locale locale = Locale.getDefault();

// Get the browser's preferred language.
    String acceptLangString = request.getHeader("ACCEPT-LANGUAGE");

// If there is an ACCEPT-LANGUAGE header, parse it.
    if (acceptLangString != null)
    {

// The accepted languages should be separated by commas, but also
// add space as a separator to eliminate whitespace.
        StringTokenizer localeParser = new StringTokenizer(
            acceptLangString, " ,");

// See whether there is a language in the list (you need only the first one).
        if (localeParser.hasMoreTokens())
        {
// Get the locale.
            String localeStr = localeParser.nextToken();
```

LISTING 22.3 Continued

```
// The locale should be in the format ll-CC where ll is the language
// and CC is the country, like en-US for English in the U.S. and
// de-DE for German in Germany. Allow the browser to use _ instead
// of -, too.
            StringTokenizer localeSplitter = new StringTokenizer(
                localeStr, "_-");

// Assume both values are blank.
            String language = "";
            String country = "";

// See whether a language is specified.
            if (localeSplitter.hasMoreTokens())
            {
                language = localeSplitter.nextToken();
            }

// See whether a country is specified (there won't always be one).
            if (localeSplitter.hasMoreTokens())
            {
                country = localeSplitter.nextToken();

            }

// Create a locale based on this language and country (if country is
// blank, you'll still get locale-based text, but currencies won't
// display correctly.
            locale = new Locale(language, country);
        }
    }
%>
<html>
<body>
Your locale language is <%=locale.getLanguage()%>.<p>
Your locale country is <%=locale.getCountry()%>.<p>
<%
// Get a formatter to display currency.
    NumberFormat currencyFormatter =
        NumberFormat.getCurrencyInstance(locale);

// Get a formatter to display dates and times.
    DateFormat dateFormatter =
        DateFormat.getDateTimeInstance(
            DateFormat.FULL, DateFormat.FULL, locale);
%>
A currency in your locale looks like this:
    <%= currencyFormatter.format(12.34) %><p>
A date in your locale looks like this:
    <%= dateFormatter.format(new Date()) %><p>
</body>
</html>
```

Figure 22.4 shows the TestLocale JavaServer Page running with a locale of en-US (English-U.S.).

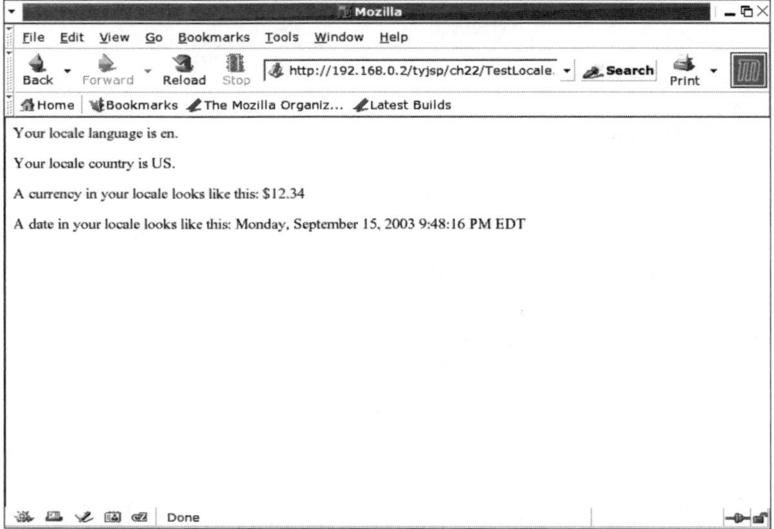

FIGURE 22.4
The java.text package can format dates and currencies.

Figure 22.5 shows the TestLocale JSP running with a locale of de (German) and no country code. Notice the odd-looking character in the currency. If you don't specify a country, you'll see this odd symbol. Also notice that the currency formatter still uses the German convention of using a comma where English text uses a period. Although the currency formatter doesn't know the currency symbol, it uses the number formatter to format the currency value, and the number formatter doesn't need to know the country.

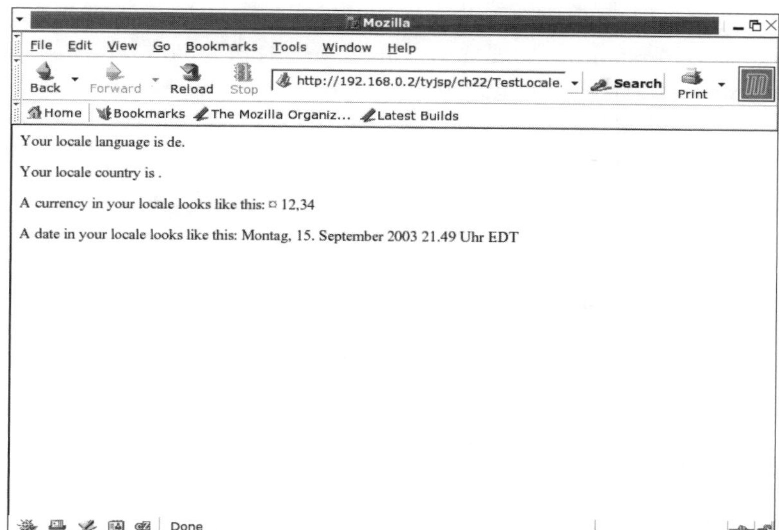

FIGURE 22.5
If you don't specify a country for a locale, the currency symbol isn't correct.

Using Resource Bundles in Web Pages

Java's I18N support includes objects known as **resource bundles**. When you create a multilingual application or Web site, you don't always want to make separate screens or pages for each language. For example, when you create an HTML form, the prompt strings can be in different languages, but the HTML for defining the form itself is the same no matter what language you use.

By using resource bundles, you can group various prompt strings and other objects that are locale dependent. When you create a resource bundle class, you decide on a base classname and then define each locale's resources in a class whose name is formed by adding the locale to the end of the classname.

For example, you might store some resources in a class called `SomeResources`. The French version of the resources would be in a class called `SomeResources_fr`, and the German version would be in a class called `SomeResources_de`. If you need to make a special German version of the resources tailored to Austria, you can put them in a class called `SomeResources_de_AT`.

Because writing resource bundles can be tedious, Java gives you some prebuilt framework classes. The `ListResourceBundle` class allows you to store the resources in an array of objects. Listing 22.4 shows an example `ListResourceBundle`. Notice that there is no locale at the end of the classname. That makes this class the default bundle if there is no bundle for the browser's locale.

LISTING 22.4 Source Code for `TestResources.java`

```
package usingjsp;

import java.text.*;
import java.util.*;

public class TestResources extends ListResourceBundle
{
    public Object[][] getContents()
    {
        return contents;
    }

    final Object[][] contents =
    {
        { "namePrompt", "What is your name: " },
        { "agePrompt", "How old are you: " },
        { "placePrompt", "Where do you live: " },
        { "greetHeading", "Hello!" },
        { "welcomeText",
            "Welcome to our web site. Please take a moment to "+
            "fill out our survey" },
        { "submitButtonText", "Submit" }
    };
}
```

Listing 22.5 shows the German version of the `TestResources` resource bundle.

LISTING 22.5 Source Code for `TestResources_de.java`

```
package usingjsp;

import java.util.*;
import java.text.*;

public class TestResources_de extends ListResourceBundle
{
    public Object[][] getContents()
    {
        return contents;
    }

    final Object[][] contents =
    {
```

LISTING 22.5 Continued

```
        { "namePrompt", "Wie hei[gb]en Sie" },
        { "agePrompt", "Wie alt sind Sie: " },
        { "placePrompt", "Wo wohnen Sie: " },
        { "greetHeading", "Guten Tag!" },
        { "welcomeText",
            "Willkommen bei unserer Web-Site. Bitte, dauern Sie einen "+
            "Moment Um unsere Umfrage auszufüllen" },
        { "submitButtonText", "Senden" }
    };
}
```

Listing 22.6 shows a JSP that displays an HTML form using the prompts from the `TestResources` resource bundle. Notice that you don't need separate pages for each language. Only the prompts need to change.

LISTING 22.6 Source Code for `ResourceBundles.jsp`

```
<%@ page language="java" import="java.text.*,java.util.*" %>
<%

// Get the default locale in case you can't determine the
// user's locale.
    Locale locale = Locale.getDefault();

// Get the browser's preferred language.
    String acceptLangString = request.getHeader("ACCEPT-LANGUAGE");

// Allow the user to override the browser's language setting. This
// lets you test with tools such as Babelfish (which isn't that great
// at translating to begin with).
    String override = request.getParameter("langOverride");

    if (override != null)
    {
        acceptLangString = override;
    }

// If there is an ACCEPT-LANGUAGE header, parse it.
    if (acceptLangString != null)
    {

// The accepted languages should be separated by commas, but also
// add space as a separator to eliminate whitespace.
        StringTokenizer localeParser = new StringTokenizer(
            acceptLangString, " ,");

// See whether a language is in the list (you need only the first one).
        if (localeParser.hasMoreTokens())
        {
// Get the locale.
            String localeStr = localeParser.nextToken();
```

LISTING 22.6 Continued

```
// The locale should be in the format ll-CC where ll is the language
// and CC is the country, like en-US for English in the U.S. and
// de-DE for German in Germany. Allow the browser to use _ instead
// of -, too.
            StringTokenizer localeSplitter = new StringTokenizer(
                localeStr, "_-");

// Assume both values are blank.
            String language = "";
            String country = "";

// See where a language is specified.
            if (localeSplitter.hasMoreTokens())
            {
                language = localeSplitter.nextToken();
            }

// See whether a country is specified (there won't always be one).
            if (localeSplitter.hasMoreTokens())
            {
                country = localeSplitter.nextToken();

            }

// Create a locale based on this language and country (if country is
// blank, you'll still get locale-based text, but currencies won't
// display correctly).
locale = new Locale(language, country);
        }
    }

// Get the bundle of resource strings for this locale.
    ResourceBundle resources = ResourceBundle.getBundle(
        "usingjsp.TestResources", locale);
%>
<html>
<body>
<h1><%= resources.getString("greetHeading")%></h1>
<p>
<%= resources.getString("welcomeText")%>:
<p>
<form action="your_form_handler_here" method="post">

<%=resources.getString("namePrompt")%>
<input type="text" name="name"><br>

<%=resources.getString("agePrompt")%>
<input type="text" name="age"><br>

<%=resources.getString("placePrompt")%>
<input type="text" name="place"><br>
```

LISTING 22.6 Continued

```
<p>
<input type="submit" value="<%=resources.getString("submitButtonText")%>">
</form>
</body>
</html>
```

Figure 22.6 shows the `ResourceBundles` JSP running in a browser with a preferred language of English.

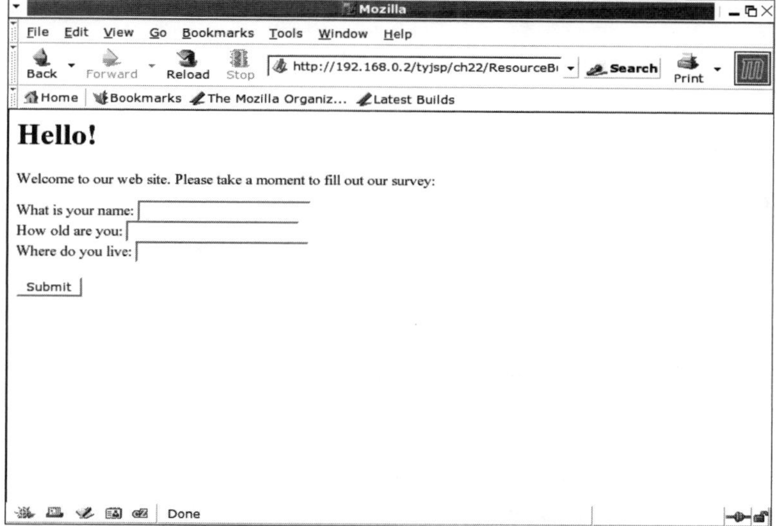

FIGURE 22.6 Resource bundles let you customize parts of a JSP or servlet.

Figure 22.7 shows the `ResourceBundles` JSP running in a browser with a preferred language of German.

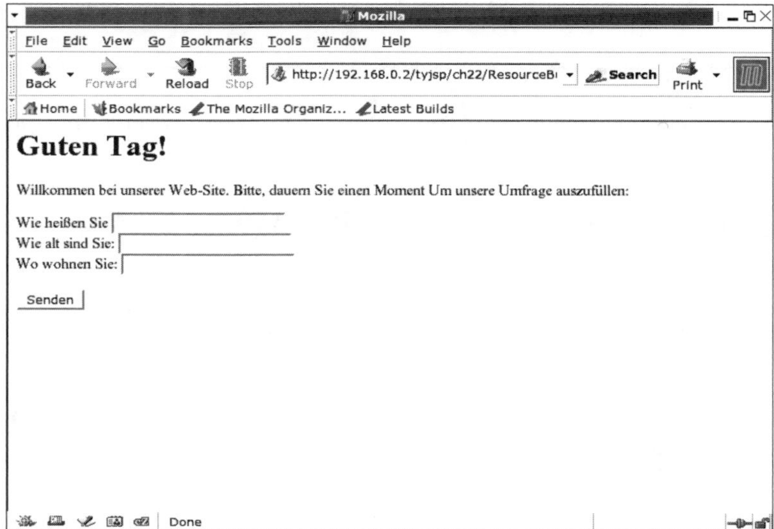

FIGURE 22.7
The `ResourceBundle` class locates a resource bundle for a particular locale.

Although the `ListResourceBundle` class makes it easy to customize various items in a Web page, the `PropertyResourceBundle` class makes it even easier. The `PropertyResourceBundle` class lets you store locale-specific strings in a properties file rather than a Java class, making it much easier to customize the resources. All you need to do to use the `PropertyResourceBundle` class is to create a properties file with lines of the form `name=value`. Listing 22.7 shows a properties file defining the same resource names as `TestResources.java`. Make sure the properties file ends with `.properties`. The `ResourceBundle` class specifically looks for files with the `.properties` extension.

LISTING 22.7 Source Code for `TestResourceProps.properties`

```
namePrompt=What is your name:
agePrompt=How old are you:
placePrompt=Where do you live:
greetHeading=Hello!
welcomeText=Welcome to our Web site.
        Please take a moment to fill out our survey
submitButtonText=Submit
```

Listing 22.8 shows the German version of the properties file. Notice that you just need to append the language to the end of the name of the properties file, right before the `.properties` extension.

LISTING 22.8 Source Code for `TestResourceProps_de.properties`

```
namePrompt=Wie hei[gb]en Sie:
agePrompt=Wie alt sind Sie:
placePrompt=Wo wohnen Sie:
greetHeading=Guten Tag!
welcomeText= Willkommen bei unserer Web-Site.
        Bitte, dauern Sie einen Moment Um unsere Umfrage auszufüllen
submitButtonText=Senden
```

The beauty of the `PropertyResourceBundle` class is that it treats the files as if they were classnames. That is, you just need to put the properties files somewhere in your classpath and call `ResourceBundle.getBundle` by using the base name of the properties file (such as `TestResourceProps`).

Instead of using the `TestResources` class, you need to change the `getBundle` statement in `ResourceBundles.jsp` to support properties files:

```
ResourceBundle resources = ResourceBundle.getBundle(
    "TestResourceProps", locale);
```

By the Way

Class Comes Before Precedence

If you have a properties file named `TestResourceProps.properties` and a class named `TestResourceProps`, the class takes precedence over the properties file. The `ResourceBundle` class loads the `TestResourceProps` class rather than the properties file.

The Format Tag Library

Java's text formatting and internationalization APIs are useful in making Web sites for users in many countries. You may need to display times, dates, and numbers in a different format, or you may need to display messages in different languages, depending on a browser's language preferences. JSTL includes a number of text formatting and internationalization tags that provide easy access to the underlying Java APIs.

Internationalization Tags

The internationalization (I18N) tags let you specify a particular locale, which controls the formatting of data. You can also access resource bundles, which contain language-specific items.

By the Way

Who Wants to Type That Much?

You might have seen "internationalization" abbreviated as I18N. The abbreviation is a clever acknowledgment of the fact that there are 18 letters between the *I* and the *N* in *internationalization*.

The `<fmt:setLocale>` Tag

The `<fmt:setLocale>` tag sets the locale used for performing any locale-specific operations. The `value` attribute specifies the locale and may be either an expression that evaluates to a `java.util.Locale` object or a string of the form `"LL"` or `"LL-ccc"` where *LL* is a two-letter language code and *ccc* is an optional country code (for example, EN, EN-us, EN-gb, DE-at). You can also specify a scope for the locale setting. A scope of `session` means that the locale setting remains active for the entire scope of this session, but it doesn't affect other sessions. A scope of `application` would set the locale for the entire application. By using a `session` scope, you avoid the trouble of setting the locale every time you process a new request.

By default, the I18N and formatting tags determine the locale based on the browser's preferences.

The `<fmt:bundle>` Tag

The `<fmt:bundle>` tag specifies a resource bundle to use for any messages enclosed within the `<fmt:bundle>` tag. The `basename` attribute specifies a fully qualified resource bundle name, without the locale-specific suffix. A resource bundle name uses the same form as a classname. If the resource bundle is a properties file, *don't* include `.properties` at the end. As you'll see in a moment, the `<fmt:bundle>` tag is used when you format messages with the `<fmt:message>` tag.

A resource bundle may contain a number of items, each associated with a key value. If the key values are long and share a common prefix, you can use the prefix attribute to specify the prefix in the `<fmt:bundle>` tag. For example, suppose several messages all begin with the key `com.wutka.i18n.msg`. Rather than using the long key name, you specify `prefix="com.wutka.i18n.msg."`, and then in your <fmt:message> tags you just supply the part of the key that comes after the common prefix.

The <fmt:setBundle> Tag

The <fmt:setBundle> tag locates a resource bundle and assigns it to a variable for later use. As with the <fmt:bundle> tag, the basename attribute specifies the name of the resource bundle. The var attribute specifies the name of the variable in which to store the bundle, and the optional scope attribute specifies the scope of the variable (page being the default).

The <fmt:message> Tag

The <fmt:message> tag retrieves a message from a resource bundle and optionally uses the java.util.MessageFormat class to format the message. The key attribute specifies the message key. If the <fmt:message> tag occurs within a <fmt:bundle> tag, the key is appended to the bundle's prefix, if there is one. If the <fmt:message> tag occurs outside of a <fmt:bundle> tag, the bundle attribute must be present and must be an expression that evaluates to a LocalizationContext object (most often, a variable initialized with the <fmt:setBundle> tag).

Rather than specify a key with the key attribute, you can put the key in the body of the <fmt:message> tag. For example, the following two tags are equivalent:

```
<fmt:message key="greeting"/>
<fmt:message>greeting</fmt:message>
```

By default, the <fmt:message> writes its output to the JSP's writer. You can also store the formatted message in a variable by specifying the variable name in a var attribute. If you store the message in a variable, <fmt:message> doesn't write the message to the JSP's writer. You can also specify a scope for the variable with the scope attribute.

The MessageFormat class can perform parameter substitution, and the <fmt:message> tag enables you to pass parameters with the <fmt:param> tag. There are two ways to specify a parameter with the <fmt:param>. You can specify the value in the value attribute or specify the value in the content of the <fmt:param> tag. For example, the following two tags are equivalent:

```
<fmt:param value="destination"/>
<fmt:param>destination</fmt:param>
```

The following tag formats a message with several parameters:

```
<fmt:message key="shipment">
```

```
   <param value="${shipDate}"/>
   <param value="${shipmentStatus}"/>
</fmt:message>
```

Listing 22.9 shows the JSTL version of the ResourceBundle.jsp page. It uses the `<jsp:bundle>` tag to load a resource bundle and the `<jsp:message>` tag to retrieve messages from the bundle.

LISTING 22.9 Source Code for `ResourceBundleJSTL.jsp`

```
<%@ taglib prefix="fmt" uri="http://java.sun.com/jstl/fmt" %>
<fmt:bundle basename="TestResourceProps">
<html>
<body>
<h1><fmt:message key="greetHeading"/></h1>
<p>
<fmt:message key="welcomeText"/>:
<p>
<form action="your_form_handler_here" method="post">

<fmt:message key="namePrompt"/>
<input type="text" name="name"><br>

<fmt:message key="agePrompt"/>
<input type="text" name="age"><br>

<fmt:message key="placePrompt"/>
<input type="text" name="place"><br>

<p>
<input type="submit" value="<fmt:message key='submitButtonText'/>">
</form>
</body>
</html>
</fmt:bundle>
```

The `<fmt:requestEncoding>` Tag

The `<fmt:requestEncoding>` tag specifies the encoding for the `request` object. Many browsers don't specify a content encoding in the HTTP header, so you often need to set the encoding yourself. By default, the `<fmt:requestEncoding>` tag uses the current locale to determine the request encoding. You can also specify a particular encoding with the `value` attribute.

Formatting Tags

The formatting tags provide access to many of the formatting objects in the java.text package. The formatting tags focus on formatting and parsing dates, numbers, percentages, and currency values.

The <fmt:timeZone> Tag

The <fmt:timeZone> tag specifies the time zone to be used by any tags contained within it (similar to the way <fmt:bundle> specifies a resource bundle to use). The <fmt:timeZone> can't determine the browser's time zone; you must always supply some kind of time zone value via the value attribute. The value attribute can be any of the time zones supported by the java.util.TimeZone class, such as America/New_York, Asia/Calcutta, or GMT-8.

The <fmt:setTimeZone> Tag

The <fmt:setTimeZone> tag stores a time zone in a variable and uses the time zone as the default time zone depending on the scope of the variable. As with the <fmt:timeZone> tag, the value attribute specifies the time zone name. The var attribute specifies the variable name (if the variable name is omitted, the time zone is stored in the default time zone variable). You can also specify a scope, which can apply to either the named variable or the default time zone variable. For example, if you specify a session scope and omit the variable name, you set the default time zone for only the current session. If you specify an application scope and omit the variable name, you specify the default time zone for the entire application.

The <fmt:formatNumber> Tag

The <fmt:formatNumber> tag formats numbers as integers, decimals, percentages, and currencies. You can specify the number to format either with an EL expression in the value attribute or as the tag's body content. The type attribute specifies the kind of formatting to perform: number, currency, or percent. The default formatting type is number. By default, the <fmt:formatNumber> tag writes the formatted number to the JSP's writer. Instead of writing the number to the JSP's writer, you can store the formatted number in a variable by supplying a variable name in the var attribute and an optional scope in the scope attribute.

The <fmt:formatNumber> tag has several attributes related to formatting, as shown in Table 22.1.

TABLE 22.1 Attributes Supported by <fmt:formatNumber>

Attribute	Description
pattern	A custom pattern for decimal numbers, as defined by the java.text.DecimalFormat class.
currencyCode	The currency code to use (only if type=currency).
currencySymbol	The currency symbol to use (only if type=currency).
groupingUsed	If true, numbers may contain grouping characters (for example, 1000 appears as 1,000 for English locales). If false, no grouping is performed. This setting is true by default.
maxIntegerDigits	The maximum number of digits to show in the integer portion of a number.
minIntegerDigits	The minimum number of digits to show in the integer portion of a number.
maxFractionDigits	The maximum number of digits to show in the fraction portion of a number.
minFractionDigits	The minimum number of digits to show in the fraction portion of a number.

To write out a decimal number with two digits to the right of the decimal point, and up to six digits to the left, use the following tag:

```
<fmt:formatNumber value="3.1415926536" maxFractionDigits="2"
    maxIntegerDigits="6"/>
```

When specifying a number pattern, there are a number of characters that may appear in the pattern. These characters are shown in Table 22.2.

TABLE 22.2 Allowable Number Pattern Characters

Character	Meaning
0	Represents a single digit, displaying leading zeros.
#	Represents a single digit with a blank or blanks for leading zeros.

TABLE 22.2 Continued

Character	Meaning
.	Represents a decimal or monetary separator (decimal point in English locales, translates to a comma in locales such as DE [German].
-	Indicates where to display the minus sign for negative numbers.
,	Represents a grouping separator.
E	Represents the separator between the mantissa and exponent in scientific notation.
;	Separates the patterns for a positive and negative number (you can specify these separately).
%	Represents the percent symbol; causes the result to be multiplied by 100 and displayed as a percent.
\u2030	Represents the per-mille symbol; causes the result to be multiplied by 1000 and displayed as a per-mille.
\u00a4	Represents a currency symbol; causes the monetary separator to be used instead of decimal separator, if different.
'	Causes the next character to be interpreted as a simple character, similar to the way \ works in Java strings. To represent a single quote, use two of them (`''`). The sequence `'0` represents a 0 instead of any digit, for example.

The `<fmt:parseNumber>` Tag

The `<fmt:parseNumber>` tag converts a string to a numeric value, including percentages and currencies. It can parse a value specified by the `value` attribute or parse the body content of the `<fmt:parseNumber>` tag.

You can store the parsed number in a variable by specifying a `var` attribute and an optional `scope` attribute. If you don't store the parsed value in a variable, the `<fmt:parseNumber>` tag writes the parsed value to the JSP's writer.

The `type` attribute specifies the kind of value to parse: number, percent, or currency. The default type is `number`. The `<fmt:parseNumber>` tag uses the default locale, although you can specify an alternate locale with the `parseLocale` attribute, which must be an EL expression that evaluates to a `java.util.Locale` object. To parse only integer values (that is, no decimal numbers), specify integerOnly="true". Finally, to parse a number using a custom pattern, specify the pattern with the pattern attribute. The custom pattern for <fmt:parseNumber> is the same as the pattern in <fmt:formatNumber> and is described by Table 22.2.

The <fmt:formatDate> Tag

The <fmt:formatDate> tag formats a date value specified either by the value attribute or by the body content of the tag itself. By default, the <fmt:formatDate> tag writes the formatted date to the JSP's writer, but you can instead store the value in a string variable named by the var attribute and optional scope attribute.

The <fmt:formatDate> tag can format both times and dates. The type attribute specifies what kind of value you want to format: time, date, or both. You can also specify the general type of a date or time with the dateStyle and timeStyle attributes. The possible styles are default, short, medium, long, and full. You can also specify a custom format with the pattern attribute. Table 22.3 shows the pattern characters for a custom pattern.

TABLE 22.3 Valid Date Pattern Characters

Character	Description
G	The era (A.D., B.C., and so on)
y	The year (yy for two-digit years, yyyy for four digits)
M	The month (MM for numeric month, MMM or longer for month names or abbreviations)
w	The week of the year (ww for two digits)
W	The week of the month
D	The day of the year (DDD for three digits)
d	The day of the month (dd for two digits)
F	The numeric day of the week
E	The text day of the week (EEEE or longer for full name)
a	AMa.m./PMp.m. indicator
H	Hour of the day (0–23)
k	Hour of the day (1–24)
K	Hour in a.m./p.m. (0–11)
h	Hour in a.m./p.m. (1–12)
m	Minutes in hour
s	Seconds in minute

TABLE 22.3 Valid Date Pattern Characters

Character	Description
S	Milliseconds in second
z	Full time zone name
Z	RFC 822 time zone (for example, 0500)

The `<fmt:parseDate>` Tag

The `<fmt:parseDate>` tag parses a date specified by either the `value` attribute or the tag's body content and stores the result in a variable named by the `var` attribute (with optional `scope`). If no variable is specified, the tag writes its output to the JSP's writer.

The `<fmt:parseDate>` tag supports all the attributes in the `<fmt:formatDate>` tag and also supports a `parseLocale` attribute that specifies the locale of the time being parsed. The value of the attribute should be an EL expression that evaluates to a `java.util.Locale` object.

Summary

Creating multilingual Web sites can be a daunting task. After all, it is difficult to provide text for so many different languages. Although Java can't solve the language barrier, it does provide simple ways to display text, numbers, dates, and currencies in a variety of formats. The JSTL formatting tags make it even easier to create multilingual Web sites. With a single tag, you can load a resource bundle and then use other simple tags to display values from the bundle. The JSTL formatting tags also allow you to format JSP EL expressions so you can display dynamic data as well.

Q&A

Q. ***How can I tell whether my Web site actually works for other languages?***

A. You can change the language setting for your browser to specify a different preferred language.

Q. ***Why can't the resource bundle find my properties file?***

A. Treat the properties file like a `.class` file. It must be visible somewhere along your classpath. Also, make sure that the browser is requesting a language that you support. If not, make sure you have a default properties file (one without a language on the end).

Workshop

The Workshop is designed to help you review what you have learned and help you further increase your understanding of the material covered in this hour.

Quiz

1. How do you tell the JSP to use a different character encoding?
2. How can you load alternate language versions of various values at runtime?
3. How can you display times and dates in different formats?

Answers

1. Use the `pageEncoding` attribute in the `page` directive.
2. Store the values in resource bundles and then look up the values from the bundles at runtime. Java will use the bundle for the appropriate language.
3. The easiest way is to use the JSTL formatting tags. Your next best alternative is to use the objects in the `java.text` package.

Activities

1. Create a Web page that displays greetings based on the browser's language preference.
2. Modify your greeting program to load its greetings from resource bundles.

HOUR 23
Security

What You'll Learn in This Hour:

- How role-based security works
- What options are available for you to use when considering your security needs
- How to use the FORM authentication method
- How to use role-based security programmatically

In Hour 12, "Saving Data Between Requests," you saw how to create a login form and keep track of a user with the `session` object. The servlet container gives you an alternative to creating your own login form. By adding additional information to the deployment descriptor for your Web application, you can force the user to log in to the application without writing specific code for login authentication.

Role-Based Security

The authentication mechanism in the servlet specification uses a technique called **role-based security**. The idea is that rather than restricting resources at the user level, you create **roles** and restrict the resources by role. A single user can have more than one role. For example, a company might have employees and contractors, so you can have an application that permits different operations, depending on whether you are an employee or a contractor. You might also have a manager role. If a contractor happens to be a manager, he would have two roles: contractor and manager.

There are no predefined roles. You can come up with role names as you see fit. As far as creating users and roles, each servlet engine has its own method for defining users and roles. In Tomcat, roles are defined in the file `tomcat-users.xml`, which is located off of Tomcat's home directory in conf. An example of this file is shown in Listing 23.1.

LISTING 23.1 An example tomcat-users.xml

```
<?xml version='1.0' encoding='utf-8'?>
<tomcat-users>
  <role rolename="tomcat"/>
  <role rolename="role1"/>
  <role rolename="manager"/>
  <role rolename="admin"/>
  <user username="tomcat" password="tomcat" roles="tomcat"/>
  <user username="role1" password="tomcat" roles="role1"/>
  <user username="both" password="tomcat" roles="tomcat,role1"/>
  <user username="admin" password="secret" roles="admin,manager"/>
</tomcat-users>
```

The Tomcat documentation briefly mentions this file in connection with the Manager application. You may recall that you must add an admin and manager role and a user in those roles to be able to use the Administration tool and Web application manager. As you can see, you add roles and users by adding <role> and <user> elements.

BASIC **Authentication**

HTTP has a built-in authentication protocol. When you log in to a page that requires authentication, the Web server first sends back a message telling the browser to send authentication information. The browser then prompts you for a username and password to send to the server. After the browser sends the username and password (assuming they are correct), the Web server displays the requested page. The browser holds on to the authentication information in case the Web server asks for it again.

To set up BASIC authentication for a Web application, you must add several new tags to your web.xml file. Listing 23.2 shows a basic web.xml file that uses authentication.

LISTING 23.2 Source Code for web.xml for the authtest Application

```
<?xml version="1.0" encoding="ISO-8859-1"?>
<web-app xmlns="http://java.sun.com/xml/ns/j2ee"
    xmlns:xsi="http://www.w3.org/2001/XMLSchema-instance"
    xsi:schemaLocation="http://java.sun.com/xml/ns/j2ee
    http://java.sun.com/xml/ns/j2ee/web-app_2_4.xsd"
    version="2.4">
    <display-name>authtest</display-name>
```

LISTING 23.2 Continued

```
    <description>A test of authentication</description>
    <security-constraint>
        <web-resource-collection>
            <web-resource-name>SecureTest</web-resource-name>
            <url-pattern>/*</url-pattern>
            <http-method>GET</http-method>
            <http-method>POST</http-method>
        </web-resource-collection>
        <user-data-constraint>
            <description>SSL not required</description>
            <transport-guarantee>NONE</transport-guarantee>
        </user-data-constraint>
        <auth-constraint>
            <description>Let only managers use this app</description>
            <role-name>manager</role-name>
        </auth-constraint>
    </security-constraint>
    <security-role>
        <description>The role of manager is one that can use our application.
        </description>
        <role-name>manager</role-name>
    </security-role>
    <login-config>
        <auth-method>BASIC</auth-method>
    </login-config>
</web-app>
```

The main tags that have been added to the basic deployment descriptor are `<security-constraint>`, `<login-config>`, and `<security-role>`.

The `<security-constraint>` Tag

The `<security-constraint>` tag tells the servlet engine what security requirements your application has. You can have more than one security constraint if necessary. Within the security constraint, you must specify a Web resource collection with the `<web-resource-collection>` tag.

A Web resource collection is a collection of URL patterns to which the security constraint applies. For instance, you might want to restrict only a single directory in your application. The `<url-pattern>` tag in your resource collection would then contain a pattern matching the directory you want to restrict. The pattern `/*` in Listing 23.1 means that the security constraint applies to all URLs in the application's directory. The `<web-resource-name>` tag specifies the name for the Web resource collection. There is no connection between the name and any of the URLs within it. The name serves little purpose but can be useful for various development and configuration tools.

The other tag you find in the Web resource collection is the `<http-method>` tag. This specifies which HTTP methods require authentication. If you do not specify an HTTP method, the security applies to all HTTP methods. You might, for example, want to perform authentication for an HTTP `POST` but not for a `GET`. You might also want to perform different kinds of authentication for `GET` and `POST`. In the latter case, you specify two separate security constraints, one with an HTTP method of `GET` and the other with an HTTP method of `POST`. You can also use authentication with other HTTP methods such as `PUT` and `DELETE`.

The `<user-data-constraint>` tag tells the servlet engine what kind of data security your application needs. You can include a `<description>` tag to describe the constraint, but it is optional. The `<transport-guarantee>` tag indicates the kind of transport-level data security your application needs. The value for the `<transport-guarantee>` tag can be one of three values:

- `NONE`—Indicates that the application doesn't require any special data security.
- `INTEGRAL`—Indicates that the client and server should ensure that the data can't be changed by anyone. Although you would typically use an encrypted protocol such as SSL for this level of security, `INTEGRAL` does not require that the data can't be observed by a third party. You could send digitally signed, unencrypted messages back and forth and still meet the requirements for `INTEGRAL`.
- `CONFIDENTIAL`—Requires that a third party can't tamper with the data or read it. You will almost always use SSL for this level unless you have another encryption transport protocol available.

The `<auth-constraint>` tag enables you to specify the various roles to which this security constraint applies. The `<role-name>` tag enables you to specify a specific role. You can include multiple `<role-name>` tags within a single `<auth-constraint>` tag.

The `<login-config>` Tag

The `<login-config>` tag enables you to control the type of authentication you want the servlet engine and browser to perform. You specify the type of authentication through the `<auth-method>` tag. The servlet specification supports four kinds of authentication methods:

- `BASIC`—Causes the browser to prompt the user for a username and password and then send them to the server without encrypting them first. If you use

BASIC authentication over an SSL (encrypted) connection, the username and password are encrypted by the SSL protocol itself. The password is encoded using Base64 encoding, which isn't really a form of encryption.

- DIGEST—Causes the browser to encrypt the password before sending it. Although this method can prevent someone from reading the password as it travels over the network, this method is not as secure as using a fully encrypted session.
- FORM—Just like the BASIC authentication method, except the server sends back a login form rather than using the browser's built-in form. The username and password are transmitted as form variables.
- CLIENT-CERT—Requires the user to provide a public key certificate for authentication. This method is frequently too cumbersome for general users because they rarely have their own digital certificates, but it does offer a reasonably high level of security, even over an unencrypted connection.

For BASIC authentication, you can specify a realm name using the `<realm-name>` tag. The realms help organize various sections of a Web site that might need authentication. By grouping applications into separate realms, you can require the user to log in to each application. The realm name isn't configured anywhere other than in the `<realm-name>` tag, so you don't need to worry about setting up different realms. A realm is basically a grouping of usernames and passwords. You can have multiple sets of users, each belonging to a different realm. For example, you might have a set of personnel Web applications with users belonging to a "manager" realm. Likewise, you might have an administration Web application with users that belong to an "admin" realm. In addition to usernames and passwords, you can define various roles for users. You can restrict parts of a Web application based on the role of a user (a user might belong to a "power-user" role or a "sysadmin" role). By granting access based on a role rather than an individual user, you can grant and revoke privileges to whole sets of users with a single operation.

Listing 23.1 uses BASIC authentication. Figure 23.1 shows the login prompt for a page in the authtest application.

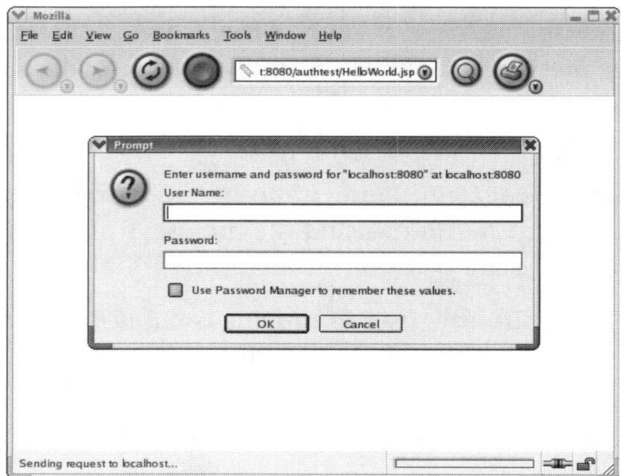

FIGURE 23.1 The browser prompts for a username and password for basic authentication.

The <security-role> Tag

The <security-role> identifies the roles that participate in an application. In this simple example, we've defined only one—manager. More-sophisticated applications will have several. It's important to note that the container is responsible for associating users and roles. As mentioned earlier, that means that you have to edit tomcat-users.xml, which is located off of Tomcat's home directory in conf. The format of that file is self-explanatory.

Creating a Custom Login Form

When you use the FORM authentication method, you must supply a login form to prompt the user for a username and password. The login form must contain form elements named j_username and j_password. The action in the <form> tag must be j_security_check. Listing 23.3 shows the HTML source for an example login form.

LISTING 23.3 Source Code for LoginForm.html

```
<html>
<body bgcolor="#ffffff">
<form action="j_security_check">
<table border="0">
<tr>
<td>Login</td>
<td><input type="text" name="j_username"></td>
```

LISTING 23.3 Continued

```
</tr>
<tr>
<td>Password</td>
<td><input type="password" name="j_password"></td>
</tr>
</table>
<input type="submit" value="Login!">
</center>
</form>
</body>
</html>
```

Figure 23.2 shows the example login form after the user has tried to access a page that requires authentication.

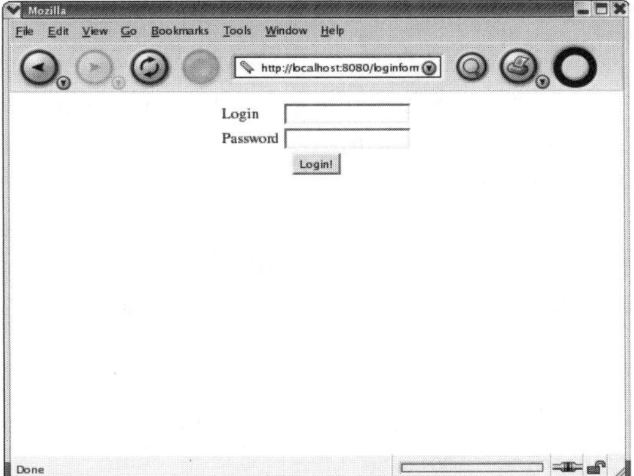

FIGURE 23.2
You can supply your own custom login form.

You can also create an error page that displays when there is an error in performing the authentication. Listing 23.4 shows a simple error page.

LISTING 23.4 Source Code for `LoginError.html`

```
<html>
<body bgcolor="#ffffff">
<h1>Sorry</h1>
An error occurred during authorization.
<p>
</body>
</html>
```

Figure 23.3 shows the simple error page in action.

FIGURE 23.3 You can supply your own custom error page for handling authentication errors.

When you supply your own custom login form, you must supply the name of the login form and the name of the error form inside the `<login-config>` tag. The `<form-login-page>` tag specifies the location of the login page, whereas the `<form-error-page>` tag specifies the location of the error page. The `<form-login-page>` and `<form-error-page>` tags are contained within the `<form-login-config>` tag. Listing 23.5 shows an example `web.xml` file for authentication with a custom login form.

LISTING 23.5 `web.xml` **for** `loginform` **Application**

```
<?xml version="1.0" encoding="ISO-8859-1"?>
<web-app xmlns="http://java.sun.com/xml/ns/j2ee"
    xmlns:xsi="http://www.w3.org/2001/XMLSchema-instance"
    xsi:schemaLocation="http://java.sun.com/xml/ns/j2ee
    http://java.sun.com/xml/ns/j2ee/web-app_2_4.xsd"
    version="2.4">
    <display-name>LoginForm</display-name>
    <description>An application that makes use of a user-defined login form
    </description>
    <security-constraint>
        <web-resource-collection>
            <web-resource-name>Test</web-resource-name>
            <url-pattern>/*</url-pattern>
            <http-method>GET</http-method>
            <http-method>POST</http-method>
        </web-resource-collection>
        <user-data-constraint>
            <description>SSL not required</description>
            <transport-guarantee>NONE</transport-guarantee>
```

LISTING 23.5 Continued

```
        </user-data-constraint>
        <auth-constraint>
            <description>Let only managers use this app</description>
            <role-name>manager</role-name>
        </auth-constraint>
    </security-constraint>
    <security-role>
        <description>The role of manager is one that can use our application.
        </description>
        <role-name>manager</role-name>
    </security-role>
    <login-config>
       <auth-method>FORM</auth-method>
       <form-login-config>
          <form-login-page>/LoginForm.html</form-login-page>
          <form-error-page>/LoginError.html</form-error-page>
       </form-login-config>
    </login-config>
</web-app>
```

Checking Security Roles Programmatically

Role-based authentication is nice when you can partition pages based on a role, but you can rarely make this kind of authentication seamless. Suppose you want to set up pages that can be run only by someone in a `manager` role. Obviously you can group the pages into a separate Web resource collection and specify a role name of `manager` in the `<auth-config>` tag for the collection. The problem is, where do you put the links to the manager-only pages?

If you put them on a page that everyone can access, the non-manager users might click the link and see an error page. Although this mechanism does secure your application, it doesn't make it pretty.

By the Way

Error Pages Should Be for Errors

If you want your site to look professional, a user should never see an error page as part of the normal operation of the site.

Rather than presenting the user with an ugly error page, you can check the user's role programmatically by calling the `isUserInRole` method in the `request` object.

For example, in a JavaServer Page that links to pages for managers, you might have the following code:

```
<% if (request.isUserInRole("manager")) { %>
<a href="managers/mgrreport.jsp">Manager Report</a>
<a href="managers/personnel.jsp">Personnel Records</a>
<% } %>
```

By checking the user's role in a JSP or servlet, you can customize the Web page to show the user only the items she can access.

If you need the user's name as it was entered in the authentication form, you can call `getRemoteUser` in the `request` object.

Listing 23.6 shows the source for a custom tag that lets you specify a required role for all the text contained in the tag body. The beauty of the custom tag is that it is more compact and more readable than using Java code embedded inside `<% %>` tags.

LISTING 23.6 Source Code for `RequireRoleTag.java`

```
package examples.taglibs;

Import java.io.*;
import javax.servlet.jsp.tagext.*;
import javax.servlet.jsp.*;
import javax.servlet.http.*;
import java.util.*;

public class RequireRoleTag extends SimpleTagSupport
{
    protected String role = null;

    public int doTag()
        throws JspException , IOException

    {
        PageContext context = (PageContext)getJspContext();
        HttpServletRequest request =
            (HttpServletRequest) context.getRequest();

        if ((role != null) && request.isUserInRole(role))
        {
            getJspBody().invoke(null);
        }
    }

    public String getRole() { return role; }
    public void setRole(String aRole) { role = aRole; }
}
```

Listing 23.7 shows a JavaServer Page that tests the custom tag in Listing 23.6.

LISTING 23.7 Source Code for `CheckRole.jsp`

```
<%@ taglib uri="/rolecheck" prefix="rc" %>
<html>
<body>

<h1>Welcome</h1>

Here are the things you can do:<br>
<a href="complain.jsp">Complain</a><br>
<a href="checkstocks.jsp">Check Your Stocks</a><br>
<a href="clock.jsp">Look At The Clock</a><br>
<rc:require-role role="manager">
    <a href="fire.jsp">Fire Someone At Random</a><br>
    <a href="meeting.jsp">Call A 10-Hour Meeting</a><br>
</rc:require-role>
</body>
</html>
```

Listing 23.8 shows the `rolecheck.tld` file used to define the custom tag library.

LISTING 23.8 Source Code for `rolecheck.tld`

```
<?xml version="1.0" encoding="ISO-8859-1"?>

<taglib xmlns="http://java.sun.com/xml/ns/j2ee"
      xmlns:xsi="http://www.w3.org/2001/XMLSchema-instance"
      xsi:schemaLocation=
              "http://java.sun.com/xml/ns/j2ee/web-jsptaglibrary_2_0.xsd"
      version="2.0">

    <tlibversion>1.0</tlibversion>
    <shortname>rolecheck</shortname>
    <info>
        A tag to require a specific authentication role for its body
    </info>

    <tag>
        <name>require-role</name>
        <tagclass>examples.taglibs.RequireRoleTag</tagclass>
        <body-content>scriptless</body-content>
        <attribute>
            <name>role</name>
            <required>yes</required>
        </attribute>
    </tag>
</taglib>
```

Listing 23.9 shows the `web.xml` file that describes the application.

LISTING 23.9 `web.xml` **File for** `rolecheck` **Application**

```
<?xml version="1.0" encoding="ISO-8859-1"?>
<web-app xmlns="http://java.sun.com/xml/ns/j2ee"
    xmlns:xsi="http://www.w3.org/2001/XMLSchema-instance"
    xsi:schemaLocation="http://java.sun.com/xml/ns/j2ee
    http://java.sun.com/xml/ns/j2ee/web-app_2_4.xsd"
    version="2.4">
    <display-name>roletest</display-name>
    <description>A test of authentication</description>
    <taglib>
        <taglib-uri>/rolecheck</taglib-uri>
        <taglib-location>/WEB-INF/tld/rolecheck.tld</taglib-location>
    </taglib>
    <security-constraint>
        <web-resource-collection>
            <web-resource-name>RoleTest</web-resource-name>
            <url-pattern>/*</url-pattern>
            <http-method>GET</http-method>
            <http-method>POST</http-method>
        </web-resource-collection>
        <user-data-constraint>
            <description>SSL not required</description>
            <transport-guarantee>NONE</transport-guarantee>
        </user-data-constraint>
        <auth-constraint>
            <description>Let managers and users use this app</description>
            <role-name>manager</role-name>
            <role-name>user</role-name>
        </auth-constraint>
    </security-constraint>
    <security-role>
        <description>The role of manager is one that can use our application.
        </description>
        <role-name>manager</role-name>
    </security-role>
    <security-role>
        <description>A regular user can also use (parts of) our application.
        </description>
        <role-name>user</role-name>
    </security-role>
    <login-config>
        <auth-method>BASIC</auth-method>
    </login-config>
</web-app>
```

Watch Out!

Package Your Applications!

This example can be used to point out some container behavior that almost always causes a few hour of frustration. In Listing 23.5, you'll note that the tag handler implementation is packaged in `examples.taglibs`. If you didn't bother to package it, you'd have a rather cryptic message when your application ran; the container would complain about not being able to locate `RequireRoleTag` when it was translating the JSP that uses it. This occurs because most containers package the JSP and assume that any unpackaged classes belong to the same package as the JSP—which is rarely the case.

Consequently, the container can't find the class and can't compile the JSP, even though you've made sure that the class is in a place that the container will find at runtime. To avoid this behavior, always package your classes.

Using Client Certificates for Authentication

There are at least two ways to use client certificates for authentication, but only one is likely to be supported by most servlet engines. The first way to do certification authentication is to set the authentication method in the `<auth-method>` tag to `CLIENT-CERT`. If you're using Tomcat, you can use this method; otherwise you may not be able to. Not all servers support this type of authentication.

After the client has been authenticated, you can access the `java.security.Principal` object that represents the user by calling `getUserPrincipal`. If `getUserPrincipal` returns null, the client isn't authenticated.

Tomcat must be set up to perform SSL client certificate authorization. Consult the documentation for instructions on how to do this. To enable your Web application to use client certificates, you simply need to create a `web-xml` that looks like this:

```
<web-app>
   <display-name>My CLIENT-CERT Web Application</display-name>
   <description>An Application that uses CLIENT-CERT for
Authentication</description>
   <login-config>
      <auth-method>CLIENT-CERT</auth-method>
      <realm-name>Authenticated Users Only Area</realm-name>
   </login-config>
...
```

If you aren't working with a server that supports `CLIENT-CERT`, your second option is to not use the normal authentication mechanism and go back to checking authentication manually, as you did in Hour 12. If you use an SSL-enabled servlet engine such as Tomcat, you might be able to access the client's certificate by accessing the `javax.servlet.request.X509Certificate` attribute in the `request` object.

The idea is that you keep a database of valid certificate numbers, and when a user accesses your site, you check the certificate number against the list of valid numbers. If the numbers match, you allow the user in. Because a trusted certificate authority digitally signs the certificates, it is almost impossible to forge a certificate.

Listing 23.10 shows a segment of code that accesses the client's certificate.

LISTING 23.10 Code to Access a Client Certificate

```
    X509Certificate cert = (X509Certificate) request.
        GetAttribute("javax.servlet.request.X509Certificate");

    if (cert != null)
    {
        String serialNumber = cert.getSerialNumber().toString();
        String issuer = cert.getIssuerDN().getName();

// validate the serialNumber/issuer against a valid list here...
    }
```

The serial number alone is not necessarily unique. The serial number is required to be unique for only a single certificate authority. For extra safety, you should check both the serial number and the name of the certificate issuer to make sure that you have the correct certificate.

Summary

JavaServer Pages and servlets make several mechanisms available to Web developers to secure applications. Resources are protected declaratively by identifying them in the application deployment descriptor and assigning a role to them. Clients that act in a role are authorized to use resources that are linked to the role. Access can also be restricted by the HTTP method used to approach the resource.

Web applications may declare a data constraint that defines the level of data integrity. One of the more important facets of this is the ability to secure the communications channel. SSL is commonly used to do this.

Several levels of authentication are available, ranging from basic authentication using identifiers and passwords to sophisticated authentication using certificates. If you use FORM authentication, you can customize the forms used to authenticate a client.

It's also easy to write applications whose behavior depends on the identity or role of the client.

Q&A

Q. *Why doesn't the servlet engine prompt me for authentication information?*

A. Most likely it's because the servlet engine doesn't support the kind of authentication you want. If the servlet engine doesn't support authentication, you might still be able to use the Web server's authentication if the servlet engine is just acting as a plug-in for a Web server such as Apache or Netscape. Another possibility is that even though you changed the servlet configuration to require authentication, you might have forgotten to restart the servlet engine to pick up the changes.

Q. *Why doesn't the servlet engine pass me the certificate information when I use SSL?*

A. Although most servlet engines support client certificates, there are still cases when you don't receive the certificate information. Occasionally, the problem is simply that the servlet engine doesn't support client certificates. The more common problem occurs when the servlet engine acts as a plug-in to a Web server. You are less likely to get the certificate information because the Web server probably isn't passing the information to the servlet engine in the first place.

Workshop

The Workshop is designed to help you review what you have learned and help you further increase your understanding of the material covered in this hour.

Quiz

1. What is `BASIC` authentication?
2. What is the difference between the `FORM` and `BASIC` authentication methods?
3. Which authentication method is most suitable for protecting sensitive information?

Answers

1. `BASIC` authentication is a simple authentication method that is built into HTTP. When a client requests a resource, the server challenges the client by asking for an identifier and password using a standard HTTP response code. It's only useful for the most basic security.

2. `FORM`-based authentication allows the container to participate in authentication and authorization. The container serves a form to the client that is used to submit an identifier and password. Once a client is authenticated, the application can obtain information about the client such as its role. In this way, `FORM` authentication is more useful that `BASIC` authentication.

3. `DIGEST` will do a reasonable job protecting a user's password. Using `CLIENT-CERT` will provide the best guarantee that a client is who he claims to be. By themselves, neither will protect the data, since that is a function of the user-data-constraint element. To ensure that data exchanged between a client and an application is secure, you should use user-data-constraint with a transport-guarantee attribute value of `CONFIDENTIAL`.

Activity

Modify the last practice activity from Hour 20 to use `FORM`-based authentication and to check security roles programmatically.

HOUR 24
Performance

What You'll Learn in This Hour:

- How to buffer pages to improve performance
- How to use static content where possible
- How to cache objects to reduce setup time
- How to choose the right session mechanism
- How to precompile JSPs
- How to set the JSP reload time
- Basic Java optimizations that help JSP performance
- How to make JSPs and servlets thread-safe
- How to use thread pools

When you're developing an application, your biggest concern is usually just getting it finished. Software engineering also recommends against "coding for performance" early in the development process. Be careful about doing too much optimization work too early. You need to let the code stabilize before you go in and work on improving its speed or resource allocation. After all, you might make a change that really speeds things up today but makes it difficult to add next week's new set of features.

Sooner or later, however, you have to work on optimizing the performance of the system. There are two parts to performance optimization. There are a few minor things that you should do that you know will help improve performance. After development is complete, or at major milestones during the development cycle, you can do performance testing and isolate areas in which you need to concentrate on optimization.

Buffering Pages to Improve Performance

Buffering Java I/O is one of the biggest performance boosts any network-centric application can make. Without buffering, every time you write to an output stream you make a system call, which takes a lot of time. By buffering the output stream, you keep the data in memory until the buffer fills. Only when the buffer fills do you incur the time for the system call. You can do this using the following code:

```
<%@ page session="false" buffer="12kb" %>
```

Buffering is a classic tradeoff between memory and speed. You use more memory for the buffering, but you improve your program's speed. Some JavaServer Pages and servlets might require different buffer sizes, and deciding on the optimal buffer size helps you keep memory usage down while keeping your server running quickly.

From a speed standpoint, you want the buffer size to be as large as the page you are returning. By default, the size of our (implicit object of `JSPWriter`) object is 8KB. That way, you perform only one system call to send the buffer back. When you look at memory usage, you want the pages with the largest buffers to execute as quickly as possible, so the memory can be reclaimed quickly. Unfortunately, it typically takes more time to generate the contents for a large buffer, especially if a lot of computation is involved.

Optimization is an iterative process. You make changes and observe the results. You should look at optimization only when it looks as if you have a problem. Before you deploy a large-scale production application, get a load-testing tool and see whether your application stands up under a heavy load. If not, look at the hotspots (statements that are executed frequently) and try to reduce the number of times you execute them.

As you start to tune your buffering, you can use `response.getBufferSize()` at the end of your JSP or servlet to find out how much buffer space you used. When doing this, set the initial buffer size to something much larger than you think you'll need. Otherwise, you might fill the buffer and then see a small buffer size because the buffer has already been flushed.

Use Static Content Where Possible

A JavaServer Page has a good mix of static content and dynamic content. Obviously, the dynamic content is not something that you can cache, and you encounter some performance hit proportional to the amount of dynamic data on that JSP. Thus, maximizing the amount of static content in a JSP is an important performance aspect.

The `jspInit()` method can be used to load static data and cache it. The `jspInit()` method is called only once in the life cycle of the JSP. However, you should remember to release all static data in the `jspDestroy()` method.

Caching Objects to Reduce Setup Time

Like buffering, caching is a speed-memory tradeoff. If an item takes a long time to create and initialize, you keep it in a cache and reuse it. Database connections are excellent examples of cached resources. It takes a relatively long time to establish a database connection, so most applications create the database connections when they start up and then store the connections in a connection pool, which is another form of a cache.

Most JSP and servlet engines even come with built-in database connection pools because they are so frequently used.

The main difference between pooling and caching is that pooled objects are meant to be shared and reused. When you need a database connection, you grab it from the pool, use it, and put it back. With a cache, you typically create an object and put it somewhere for safekeeping until you need it the next time, but you don't necessarily want to share the object.

For example, when a user logs in to your application, you might query the database for information about the user. You might need this information every time the user makes a request, but you don't want to go back to the database every time to get it. Instead, you store the information in the user's `session` object. The `session` object makes an excellent cache.

In most applications, there is always some data that is pretty much read-only—for example, a list of countries or states. This is another good example of data that should be cached so that you do not have a database hit each time you need that data.

Choosing the Right Session Mechanism

It is typical when using JSPs to maintain some client information or other data caches across multiple JSP invocations. There are several stores that are available for storing information that needs to be maintained across a request-response cycle. These include the following:

- HTTP Session—This data store is provided by the Servlet API. This is generally a good idea from a performance standpoint. The data is stored on the server, and only a session ID needs to be maintained over the network (generally using the URL rewriting method).
- Hidden fields—Developers sometimes use hidden HTML form fields on the JavaServer Page to maintain information. The use of hidden fields is slow and limited to a maximum size of an HTTP `get` or `post`.
- Cookies—Browser-based cookies are also used to store session information. Cookies are relatively slow and limited to a maximum size of 4K. Furthermore, client might turn off cookies, which might cause errors on the JavaServer Page.
- URL rewriting—You can encode the data that you need to persist across sessions in the URL. URL rewriting is similar to the use of hidden fields. The more data you need to pass over the network, the slower your application will perform.
- Persistent mechanism—You can use a database or some other data store and persist the data to that store. This goes against various design patterns for J2EE programming and is definitely the biggest performance hit.

Precompiling JSPs

Converting a JSP into a servlet and then compiling the servlet can be a time-consuming task for a JSP engine. Although the compilation happens only when the page has changed, you might want to compile all the pages ahead of time to make sure your users never see any delay when accessing recently changed JSPs.

The JSP specification includes a special precompilation directive that asks the JSP engine to precompile a JSP rather than execute it. You just need to send a `jsp_precompile="true"` parameter or an empty `jsp_precompile` parameter to tell the JSP engine that you want it to precompile a page.

Listing 24.1 shows a program that takes a base URL and a base directory and asks the JSP engine to precompile every JSP in the directory, including those in subdirectories. You can use this utility to eliminate compilation delays and also to locate JSPs that no longer compile cleanly. Because you normally see compile errors only when you access a page, you often don't discover a broken JSP until a user stumbles upon it, especially when it's a rarely used page. The program in Listing 24.1 helps you locate those pages before the user does.

LISTING 24.1 Source Code for `Precompile.java`

```
package usingjsp;

import java.io.*;
import java.net.*;

/** A class to recursively visit JSP files and precompile them using
 *  a JSP engine
 */
public class Precompile
{
    public static FileFilter fileFilter = new PrecompileFileFilter();
    public URL rootURL;

    public Precompile(URL aRootURL)
    {
        rootURL = aRootURL;
    }

/** Precompiles an entire directory of files */
    public void precompileDirectory(File dir, String startDir)
    {
// Get all the files that are either directories or JSP files (the filter
// source code is at the bottom of this file)
        File[] files =  dir.listFiles(fileFilter);

        for (int i=0; i < files.length; i++)
        {
// If the current file is a directory, precompile its contents
            if (files[i].isDirectory())
            {
                precompileDirectory(files[i], startDir+"/"+dir.getName());
            }
            else
            {
// Otherwise precompile the current file
                precompileFile(files[i], startDir+"/"+dir.getName());
            }
        }
    }

    public void precompileFile(File file, String startDir)
    {
        try
        {
// Create the URL for precompiling
            URL precompileURL = new URL(rootURL, startDir+"/"+
                file.getName()+"?jsp_precompile=true");

// Create a URL connection to the JSP
            HttpURLConnection conn = (HttpURLConnection) precompileURL.
openConnection();
```

LISTING 24.1 Continued

```
// Check the response code (this also forces the connection to contact
// the Web server and precompile the JSP)
            int responseCode = conn.getResponseCode();

            System.out.println(startDir+file.getName()+": "+responseCode);
        }
        catch (Exception exc)
        {
            System.out.println("Exception: "+exc.toString()+
                " for "+startDir+file.getName());
        }
    }

    public static void main(String[] args)
    {
        if (args.length < 2)
        {
            System.out.println(
                "Please supply a base URL and a base directory");
            System.exit(0);
        }

        try
        {
            String startURL = args[0];
            File start = new File(args[1]);

            Precompile precomp = new Precompile(new URL(startURL));

            if (start.isDirectory())
            {
                precomp.precompileDirectory(start, "");
            }
            else
            {
                precomp.precompileFile(start, "");
            }
        }
        catch (Exception exc)
        {
            exc.printStackTrace();
        }
    }
}

class PrecompileFileFilter implements FileFilter
{
    public boolean accept(File f)
    {
        if (f.isDirectory()) return true;
        if (f.getName().endsWith(".jsp")) return true;
        return false;
    }
}
```

Setting the JSP Reload Time

Most servlet containers have the ability to set an interval for when to check for updated JSPs. This feature is very useful during development, allowing you to quickly redeploy your JSPs. Thus, you do not have to bounce the server every time you want to test a change.

As you can imagine, this feature comes with a performance hit. It is wise to check for a new JSP every few seconds or minutes in a development environment. However, you should most definitely turn this off in a production setting.

Simple Java Optimizations

In addition to optimizing the performance of your servlet engine by manipulating the threads, or increasing throughput by modifying the buffering, you can do many simple things in your Java code to speed it up. These optimizations are always useful, whether you're writing a Web application, a GUI application, or an applet.

Use the `StringBuffer` Class

This is a very basic Java performance issue that applies just as much to JavaServer Pages. Many Java programmers never take the time to use the `StringBuffer` class. Some programmers, who should know better, frequently ignore it even in situations in which it should be used. Most programmers concatenate two strings with a statement like this:

```
String foobar = "foo" + "bar";
```

When you look at this statement, you naturally assume that the Java Virtual Machine must have some built-in string concatenation operation. What most people don't realize, however, is that the Java compiler generates code similar to this:

```
StringBuffer a = new StringBuffer("foo");
a.append("bar");
foobar = a.toString();
```

Creating one string buffer isn't so bad, but things slow down when you have a series of concatenations, like this:

```
String name = prefix;
name = name + "  "+firstName ;
name = name + "  "+middleName;
```

```
name = name + " "+lastName;
name = name + " "+suffix;
```

Each new assignment creates a new `StringBuffer` object. When you execute this code many times, you start creating a lot of `StringBuffer` objects. You are much better off creating a single `StringBuffer` object yourself and appending the strings to it, like this:

```
StringBuffer nameBuff = new StringBuffer(prefix);
nameBuff.append(" ");
nameBuff.append(firstName);
nameBuff.append(" ");
nameBuff.append(middleName);
nameBuff.append(" ");
nameBuff.append(lastName);
nameBuff.append(" ");
nameBuff.append(suffix);
String name = nameBuff.toString();
```

When you need to optimize your programs, start looking for places where you use + to concatenate strings. If you do several concatenations, replace them with `StringBuffer` and you'll see a reasonable performance increase.

Parsing Numbers

When you need to convert a string into a number, you use the various object wrapper classes, such as `Integer`, `Double`, `Long`, and so on. There are several ways to convert a string into a number when using these classes, but there is only one optimal way (assuming that you want a native type as the end result).

When you want to convert a string into an `int`, for example, you might use one of the two following statements:

```
int i = (new Integer("12345")).intValue();
int i = Integer.valueOf("12345").intValue();
```

The problem with both these statements is that they create a new `Integer` object first and then extract the `int` value from the object. The most efficient way to convert a string into an `int` is by the `parseInt` method:

```
int i = Integer.parseInt("12345");
```

In fact, both the string constructor for `Integer` and `Integer.valueOf` use `parseInt` to first create an `int` and then wrap an `Integer` object around it. The other classes have their own parse methods, such as `parseDouble` and `parseLong`.

Creating Objects

As you might have noticed, the previous two optimization tips centered around reducing the number of objects you create. Object creation consumes time and memory, and the fewer times you do it, the faster your program runs. In fact, with a good just-in-time compiler, a Java program that doesn't create any objects can run about as fast as a C program that doesn't allocate memory. For example, Java programs that analyze chess moves recursively and reuse the same memory for the board tend to run at about the same speed as their C counterparts. Although situations like this are rare in a typical business application, you can see that object creation does contribute to the relative slowness of Java.

Making JSPs and Servlets Thread-Safe

One of the key features for high-performance server applications is the heavy use of threads. The Java networking classes do all their data transfer via blocking operations, meaning the executing thread waits until the data has been transferred. Many times, however, the server can be doing other things while waiting for the data to transmit. Most servers generally have one thread per client, with each thread listening for incoming requests. Some servers might also have a pool of threads to execute requests (the reader thread hands the request off to an execution thread and then looks for more incoming requests).

By the Way

New I/O

JDK 1.4 introduced a new IO system called **NIO** (**New I/O**), which includes nonblocking IO. With nonblocking IO, you don't have to dedicate a separate thread per connection. For high-volume applications, NIO lets you reduce the number of active threads, conserving precious system resources. Of course, to really take advantage of NIO with JSP and servlets, you need a JSP/servlet container that supports NIO.

At the time of writing this book, Tomcat 5 does not support NIO, because it works on JDK 1.3. However, more than likely you will see a patch for it in the very near future (maybe even by the time this book is published).

Almost all JSP and servlet engines are multithreaded, and by default, JavaServer Pages are assumed to be thread-safe. Unless you specify otherwise, multiple threads might be executing a JavaServer Page at the same time. The `<%@ page isThreadSafe="false"%>` directive tells the JSP engine that a JavaServer Page is not thread-safe. If you expect fairly high volume on your JSP, you should make sure it is thread-safe. Restricting a JSP to a single thread can really slow things down.

Servlets are also assumed to be multithreaded, but there is no simple directive to mark the servlet as not being thread-safe. Instead, you must declare either the `service` method or the individual `doPost` and `doGet` methods as being synchronized. Marking the whole method as synchronized is a brute-force method, just like marking an entire JSP as non-thread-safe. You are much better off finding the places where threading is a problem and fixing them.

There are certain things you can look for when searching for areas of your program that might not be thread-safe:

- Does the JSP access a variable defined with the `<%! %>` tag?
- Does the servlet access any member variables?
- Does the JSP or servlet modify the contents of an object stored in either the `session` or `application` (`ServletContext`) objects?
- Does the JSP or servlet use any libraries that might not be thread-safe?

Even if the answer to any of these questions is "yes," you don't necessarily have a threading issue. If you are always reading the value of a member variable, you probably don't have a threading issue. Sometimes you set up some variables during the initialization of a JSP or servlet and then don't change the value during execution. You can safely assume that multiple threads can read the value of the variables without any problems.

When you store an object in the `session` or the `application` object, you need to consider the circumstances in which multiple threads might be using the same data. Because each browser has its own session, the only threading issues for objects stored in the `session` will occur when the browser requests several JSPs or servlets at once. When you store objects in the `application` object, consider whether another thread might also be trying to store the same object.

Often you create an object that is shared across multiple servlets, but you create the object only if there isn't one already stored in the `application` object. When you discover that you need to create the object, synchronize on the `application` object and then check again to see whether the object needs to be created. Then, within the synchronized block, create the shared object. Listing 24.2 shows a segment of code that creates a shared object.

LISTING 24.2 Code Fragment to Create a Shared Object

```
// Synchronize on the application object
    synchronized(context)
    {
// See whether the connection pool has already been created.
        IConnectionPool pool = (IConnectionPool) context.getAttribute(
            "connectionPool");

// If not, the pool must be created.
        if (pool == null)
        {

// Make sure the database driver is available.
            try {
                Class.forName("org.gjt.mm.mysql.Driver").
                    newInstance();
            } catch (Exception exc) {
                getServletContext().log(
                    "Error loading JDBC driver", exc);
            }

// Create the connection pool and store it in the application object.
            pool = new SimpleConnectionPool(
                "jdbc:mysql://localhost/usingjsp",
                "", "");
            context.setAttribute("connectionPool", pool);
        }
    }
```

Because the test for the presence of the object is in the same synchronized block as the code that creates the object, you can be sure that only one thread actually creates the object.

You must also take special care with the objects you store in the `application` and `session` objects. If you store objects that aren't thread-safe, you must synchronize any method calls that modify the state of those objects. Most of the objects in the Java API, such as `Vector`, `ResultSet`, `Connection`, and so on, are thread-safe. If you use third-party libraries, consult your documentation to find out whether any objects are known to be unsafe for threading.

Using Thread Pools

Threading is more than just a programming issue, of course; it's also a tuning issue. The more threads your Java Virtual Machine or operating system must keep track of, the slower your overall performance.

Many JSP/servlet engines let you configure the number of threads for performing various operations. They allow you to create a thread pool with a minimum and maximum number of available threads. You should have some idea of how many requests the server should be handling during a peak load, and the documentation for your JSP/servlet engine should give you an idea of how it uses threads and what numbers you can set for threading.

You also need to decide whether you should gear your server for best performance under peak load or for better performance the rest of the time but some degradation at peak time. If you expect a huge load at peak time but peak time is only a small part of the day, and if gearing your server for peak time hogs resources the rest of the time, you might consider lowering your resource allocation.

Summary

In this hour you saw various aspects of performance tuning that impact the performance of JavaServer Pages. It is important to understand the issues around threading, as this not only affects performance but also can lead to unexpected outputs such as mixing of client data.

Precompiling JSPs is a very important technique to use once you are in production. This is a good example where performance tuning need not be done during development. During development, you want to be able to redeploy JSPs without constantly re-cycling the servlet engine. On the same token, it is a no-brainer to turn this on in a production setting.

We concluded this hour by going over some very basic Java optimizations. These are specifically important in JavaServer Page programming, because JavaServer Pages do a lot of dynamic data presentation. The data, whether stored in a JavaBean or some other Java component, might need this sort of tuning, which ultimately affects the performance of the JSP.

Q&A

Q. ***I marked my pages as not being safe for threading. Why do some users still see data belonging to other users?***

A. Usually these situations happen because different servlets and JSPs are sharing objects that aren't thread-safe. Remember that the JSP/servlet engine ensures only that a specific JSP or servlet will be accessed by one thread at a time. You might need to synchronize on any shared objects to make sure that only one user at a time can access the object.

Q. ***I asked the JSP engine to precompile a page. Why didn't it compile the page?***

A. The precompile option is only a hint to the JSP engine. It is up to the JSP engine whether or not to precompile the page. You need to set the appropriate flag in your servlet engine to do this.

Workshop

The Workshop is designed to help you review what you have learned and help you further increase your understanding of the material covered in this hour.

Quiz

1. How do you indicate that a JSP is not thread-safe?
2. How do you indicate that a JSP should be precompiled?
3. My JSP engine does not support precompiling of my JSP. What do I do?

Answers

1. By using the `<%@ page isThreadSafe="false"%>` tag.
2. You just need to send a `jsp_precompile="true"` parameter to the JSP engine.
3. Which world are you living in! The best option is to upgrade to a newer version of your JSP engine. Another solution would be to use the `precompile` class shown earlier in this hour.

Activities

1. Turn on JSP precompilation in your servlet engine.
2. Flag your JSP to precompile.

Appendixes

Appendix A, “Apache Tomcat,” will help you get started with Apache Tomcat. On CD.
Appendix B, “Packaging a Web Application,” reveals the details of how to package and deploy your Web applications. On CD.

Index

*Page numbers preceded by "PDF:" indicate a reference to information found in the appendixes on the CD-ROM.

Special Symbols

<% %> tags

versus <c:out> tag, 357

in output, 352

used in JavaServer Pages, 9-10

<%@page%> tag, 388

<%@ page errorPage="xxx" %> directive, 229

<%@ page isErrorPage="true" %> directive, 229

<%= %> tags, 11-13

out.write and, 13

troubleshooting, 12

<%= action, 296

<%= tag, 297

<%! %> tags, 15-16

writing to out, 16

<!DOCTYPE> tag, 391

<?xml?> tag, 33

A

Accept-Charset header, 72

Accept header, 71-72

Accept-Language header, 72

ACCEPT-LANGUAGE header value, 446

locale codes for, 452

access operators, 317-318

ActionErrors object, 432

ActionForms, 432-433

actionRef tags, 440

actions

<%=, 296

capitalization, 63

<jsp:doBody>, 349

jsp:getProperty, 296

<jsp:invoke>, 349

jsp:setProperty. *See* jsp:setProperty action

jsp:useBean. *See* jsp:useBean action

standard, 187

addCookie method, 123

addDateHeader method, 122

addHeader method, 122

addIntHeader method, 122

addItem method, 270

AddToShoppingCartServlet class, 273-274

ALTER command, 374

Ant configuration tool, 37

Apache

- Ant configuration tool, 37
- Tomcat. *See* Tomcat

Appenders component, 217, 218

applets

- embedding in Web page, 208
- function of, 207
- in Internet Explorer, 209
- passing parameters to, 208

<applet> tag, 207

application event facilities, 92-96

application object, 155, 496

- versus static variable, 256
- storing data in, 255-256

applications. *See also* Web applications

- accessing resources for, 119
- JSP, 200-207
- Manager, PDF:509-511
- shopping cart. *See* shopping cart applications

application scope, 295

architectures

- designing for Web applications, 411-412
- Model 1, 412-413
- Model 2, 413-414

arithmetic operators, 318

attribute directive, 348, 349

attributes

- accessing, 103, 335-337
- action element, 339-340
- capitalization action, 63
- className, PDF:507
- configuring in tag library descriptor (TLD), 336
- connectionName, PDF:507
- connectionPassword, PDF:507
- connectionURL, PDF:507
- context, 364
- of custom tags, 337-338
- dataSource, 381
- debug, PDF:508
- declaring, PDF:520
- digest, PDF:508
- directive for, 348, 349
- display-name, 348
- driverName, PDF:507
- dynamic, 337-338
- escapeXML, 357
- flush, 190
- pageEncoding, 173
- request, 103
- reserved names of, 103
- roleNameCol, PDF:507
- scope, 350, 380-381
- storing, 103
- tag, 335-337
- type, 304-306
- userCredCol, PDF:507
- userNameCol, PDF:507
- userRoleTable, PDF:507
- userTable, PDF:507
- using with SimpleTag interface, 346-347
- var, 349-350
- versus variables, 339
- varReader, 349-350, 365

<attribute> tag, 336

<auth-config> tag, 479

<auth-constraint> tag, 474

authentication

- BASIC, 472-476
- CLIENT-CERT, 475
- DIGEST, 475
- FORM, 475
- role-based, 471-472
  - checking programmatically, 479-483
- of Tomcat, PDF:506-508
- using client certificates for, 483-484

<auth-method> tag, 474

autoFlush option, 177

B

BASIC authentication

- <login-config> tag, 474-476

<security-constraint> tag, 473-474
<security-role> tag, 476
setting up, 472-473

beans
adding to JavaServer Pages, 294-295
getting properties of, 296
initializing new, 302-304
setting properties of, 296-297
from parameters, 298-302
troubleshooting tips for, 312
type attribute for, 304-306
using scopes for, 294-295

binary data, sending to browser, 29

BindListener class, 247-248

<body-content> tag, 329

BodyTag interface, 326, 332-333

body tags, 332-334

BodyTagSupport class, 325-326

body.writeOut method, 334

bookmarking, 53

breakpoints, 223

browsers
interaction with servlets, 245
redirecting, 122
and request headers, 78
sending cookies to, 123
sending response to, 40-42
sending URLs to, 123

buffering, 488
when forwarding, 197

buffer option, 177

buffers
accessing information about, 156
control of, 157-158

built-in JSP objects, 153-155

C

Cache-Control header, 74

caches, 489

capitalization action attribute, 63

catalina script, 222

<c:catch> tag, 360

<c:choose> tag, 361-362

certification authentication, 483

<c:forEach> tag, 362

<c:forTokens> tag, 363

character encoding, 106

<c:if> tag, 360-361

<c:import> tag, 365-366

classes
AddToShoppingCartServlet, 273-274
BindListener, 247-248
BodyTagSupport, 325-326
Cookie, 287-288
creating, 265-267
DateFormat, 450
Element, 402
GenericServlet, 29, 84-85
grouping attributes and behaviors of, 306
HttpServlet, 29, 42, 84-85, 244
HttpSession, 124-125, 244, 255
Item, 279-280
JspEngineInfo, 165-166
JspFactory, 165, 166
JspWriter. *See* JspWriter class
ListResourceBundle, 455-459, 460
Logger, 218
MessageFormat, 463
NumberFormat, 451
PageContext, 160-163
PrintWriter, 8, 156
PropertyResourceBundle, 460-461
ReloadedClass, 90-91
reloading of, 89-92
ReloadTest, 91
ServletRequest, 101
shopping cart, 265-267, 281-282
ShoppingCartException, 267
SimpleDateFormat, 449
SimpleTagSupport, 343
StringBuffer, 493-494
Struts action, 430-432
TagExtraInfo, 342
TagSupport, 325

VariableInfo, 340
wrapper, 139
classic tag handlers, 326
className attribute, PDF:507
classpath, modifying, 31
CLASSPATH variable, 27
clearBuffer method, 158
clear method, 157-158
CLIENT-CERT authentication, 475
client certificates, 483-484
Cloudscape, 376-377
commands
ALTER, 374
cont, 224
for cookies, 130-131
CREATE, 374
DDL, 374-375
DELETE, 375
DROP, 374
GET, 74, 75-76
jre, 232
list, 223
POST, 74-76
telnet, 66-67
UPDATE, 375
comments
adding to JavaServer Pages, 13-15
debugging with, 14
function of, 13
using a JSP comment tag, 14-15
using HTML, 14
using Java, 14
Communiqué JSP Debugger, 225
compilation, of JavaServer Pages, 87
compile errors, 214-215
compile time, including files at, 183, 188
components
Appenders, 217, 218
of J2EE, 412
Layouts, 218
Levels, 217
of Log4J, 217
Loggers, 217
page, 388
in Struts, 430, 432, 435
of user interface, 441
conditional operator, 319
config object, 155
connectionName attribute, PDF:507
connectionPassword attribute, PDF:507
connectionURL attribute, PDF:507
containers
errors communication with Web servers, 23
functions of, 81
servlets and, 7
containsHeader method, 122
cont command, 224
content, 120
Content-Length header, 73-74
content type, 40-41
Content-Type header, 73
contentType option, 172-173
context
defined, 34
getting name of, 116
obtaining path information, 114
context attribute, 364
context-param option, PDF:518
context path, 95
Context Servlet, 119
controllers
calling multiple, 421-425
defined, 414
example of, 417-418
Struts implementation of, 435
Cookie class, 287-288
cookie object, 321
cookies
abuse of, 252
commands for, 130-131
creating, 127-128, 288
expiration of, 129
function of, 127
protocol versions of, 130
retrieved by servlet, 289-290
retrieving, 116
retrieving values of, 289
security of, 129-130
sending to browser, 123, 243
sent by servlet, 288-289
as session identifiers, 244
setting domain and path, 128-129
storing data in, 287-290, 490

storing on browser, 288
storing session identifiers with, 115
Core tag library
conditional tags
<c:choose> tag, 361-362
<c:if> tag, 360-361
directive for, 356
general-purpose tags
<c:catch> tag, 360
<c:out> tag, 357-358
<c:remove> tag, 360
<c:set> tag, 358-359
iterator tags
<c:forEach> tag, 362
<c:forTokens> tag, 363
loop status, 363
URL-related tags
<c:import> tag, 365-366
<c:redirect> tag, 366
<c:url> tag, 364
<c:out> tag, 357-358
<c:param> tag, 364
using within <c:import> tag, 365-366
CREATE command, 374
<c:redirect> tag, 366
<c:remove> tag, 360
<c:set> tag, 358-359
<c:url> tag, 364
currency
country code and, 454
formatting, 451-452
custom tags
accessing attributes of, 335-337
adding scripting variables in, 338-342
advantage of, 480-481
and compile errors, 352
conditionally including body of, 330-332
creating, 325
with Simple Tag extensions, 343
dynamic attributes of, 337-338
and exceptions, 334-335
processing body content with, 332-334
seeing in HTML output, 352

D

data
retrieving encoding type, 106
retrieving size information, 105-106
retrieving type information, 105-106
storing in application objects, 255-256
storing in cookies, 287
storing in hidden form variables, 235-238
databases
Cloudscape, 376-377
and Data Definition Language (DDL), 374-375
defined, 373-374
Java Database Connectivity (JDBC). *See* Java Database Connectivity (JDBC)
and SQL tag library, 380-383
troubleshooting connection problems in, 384
Data Definition Language (DDL), 374-375
Data Manipulation Language (DML), 375
data objects, 262-265
Data Query Language, 376
data source, specifying, 381
data storage
in application objects, 255-256
in cookies, 287
in hidden form variables, 235-238
in shopping cart applications. *See* shopping cart applications
dataSource attribute, 381
DateFormat class, 450
dates, formatting, 449-451
DDL commands, 374-375
debug attribute, PDF:508
debuggers
graphical, 225-226
for Java, 221
jdb, 222-224
using, 221-228

debugging
- difficulties in, 213-214
- with graphical debugger, 225-226
- of JavaServer Pages, 226-228
- with jdb debugger, 222-224
- with log files, 215-216
  - and tracing method execution, 220-221
  - using Log4J, 217-220
  - using servlet-logging API, 216-217
  - using system.out and system.err, 216
- remote, 222

<declare> element, 338

default factory, 165

DELETE command, 375

deployment descriptor, 32, 144, 150
- adding initialization parameter to, 83-84, 138
- creating, 33-35
- default, PDF:515
- in a JavaServer Page, 94-95
- location of, 36

description option, PDF:517

<description> tag, 33, 328, 339

destroy method, 39, 86
- of servlet filter, 136

detailed logging, 217-220

digest attribute, PDF:508

DIGEST authentication, 475

directives. *See also* JSP directives
- <%@ page errorPage="xxx" %>, 229
- <%@ page isErrorPage="true" %>, 229
- attribute, 348, 349
- for Core tag library, 356
- for format tag library, 356
- include, 183, 189
- in JavaServer Pages, 171-172
- <jsp:param>, 192-193
- page. *See* page directives
- for SQL tag library, 356
- tag, 348-349
- of tag files, 348-349
- taglib, 183-184, 371
- variable, 348, 349
- for XML tag library, 356

dispatchers, 421-425

<dispatcher> tags, 138

display-name attribute, 348

display-name option, PDF:517

<display-name> tag, 33, PDF:520

distributable option, PDF:517

DML. *See* Data Manipulation Language (DML)

DML statements, 375

doAfterBody method, 333

<!DOCTYPE> tag, 391

document elements, 388

Document Object Model. *See* DOM (Document Object Model)

Document Type Definition (DTD)
- parsers for, 393
- for XML pages, 391-392

doEndTag method, 330

doFilter method, 136

doGet method, 29, 42

DOM (Document Object Model)
- parsing XML with, 397, 402-404
- versus SAX, 402

doPost method, 57

-d option, 28

doStartTag method, 330

driverName attribute, PDF:507

DROP command, 374

Dumper program, 69-70
- and firewalls, 78
- port number of, 78
- after receiving POST request, 75

DynaForms, 433

dynamic attributes, 337-338

DynamicAttributes interface, 337

E

Eclipse, 225

Element class, 402

elements
- action, 339-340
- <declare>, 338
- <jsp-file>, PDF:521

<Realm>, PDF:507-508
root, 388
<scope>, 338
<tag-file>, 348
<url-pattern>, 34, 137
<web-app>, PDF:514
in web.xml file, PDF:516

<el-ignored> tag, PDF:522

<embed> tag, 208

empty operator, 319

encodeRedirectURL method, 123, 252-253

encodeURL method, 123, 252-253

end tags, 193

<error-code> tag, PDF:519

error handlers
for bean-based Web applications, 310-311
specifying for Web server errors, 230

error handling, 228-230

errorPage option, 178, 310-311, PDF:518-519

error pages
creating, 477-478
specifying for JavaServer Pages, 228-229

errors
compile, 185, 214-215, 352
500 (Internal Server Error), 46
404 (File Not Found), 46
handling, 228-230. *See also* error handlers
HTTP, PDF:518-519
runtime, 176, 214-215
Web server, 230

escapeXML attribute, 357

exception object, 155

exceptions
handling in custom tags, 334-335
IllegalStateException, 106, 241
stack traces and, 9
using to trace execution, 220

expression evaluator, 316

extends option, 180-183

Extensible Markup Language (XML)
advantages for using, 392-393
data representation and, 387-388
versus HTML, 388
page components, 388
parsing
with DOM, 397, 402-404
with JOX, 404-405
with SAX, 397-402
rules for creating pages, 391-392
serializing Java objects, 393
setting content type
for JavaServer Pages, 388-389
for servlets, 389-390
tag library. *See* XML tag library

extension mapping, 34

F

files
creating for tag library descriptor (TLD), 328-329
generated source, 8
including. *See also* included file
at compile time, 188-190
with include directive, 189
at Runtime, 190-192
from a servlet, 194-196
log. *See* log files
servlet binary class, 8
tag, 347-351
uploading
from HTML pages, 110-112
from Java clients, 106-109
WAR. *See* WAR (Web Archive) files
web.xml. *See* web.xml file
XML, 33

FilterConfig object, 138

Filter interface
configuration of, 137-138
lifecycle of, 136
methods of, 135-136
request and response wrappers in, 139
session logging, 145-150

filters, troubleshooting tips for, 152

firewalls, 221
500 (Internal Server Error), 46
flush attribute, 190
flush method, 157
<fmt:bundle> tag, 462
<fmt:formatDate> tag, 357-358, 468-469
<fmt:formatNumber> tag, 465-467
<fmt:message> tag, 463-464
<fmt:parseDate> tag, 469
<fmt:parseNumber> tag, 467-468
<fmt:requestEncoding>, 464
<fmt:setBundle> tag, 463
<fmt:setLocale> tag, 462
<fmt:setTimeZone> tag, 465
<fmt:timeZone> tag, 465
fn:contains function, 366
fn:containsIgnoreCase function, 367
fn:endsWith function, 367
fn:escapeXml function, 367
fn:indexOf function, 367-368
fn:join function, 368
fn:length function, 368
fn:replace function, 368
fn:split function, 368-369
fn:startsWith function, 369
fn:substringAfter function, 369
fn:substringBefore function, 369
fn:substring function, 369
fn:toLowerCase function, 370
fn:toUpperCase function, 370
fn:trim function, 370
format tag library, 461
  directive for, 356
  formatting tags
    <fmt:formatDate>, 468-469
    <fmt:formatNumber>, 465-467
    <fmt:parseDate>, 469
    <fmt:parseNumber>, 467-468
    <fmt:setTimeZone>, 465
    <fmt:timeZone>, 465
  internationalization (I18N) tags
    <fmt:bundle>, 462-463
    <fmt:message>, 463-464
    <fmt:requestEncoding>, 464
    <fmt:setBundle>, 463
    <fmt:setLocale>, 462
formatting tags
  <fmt:formatDate>, 468-469
  <fmt:formatNumber>, 465-467
  <fmt:parseDate>, 469
  <fmt:parseNumber>, 467-468
  <fmt:setTimeZone>, 465
  <fmt:timeZone>, 465
FORM authentication, 475
  and login forms, 476-477
form data
  detection of, 60-61
  protection of, 76
<form-error-page> tag, 478
form handlers
  arrangements of, 59-61
  combining with input form, 60-61
form handling code, 59-61
<form-login-page> tag, 478
form values, 54-57
form variables, 52-53
  getting values of, 63
  hidden
    security concerns with, 238-239
    storing data in, 235-238
  looking for, 60-61
  retrieving in servlet, 57-59
forwarding
  defined, 196
  from a JavaServer Page, 196-197
  from a servlet, 198
404 (File Not Found) error, 46
Front Controller design pattern, 435
functions
  fn:contains, 366
  fn:containsIgnoreCase, 367
  fn:endsWith, 367
  fn:escapeXml, 367
  fn:indexOf, 367-368
  fn:join, 368
  fn:length, 368
  fn:replace, 368
  fn:split, 368-369
  fn:startsWith, 369

fn:substring, 369
fn:substringAfter, 369
fn:substringBefore, 369
fn:toLowerCase, 370
fn:toUpperCase, 370
fn:trim, 370
in JSP Expression Language (EL), 321, 366-370
using tags to perform, 188
Functions tag library, 356

G

GenericServlet, 42
GenericServlet class, 29, 84-85
getAttribute method, 103, 117, 124-125, 240-241, 242, 255
getAttributeNames method, 117
getBufferSize method, 121, 158
getCharacterEncoding method, 106, 120
GET command, 74. *See also* GET request
versus POST command, 75-76
getBegin() method, 363
getComment method, 131
getContentLength method, 105-106
getContentType method, 105-106
getContextPath method, 114
getCookies method, 116
getCount() method, 363
getCreationTime method, 126
getCurrent() method, 363
getDateHeader method, 113
getDateTimeInstance method, 450
getDomain method, 129
getEnclosingWriter method, 334
getEnd() method, 363
getHeader method, 113
getHeaderNames method, 113
getIndex() method, 363
getInitParameter method, 117
getInitParameterNames method, 117
getInputStream method, 106
getIntHeader method, 113
getJspContext method, 343
getLastAccessedTime method, 126
getLocale method, 112
getLocales method, 112
getMajorVersion method, 116
getMaxAge method, 129
getMethod method, 114
getMinorVersion method, 116
getNamedDispatcher method, 118-119
getName method, 127
getOutputStream method, 29, 120
getParameter, 102-103
getParameter method, 52
getParameterNames method, 55-56
getParameterValues, 102-103
getParameterValues method, 55
getPath method, 129
getProtocol method, 105
getQueryString method, 114
getReader method, 106
getRealPath method, 119
getRemaining method, 158
getRemoteAddr method, 104
getRemoteHost method, 104
getRemotePort method, 104
GET request. *See also* GET command
hidden form variables and, 239
passing parameters, 102
getRequestDispatcher method, 118
getRequestURL method, 114
getResourceAsStream method, 108, 119
getResource method, 119
getResourcePaths method, 119
getScheme method, 105
getSecure method, 129
getServerInfo method, 116
getServerName method, 104
getServerPort method, 104
getServletConfig method, 40
getServletContext method, 125, 256
getServletContextName method, 116
getServletInfo method, 40
getServletPath method, 114
getSession method, 115, 242, 246
getStep() method, 363
getTimeInstance method, 450

getValue method, 127

getWriter method, 120

graphical debugger, 225-226

H

header information, 189

header objects, 321

headers

- Accept, 71-72
- Accept-Charset, 72
- Accept-language, 72
- Cache-Control, 74
- Content-Length, 73-74
- Content-Type, 73
- request, 68-70, 71-73, 78
- response, 73-74
- setting variables for, 122
- User-Agent, 72-73

header values

- ACCEPT-LANGUAGE, 446
- getting, 113

headerValues objects, 321

"Hello World" servlet, 26-30

"Hello World" tag, 325-327

hidden fields, 490

hidden form variables

- security concerns with, 238-239
- storing data in, 235-238

HTML

- indicating Java code in, 9
- used in JavaServer Pages, 6
- versus XML, 388

HTML form

- GET command versus POST command, 75-76
- simple, 49-52

HTML pages, uploading files from, 110-112

HTTP, 65, 66-71

- authentication protocol, 472
- mapping errors in, PDF:518-519
- POST command, 74-75
- versus Secure Sockets Layer (SSL), 76-77
- as a stateless protocol, 115

HTTP errors, PDF:518-519

HTTP GET request. *See* GET request

HTTP methods, authentication for, 474

<http-method> tag, 474

HTTP 1.1, 67-68

HTTP Post request. *See* Post request

HTTPS, 76-77

HttpServlet class, 29, 42, 84-85

- using HttpSession, 244

HttpServletRequest, 102, 114

- checking request methods, 113-114
- getting header values, 113
- managing cookies, 115
- retrieving cookies, 116
- retrieving query strings, 114
- ServletRequest and, 112

HttpServletResponse object

- encoding URLs, 123
- function of, 121
- passing session ID to pages, 252
- redirecting browsers, 122
- returning status, 122-123
- sending cookies, 123
- setting header variables, 122
- tracking sessions, 253

HTTP session, 490

HttpSessionActivationListener interface, 252

HttpSessionBindingListener interface, 247-251

HttpSession class, 255

- function of, 124
- HttpServlet and, 244
- storing and retrieving objects, 124-125
- terminating sessions, 125

HttpSessionListener interface, 251

Hypertext Transfer Protocol. *See* HTTP

I

icon option, PDF:517

IllegalStateException, 106, 241

implicit objects, 320-321

import option, 174-175

<include-coda> tag, PDF:522

included file, passing parameters to, 192-194. *See also* files, including

include directive, 183

including a file with, 189

<include-prelude> tag, PDF:522

incoming requests, logging of, 145-150

info option, 175

initialization parameters, 83-84

adding to deployment descriptor, 138

associating with JavaServer Page, 88-89

retrieving, 117

initialization phase

of JavaServer Pages, 88-89

of servlets, 82, 83-85

initial values, passing to input form, 61

init method, 38-39, 83

of server filter, 136

simplified, 85

troubleshooting tips for, 98

<init-param> tag, PDF:520

input form, 60-61

INSERT statement, 375

installation, checking, 46

interfaces

BodyTag, 326, 332-333

DynamicAttributes, 337

Filter. *See* Filter interface

HttpSessionActivationListener, 252

HttpSessionBindingListener, 247-251

HttpSessionListener, 251

JspFragment, 344

JspPage, 180-181

LoopTagStatus methods for, 363

Nameable, 304-306

NODE, 402

Result, 382

servlet, 29, 37

ServletContext, 256

SimpleTag, 342-347

internationalization (I18N) tags, 462-464

Internet Explorer, as Mozilla, 78

Internet standards, 130

invalidate method, 247

invoke method, 344

invoker servlet, 30-31, 83, PDF:521

IP addresses, 104

isELIgnored option, 174

isErrorPage option, 178-180

isFirst() method, 363

isLast() method, 363

isNew method, 126

isSecure method, 105

isThreadSafe option, 177-178

isUserInRole method, 479-480

Item class, 279-280

Item object

creating, 270-271

passing from browser, 271-274

J

Java

execution of in JavaServer Pages, 6

indicating code in HTML, 9-10

inserting declarations in JavaServer Pages, 15-16

packages for locale-based formatting, 448

printing expressions with <%= %> tags, 11-12

scriptlets and, 6

Java 1.4, logging in, 220

JavaBeans. *See* beans

Java clients, uploading files with, 106-109

Java Database Connectivity (JDBC), 377-378

realms in, PDF:507-508

using from JavaServer Pages and servlets, 379-380

Java Development Kit (JDK), PDF:501

installing, PDF:502

version 1.4, 495

Java I/O, 488

Java objects, 199

Java Plug-In, 208

Java Secure Sockets Extension (JSSE), 86

JavaServer Faces (JSF)
- components of user interface, 441
- features of, 437-438
- life cycle of, 438-440
- using with Struts, 441-443

JavaServer Pages (JSPs)
- adding a bean to, 294-295
- advantages and disadvantages of, 5, 43
- and beans, 294
- bookmarking, 53
- buffered responses and, 121
- buffering, 488
- cleanup of, 89
- comments for, 13-15
- compilation of, 87
- containers and, 7
- creating custom tags in, 183-184
- creation and management of, 81
- debugging
  - difficulty of, 213-214
  - with Tomcat, 226-228
- declaring methods and variables in, 15-16
- decoupling of, 161
- default package for, 227
- directives in, 171-172
- enhancing portability between, 160
- execution, 89
- execution of Java Code in, 6
- execution statistics display, 143-144
- execution statistics for, 139-141
- Expression Language. *See* JSP Expression Language (EL)
- forwarding to another page from, 196
- getting bean properties in, 296
- implicit objects, 320-321
- including files at runtime, 190-192
- initialization of, 88
- initializing new beans in, 302-304
- life cycle of, 87-89
- loading of, 87-88
- log method, 94
- making more modular, 200-207
- making thread-safe, 495-497
- Model 1 architecture and, 412-413
- Model 2 architecture and, 413-414
- Nameable interface in, 304-306
- objects, 153-155
- passing Java objects between servlets and, 199
- performance optimization. *See* performance optimization
- precompiling, 490-492
- putting on shopping cart application, 268-270
- reducing setup time in, 489
- reloading classes in, 89-92
- reload time, 493
- scriptlets and, 6, 320
- sending output in, 156-157
- sending XML from, 388-389
- versus servlets, 40, 42-45
- servlets and, 7
- setting bean properties in, 296-297
  - from parameters, 298-302
- sharing objects and, 117
- shorthand for printing out variables, 11-12
- specifying an error page for, 228-229
- standard actions, 187
- storing information in, 489-490
- superclasses for, 180-183
- tag extensions, 325
- thread safety in, 495-497
  - encapsulation and, 20-21
  - external variables and, 17
  - problems with multiple threads, 19
  - synchronizing variables and, 19-20
- timing filter for, 141-143

and Tomcat. *See* Tomcat
using cookies in, 287-290
using for input form and form handler, 60-61
using Java Database Connectivity (JDBC) from, 379-380
using static content in, 488-489
using thread pools in, 497-498
WAR file configuration options for, PDF:521-523
JavaServer Pages API, 183-184
Java Standard Tag Library (JSTL)
Core library
conditional tags, 360-362
functions of, 366-370
general-purpose tags, 357-360
iterator tags, 362-363
URL-related tags, 364-366
finding tags in, 371
format tag library
directive for, 356
formatting tags, 465-469
internationalization (I18N) tags, 462-464
installing and using, 355-356
internationalization (I18N) tags
<fmt:bundle>, 462-463
<fmt:setLocale>, 462
library types, 356
SQL tag library
directive for, 356
<sql:query> tag, 381-382
<sql:setDataSource> tag, 380-381
<sql:transaction> tag, 382
<sql:update> tag, 382-383
Struts tag libraries and, 434
XML tag library. *See also* XML tag library
<xml:out> tag, 407
<xml:parse> tag, 406
<xml:set> tag, 406
<xml:transform>, 407-408
XPath expressions, 405-406
Java 2 Enterprise Edition (J2EE). *See* J2EE
JDBC. *See* Java Database Connectivity (JDBC)
jdb debugger, 222-224
JDK 1.4, 495. *See also* Java Development Kit (JDK)
JNDI, using a data source with, 381
JOX (Java Objects in XML), 393
parsing XML with, 404-405
JRE (Java Runtime Environment), 23
jre command, 232
JSF. *See* JavaServer Faces (JSF)
JSP application, 200-207
JSP cleanup, 89
JSP compiler, 175
jsp-config option, PDF:522
jspDestroy method, 89, 489
JSP directives, 171-172
include directive, 183, 189
page directive, 172
autoFlush option, 177
buffer option, 177
contentType option, 172-173
errorPage option, 178
extends option, 180-183
import option, 174-175
info option, 175
isELIgnored option, 174
isErrorPage option, 178-180
isThreadSafe option, 177-178
language option, 173
pageEncoding attribute, 173
session option, 175-176
taglib directive, 183-184
<jsp:doBody> action, 349
JSP engine, troubleshooting tips for, 98
JspEngineInfo class, 165-166
JSP execution, 89

JSP Expression Language (EL), 315
- access operators, 317-318
- advantages of, 322
- arithmetic operators, 318
- conditional operator, 319
- empty operator, 319
- function of, 316
- functions in, 321, 366-370
- implicit objects, 320-321
- logical operators, 319
- relational operators, 319
- using strings with, 317

JspFactory class, 165, 166
<jsp:fallback> tag, 208
<jsp-file> element, PDF:521
jsp-file option, PDF:521
<jsp-file> tag, PDF:520
<jsp:forward> tag, 102
JspFragment interface, 344
JSP fragments, 191, 344
- configuring in tag library descriptors (TLDs), 346-347

jsp:getProperty action, 296
<jsp:import> tag, 365
<jsp:include> tag
- creating reusable modules with, 200
- passing parameters and, 102

jspInit method, 88, 489
<jsp:invoke> action, 349
JSP loading, 87-88
JSP objects, 153-155
JspPage interface, 180-181
<jsp:param> directive, 192-193
<jsp:params> tag, 208
jsp_precompile parameter, 490
jsp-property-group option, PDF:522
JSPs. *See* JavaServer Pages (JSPs)
JSP segments, 191
jspService method, 89, 181
jsp:setProperty action
- automatic type conversions performed by, 297
- and bean-based Web applications, 307-311
- null parameters and, 298
- scanning for property matches with, 300
- setting bean properties directly from parameters, 298-302

JSP tags, 315-316
<jsp:text> tag, 316
JSP 2.0
- decoupling of JavaServer Pages, 161
- functions in expression language of, 366-370. *See also* JSP Expression Language (EL)
- SimpleTag interface, 342-347

jsp:useBean action, 293-294
- adding beans to JavaServer Pages with, 294
- and bean-based Web applications, 307-311
- getting bean properties with, 296
- initializing new bean with, 302-304
- setting bean properties with, 296-297
  - from parameters, 298-302
- type attribute in, 304-306

<jsp:useBean> tag, 315
JspWriter, handling threads in, 17-21
JspWriter class, 8
- buffer control, 157-158
- versus PrintWriter class, 156
- sending output in, 156-157
- threads and, 17-21
- using a PrintWriter in, 158-159

JSSE, 86
JSTL. *See* Java Standard Tag Library (JSTL)
JSwat, 225
J2EE, 28
- components of, 412
- locating servlets in, 27, 28

Just-in-Time (JIT) compiler, disabling, 217

L

language option, 173
Layouts component, 218

LDAP, realms in, PDF:508
Leader Values, 113
Levels component, 217
Linux, installing Tomcat on, PDF:504
list command, 223
listeners
invocation order of, 98
using, 92-96
ListResourceBundle class, 455-459
PropertyResourceBundle class versus, 460
<load-on-startup> tag, PDF:520
local echo, 67
locales
creating objects for, 449
detecting in browsers, 446
function of, 112
obtaining preferred language, 452-453
resource bundles and, 445
setting information for, 120
text formatting for, 448
log files
absence of messages in, 232
using to debug applications, 215-216
with Log4J, 217-220
with servlet-logging API, 216-217
with System.out and System.err, 216
and tracing method execution, 220-221
Log4J
components of, 217
configuration of, 219
detailed logging with, 217-220
logical operators, 319
<login-config> tag, 474-476, 478
login forms, creating, 476-479
Logger class, 218
loggers, 217-218
Loggers component, 217
logging, 217-220
log methods, 94
accessing, 216
loop status variable, 363
LoopTagStatus interface methods, 363

M

McClanahan, Craig R., 429, 437
Manager application, PDF:509-511
MessageFormat class, 463
method execution, 220-221
methods
addCookie, 123
addDateHeader, 122
addHeader, 122
addIntHeader, 122
addItem, 270
authentication, 474-475
body.writeOut, 334
clear, 157-158
clearBuffer, 158
containsHeader, 122
declaring
with <%! %> tags, 15
in JavaServer Pages, 15-16
destroy, 39, 86, 136
doAfterBody, 333
doEndTag, 330
doFilter, 136
doGet, 29, 42
doPost, 57
doStartTag, 330
encodeRedirectURL, 123, 252-253
encodeURL, 123, 252-253
execution of, 220-221
of Filter interface, 135-136
flush, 157
getAttribute, 117, 124-125, 240-241, 242, 255
getAttributeNames, 117
getBegin(), 363
getBufferSize, 121, 158
getCharacterEncoding, 106, 120
getComment, 131
getContentLength, 105-106
getContentType, 105-106
getContextPath, 114
getCookies, 116
getCount(), 363
getCreationTime, 126

getCurrent(), 363
getDateHeader, 113
getDateTimeInstance, 450
getDomain, 129
getEnclosingWriter, 334
getEnd(), 363
getHeader, 113
getHeaderNames, 113
getIndex(), 363
getInitParameter, 117
getInitParameterNames, 117
getInputStream, 106
getIntHeader, 113
getJspContext, 343
getLastAccessedTime, 126
getLocale, 112
getLocales, 112
getMajorVersion, 116
getMaxAge, 129
getMethod, 114
getMinorVersion, 116
getName, 127
getNamedDispatcher, 118-119
getOutputStream, 120
getParameter, 52
getParameterNames, 55-56
getParameterValues, 55
getPath, 129
getProtocol, 105
getQueryString, 114
getReader, 106
getRealPath, 119
getRemaining, 158
getRemoteAddr, 104
getRemoteHost, 104
getRemotePort, 104
getRequestDispatcher, 118
getRequestURL, 114
getResource, 119
getResourceAsStream, 108, 119
getResourcePaths, 119
getScheme, 105
getSecure, 129
getServerInfo, 116
getServerName, 104
getServerPort, 104
getServletConfig, 40
getServletContext, 125, 256
getServletContextName, 116
getServletInfo, 40
getServletPath, 114
getSession, 115, 242, 246
getStep(), 363
getTimeInstance, 450
getValue, 127
getWriter, 120
HTTP, 474
init. *See* init method
invalidate, 247
invoke, 344
isFirst(), 363
isLast(), 363
isNew, 126
isSecure, 105
isUserInRole, 479-480
jspDestroy, 89, 489
jspInit, 88, 489
jspService, 89, 181
log, 94, 216
LoopTagStatus, 363
overloaded, 223
parseInt, 494
print, 156-157
println, 156-157
removeAttribute, 103, 117, 124-125, 240, 255
secureFlag, 129
sendRedirect, 122
service, 29, 38, 57
ServletContextListener, 92, 93, 94
ServletRequestAttribute Listener, 96
sessionCreated, 251
sessionDestroyed, 251
setAttribute, 103, 117, 124-125, 240-241, 242, 255
setBufferSize, 121
setCharacterEncoding, 106
setComment, 131
setDateHeader, 122
setDomain, 129, 288
setError, 123
setHeader, 122
setIntHeader, 122
setLocale, 120
setMaxAge, 129
setPath, 129, 288
setSecure, 129
setStatus, 123

setValue, 128
toString, 12
valueBound, 247
valueUnbound, 247

mime-mapping option, PDF:518

models

defined, 414
Struts action classes and, 430-432

Model 1 architecture, 412-413

Model 2 architecture, 413-414

Model-View-Controller (MVC), 262

controllers, 414, 417-418, 421-425
models, 414
reasons for using, 416
Struts and, 429-430
using in Web applications, 414-416
views, 414, 419-420, 421-425

modules, creating reusable HTML, 200-207

Mozilla, 72-73

multihomed servers, 103-104

N

Nameable interface, 304-306

NetBeans, 225, 226, 228

NIO (New I/O), 495

NODE interface, 402

NumberFormat class, 451

O

objects

ActionErrors, 432
application. *See* application object
associating with sessions, 247
built-in JSP, 153-155
caching, 489
cookie, 321
config, 155
creating
for locales, 449
for performance optimization, 495
for shopping cart applications, 262-265
data, 262-265
exception, 155
FilterConfig, 138
header, 321
headerValues, 321
HttpServletResponse. *See* HttpServletResponse object
implicit, 160, 320-321
Item, 270-274
Java, 199. *See also* JOX (Java Objects in XML)
JSP, 153-155
out, 51, 154
page, 155
pageContext, 155, 320
param, 320
paramValues, 320
PrintWriter, 41, 158
request. *See* request objects
RequestDispatcher, 198
response, 154
scope, 320
ServletConfig, 83-84, 256
ServletContext, 84, 92
ServletRequest, 92
ServletResponse, 41-42, 101, 119
session, 155, 176, 261, 489, 496
sharing, 117
storing and retrieving, 124-125
Times, 141

<object> tag, 208

operators

access, 317-318
arithmetic, 318
conditional, 319
empty, 319
in JSP Expression Language (EL), 317-319
logical, 319
relational, 319
unary -, 318

options

autoFlush, 177
buffer, 177
contentType, 172-173
context-param, PDF:518
-d, 28

description, PDF:517
display-name, PDF:517
distributable, PDF:517
errorPage, 178, 310-311, PDF:518-519
extends, 180-183
icon, PDF:517
import, 174-175
info, 175
isELIgnored, 174
isErrorPage, 178-180
isThreadSafe, 177-178
jsp-config, PDF:522
jsp-file, PDF:521
jsp-property-group, PDF:522
language, 173
mime-mapping, PDF:518
pageEncoding, 173
servlet, PDF:519-520
<servlet-mapping>, PDF:520-521
session, 175-176
session-config, PDF:519
for WAR files, PDF:517-523
welcome-file-list, PDF:518

orderQuantity property, 281-282

out object, 51, 154

output streams, 120

out.write statement, 10
<%= %> tags and, 13

overloaded methods, 223

P

PageContext class, 160-163

pageContext object, 155, 320
forwarding and including in, 164
function of, 159-160
implicit objects of, 160
searching scopes of JavaServer Pages, 161-162

page directives, 172
autoFlush option, 177
buffer option, 177
compile errors in, 185
contentType option, 172-173
errorPage option, 178
extends option, 180-183
import option, 174-175
info option, 175
isELIgnored option, 174
isErrorPage option, 178-180
isThreadSafe option, 177-178
language option, 173
pageEncoding option, 173
session option, 175-176

page encoding, 445-446

pageEncoding option, 173

<page-encoding> tag, PDF:522

page object, 155

page scope, 294

parameters
accessing, 102-103
distribution, 117
initialization, 83-84, 138
jsp_precompile, 490
manually passing, 57
null, 298
passing
to applets, 208
to forwarded page, 199
to included file, 192-194
to servers, 102
providing to servlets, 196
Request, 102-103
retrieving multiple, 55
setting properties of beans from, 298-302

param object, 320

paramValues object, 320

parseInt method, 494

path-mapping, 34

performance optimization, 487
buffering pages for, 488
caching objects for, 489
in Java
by creating objects, 495
by parsing numbers, 494
using StringBuffer class, 493-494
precompiling JavaServer Pages for, 490-492
and session mechanisms, 489-490
and use of threads, 495-497

using static content for, 489
using thread pools for, 497
persistent connections, 240
persistent mechanism, 490
pools, 489
POST command, 74-75
versus GET command, 75-76
POST request, 75, 102, 239
preferred languages
getting locale for, 452-453
setting, 448
println method, 156-157
print method, 156-157
PrintWriter
JspWriter versus, 8
versus ServletOutputStream, 124
PrintWriter class, 8, 156
PrintWriter object, 158
returning, 41
PropertyResourceBundle class, 460-461

Q

query strings, retrieving, 114

R

<Realm> element, PDF:507-508
realm name, specifying, 475
<realm-name> tag, 475
realms
configuration of, PDF:507
function of, 475
in Java Database Connectivity (JDBC), PDF:507-508
in LDAP, PDF:508
in Tomcat, PDF:506
relational operators, 319
ReloadedClass class, 90-91
ReloadTest class, 91
remote debugging, 222
removeAttribute method, 103, 117, 124-125, 240, 255
request attributes, 103
request dispatcher
obtaining, 118, 195
retrieving, 164
RequestDispatcher object, 198
request headers, 71-73
browser display of, 78
viewing, 68-70
request objects, 51, 57, 154
accessing information in, 192
function of, 101
storing Java objects in, 199
using, 52-57
Request parameters, 102-103
requests
for attributes, 103
checking methods of, 113-114
determining method used, 113-114
in Filter interface, 139
GET, 102, 239
for hostname, 104
incoming, 145-150
for IP address, 104
issuing to Web servers, 34
and multihomed servers, 103-104
for parameters, 102-103
for port information, 104
POST, 75, 102, 239
for protocol information, 105
reading content of, 106
receiving in servlets, 57
request scope, 295
request URL, 115
request wrappers, 139
<required> tag, 336
resource bundles
and locales, 445
reasons for using, 455
using ListResourceBundle class, 455-459
using PropertyResourceBundle class, 460-461
resource collection, 473-474
resources, assessing for applications, 119
response headers, 73-74
response object, 154
responses, buffering, 121
response wrappers, 139
Result interface, 382

role-based security, 471-472
checking programmatically, 479-483
roleNameCol attribute, PDF:507
<role-name> tag, 474
RollingFileAppender, 219
root elements, 388
<rtexprvalue> tag, 336
runtime errors
compile errors versus, 214-215
when using session object, 176

S

SAX (Simple API for XML)
versus DOM, 402
parsing XML with, 397-402
schemes, 105
scope
application, 295
of <c:set> variables, 358
object variables, 320
page, 294
problems involving, 312
request, 295
of scripting variables, 338
session, 295
scope attribute, 350
specifying scope of default variable with, 380-381
<scope> element, 338
scope objects, 320
scripting variables
adding, 338-342
defining, 340
scriptless value, 346
scriptlets, 6
ScriptTag custom tag, 341
secureFlag method, 129
secure HTTP, 76-77
secure protocol, 105
Secure Sockets Layer (SSL), 76-77
Secure Sockets Layer (SSL) API, 86
security
authentication methods for, 474-475
BASIC authentication, 472-476
constraints for, 473-474
custom login forms, 476-479
role-based, 471-472
checking programmatically, 479-483
using client certificates for, 483-484
<security-constraint> tag, 473-474
<security-role> tag, 476
sendRedirect method, 122
service method, 29, 38, 57
Servlet API, 252
<servlet-class> tag, PDF:520
servlet cleanup, 86
servlet code, 25
ServletConfig object, 83-84
servlet context and, 256
servlet containers
finding log files in, 95-96
initialization of filter method, 136
installing WAR files in, 36
using listeners in, 92-96
ServletContext
getting context name, 116
getting distribution parameters, 117
getting server versions, 116
logging messages for, 117
purpose of, 116
sharing objects and, 117
ServletContext interface, 256
ServletContextListener method, 92, 93, 94
ServletContext object, 84, 92
servlet engines. *See* servlets
servlet execution, 85-86
servlet filters, 135
servlet initialization, 83-85
ServletInputStream, 106
function of, 123
servlet interface
definition of, 37
implementing, 29
servlet loading, 82-83
servlet-logging API, 216-217
<servlet-mapping> option, PDF:520-521
<servlet-mapping> tag, 34, PDF:519

<servlet-name> tag, 34, PDF:519
servlet option, PDF:519-520
ServletOutputStream, 124
servletPath, 34
/servlet path, 83
ServletRequest
- accessing attributes with, 103
- accessing parameters with, 102-103
- availability of, 102
- getting locale information, 112
- HTTPServletRequest and, 102, 112
- obtaining host information with, 104
- obtaining IP addresses with, 104
- obtaining port information with, 104
- obtaining protocol information with, 105
- obtaining request dispatchers with, 118
- retrieving data information with, 105-106
- uploading files
  - from HTML pages, 110-112
  - with Java clients, 106-109

ServletRequestAttributeListener method, 96
ServletRequest object, 92
ServletResponse
- function of, 101, 119
- opening output streams, 120
- response buffering, 121
- setting content information, 120
- setting locale information, 120

ServletResponse object, 41-42
- function of, 101, 119

servlets
- accessing beans in, 295
- advantages and disadvantages of, 43-45
- anatomy of, 37
- authentication methods for, 474-475
- authentication problems in, 485
- cleanup in, 39
- cleanup of, 86
- compiling, 27-28
- creation and management of, 81
- debugging with Tomcat
  - using graphical debugger, 225-226
  - using jdb, 222-224
- declaring attributes of, PDF:520
- defining, 33
- eliminating old sessions, 245
- execution of, 85-86
- execution statistics for, 139-141
- forwarding to another page from, 198
- functions of, 25
- "Hello World," 26-30
- including files from, 194-196
- initialization of, 83-85
- initialization phase, 82
- interactions with browsers, 245
- versus JavaServer Pages, 40, 42-45
- JSP containers and, 7
- lifecycle of, 82-86
- loading, 82-83
- location of, 27
- making default, 35
- making thread-safe, 495-497
- passing Java objects between JavaServer Pages and, 199
- performance optimization. *See* performance optimization
- precompiling, 490-492
- providing parameters to, 196
- putting on shopping cart application, 268-270
- receiving requests in, 57
- reducing setup time in, 489
- reloading on Tomcat, 291
- retrieving form variables in, 57-59
- sending response to browser in, 40-42

- sending XML from, 389-390
- sharing objects and, 117
- TableServlet, 206
- timing filter for, 141-143
- and Tomcat. *See* Tomcat
- using cookies in, 287-290
- using invoker to run, 30-32
- using Java Database Connectivity (JDBC) from, 379-380
- using sessions in, 242-244
- using thread pools in, 497-498
- WAR file configuration options for, PDF:519-521

session-config option, PDF:519

sessionCreated method, 251

sessionDestroyed method, 251

session identifiers, 244

session keys, 244

session logging, 145-150

session mechanisms, 489-490

session object, 155, 489, 496

- for shopping cart data, 261

session option, 175-176

sessions

- activating, 251
- associating with objects, 247
- controlling termination, 125
- eliminating, 245
- forcing creation of, 245-246
- function of, 115
- getting status of, 126-127
- handling without cookies, 252-255
- HTTP, 490
- invalidating, 241
- logging of, 145-150
- managing identifiers, 115
- passivating, 251
- saving data in shopping cart application with, 261. *See also* shopping cart applications
- termination of, 125, 247
- tracking in HttpServletResponse object, 253
- turning off, 175-176
- using
  - in JavaServer Pages, 240-242
  - to save data in shopping cart applications, 261
  - in servlets, 242-244

session scope, 295

setAttribute method, 103, 117, 124-125, 240-241, 242, 255

setBufferSize method, 121

setCharacterEncoding method, 106

setComment method, 131

setContentLength, 120

setContentType, 120

setDateHeader method, 122

setDomain method, 129

- in cookies, 288

setError method, 123

setHeader method, 122

setIntHeader method, 122

setLocale method, 120

setMaxAge method, 129

setPath method, 129

- in cookies, 288

setSecure method, 129

setStatus method, 123

setValue method, 128

shopping cart applications

- adding and removing items in, 270-283
- allowing multiple quantities in, 279-282
- completing order in, 284-287
- creating data objects for, 262-265
- creating shopping cart class for, 265-267
- designing, 262
- displaying contents of, 268-270
- keeping items in memory, 274-279
- removing items in, 282-283
- using sessions to save data in, 261

shopping cart class

- creating, 265-267
- modifying to update orderQuantity property, 281-282

ShoppingCartException class, 267

shopping cart items
- keeping in memory, 274-279
- removing, 282

<short-name> tag, 328

showtext.jsp, 351

Simple API for XML. *See* SAX (Simple API for XML)

SimpleDateFormat class, 449

SimpleFormHandler JSP, 50-52

SimpleTag, accessing body of, 344-346

Simple Tag extensions, 343

simple tag handlers, 346-347

SimpleTag interface, 342-343
- creating custom tags with, 343
- JSP fragments, 344
- using attributes and variables with, 346-347

SimpleTagSupport class, 343

special characters, in URLs, 53

SQL. *See* Structured Query Language (SQL)

<sql:query> tag, 381-382

<sql:setDataSource> tag, 380-381

SQL tag library
- directive for, 356
- <sql:query> tag, 381-382
- <sql:setDataSource> tag, 380-381
- <sql:transaction> tag, 383
- <sql:update> tag, 382-383

<sql:transaction> tag, 383

<sql:update> tag, 382-383

SSL. *See* Secure Sockets Layer (SSL)

stack traces, 9
- printing, 158-159

standard actions, 187

stateless protocols, 115

statements
- DML, 375
- INSERT, 375
- out.println, 8
- out.write, 10

static content, 488-489

static variable, 256

status code, 122-123

StringBuffer class, 493-494

Structured Query Language (SQL)
- Data Definition Language (DDL), 374-375
- Data Query Language, 376
- Data Manipulation Language (DML), 375
- data types of, 374
- tag library. *See* SQL tag library

Struts
- action classes in, 430-432
- ActionForms and, 432-433
- controller component in, 430, 435
- DynaForms and, 433
- implementing Model-View-Controller design with, 429-430
- JavaServer Faces (JSF) versus, 438
- model component in, 430
- setting up, 436-437
- tag libraries for, 433-434
- using, 429
- using JavaServer Faces (JSF) with, 441-443
- view component in, 432
- Web site for, 436

Sun, Java Plug-In, 208

superclass, creating, 180-181

System.err, 216

System.out, 216

T

TableServlet servlet, 206

tag attributes, 335-337

<tag-class> tag, 329

tag directive, 348-349

tag extensions, 325

TagExtraInfo class, 342

<tag-file> element, 348

tag files
- creating, 347
- deploying, 347-348
- directives of
  - attribute directive, 348, 349
  - tag directive, 348-349
  - variable directive, 349
- function of, 347
- standard actions used with, 349-350
- using, 350-351

tag handlers, 346-347

taglib directive, 183-184, 371

<taglib-location> tag, 329

tag libraries, 183-184

- Core. *See* Core tag library
- descriptor; tag library descriptor (TLD)
- format. *See* format tag library
- function of, 355
- Functions, 356
- Java Standard. *See* Java Standard Tag Library (JSTL)
- SQL. *See* SQL tag library
- Struts, 434
- XML. *See* XML tag library

tag library descriptor (TLD)

- configuring attributes in, 336
- configuring JSP fragments in, 346-347
- creating file for, 328-329
- processing body content in, 331-332
- for SimpleTag, 345-346
- using action element attribute in, 339-340

<taglib> tag, 328, 329

<taglib-uri> tag, 329

tag names, 328-329

tags

- <% %>, 9-10, 352, 357
- <%=, 297
- <%= %>, 9-10, 11-13
- <%! %>, 15-16
- <%@page%>, 388
- <!DOCTYPE>, 391
- actionRef, 440
- <applet>, 207
- <attribute>, 336
- attributes of, 335-337
- <auth-config>, 474
- <auth-constraint>, 474
- <auth-method>, 474
- body, 332-334
- <body-content>, 329
- <c:catch>, 360
- <c:choose>, 361-362
- <c:forEach>, 362
- <c:forTokens>, 363
- <c:if>, 360-361
- <c:import>, 365-366
- comment, 14-15
- conditional, 360-362
- in Core tag library. *See* Core tag library
- <c:out>, 357-358
- <c:param>, 364
- <c:redirect>, 366
- <c:remove>, 360
- <c:set>, 358-359
- <c:url>, 364
- custom. *See* custom tags
- <description>, 33, 328, 339
- <dispatcher>, 138
- <display-name>, 33, PDF:520
- <el-ignored>, PDF:522
- <embed>, 208
- end, 193
- <error-code>, PDF:519
- files of. *See* tag files
- finding in Java Standard Tag Library (JSTL), 371
- flow, 407
- <fmt:bundle>, 462
- <fmt:formatDate>, 357-358, 468-469
- <fmt:formatNumber>, 465-467
- <fmt:message>, 463-464
- <fmt:parseDate>, 469
- <fmt:parseNumber>, 467-468
- <fmt:requestEncoding>, 464
- <fmt:setBundle>, 463
- <fmt:setLocale>, 462
- <fmt:setTimeZone>, 465
- in format tag library. *See* format tag library
- formatting. *See* formatting tags
- <form-error-page>, 478
- <form-login-page>, 478
- general-purpose, 357-360
- handlers of, 346-347
- "Hello World," 325-327
- <http-method>, 474
- <include-coda>, PDF:522
- <include-prelude>, PDF:522
- <init-param>, PDF:520
- internationalization (I18N), 462-464
- iterator, 362-363

JSP, 315-316
<jsp:fallback>, 208
<jsp:file>, PDF:520
<jsp:forward>, 102
<jsp:import>, 365
<jsp:include>, 102, 200
<jsp:params>, 208
<jsp:text>, 316
<jsp:useBean>, 315
library of. *See* tag libraries
<load-on-startup>, PDF:520
<login-config>, 474-476, 478
<object>, 208
packaging and installing, 328-330
<page-encoding>, PDF:522
<realm-name>, 475
<required>, 336
<role-name>, 474
<rtexprvalue>, 336
<security-constraint>, 473-474
<security-role>, 476
<servlet-class>, PDF:520
<servlet-mapping>, 34, PDF:519
<servlet-name>, 34, PDF:519
<short-name>, 328
<sql:query>, 381-382
<sql:setDataSource>, 380-381
in SQL tag library. *See* SQL tag library
<sql:transaction>, 382
<sql:update>, 382-383
<tag-class>, 329
<taglib>, 328, 329
<taglib-location>, 329
<taglib-uri>, 329
<tlib-version>, 328
transform, 407-408
<transport-guarantee>, 474
<url-pattern>, 473
URL-related, 364-366
<user-data-constraint>, 474
using to perform functions, 188
<web-app>, 33
<?xml?>, 33
<xml:out>, 407
<xml:parse>, 406
<xml:set>, 406
in XML tag library. *See* XML tag library
<xml:transform>, 407-408

TagSupport class, 325

telnet command, 66-67

Telnet window, 67

thread pools, 497-498

threads
encapsulation and, 20-21
external variables and, 17
function of, 495
pools of, 497-498
problems executing multiple, 19
safety of, 495-497
synchronizing variables and, 19-20

Times object, 141

timing filter, 141-143

TLD. *See* tag library descriptor (TLD)

<tlib-version> tag, 328

Tomcat
adding administrators to, PDF:510
application manager, 95
authentication of, PDF:506-508
configuration of, PDF:505-506
debugging JavaServer Pages in, 226-228
debugging servlets in
using graphical debugger, 225-226
using jdb, 222-224
defining roles in, 471-472
downloading, PDF:501-502
function of, PDF:501
installing
on Linux or Unix, PDF:504
on Windows, PDF:502-503
installing WAR file in, PDF:515-516
locating servlets in, 27, 28
location of generated source files in, 8
location of servlet binary class files in, 8
Manager application in, PDF:509-511
realms in, PDF:506-508
reloading servlets on, 291
running, PDF:505
in a JVM, 224

- setting classpath for, PDF:506
- starting under jdb, 222
- testing installation of, PDF:503
- Tomcat Manager, 37
- using Log4J with, 219
- WAR files in, PDF:511
- Web Server Administration Tool, PDF:508-509
- Web site for, PDF:501

Tomcat 5, 227
Tomcat Manager, manager application, 37, PDF:509-511
toString method, 12
translation, problems that occur during, 214-215
<transport-guarantee> tag, 474
type attribute, 304-306

U

unary - operator, 318
Uniform Resource Locators. *See* **URLs (Uniform Resource Locators)**
Unix, installing Tomcat on, PDF:504
UPDATE command, 375
URI (Uniform Resource Identifier), 34
url-pattern, 34-35
<url-pattern> element, 34, 137
<url-pattern> tag, 473
URL rewriting, 490
URLs (Uniform Resource Locators)
- encoding, 123
- inserting session IDs into, 252
- mapping to servlets, 83
- rewriting of, 364
- special characters in, 53
- specifying alternate context of, 365
- specifying context-relative, 364
- versus URI (Uniform Resource Identifier), 34

useBean ID, 294
User-Agent header, 72-73
userCredCol attribute, PDF:507
<user-data-constraint> tag, 474
userNameCol attribute, PDF:507
userRoleTable attribute, PDF:507
userTable attribute, PDF:507

V

valueBound method, 247
valueRef expressions, 440
values
- form, 54-57
- of form variables, 63
- getting, 63, 113
- header, 113, 446
- initial, 61
- Leader, 113
- retrieving cookie, 289
- scriptless, 346

valueUnbound method, 247
var["attr"], 318
var attribute, 349-350
variable directive, 348, 349
VariableInfo class, 340
variables
- versus attributes, 339
- CLASSPATH, 27
- <c:set>, 358
- declaring
  - with <%! %> tags, 16
  - in JavaServer Pages, 15-16
- directives for, 348, 349
- external, 17
- form. *See* form variables
- hidden form. *See* hidden form variables
- loop status, 363
- object, 320
- printing out, 11-12
- scripting, 338-342
- setting for headers, 122
- static, 256
- synchronizing in JavaServer Pages, 19-20
- using with SimpleTag interface, 346-347

varReader attribute, 349-350, 365
views
- calling multiple, 421-425
- defined, 414
- example of, 419-420

in Model-View-Controller (MVC), 414, 419-420, 421-425
Struts ActionForms and, 432

Virtual Network Computing (VNC), 221

W

WAR (Web Archive) files, 32
configuration of
general application options for, PDF:517-519
JSP options for, PDF:521-523
servlet options for, PDF:519-521
creating, 35
deploying, 36-37
deploying servlets in, 390
example of, PDF:513-515
installing under Tomcat, PDF:515-516
purposes of, PDF:513
recognizing in Tomcat, PDF:511
using to reload classes, 91

<web-app> element, PDF:514

Web applications
bean-based, 307-311
debugging with log files, 215-216
with Log4J, 217-220
servlet-logging API, 216-217
with System.out and System.err, 216
and tracing method execution, 220-221
designing architecture for, 411-412
difficulty in debugging, 213-214
enabling use of client certificates in, 483
Model 1 architecture and, 412-413
Model 2 architecture and, 413-414
performance optimization for. *See* performance optimization
setting up BASIC authentication for, 472-473
shopping cart. *See* shopping cart applications
using Model-View-Controller in, 414-416
WAR file configuration options for, PDF:517-519

<web-app> tag, 33

Web archive file. *See* WAR (Web Archive) files

Web server errors, 230

Web servers
issuing request to, 34
Tomcat. *See* Tomcat

Web sites
for Cloudscape, 376
for Struts, 436
for Tomcat, PDF:501-502

web.xml file, PDF:514, PDF:515
order of elements in, PDF:516
servlet definitions in, 33

welcome-file-list option, PDF:518

Windows, installing Tomcat on, PDF:502-503

wrapper class, 139

X

XML. *See* Extensible Markup Language (XML)

XML files, 33

<xml:out> tag, 407

<xml:parse> tag, 406

XMLSchema, 392

<xml:set> tag, 406

<?xml?> tag, 33

XML tag library
directive for, 356
flow tags, 407
function of core tags, 405
transform tags, 407-408
<xml:out> tag, 407
<xml:parse> tag, 406
<xml:set> tag, 406
<xml:transform>, 407-408
XPath expressions, 405-406

<xml:transform> tag, 407-408

XPath expressions, 405-406
flow tags and, 407

Related Titles

STY Web Services in 24 Hours
Stephen Potts and Mike Kopack
0-672-32515-2
$24.99 US/$37.99 CAN

Extreme Programming with Ant
Glenn Niemeyer and Jeremy Poteet
0-672-32562-4
$34.99 US/$52.99 CAN

Java Web Development with Servlets, JSP, and EJB, 2nd edition
Budi Kurniawan
0-672-32626-4
$49.99 US/$75.99 CAN

XSLT 2.0 Kick Start
Andrew H. Watt
0-672-32437-7
$34.99 US/$52.99 CAN

J2EE Developer's Handbook
Paul Perrone, et al
0-672-32348-6
$59.99 US/$90.99 CAN

Java Primer Plus
Steven Haines and Stephen Potts
0-672-32415-6
$44.99 US/$67.99 CAN

XQuery Kick Start
James McGovern, et al
0-672-32479-2
$34.99 US/$52.99 CAN

XPath Kick Start: Navigating XML with XPath 1.0 and 2.0
Steven Holzner
0-672-32411-3
$34.99 US/$52.99 CAN

SAMS
www.samspublishing.com

JavaServer Page Developer's Handbook
Nick Todd and Mark Szolkowski
0-672-32438-5
$49.99 US/$75.99 C

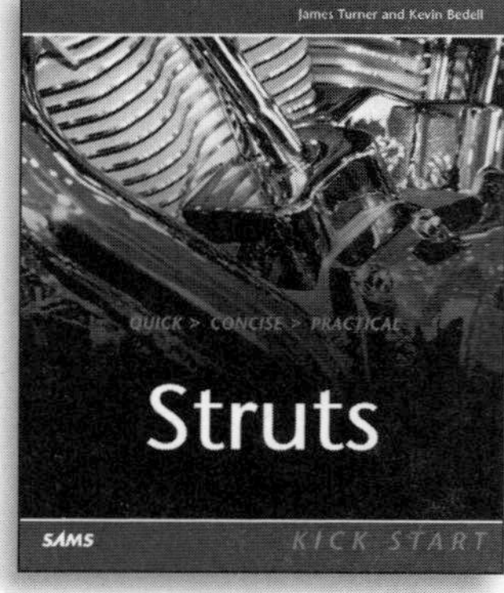

Struts Kick Star
James Turner and Kevin Bedell
0-672-32472-5
$34.99 US/$52.99 C

STY XML in 21 Days
Steven Holzner
0-672-32576-4
$39.99 US/$60.99 C

All prices are subject to change.